New College
1975

ECONOMIC ANALYSIS

Economic Analysis

C. E. FERGUSON
Late Professor of Economics, Texas A&M University

S. CHARLES MAURICE
Associate Professor of Economics, Texas A&M University

 Revised Edition • 1974

RICHARD D. IRWIN, INC. Homewood, Illinois 60430
Irwin-Dorsey International, London, England WC2H 9NJ
Irwin-Dorsey Limited, Georgetown, Ontario L7G 4B3

Revised Edition

First Printing, March 1974
Second Printing, August 1974
Third Printing, December 1974
Fourth Printing, February 1975

ISBN 0-256-01548-1
Library of Congress Catalog Card No. 73–89108
Printed in the United States of America

LEARNING SYSTEMS COMPANY—
a division of Richard D. Irwin, Inc.—has developed a
PROGRAMMED LEARNING AID
to accompany texts in this subject area.
Copies can be purchased through your bookstore
or by writing PLAIDS,
1818 Ridge Road, Homewood, Illinois   60430.

To Charlie

Preface

This textbook is designed for undergraduate courses in the microeconomic theory of value and distribution. Its primary object is to present the basic fundamentals of price theory that can be covered in a one-semester course along with enough analysis and applications to give the student intense practice in using theory.

While *Economic Analysis* remains a text in basic price theory, the fundamental revisions from and additions to the first edition have been made in the area of analysis and application. Many users of the first edition suggested the inclusion of additional examples of applications of theory, particularly applications to contemporary economic and business problems. Many felt, and I feel also, that students want and should have more practice in how to use economic theory to analyze prototypes of real-world situations; students want to know how to solve problems. They want to know what economists are doing about current problems in the economy as a whole, or about certain business problems.

To this end I have greatly expanded the material on the application of theory and the number of empirical examples. I have attempted to use varied, interesting, and particularly timely applications from recent articles in the more important economic journals. Thus, the student should get some "feel" for what professional economists are doing *now* about problems such as pollution, population, discrimination in employment, crime, and so forth. Included also are a few slightly older articles that have become classics.

Every chapter except the first and last contains examples and analysis of applications of the theoretical material in the chapter. Chapter 2 contains a section on how to estimate demand curves, for example; Chapter 5, which is all new, consists entirely of analytical material on the economics of crime, fertility, job choice, slum clearance, and similar areas.

I want to mention in passing that the authors of this text did not necessarily agree with all of the material presented in the applications. I feel that in one or two cases the interpretations of some results may not be quite correct. Furthermore, some of the articles cited were commented upon by other economists. This is not to say that the articles are wrong, but to point out there is the possibility of differing interpretation of results. I emphasize, however, that the disagreement concerns interpretation and not the theory itself. In any case the student will become familiar with the way in which economists apply theory to problems.

While every effort has been made to keep technical language out of the empirical applications, a few elementary statistical terms are necessary from time to time in the reporting of statistical results. For this reason I have included a very short statistical appendix at the end of Chapter 1, to familiarize those who have not had a statistics course with some of the commonly used terms.

There have been several other important changes in this edition. Again at the suggestion of users of the first edition, I have added several numerical examples where they seem to aid understanding of the previously graphical exposition. I have also added many numerical problems and, in fact, the number of problems, questions, and exercises has been more than doubled.

I have included a few additional theoretical concepts. The Edgeworth box analysis of exchange in production and consumption has been added to the chapter on general equilibrium, for example; a section on consumer surplus has been added to demand theory; and I have added several new points on imperfect competition.

These are only the principal changes. I have corrected several errors in the first edition, most of which were pointed out by users of the text. I have expanded upon many sections that seemed obscure. Even though a large part of the text has been changed, I have attempted everywhere possible not to change the lucid exposition of the late Charles Ferguson. He remains in every sense a coauthor.

I would like to thank several people who helped much with this edition. Joe Hulett and Mark Jackson, colleagues at Texas A&M, read much of the text and suggested many improvements. Three other colleagues Sam Gillespie, Ray Battalio, and John Kagel gave valuable suggestions. Richard B. Westin of Northwestern University read all of the revision and helped greatly on several points. Bob Nash of Texas A&I pointed out mistakes in the first edition that I subsequently corrected. As noted, many users of *Economic Analysis* indicated areas of improvement, particularly the addition of many more applications.

Regretfully, I alone am responsible for errors.

February 1974   S.C.M.

Contents

ix

Diminishing *MRS*. The Budget Line: *Limited Money Income. Shifting the Budget Line.* Consumer Equilibrium: *Maximizing Satisfaction Subject to a Limited Money Income. Marginal Utility Interpretation of Equilibrium. Corner Solutions.* Analyses and Applications: *Price Search and the Wage Rate. Application: The Economics of Philanthropy.*

Competitive Aspects of Monopolistic Competition. Comparisons of Long-Run Equilibria: *Equilibrium in the Firm. Long-Run Equilibria in Industries and Product Groups. Conclusion.* Oligopoly. Oligopoly and Price Rigidity: Theory and Evidence: *Kinked Demand Curve. Sticky Oligopoly Price: Some Empirical Investigations.* Some "Market" Solutions to the Oligopoly Problem: *Cartels and Profit Maximization. Cartels and Market Sharing. Short and Turbulent Life of Cartels. Price Leadership in Oligopoly.* Competition in Oligopoly Markets. Welfare Effects of Oligopoly. Barriers to Competition. Oligopoly and Economic Analysis. Economic Analysis: Oligopoly, Competition, and Pollution.

chapter 1

Scope and Methodology of Economics

1.1 SCOPE OF ECONOMICS

Over the past hundred years or more, economics has become a well-defined member of the social sciences. While several disciplines are concerned with social action dominated by a means-end relation, the particular relation unique to economics can be stated with some precision. As most *Principles* texts avow, economics is a study of the proper method of allocating scarce physical and human means (resources) among competing ends—an allocation that achieves some stipulated *optimizing* or *maximizing* objective. The area of study is circumscribed by the stipulation that the means consist of human, natural, and manmade resources and that the ends be economic goods or economic objectives.

1.1.a—Ends and Goals

It is helpful to distinguish ends and goals. The combined process of production and exchange is one in which a collection of resources distributed among individuals is transformed into a collection of goods, which are distributed among those responsible for production. The two distributions are, of course, not necessarily the same. Let us define economic goods themselves as "ends." Then the word "goal" may be used to describe the fundamental motivations of the various economic agents. For example, economists frequently assume that consumers attempt to maximize satisfaction and that entrepreneurs attempt to maximize profit. So defined, the goals of economic agents provide the economist with a frame of reference that permits systematic analysis of individual economic behavior. In general, every economic agent competes with every other agent in the sense that each tries to obtain "as much" as possible.

1

and total possibilities are limited by the resource base. But in a broader view, it is the mutual cooperation of agents with conflicting goals that is ultimately responsible for the production of economic goods and services.

When the principles of microeconomic behavior have been discovered, our attention can be focused on a macroeconomic problem that has beset economics since its inception as a science. Indeed, one might say it was the attempt to resolve this problem that caused economics to become a science. The problem may be stated as a question: Will the independent maximizing behavior of each economic agent eventually result in a social organization that, in a *normative* sense, maximizes the well-being of society as a whole? Adam Smith suggested an answer to this when he presented his doctrine of the "invisible hand." According to Smith, each individual, bent on pursuing his own best interest, is inevitably led, as if by an unseen hand, to pursue a course of action that benefits society as a whole. This is a happy and optimistic doctrine. It has, however, been increasingly questioned as the social and industrial milieu has undergone great change. If all economic agents are atomistic in size relative to the total economic society, either Smith's "invisible hand" or an IBM machine will seek out an optimal organization of economic activity. But if all agents are not atomistic, one must ask if this optimum will be reached. Or will the very large agents "play" an economic game in which they achieve gains at the expense of counterbalancing losses on the part of smaller units? The answers to these questions are not at all clear. But they are very important, both from the standpoint of theory and from that of policy. Some tentative answers are suggested in the concluding chapter of this book.

1.1.b—Norms and Policy

The discussion of ends and goals, especially in the last paragraph above, leads to a further discussion of *welfare norms* and economic policy (*positive* economics). Economists, in their role as economists, cannot establish normative objectives for a society. For example, an economist cannot say that free public education is desirable or that some minimum level of income should be received by each family unit. Of course, as a citizen he can vote for school bond issues and for legislators who favor income redistribution; but an economist *as an economist* cannot determine social goals.

The business of an economist is a positive, not a normative, one. That is, given a social objective, the economist can analyze the problem and suggest the most efficient means by which to attain the desired end. This book is accordingly devoted to the positive aspects of economic analysis, not to the normative decisions that a society must make.

1.1.c—Relation of Economics to Other Social Disciplines[1]

Broadly conceived, social science is the study of the totality of man's social behavior. However, this totality is so extensive in scope that no individual can confidently hope to gain knowledge of every aspect of social behavior. As Adam Smith long ago pointed out, the division of labor tends to augment total physical production; similarly, the division of academic labor tends to enhance our total understanding of man's social action. But the division of a social totality into compartments is not so easily accomplished as the division of jobs along an assembly line; nor do the division lines tend to stay put once they are drawn. The various areas of study are interrelated, and it is only by somewhat arbitrary decisions that the subject matter of social science is divided among the various specialties.

In this light, J. J. Spengler says that "since the several segments of social studies are mutually interrelated, a specialist's mastery of the behavior-forms allotted to his social science is governed by his understanding of related behavior-forms treated by other social sciences."[2] Yet this understanding is, to some extent, made more difficult by the very process of specialization itself. In the first place, "important modes of collective behavior have escaped significant analysis because no unseen hand has been present to coordinate the activities of diverse specialists and insure analysis of *all* significant forms of interpersonal behavior." Second, "developments within fields of specialization frequently have weakened and sometimes have nearly destroyed interfield communication. The comparatively homogeneous tongue of what passed for social science in the past seemingly has given place to a Babel of symbol-ridden jargons."[3]

Accordingly, to promote a wider general understanding of social behavior, there is need for interdisciplinary cooperation in the study of certain problems that transcend any one special field and, furthermore, for the development of a comparatively uniform language base. Through foundation grants and certain university-sponsored interdisciplinary projects, some advances have been made in the direction of greater cooperation among specialists. This, in turn, has been facilitated by the recent introduction of a new language that permits specialists to communicate with one another with precision and clarity. Specifically, the utilization of mathematics, its language and its logic, has stimulated, perhaps more than ever before, interdisciplinary understanding and cooperation.[4]

---

[1] For a thorough discussion, see J. J. Spengler, "Generalists versus Specialists in Social Science: An Economist's View," *American Political Science Review*, Vol. XLIV (1950), pp. 358–79.

[2] Ibid., p. 359.

[3] Ibid., p. 360.

[4] As examples, see Paul Lazerfeld (ed.), *Mathematical Thinking in the Social*

1.2 METHODOLOGY

A person observing the real world of economic phenomena is confronted with a mass of data that is, at least superficially, meaningless. To discover order in this morass of facts and to arrange them in a meaningful way, it is necessary to develop theories to explain various aspects of human behavior, and thus to explain the otherwise meaningless data. By abstracting from the real world, it is possible to achieve a level of simplicity at which human action may be analyzed. But in the process of abstraction, the analyst must be careful to preserve the essential features of the real world problem with which he is concerned. That is to say, simplification is necessary; but at the same time a theory must capture the essence of the fundamental economic problem it is designed to solve.

1.2.a—Model Analysis

Since this text is entirely concerned with economic models and their use in analyzing real world economic problems, it is important to give attention to the use of model analysis in general before undertaking a study of specific economic models. It is convenient to do this schematically with the aid of the diagram in Figure 1.2.1.[5]

The real world usually serves, at least tentatively, as the starting point. A particular problem, or merely a desire to understand, motivates one to move from the complicated world of reality into the domain of logical simplicity. By means of theoretical abstraction, one reduces the complexities of the real world to manageable proportions. The result is a logical model presumably suited to explain the phenomena observed. By logical argument (i.e., deduction) one then arrives at logical or model conclusions. However, these must be transformed, by means of theoretical interpretation, into conclusions about the real world.

Let us summarize to this point. The economist, having begun with a portion of the real world, proceeds, through the use of completely theoretical means, to arrive at conclusions about the real world. His first step entails abstraction from the real world into a simplified logical model. His second step requires the use of logical argument to arrive at an abstract conclusion. His final step consists of a return to the real world by means of an interpretation that yields conclusions in terms of the concrete, sensible world of physical reality.

Another approach provides a different method of achieving the same goal. Let us call it the "statistical method" to distinguish it from the

---

Sciences (Glencoe: Free Press, 1954); and Herbert Simon, *Mathematical Models of Man* (New York: John Wiley & Sons, Inc., 1957).

[5] Adapted from a diagram appearing in C. H. Coombs, Howard Raiffa, and R. M. Thrall (eds.), "Mathematical Models and Measurement Theory," *Decision Processes* (New York: John Wiley & Sons, Inc., 1954), p. 22.

FIGURE 1.2.1
Model Analysis

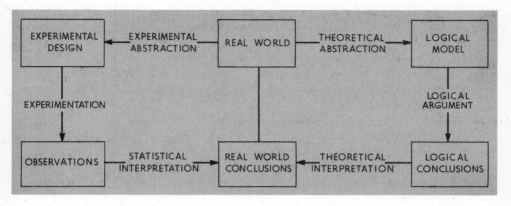

"deductive method" previously discussed. Again starting from the real world, we may, by means of experimental abstraction, arrive at an experimental design. That is, we may, by a process of simplification, design a statistical model that is useful in analyzing the real world. In this instance, however, we obtain observations by experimentation, rather than theorems by logical deduction. These observations, given proper statistical interpretation, yield conclusions concerning the real world.

Although there is some disagreement over the relative merit of the two methods, the tenor of present thinking is that they are complementary. That is to say, deductive and statistical methods are mutually reinforcing, rather than completely alternative, instruments of analysis. However, since professional opinion regarding methodology is not uniform, we mention briefly three positions commonly held.[6]

One group embraces theorists who feel that *only* the right-hand portion of our diagram is applicable. This group, prominent since the time of John Stuart Mill, presumably believes that economic theory is not amenable to verification or refutation on purely empirical grounds. Instead, they think that "economic science is a system of a priori truths, a product of pure reason . . . , a system of pure deduction from a series of postulates. . . ."[7]

One of the clearest explanations of the position held by these writers is found in Ludwig von Mises' definition of a praxeologist, or what Fritz Machlup calls an extreme apriorist. According to Mises, a praxeologist is

---

[6] For a complete discussion of the material in the remainder of this section see Fritz Machlup, "The Problem of Verification in Economics," *Southern Economic Journal*, Vol. XXII (1955), pp. 1–21.

[7] Machlup, *Journal*, p. 5.

one who believes (*a*) that the fundamental premises and axioms of economics are absolutely true; (*b*) that the theorems and conclusions deduced from these axioms by the laws of logic are, therefore, absolutely true; (*c*) that, consequently, there is no need for empirical testing of either the axioms or the theorems; and (*d*) that the deduced theorems could not be tested, even if it were desirable to do so. Thus the extreme apriorist relies upon introspection and logic to develop the whole body of economic principles.

At the opposite extreme is a group whose members Machlup calls ultraempiricists. Fundamentally, these economists "refuse to recognize the legitimacy of employing at any level of analysis propositions not independently verifiable."[8] Instead of beginning with a system of axioms, the ultraempiricists presumably prefer to start with a body of what they call facts. Starting with facts of course entails sacrificing the very simplicity that is sought. One's approach immediately involves all the complexities of the real world; and he is deprived of the use of the single tool—model analysis—that enables him to escape the morass of meaningless facts and to reach conclusions of some generality.

The final methodological position is labeled "logical positivism." It finds wide acceptance among modern economists. The positive economists agree that the basic axioms or assumptions of theory are not subject to independent empirical verification. At the same time, they consider it both possible and desirable to test the deduced hypotheses, and thereby to test indirectly the system of axioms underlying economic theory.

In sum, the apriorists believe that no aspect of economic theory is susceptible of empirical test, whereas the empiricists think that every facet of theory can and must be proved empirically at each step in a chain of analysis. The positive economists take a middle position. They assert that the conclusions (or theorems) of a model should be tested. If these conclusions are found to be in sufficiently close correspondence with reality, the basic assumptions underlying the model are deemed acceptable. Accordingly, positive economics puts primary emphasis upon the predictive powers of a model: if the predictions derived from one model prove "better" than the corresponding predictions drawn from another model, the former is tentatively selected as preferable. If subsequently a theory is advanced that explains more of the relevant facts or, in a probabilistic sense, conforms more closely to reality, this new theory is deemed superior to the one previously accepted. In every case the test is a pragmatic one: that theory is preferred that best explains the observable phenomena of economic life.

---

[8] Ibid, p. 7.

1.3 EQUILIBRIUM AND COMPARATIVE STATICS

Methodologically, we side with the logical positivists. Theory comes first, and then an empirical or statistical investigation to determine whether the results of that theory correspond to the real world. In this course, however, we are concerned primarily with economic theory and economic analysis—the right-hand side of Figure 1.2.1.

To reemphasize, this course is concerned first with developing well-established microeconomic theories and second with analyzing real world problems by means of these theories and empirical data. To elucidate more, and perhaps to give some warning to the student, we quote what Donald Dewey said of one of his own books, but which applies equally well to this one: "this book employs the method of austere, sustained, and, I regret, largely humorless abstraction that has served economics so well in the past. Given the excruciating complexity of so many of the problems . . . , I cannot see that any other method will allow us to cut through to first principles and deal with these problems according to their importance. Either we simplify drastically . . . , or we wander forever in the wilderness. . . ."[9]

1.3.a—Equilibrium

Most of economic theory can conveniently be divided into "equilibrium statics," "comparative statics," and "equilibrium dynamics." This text concerns only the first two, which contain by far the larger part of economic theory. The word "statics" denotes that our attention is focused on one moment in time and, in particular, that we do not allow time to enter our analysis in such a way as to affect the results. Thus we cannot analyze speculation in commodity markets, nor can we decide when to cut a tree or to stop maturing wine; but we can analyze a very wide variety of economic problems.

"Equilibrium" means balance; more specific to our needs, it means *balancing of forces*. This is something that it will be well to remember, because throughout the rest of the book we determine equilibrium by balancing opposing forces. For example, in the theory of consumer behavior we balance what a consumer would *like* to do with what he is *able* to do with his limited money income. In the theory of the firm, we balance the demand for a producer's output with the technical and market forces that determine supply.

These examples could be multiplied many times over. In the remainder of this chapter we explain the meaning of equilibrium and comparative

---

[9] Donald J. Dewey, *Modern Capital Theory* (New York: Columbia University Press, 1965), p. vii.

statics by means of the simplest and most important model in economic theory—the model of demand and supply. This model is analyzed in detail in Chapter 2; and most of the rest of the book is concerned with the determinants of demand and supply. At present, but not subsequently, we assume that the student has a rudimentary familiarity with the demand-supply model. For those not familiar with elementary demand and supply models it would be best to go immediately to Chapter 2 and then return to the rest of this chapter.

Consider Figure 1.3.1. The negatively sloped *DD'* curve shows, let us

FIGURE 1.3.1

Demand and Supply

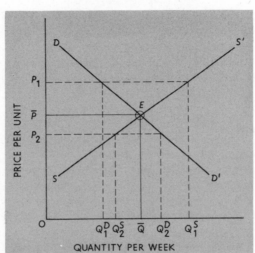

say, the weekly demand for apples in a certain city. The positively sloped *SS'* curve shows the supply. The negative and positive slopes simply indicate that the lower the price buyers are willing to take more and sellers to offer less. Our object is to prove that point *E* (with price $O\bar{P}$ and quantity $O\bar{Q}$) is the market equilibrium, the point where the two opposing forces are in balance. To get the proof, we show that at any price other than $O\bar{P}$, there will be forces that push the price in the direction of $O\bar{P}$.

First, suppose price is *anywhere* above $O\bar{P}$, say OP_1. At this price grocers wish to sell OQ_1^S apples per week. They place their orders and stock their shelves accordingly. But at the price OP_1, buyers are only willing to purchase OQ_1^D apples per week. As a result, sellers accumulate costly and unwanted inventories of apples. The grocers have a clear incentive to reduce the price of apples so as to get rid of their undesired inventories.

Further, this is not only true of the price OP_1 but of *any* price above $O\bar{P}$. At any price above $O\bar{P}$, the quantity sellers wish to offer exceeds the quantity buyers are willing to purchase. Thus at any point above $O\bar{P}$, price must be reduced in the direction of $O\bar{P}$ to clear out undesired accumulations of stock.

Let us now look at the other side. When price is "too low," buyers take the initiative. Suppose price is anywhere below $O\bar{P}$, say OP_2. Buyers wish to purchase $OQ_2{}^D$ apples per week; but at this price grocers are only willing to supply $OQ_2{}^S$ per week. All who wish to buy apples at the price OP_2 cannot do so. Some of the dissatisfied buyers therefore bid slightly more for apples in the hope of getting them away from others. In part they are successful because some people are only willing to buy apples at the price OP_2 or less. But others are willing to pay more than OP_2; and until the price is bid up to $O\bar{P}$, there will be dissatisfied buyers in the market who will offer more for apples.

Here we have two opposing forces: buyers who are willing to purchase larger quantities at lower prices, and sellers who are only willing to offer larger quantities at higher prices. The two forces are in balance at E, the point of equilibrium.

The above account may seem to be somewhat unrealistic in that consumers seldom make price bids (except in the stock market). Prices are set by sellers and are not changed *immediately* to establish an equilibrium. However, sellers are sensitive to sales and will not hesitate to raise price in order to ration existing quantities. If they do not, a second market—called a black market—will develop; and in this market, consumers truly make price bids.

1.3.b—Comparative Statics

When our equilibrium position is determined, as in Figure 1.3.1, we can say that the price of apples will be $O\bar{P}$ and that $O\bar{Q}$ apples will be sold per week. This analysis is based upon the *given* demand and supply curves. But demand and/or supply can change; and we should like to be able to say what will happen to equilibrium price and quantity. This is the object of comparative statics.

Briefly, comparative statics involves the comparison of two static equilibria for the purpose of determining what happens to the variables when there is a shift from one equilibrium to another. Now consider Figure 1.3.2. D_1D_1' and SS' are again the demand and supply of apples per week in a certain city. Our equilibrium analysis shows us that market price is OP_1 and quantity demanded and supplied is OQ_1.

The demand for apples depends upon several things, especially taste,

FIGURE 1.3.2

Comparative Statics

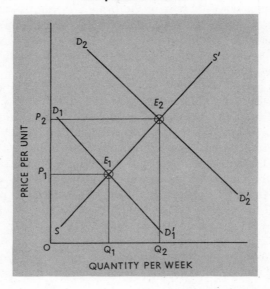

money income, and the prices of related commodities such as oranges. Let us suppose there is a severe freeze in Florida that kills a large portion of the orange crop. As a result the *rationing price*[10] of oranges goes up, and the demand for apples increases from D_1D_1' to D_2D_2'. Our equilibrium moves from E_1 to E_2; price rises from OP_1 to OP_2, and quantity increases from OQ_1 to OQ_2.

This is the method of comparative statics. We postulate a basic change in one of the functional relations in the model and then inquire how this affects the equilibrium values of the variables. From this example we can say that an increase in demand, supply remaining constant, will cause an increase in both equilibrium price and quantity.

1.4 EQUILIBRIUM: PARTIAL AND GENERAL

As we have seen, our study of microeconomic theory is to be the analysis of equilibrium and the comparative static analysis of changes between equilibria. But even then there are two fundamental approaches to static and comparative static analysis—called the "general equilibrium method" and the "partial equilibrium method." Curiously enough, both methods had their basic development at about the same time, in the late 19th century.

---

[10] If this term is not obvious, it is explained in Chapter 2.

There is no doubt that all facets of an economy are interrelated. If pressed far enough, the price of beef depends not only on the price of pork but upon the prices of buttons, color television sets, and tickets to the Masters golf tournament. The wages of unskilled labor depend not only on the wages of semiskilled labor but on the charges of neurosurgeons as well. Everything is related to everything else; and a *complete* treatment of economic theory must take this into account. This was the approach of Leon Walras in his pathbreaking *Elements of Pure Economics*. He analyzed—mathematically, to be sure—the *general equilibrium* of the entire economic system when all interdependencies are recognized.

The resulting system of equations, theorems, and proofs—and it should be emphasized that general equilibrium theory is *essentially* mathematical —is a delight to mathematicians and mathematical economists alike. Indeed, the work of John von Neumann and others on general equilibrium theory has contributed significantly to the development of pure mathematics.

But if the equilibrium system of general equilibrium economics is beautiful, the comparative static system is indescribably messy. Except for very restrictive and specialized cases, one simply cannot say what will happen when there is some change in the economy. Yet surely economists and intelligent laymen must be able to do so. What will happen if minimum prices are set for agricultural products or labor? when an excise tax is imposed on beer, color television sets, and perfume? when there is a freeze in Florida?

There are thousands of questions of this type that are important both to individuals and to governments; and they can be given answers that are *approximately* correct. To get these comparative static answers we must sacrifice the beauty of general equilibrium models for the practicality of partial equilibrium models.

The development of partial equilibrium theory is the most significant contribution Alfred Marshall made in his *Principles of Economics*. Everything depends upon everything else; but most things depend in an essential way upon only a *few other things*. Basically, Marshall suggested that we ignore the general interdependence of everything and concentrate only upon the *close interdependence* of a few variables.

The demand for beef obviously depends upon the prices of other meats and fowl. On the other hand, as a first approximation we can ignore the price of automobiles, airplane fares, and so forth. According to Marshall and his many followers, we can temporarily hold *other things constant*—impound them in a *ceteris paribus* assumption, in the jargon of economics—and concentrate our attention on a few closely related variables.

Thus in the previous section we were able to say that when the supply of oranges decreased and the price of oranges increased, the demand for apples and the price and quantity of apples sold increased. We could not have done this—and certainly we could not have done it graphically—if we had to consider the remote and tedious relations that run through thousands of markets.

In this text we adopt the approach of Marshall. We assume that *most*, but not *all*, of the economic interrelations can be ignored. We analyze our problems and realize that our answers are first approximations. But now return to Figure 1.2.1. We build our model on the basis of real world conditions, and then we go through purely logical analysis. Before we make any definite statements or predictions about the real world, we must go through the "interpretation" stage. Here it is necessary to realize that we have held many "other things" constant. Thus we must conclude that a decrease in the supply of oranges will *tend* to cause an increase in the price of apples. If our partial equilibrium theory is sound, as it is in the oranges-apples example, our answers—even though first approximations—will be qualitatively correct. This is about all one can demand of economic theory. Quantitative results are up to the econometricians; that is, those interested in testing economic theories. This text consists mostly of the theory, but the testing aspect will not be ignored.

1.5 ANALYTICAL EXERCISE

Consider Figure 1.5.1. First, begin at point 1, then explain the basic changes in the functional relations that give rise to the points labeled

FIGURE 1.5.1

Shifts in Demand and Supply

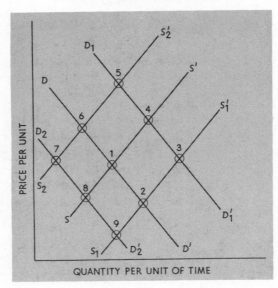

QUANTITY PER UNIT OF TIME

2–9. Second, explain the comparative static shifts in price and quantity that take place in each of the eight cases. In the graph, DD' and SS' are the initial demand and supply curves. D_1D_1' and S_1S_1' indicate increases in demand and supply respectively, while D_2D_2' and S_2S_2' reflect decreases.

1.6 CONCLUSION

Do not worry if some sections of this chapter are a bit unclear. Complete understanding of methodology requires some knowledge of economic theory. After working through the remainder of the text, reread those sections that were at first quite difficult to interpret. We believe that they will be far less hazy at that time.

For now, remember that we will deal primarily with abstract economic theory and with applications of that theory to the solution of complex real-world problems. While we are not interested in the exposition of statistical techniques we will show from time to time how economists have attempted to measure certain economic variables. We will show how economists have used theories as simple as those to be presented here to solve interesting, sophisticated, and highly relevant business and social problems. For example, what will be the effect of a guaranteed minimum income? Did the ban on television advertising by cigarette manufacturers cut down cigarette smoking? One economist has presented some evidence that the ban has caused smoking to increase. Are we doomed to an ever increasing level of population until we smother in a mass of humanity? The economic theory of fertility predicts quite the contrary. What can be done about slum deterioration? How much crime does society want? How much air and water pollution? The answer is not zero in either case. Why is the heroin trade seemingly inefficient? Why do the young compose the major portion of unemployed labor in the United States? We will discuss these and many other economic topics throughout the text. Most of the applications of theory have been taken from articles appearing quite recently in economic journals. We want you to be familiar with what is being done *now* in economics. We usually present the analysis of these economists without criticism or comment. This is not to say that we agree with all of it. We simply want you to see what is now being written. You will gain a great deal by reading and criticizing the entire article in cases in which the applications interest you.

We should stress though that the purely theoretical sections make up a large part of the text and form a self-contained unit. Very little new theoretical material is introduced in the applications. These applications are designed to show how theory can be used—and just possibly to enhance your appreciation of theory.

1.7 STATISTICAL APPENDIX

Many times in this book we will present applications of the theories developed or empirical examples of these applications. The examples and applications are designed to strengthen the student's understanding of the theoretical concepts and to give some feeling and insight into the way in which economists use their theories to make statements about real world economic problems. When we present empirical evidence, we frequently use certain elementary statistical terms in the explanation. This brief appendix defines these terms (very non-rigorously) and explains how the terms are generally used. As such, the section is designed only for those students who have had no statistics courses that covered simple and multiple regression. Others will wish to skim or even omit the appendix.

1.7.a—Regression

The most frequently used statistical tool in economics is regression analysis. Regression is a statistical procedure that economists use to examine the relations among variables. Simple regression concerns the relation between two variables, while multiple regression is used to analyze more than two variables.

Let us begin the discussion of regression with an example. Suppose that a statistician observed over time the following relations between price in a particular market and per capita income:

Price	*Income*
$4	$5,000
7	5,800
6	5,400
9	6,200
8	6,400

Next let us plot each price-income point on a graph as in Figure 1.7.1. We can see from the graph that the relation between price and income is generally upward sloping; that is, in general, higher incomes are associated with higher prices, but not always.

Suppose we wished to approximate the relation with a straight line. The dotted line in 1.7.1 seems to "fit" the points rather well. But many other straight lines may also fit the observations. Which line gives the best fit? Statisticians use the straight line that minimizes the sum of the squared vertical distances of each dot from the line. They call this line the simple regression line. There is a relatively simple mathematical formula for finding the equation for such a line, but we will leave the mathematics to statistics classes. The variable on the horizontal axis is called the *independent* variable; the one on the vertical axis is the *dependent* variable. In our example we analysed the regression of the dependent variable, price, upon the independent variable, income. Obviously we

FIGURE 1.7.1

Fitting a Regression Line

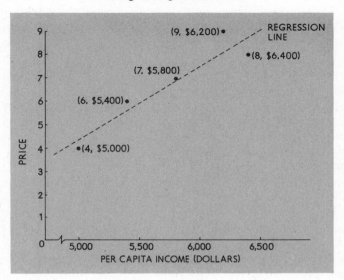

could have drawn a line that connected each point but this line would lose all simplicity.[11]

The regression line is usually expressed mathematically in the form

$$Y = a + bX,$$

where X is the independent variable and Y is the dependent. This, of course, is the equation for a straight line. The slope of the line is "b"; a one-unit change in X leads to a change in Y of "b" units. Certainly "b" can be either positive or negative. When X is equal to zero, Y equals "a"; thus, "a" is the "Y intercept," or the point at which the regression line intersects the vertical axis.

1.7.b—Tests of Significance

Let us assume that we take a sample of households from society to obtain the income and the yearly quantity of wine consumed. We regress quantity on income and obtain a simple regression equation of the above form. For example, we obtain

$$W = 20 + 3I,$$

where W is quarts of wine consumed and I is income in thousands of dollars. This equation says that wine consumption rises by three quarts

---

[11] Statisticians do, at times, attempt to find curved lines that fit the data, but we will ignore these for now.

for every increase of $1,000 in income. Is this a reliable method of prediction for society as a whole? Recall that the equation was obtained from a sample. The observed variation of W with I could be due to other influences. For society as a whole, there may be no relation between W and I, and the relation in the sample would be obtained because of random influences.

Statisticians test the regression equations by determining whether the value for "b," in this case 3, is "too close" or "too far away" from zero. If there was no relation between wine and income, the true value of "b" would be zero, and 3 would have been obtained by chance.

Let us see what we mean by "too far" and "too close" by means of an example. Suppose that a friend tells you that he believes from his observations that his student body of 10,000 consists of 5,000 males and 5,000 females. You do not believe him, so you wish to test this assertion by walking through the campus and counting males and females. You set up a hypothesis that the student body is split fifty-fifty between males and females. Statisticians call this the *null* hypothesis. On the basis of your count you will accept or reject the hypothesis.

On your stroll through the campus you see 200 students, of whom three are females. Do you accept the null hypothesis that the entire student body is split fifty-fifty? On the basis of this sample, probably you would not. The 197 to 3 split is so far from the fifty-fifty split hypothesized, that you would reject the hypothesis. Since you reject the *null* hypothesis you accept the *alternative* hypothesis that the student body is *not* evenly divided between males and females. Of course, you could be making a mistake in the rejection. Certain unusual circumstances, such as a massive women's rally at the time of your stroll could have caused such an uneven division, even though the null hypothesis was in fact correct. On the other hand, if you counted 105 males and 95 females on your stroll, you would probably say that the division was close enough to half-and-half to accept the null hypothesis and reject the alternative. Of course, you could again be making an error because of circumstances.

Returning to our regression equation, there is a technical method in statistics to determine whether "b," the estimate of the regression coefficient, is too far away from zero to accept that the true relation is zero. In this case we say that the regression equation is statistically significant; that is, that the value of b is significantly different from zero. Or if "b" is close to zero, we would say that "b" is not statistically significant. The boundary of acceptance or rejection of the null hypothesis that $b = 0$ is set with the use of a complicated formula. One usually hears that something is significant at the 5 percent, or 1 percent, or 10 percent level of significance. The percentage figure simply means that the boundaries of acceptance are set so that the probability of *rejecting* the null hypothesis that $b = 0$, when in fact the true value of b is zero and there is no true relation between the variables, is 5 percent, or 1 percent, or 10 percent. Thus, if we say that wine and income in our example are significantly related at the 5 percent level of significance, we mean that 3 is far enough from zero, when the boundaries of rejection are set, so that the probability is 5 percent of rejecting that the true $b = 0$, when in fact that is the case. We say that the relation is significant, but we might have made a mistake.

Note that statistical significance does not mean that we cannot ignore the relation in economics. For example, price and income might be significantly related, but we may choose to ignore the relation when drawing up a demand function. Significance does not mean economic significance. A statistician knows that significance only means that the independent variable has a statistically discernable association with the dependent variable, but this association may not imply an important economic relation.

1.7.c—Correlation

The *degree* of relation between two variables is called the simple correlation coefficient, usually called *r*. The more closely the observation points are clustered around the regression line, the higher is the correlation between the dependent and independent variables. For example, in Figure 1.7.2, panel *a*, the observations all lie very close to the regression line. Since the deviations from the line are small, the correlation between X and Y is high. If, at the extreme, all of the observations were on the line, the correlation would be either 1, if the regression line was upward sloping, or -1, if it was downward sloping. In panel *b* the observations are scattered broadly about the line. The correlation between X and Y in this case is close to zero. Therefore, the coefficient of correlation lies

FIGURE 1.7.2

High and Low Correlation

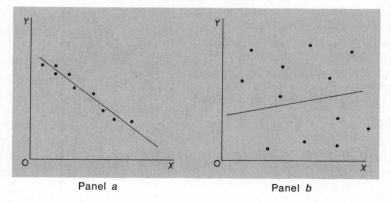

Panel *a*   Panel *b*

between zero and 1 (for a positively sloped regression line) or zero and -1 (for negative slopes). Statisticians can test whether the coefficient of correlation is statistically significant just as they do the regression coefficient.

One word of warning may be in order. High correlation between two variables or a statistically significant regression coefficient *does not* necessarily mean that variations in the independent variable *cause* variation in the dependent. Variations in the two may be caused by something else. For example, high correlation has been noted between the number of storks spotted in European villages and the number of births in the villages. But, numerous births and numerous storks are caused by something else—large population. In larger villages there were more chimneys for storks to nest on and also more children born.

1.7.d—Multiple Regression

Thus far we have dealt with simple regression and correlation involving only two variables. Frequently we regress two or more independent variables with one dependent variable. Again, we are interested in deriving the equation for the line that gives the best fit. In terms of the example used above, we may assume that wine consumption depends not only upon income but also upon the price of wine and the price of beer. The regression equation would be

$$W = a + b_1 I + b_2 P_W + b_3 P_B,$$

where P_W and P_B are the prices of wine and beer. For a sample of households we could compute "a" (the intercept) and b_1, b_2, and b_3, the three regression coefficients. These coefficients tell us how each of the independent variables affects W. Their statistical significance can be tested similarly to the test used in simple regression. Thus, the effect of all three variables can be analyzed.

As in simple regression, the coefficient of multiple regression measures the degree of variation in the independent variable associated with variation in the dependent variable. In other words, it measures the fit of the regression line. This term can be computed mathematically. If R is the correlation coefficient, R^2 is the coefficient of determination, which measures the proportion of the variation in the dependent variable, explained by variation in the independent variables. R^2 varies between 0 and 1; an R^2 of 1 means that all of the variation in the dependent variables is associated with variation in the independent variables. Obviously, zero shows no association. The significance of R^2 can be easily tested.

This material is about all you will need to understand the empirical examples used in the text. If any slight deviations are necessary, we will pause briefly and introduce them.

chapter
2

Demand and Supply

2.1 INTRODUCTION

In Chapter 1 we mentioned that economics is concerned with the problem of scarcity. Because goods are scarce, they have a price. Therefore, one of the fundamental tasks of economics is to analyze the factors that determine the prices and purchases of commodities. The more important determinants are usually separated into two categories: those affecting the demand for a good and those affecting supply. The purpose of this chapter is to explain what demand and supply are and to show how they determine price and quantity in the market.

Thomas Carlyle, a Scottish historian of some repute, was fond of criticizing economists. It was he who referred to Malthus and Ricardo as the "respectable professors of the Dismal Science," and thereby gave economics a name it has never quite overcome—possibly, as Galbraith said, because it has never quite deserved to. But more to the point, Carlyle said that "it is easy to train an economist; teach a parrot to say Demand and Supply." This is another epigram that has survived because it is humorous and contains a large measure of truth.

In fact, demand and supply are such important tools of analysis that we will devote several complete chapters to investigating the underlying forces behind these two concepts. In this chapter, however, we take many of these underlying forces as given in order to discuss rather generally what demand and supply are and rather specifically how demand and supply determine prices in markets. We first examine demand, supply, and their determinants; we then put the two together to investigate how they determine price. We will use some of these simple concepts in order to analyse some complex real-world problems.

Much of the material in this rather long chapter may be reasonably familiar, particularly to those who have recently taken a course in *Principles*. If so, treat the theoretical material as a review, possibly analyzing

19

the sections of applications, then go on to Chapter 3. If the material is somewhat unfamiliar, a good bit of time may be necessary to absorb it, since the theory and analysis here are quite basic to a thorough understanding of economics.

2.2 INDIVIDUAL AND MARKET DEMAND SCHEDULES

An individual's demand schedule for a specific commodity is the quantity of that commodity he is willing and able to purchase at each price in a list of prices during a particular time period. For example, if someone (or a household) would buy during some time period, say a week, 15 units of a particular item at $6 each, 10 units at $5 each, and 6 units at $4 each, that would be his (or its) demand schedule for that commodity. Of course, we could extend the list of prices to $3 and $2 and determine how many units would be purchased at these prices also. That list is also a demand schedule.

As you would expect, consumers are willing and able to buy more at lower prices. This result follows from the *law of demand.* If you doubt the law of demand, try to think of a specific item you would buy in larger amount if its price were higher. A major reason for the law of demand is that consumers tend to substitute relatively cheaper goods when the price of other goods rises. Since a considerable portion of Chapters 4 and 5 are devoted to analyzing the law of demand and this "substitution effect," we now simply assume that the following is correct: people are willing and able to buy more at lower than at higher prices.

Principles: An individual's demand schedule is a list of prices and of the corresponding quantities that an individual is willing and able to buy in some time period. Consumers generally are willing and able to buy more of an item the lower its price; that is, quantity demanded per time period varies inversely with price.

2.2.a—Aggregating and Graphing Demand Schedules

Suppose a very large group of people gather together to buy their week's supply of some commodity, call it X. Suppose also that an auctioneer in the market has everyone turn in a list indicating the amount of X he is willing and able to purchase that day at each price, $1, $2, $3, $4, $5, $6, and so forth. When the auctioneer adds up the amounts that each person is willing and able to buy at each of the prices, he obtains the figures shown in Table 2.2.1. The Table shows a list of prices and of quantities that consumers demand per period of time at each price in the list. This list of prices and quantities is called a *market demand schedule.* It is the *sum* of the demand schedules of all the individuals in the market.

TABLE 2.2.1

Market Demand Schedule

Quantity Demanded (Units of x)	Price per Unit (Dollars)
2,000	6
3,000	5
4,000	4
5,000	3
5,500	2
6,000	1

Again, since people are willing to buy more at lower prices than at higher prices, quantity demanded and price vary inversely in the market.

Principles: The market demand schedule is the sum of the quantities that all individual consumers in the market demand at each price. In the market, quantity demanded varies inversely with price.

Quite often it is more convenient to work with the graph of a demand schedule, called a *demand curve,* rather than with the schedule itself. Figure 2.2.1 is the graph of the schedule in Table 2.2.1. Each price-quantity combination ($6–2,000, $5–3,000, and so on) is plotted; then the six points are connected by the curve labeled *DD'.* This curve indicates the quantity of X consumers are willing and able to buy per unit of time at *every* price from $6 to $1. Since consumers demand more at lower prices, the curve slopes downward.

Note that when deriving a demand curve from a set of price-quantity data given by a demand schedule, one assumes that price and quantity are infinitely divisible. Price can be *any* number between $6 and $1; quantity demanded can also be any number. This assumption is not too unrealistic when we consider that the quantity is *per unit of time.* In any case the sacrifice in realism is more than counterbalanced by the gain in analytical convenience.

2.2.b—Changes in Demand

When price falls (rises) and consumers purchase more (less) of a good, other things remaining the same, we say that *quantity demanded* increases (decreases). We do not say that *demand* increases or decreases when price changes. Demand increases or decreases only when one or more of the factors held constant in deriving demand change. For example, if consumers' incomes change, causing them to demand more of a good at each price than they did previously, the demand for that good increases. Demand decreases if the change in income causes consumers to demand less than before at each price.

FIGURE 2.2.1
Market Demand Curve

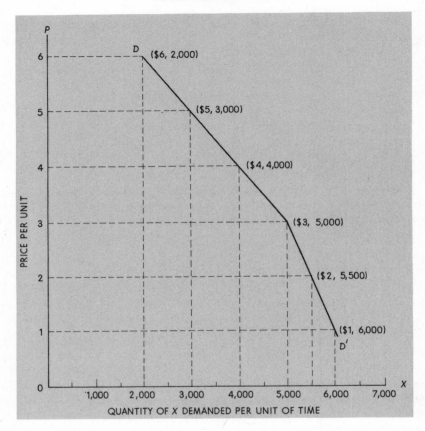

QUANTITY OF X DEMANDED PER UNIT OF TIME

Figure 2.2.2 illustrates changes in demand. The demand curve for X is at first D_0D_0'; at the price Op, consumers buy Ox_0 units per period of time. Tastes change and demand decreases (shifts to the left) to D_1D_1'. Now consumers buy only Ox_1 units per period at the price Op. In fact it is easy to see that at every price consumers buy less X after the shift than before. Now, perhaps something occurs that causes demand to increase (shift to the right) to D_2D_2'. At Op consumers purchase Ox_2 units per period; and at every other relevant price they buy more than before. If, however, demand is D_0D_0' and price falls from Op to Op', other things remaining the same, we say that *quantity demanded* changes from Ox_0 to Ox_0'. These relations may be summarized as follows:

Relations: When price falls (rises), other things remaining the same, quantity demanded rises (falls). When something held constant in deriving

FIGURE 2.2.2

Shifts in Demand

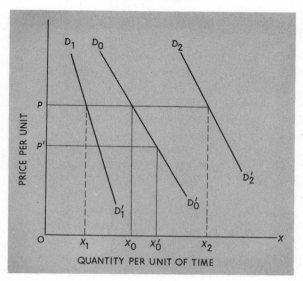

the demand curve changes, demand increases or decreases. An increase in demand indicates consumers are willing and able to buy more at each price in the list. A decrease in demand indicates they are willing and able to buy less at each price. Thus, changes in demand are represented by shifts in the demand curve; changes in quantity demanded are shown by movements along the original demand curve. Do not confuse changes in quantity demanded with increases or decreases in demand.

2.2.c—Factors Influencing Demand

Why is the demand schedule in Table 2.2.1 what it is? That is, why do consumers demand 2,000 units of X rather than 3,000 units at $6 per unit? Or why do they not demand more at every price in the list? Similarly, what would cause the increase in demand from D_0D_0' to D_2D_2' in Figure 2.2.2? Or what would cause consumers to demand less of a good at each price in the list? For answers to these questions let us consider the factors that could, in fact, cause people to be willing and able to purchase more or less at each price.

First, a consumer's income influences his demand. For some commodities at some set of prices an increase in income causes consumers to demand more of these commodities at each price in the relevant range. It may be that steak and imported wines are examples. For other commodities an increase in income causes consumers to demand less at each price. Perhaps hamburger and margarine are examples. Since the effect of income on demand is analyzed in Chapter 4, we do not discuss it here. We need only note that when income changes, demand changes. Therefore, when economists draw up demand schedules, they generally hold mony income constant.

Second, changes in consumers' tastes can change demand. If some influential movie or television stars are photographed wearing a new style of clothing, consumers who wish to emulate would probably be willing to buy more of that clothing style at the prevailing price. Since changes in tastes affect the demand for commodities, economists hold tastes constant when deriving demand.

Third, the prices of *other* goods affect the demand for a given good. More specifically, when the price of a closely related good changes, the demand for the good in question is affected. For example, suppose both beef and pork sell for $1 per pound; now let the price of beef fall to $.50 a pound. Consumers may buy less pork at $1 than they did before the price of beef fell.

Finally, people's expectations affect demand. When people think the price of a good is going to rise, they have an incentive to increase their rates of purchase before price rises. On the other hand, expecting price to fall causes some purchases to be postponed.

Therefore, when economists draw up a demand curve such as that in Figure 2.2.1, they do so under the assumption that *other things remain the same*. The other things are (1) consumers' incomes (and the income distribution among consumers), (2) tastes, (3) the prices of other goods, and (4) expectations. It is not that economists think price is the sole determinant of the quantity of a good consumers demand. They realize many other things affect quantity, but they are interested in *isolating* the effect of price changes.[1]

2.3   ANALYSIS AND APPLICATION—PSYCHOLOGICAL PRICING

Marketing experts frequently cite certain examples from the business world that supposedly violate the law of demand. Evidence of these alleged departures is that some goods have sold better at higher prices than at lower prices. We will first discuss some of these marketing examples then show that the law of demand still holds and even explains these seeming exceptions.

Marketing experts call departures from the law of demand "psychological pricing." One example of a departure from the law of demand,

---

[1] At times economists also examine the effect of changes in one of the "other things"; for example, the effect of income or prices of other goods upon quantity. We will see examples of this in Chapter 4. This is a problem in comparative statics, as discussed in Chapter 1.

recently told to us by a friend in marketing, concerns the way in which a certain brand of nasal spray gained a national market. The spray sold at 69¢ for a four ounce container. It had a small but loyal local market in the area surrounding the city in which it was manufactured. Supposedly the brand in question was equal in quality to national brands selling for about $1.39 for a two ounce container. The manufacturer, wishing to distribute nationwide, hired a marketing consultant team (including the friend who related this tale). An extensive advertising and marketing campaign in several of the surrounding states was undertaken, with practically zero success, while the spray was still selling at 69¢ for four ounces. After a certain period of failure, price was raised to $1.39 for two ounces. The marketing technique remained essentially the same, but sales increased tremendously. At the new higher price consumers seemed to believe that this spray was equivalent to the national brands; at the substantially lower price, apparently they did not. Thus far the expansion campaign has been quite successful.

A description of another case of a firm's "raising price to increase sales" appeared recently in *Business Week*.[2] This example concerns hosiery, an industry composed of many companies of widely differing sizes. The Hanes Corporation, one of the top three manufacturers, found that the influx of private brands, discount operations, supermarket and drugstore sales drastically reduced their product's visability. While Hanes pantyhose were sold only in department stores, other companies were experiencing a significant boom in supermarket sales. However, the influx of private brands, as one would expect, drove the price as low as 39¢ to 49¢ a pair. With so many brands from which to choose, customers were confused about the quality differentials. When Hanes entered this market, they began selling their pantyhose in supermarkets at $1.39. This price was at least 30¢ above most other brands, and much more above the others. Sales picked up substantially at the new higher price. Admittedly the company then keyed its advertising and merchandising methods toward emphasizing higher quality. On the other hand, the higher price fostered the image of higher quality in consumers' minds, and certainly had much to do with the sales success.

These are merely two examples of this phenomenon. The marketing literature abounds with other examples in which a firm raised the price of its products and increased sales. For example, a recently published marketing book gives an example in which an increase in the price of a car wax from 69¢ to $1.69 was followed by a substantial increase in sales. The same book also cites a market experiment in which a particular brand of ink sold better at 25¢ than at 15¢. Other carefully designed market experiments show essentially the same thing: some items sell

[2] *Business Week,* March 25, 1972.

better at a higher than at a lower price (in a certain range) under specified circumstances.[3]

The question is, do these and similar empirical examples mean that the law of demand does not hold under these circumstances? The answer is, "No, these examples imply no such thing." The problem is one of ignorance.[4] Return to the question asked in Section 2.2; is there anything you buy that you would be willing to buy more of if the price rises? Even if your answer is no, you may well judge quality by price when you are uncertain (ignorant) about product quality. This is not irrational behavior; in fact, it is quite easy to explain why this type of behavior (products that sell more at higher than at lower prices) does not violate the law of downsloping demand.

First of all, your time is valuable. Since time is scarce, no one takes the time to become an expert on every item available. While you are shopping around gaining information about products, you could be working or consuming leisure. The time that you spend shopping has value in the sense that you are allocating time (a scarce resource) away from other activities. Thus, economists say that the time spent shopping has an opportunity cost, and the total cost of a good is the price of that good plus the value of the time spent shopping.

Secondly, people note from past experience that frequently, although not always, price and quality are directly related. Thus, price is often used in lieu of research as an indicator of product quality. This would be expected when the monetary saving anticipated from buying the lower rather than the higher priced item is low relative to the cost (in time) of gaining information that might save money. When absolute price variations among products are low relative to income, as would be expected in the case of relatively low priced items, one would expect people to do less systematic research and to judge quality more on prices. The absolute price variation among higher priced goods is greater. Since the absolute difference between the higher and lower priced goods is greater, the cost of judging quality by price has risen relative to the cost of systematic quality research. Thus, as one would expect, consumers do depend more upon research and less upon price as an indicator of quality when purchasing high cost (relative to income) items, such as housing, automobiles, and major household appliances. In other words, as the cost of taking price as an indicator of quality rises, people do it less.

---

[3] For these and other instances, see Chapter 10, "Demand Curve Estimation and Psychological Pricing," in F. C. Sturdivant, et. al., *Managerial Analysis in Marketing* (Glenview, Ill.: Scott, Foresman, and Co., 1970).

[4] Do not equate ignorance with stupidity. Ignorance means lacking knowledge about something. Even the smartest people are ignorant about many, many things, possibly through lack of interest. If I value the use of my time more in some other alternative than in learning about the diet of the ancient Incas, I will remain ignorant in that area. As in all things, overcoming ignorance has a cost.

Furthermore, as the returns to quality research rise, we should expect people to rely more on research and less on price as an indicator of quality. This again would be the case for higher priced goods where the cost of making a purchasing mistake is greater. The penalty for misjudging quality in an automobile is greater than that for misjudging a 25¢ bottle of ink.

Finally, when consumers believe that quality differences among different brand names are great they will tend to buy higher priced brands than when they expect little quality differences. That is, when consumers believe they will gain little quality at higher prices they tend to pay lower prices. Marketing experiments on brands of razor blades, floor wax, cooking sherry, mothballs, salt, aspirin, and beer tend to verify this hypothesis.[5]

Thus, we can easily explain apparent exceptions to the law of demand. If consumers *knew* two goods were exactly alike in every way (including prestige) and chose the higher priced good, it would be an exception. For some goods, the imputed quality is judged by price when the cost of other research on quality is high relative to expected return. These are different goods at different prices in the mind of some consumers and the cases cited are not violations of the law of demand.

2.4 DEMAND ELASTICITY

We have noted without full explanation that quantity demanded varies inversely with price along a demand curve. Frequently economists and businessmen are interested not only in the direction in which quantity varies when price changes but also in the *responsiveness* of quantity demanded to changes in price. The measure of responsiveness along a given demand curve is called the *elasticity of demand*.

2.4.a—Responsiveness of Quantity Demanded to Price

For some products, a small change in price over a certain range of the demand curve results in a significant change in quantity demanded. In this case, quantity demanded is very responsive to changes in price. For other products, or perhaps for the same product over a different range of the demand curve, a relatively large change in price leads to a correspondingly smaller change in quantity demanded. That is, quantity demanded is not particularly responsive to price changes.

Economists classify demand as *elastic* or *inelastic* on the basis of the relative responsiveness of quantity demanded to changes in price. More specifically, demand is said to be elastic if the proportional change in

[5] For a description of these experiments see Sturdivant, et. al., *Managerial Analysis.*

quantity demanded exceeds the proportional change in price, whereas it is inelastic if the proportional change in quantity demanded is less than the proportional change in price. In fact it is possible to give a precise measure to relative responsiveness or elasticity. Before turning to specifics, however, it is instructive to examine the relation between elasticity and the total expenditure on a commodity (that is, the total revenue received by the sellers of the commodity).

2.4.b—Elasticity and Total Expenditure

The total expenditure on a commodity is product price multiplied by the quantity bought. Along a particular demand curve, quantity rises when price falls, and vice versa; thus three things can possibly happen to total expenditure when there is a change in price. First, suppose the price change "outweighs" the quantity change—that is, quantity demanded is not particularly responsive to price. Then total expenditure falls when price falls and rises when price rises. In this case, demand is inelastic.

TABLE 2.4.1

**Relations between Price Elasticity
and Total Expenditure (TE)**

	Elastic Demand	*Unitary Elasticity*	*Inelastic Demand*
Price rises...........	*TE* falls	No change	*TE* rises
Price falls...........	*TE* rises	No change	*TE* falls

If, on the other hand, a price rise leads to a decrease in total expenditure —or a price decline to an increase in total expenditure—demand is elastic. In this case quantity demanded is very responsive to price changes. Demand has *unitary elasticity* if a change in price and the corresponding quantity change cause no change in total expenditure. These relations are summarized in Table 2.4.1.

We should now emphasize that it is not accurate to say that a given demand curve is elastic or inelastic. In almost all cases, demand curves have both an inelastic and an elastic range, along with a point or range of unitary elasticity. We can only speak of demand as being elastic or inelastic over a particular range of price or quantity magnitudes.

2.4.c—Computation of Elasticity

As noted above, the elasticity of demand refers to the relative responsiveness of quantity demanded to changes in price. It is useful at times to have a specific measure of relative responsiveness rather than merely to speak of demand as being elastic or inelastic. For example, we might wish to determine, over a certain range of prices, which of two demand curves is more elastic. For this we need a measuring device. That device is the coefficient of price elasticity (η):

$$\eta = -\%\Delta Q/\%\Delta P = -\frac{\Delta Q/Q}{\Delta P/P} = -\frac{\Delta Q}{\Delta P}\frac{P}{Q},$$

where Δ is "the change in," and P and Q denote price and quantity demanded.

Since price and quantity vary inversely, a minus sign is used in the formula to make the coefficient positive. From the formula we see that the relative responsiveness of quantity demanded to changes in price measures the ratio of the proportional change in quantity demanded relative to that of price. If η is less than one, demand is inelastic; $\%\Delta Q < \%\Delta P$. If η is greater than one, demand is elastic; $\%\Delta Q > \%\Delta P$. If $\eta = 1$, demand has unitary elasticity; $\%\Delta Q = \%\Delta P$.

TABLE 2.4.2
Demand and Elasticity

Price	Quantity Demanded	Total Expenditure	Elasticity
$1.00	100,000	$100,000	ELASTIC
.50	300,000	150,000	UNITARY
.25	600,000	150,000	INELASTIC
.10	1,000,000	100,000	

The process of deriving the coefficient of elasticity between two price-quantity relations involves a simple computation; certain problems, however, are involved in selecting the proper base. As an example, let us consider the demand schedule given in Table 2.4.2. Suppose price falls from $1 to $0.50; quantity demanded rises from 100,000 to 300,000 and $P \times Q$ or TE rises to $150,000. By the analysis of subsection 2.4.b, demand is elastic since total expenditure increases.

Let us now compute η:

$$\eta = -\frac{\Delta Q/Q}{\Delta P/P} = -\frac{(100,000 - 300,000) \div 100,000}{(\$1 - \$0.50) \div \$1} = -\frac{-2}{1/2} = 4.$$

As expected, the coefficient is greater than one. But some caution must be exercised. ΔQ and ΔP are definitely known from Table 2.4.2; but we really do not know whether to use the value $Q = 100,000$ or $Q = 300,000$

and the value $P = \$1$ or $P = \$0.50$. Try the computation with the "other" values of P and Q:

$$\eta = -\frac{(300{,}000 - 100{,}000) \div 300{,}000}{(\$0.50 - \$1) \div \$0.50} = \frac{2}{3}.$$

It actually looks as though demand is inelastic, despite the fact that we know it is elastic from the total expenditure calculation.

The difficulty lies in the fact that elasticity has been computed over a wide arc of the demand curve but evaluated at a specific point. We can get a much better approximation by using the *average* values of P and Q over the arc. That is, for large changes such as this, we should compute η as

$$\eta = -\frac{Q_1 - Q_0}{Q_1 + Q_0} \div \frac{P_1 - P_0}{P_1 + P_0},$$

where subscripts 1 and 0 refer to new and to initial prices and quantities demanded. Using this formula, we obtain

$$\eta = -\frac{(100{,}000 - 300{,}000) \div (100{,}000 + 300{,}000)}{(\$1 - \$0.50) \quad \div \quad (\$1 + \$0.50)} = \frac{3}{2}.$$

Demand is indeed elastic when allowance is made for the very discrete or finite change in price and quantity demanded.

Exercise: Compute η for a change in price from $0.25 to $0.10 and from $0.50 to $0.25.

Summary: Demand is said to be elastic, of unitary elasticity, or inelastic according to the value of η. If $\eta > 1$, demand is elastic; a given percentage change in price results in a greater percentage change in quantity demanded. Thus small price changes result in more significant changes in quantity demanded. When $\eta = 1$ demand has unit elasticity, meaning that the percentage changes in price and quantity demanded are precisely the same. Finally, if $\eta < 1$, demand is inelastic. A given percentage change in price results in a smaller percentage change in quantity demanded.

2.4.d—Graphical Computation of Elasticity

The formulas developed in Section 2.4.c are relevant for arc elasticity, the price elasticity for movements between two discrete points on a demand curve. At times, however, we are interested in elasticity at a specific point or the elasticity for very small changes in price and quantity. Understanding the method of graphical computation of point elasticity permits one to estimate price elasticity by a visual inspection of the demand curve.

In Figure 2.4.1 the line CF is a linear demand curve for commodity X. The problem is to measure price elasticity at point E, where price is Op_1 and quantity demanded is Ox_1. First, let price fall very slightly from

FIGURE 2.4.1

Computation of Point Elasticity

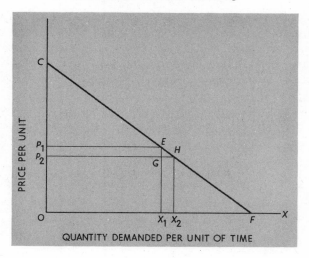

Op_1 to Op_2, so quantity demanded increases from Ox_1 to Ox_2; that is, p_2 and x_2 are very near p_1 and x_1.

Next, consider the formula for point elasticity:

$$\eta = -\Delta Q/Q \div \Delta P/P.$$

From the figure, $\Delta Q = x_1x_2$ and $Q = Ox_1$ at E. Similarly $\Delta P = p_1p_2$ and $P = Op_1$ at E. Thus,

$$\eta = -\frac{x_1x_2/Ox_1}{p_1p_2/Op_1} = \frac{x_1x_2}{p_1p_2} \cdot \frac{Op_1}{Ox_1}.$$

Since $x_1x_2 = GH$ and $p_1p_2 = EG$,

$$\frac{x_1x_2}{p_1p_2} = \frac{GH}{EG}.$$

Furthermore EGH and Ex_1F are similar right triangles inasmuch as each corresponding angle is equal. Thus

$$\frac{GH}{EG} = \frac{x_1F}{Ex_1} = \frac{x_1F}{Op_1},$$

since $Ex_1 = Op_1$. Hence

$$\eta = \frac{GH}{EG} \cdot \frac{Op_1}{Ox_1} = \frac{x_1F}{Op_1} \cdot \frac{Op_1}{Ox_1} = \frac{x_1F}{Ox_1}.$$

But $x_1F/Ox_1 = Op_1/p_1C = EF/EC$. Thus graphically the coefficient of price elasticity at the point E is

$$\eta = \frac{EF}{EC} \cdot$$

Utilizing this formula, it is easy to determine the ranges of demand elasticity for a linear demand curve. First note the following relations in Figure 2.4.1. When $EF = EC$, $EF/EC = 1$; hence, at that point the demand curve has unit elasticity. Second, when $EF > EC$, $EF/EC > 1$ and demand is elastic. Finally, when $EF < EC$, $EF/EC < 1$ and demand is inelastic.

Thus we can locate a point on DD', the linear demand curve in Figure 2.4.2, such that $DP = PD'$; at this point, demand has unitary price elastic-

FIGURE 2.4.2

**Ranges of Demand Elasticity
for Linear Demand Curve**

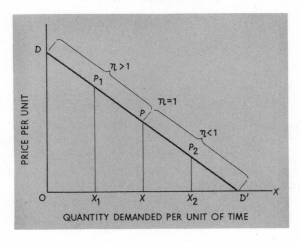

QUANTITY DEMANDED PER UNIT OF TIME

ity, or $\eta = 1$. Next consider *any* point to the left of P, such as P_1. At P_1, $\eta = (P_1D'/DP_1) > 1$. Thus for a linear demand curve the coefficient of price elasticity is greater than unity at any point to the left of the midpoint on the demand curve. Demand is elastic in this region. Finally, at any point to the right of P, say P_2, the coefficient of price elasticity is $\eta = (P_2D'/DP_2) < 1$. Over this range, demand is inelastic.

When demand is not linear, such as DD' in Figure 2.4.3, one can easily approximate point elasticity in the following manner. Suppose we want to compute the elasticity of DD' at point E. First draw the straight line AB tangent to DD' at E. Note that if AB were actually the demand curve, EB/AE would be its elasticity at point E. Note also that for very small movements away from E along DD', the slope of AB is a relatively good estimate of the slope of DD'. Now the elasticity formula may also be written as

$$\eta = \frac{1}{\Delta P / \Delta Q} \cdot \frac{P}{Q} \cdot$$

Since the slopes of DD' and AB (which are tangent at E) are approximately equal in the neighborhood of E, $\Delta P / \Delta Q$ is the same for each curve. Therefore, the elasticity of AB at E is approximately equal to the elasticity of DD' at E. The point elasticity of DD' at E is approximately EB/AE.

FIGURE 2.4.3

Computation of Point Elasticity for Nonlinear Demand Curve

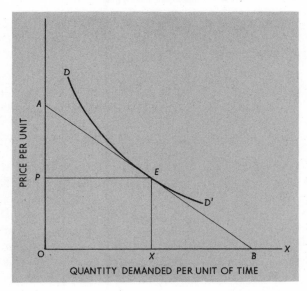

QUANTITY DEMANDED PER UNIT OF TIME

These results may be summarized as follows:

Relation: given any point E on a demand curve, construct the straight line from the vertical to the horizontal axis tangent to the curve at E. Call this line AEB. The coefficient of price elasticity is approximately EB/AE. If the demand curve is linear this measure is precise. Furthermore, for a linear demand curve: (a) demand is elastic at higher prices, (b) has unit elasticity at the midpoint of the demand curve, and (c) is inelastic at lower prices. Thus, in case of linear demand, elasticity declines as one moves downward along the curve.

2.4.e—Factors Affecting Price Elasticity

Whether demand is elastic or inelastic is an important consideration, especially for government policy in individual commodity markets. For example, suppose the demand for wheat is elastic. An increase in the price of wheat would accordingly result in a proportionately greater reduction in quantity demanded. Farmers would thus obtain a smaller total revenue from the sale of wheat. Now suppose the government establishes a minimum wheat price above the market equilibrium price. Wheat sales would be reduced, and so too would farmers' incomes, unless the price support were accompanied by a minimum sales guarantee. On the other hand, if the demand for wheat is inelastic, a minimum price above the equilibrium price would increase farmers' total revenue.

Price elasticities range quite widely. Two basic factors determine elasticity: availability of substitute goods and the number of uses to which a good may be put. These factors go a long way toward explaining variations in elasticities.

The more and better the substitutes for a specific good, the greater its price elasticity will be at a given set of prices. Goods with few and poor substitutes—wheat and salt, for example—will always tend to have low price elasticities. Goods with many substitutes—wool, for which cotton and manmade fibers may be substituted, for instance—will have higher elasticities.

Of course, the definition of a good affects greatly the number of substitutes and thus its elasticity of demand. For example, if all of the gasoline stations in a city raised the price of gasoline five cents a gallon, the total sales would undoubtedly fall off some but in the absence of close substitutes, probably not much. If all of the Gulf stations—but no others—raised price a nickel, the sale of Gulf gasoline would probably fall substantially. There are many good substitutes for Gulf gasoline at the lower price. If one service station alone raised price, its sales in the long run would probably fall almost to zero. Some might continue buying there, perhaps the owner's wife and mother, but the availability of so many easily accessible substitutes would encourage most customers to trade elsewhere, since the cost of finding a substitute service station is so small. Thus, the way in which a good is defined means a great deal.

Similarly, the greater the number of uses a commodity has, the greater its price elasticity will be. Thus a commodity such as wool—which can be used in producing clothing, carpeting, upholstery, draperies, and tapestries, and so on—will tend to have a higher price elasticity than a commodity with only one or a very few uses—butter for example.

2.4.f—Effect of Time upon Elasticity—Some Empirical Evidence

When we consider dynamic effects, the time period during which consumers can adjust greatly affects demand elasticity. For example, consider a department store that lowers its price on a particular item. At first, the change in the rate of sales may be insignificant. Consumers have not yet become informed of the price changes. Later, as information is gained, the rate of sales may increase, until an equilibrium rate is reached. Of course, if competitors match the price change after a period of time, that will damage sales also. Generally, however, when speaking of elasticity, we assume that other prices remain constant.

On the other hand, whether or not consumers regard the price change as permanent or temporary certainly affects the path of quantity adjustment over time. In one empirical study, it was found that consumers responded immediately to a price reduction.[6] During the first week sales increased substantially. The second week sales fell below the average rate prevailing before the price reductions. Then sales slowly increased until they reached the previous average rate of sales. The cumulative effect was positive. The investigators found that consumers, probably considering the price decrease as temporary, did considerable stocking up during the first week. This accumulation of consumers' inventories cut into sales during the following weeks. Later, as prices were reduced on competitive brands, sales leveled off to about the level that prevailed prior to the price change.

Thus, demand was very elastic at first but later became rather inelastic. It was found also that demand was far more inelastic in large chain stores that sold the product than in the smaller independents. The authors explain this by noting that the chain stores were very responsive in reducing the prices of their competing private brands, wherein the independents had no private brands. Of course, in this case we violate our other-things-held-constant assumption, and we cannot speak precisely about demand elasticity. Therefore, these measured demand elasticities do not conform with our theoretical definition of demand. Recall that we hold *other things constant,* including competitive prices, when deriving demand schedules. One would expect, as the evidence shows, that demand is more inelastic if competitive prices are allowed to change also. As we will see later, however, when actually estimating the elasticity of demand for "real" products, it is quite difficult to hold other things constant. In the real world other things have a way of changing.

2.4.g—Other Elasticities

At times, economists are concerned with the relative responsiveness of quantity demanded to changes in either income or the price of some related good. To measure this responsiveness we use the coefficients of income elasticity and cross-elasticity.

As you will recall, when deriving a demand curve for a good X, we held constant such things as income and the prices of related goods. The

---

[6] For details see Roland E. Frank and William F. Mussy, "Market Segmentation and the Effectiveness of a Brand's Price and Dealing Policies," *The Journal of Business,* XXXVIII, April, 1965, pp. 186–200.

price of X determines the *point* on the demand curve the consumer selects; income and the prices of related goods, among other things, determine the *position* of the demand curve; that is, how far from or close to the axes the curve stands.

The responsiveness of quantity demanded to income changes, other things remaining the same (including the price of the commodity in question), is measured by the coefficient of income elasticity (η_M). Specifically, the income elasticity of demand is the ratio of the percentage change in quantity demanded to the percentage change in money income. Symbolically

$$\eta_M = \frac{\Delta Q/Q}{\Delta M/M} = \frac{\Delta Q}{\Delta M} \cdot \frac{M}{Q} \,.$$

Note that we do not put a minus sign in the equation. As we shall show in Chapter 4, quantity demanded can vary either directly or inversely with income; that is, $\Delta Q/\Delta M$ can be either positive or negative. Therefore, η_M can be either positive or negative.

Similarly, it is possible to measure the responsiveness of quantity demanded to changes in the price of some related good. This is called price cross elasticity of demand. Hold everything constant except the price of some related good Y. The cross elasticity is the ratio of the percentage change in quantity demanded to the percentage change in the price of Y. More specifically,

$$\eta_{xy} = \frac{\Delta x/x}{\Delta p_y/p_y} = \frac{\Delta x}{\Delta p_y} \cdot \frac{p_y}{x} \,.$$

As in the case of income elasticity, one can make no general statement about the sign of η_{xy}. At a given price of X, quantity demanded may vary directly with the price of some related good; that is, $\Delta x/\Delta p_y$ is positive. For example, the quantity of Fords demanded at a particular price will increase if the price of Chevrolets rises and will decrease if the price of Chevrolets falls. Goods such as these are sometimes called substitutes; η_{xy} is positive. On the other hand, if the price of gasoline rises and the quantity of Fords demanded decreases at a particular price, η_{xy} would be negative. Fords and gasoline, and similarly related pairs of goods, are sometimes called complements. It should be emphasized that in these examples, *demand* shifts; we are not considering changes in quantity demanded along a stationary demand curve.

2.4.h—Summary

Demand is price inelastic, elastic, or unitary accordingly as $-\%\Delta Q/\%\Delta P$ is less than, greater than, or equal to one. A decrease in price occasions a decrease, an increase, or no change in total expenditure respectively. The elasticity of a good is influenced primarily by the availability of substitute goods and by the number of uses to which a good may be put. Economists also use income elasticity to measure the effect of income changes upon quantity demanded and cross elasticity to measure the effect of changes in the prices of related goods upon quantity demanded of the good in question. We shall subsequently see that these are important concepts in economic analysis.

2.5 APPLICATION—ESTIMATING INCOME ELASTICITY

The federal government has recently become quite interested in private housing. In making their development plans governmental officials were naturally quite interested in the income elasticity of demand for housing. This elasticity has been extremely difficult to estimate. Frank de Leeuw, in a recent study of the income elasticity of the demand for housing, states that past estimates of this income elasticity range from 0.4 to 2.1. He notes that such a wide range of estimates makes it very difficult to draw quantitative conclusions about many housing developments or policies.[7]

One possible source of discrepancy is the difference between normal or permanent income and current income. Current income is simply the income actually received during a particular period of time, say a year. The concept of permanent or normal income and the way in which this affects the demand for housing are harder to isolate.[8] Perhaps an example will best illustrate. Consider a master carpenter earning, on the average, about $15,000 a year. (We ignore any inflationary price changes.) He probably lives in about a $20,000 home. If, because of a series of strikes or a run of very bad weather, his earnings fall to $10,000 in one year, he would cut expenses in some things, but probably would not change houses. He considers $15,000 as his normal income. Neither would he change houses in certain very good years when his income rises above $15,000. On the other hand, a young medical doctor who earns $15,000 a year during his first few years of practice would probably consume much more housing than our carpenter. The doctor knows $15,000 is far below his expected normal income. He believes his earnings will quickly rise to the "normal" level of those in his profession. It appears that a family's normal, or expected normal, income has a greater affect upon the purchase of some items than does the actual income in any one year.

For this reason economists generally believe that the elasticity of demand for housing with respect to normal income is higher than the

---

[7] Frank de Leeuw, "The Demand for Housing: A Review of Cross-Section Evidence," *The Review of Economics and Statistics,* LIII, Feb. 1971, pp. 1–10.

[8] For an exposition see Milton Friedman, *A Theory of the Consumption Function* (New York: National Bureau of Economic Research, 1957.)

elasticity with respect to the income of a single year.[9] However, since there is considerable variation in the estimates of elasticity, even with respect to normal income, economists must have other reasons for arriving at different estimates of income elasticity.

In the article previously cited, de Leeuw suggests several possible sources of variation. First, many studies use market value rather than expense per unit of time (perhaps a year) as a measure of housing demand. There is strong evidence that housing expense per year is a smaller proportion of market value for high-value homes than for low-value homes. Most of the decrease is due to insurance, maintenance, and utility costs. Measuring housing demand by market value, therefore, biases the elasticity upward. Second, according to de Leeuw, most studies do not consider the *nonmonetary* income owner-occupants derive from the rental value of their homes. If the owner did not live in his home, he could rent it at the going rental price. Omitting net rental value (rent less maintenance, taxes, etc.) from total income tends to bias the estimates away from unity; that is, the owner's relevant income is his money income plus the rental value of his home. Third, most studies deal in current dollars. They take no account of the price level of housing or the general price level even though studies have shown vast price differences among regions. The effect of this omission depends on the price elasticity of demand. Finally, the samples may not have been representative.

Taking account of many of these sources of bias, de Leeuw estimates the elasticity of rental expenditure with respect to normal income as between 0.8 and 1.0. There is more uncertainty for owner-occupants; their estimated elasticity lies between 0.7 and 1.5. The evidence supports the hypothesis of an elasticity of owner-occupants slightly above 1.0.

The purpose of this section is not to give you simple estimates of elasticity but to emphasize the problems involved in actually assigning numbers to some of the theoretical concepts we discuss. As you will see in future examples, the empirical work is frequently quite involved.

2.6 SUPPLY SCHEDULE

To get at an understanding of supply, suppose that a large number of farmers sell cabbage in the same market. One particular farmer is willing to grow and sell 1,000 cabbages per season if the price per unit of cabbage is $0.25. If the price of cabbage were $0.35, he would be willing to grow more, say 2,000. The higher price induces the farmer to take land out of cultivation of other crops and put it into the cultivation of the now relatively more lucrative cabbage. A still higher price, $0.50 perhaps, would

---

[9] See de Leeuw, "The Demand for Housing," pp. 1–10. The remainder of this section is based on that article.

be required to induce him to market 3,000 cabbages, and so on. That is, the farmer allocates his time and land so as to make as much money as possible. Higher and higher prices are required to induce him to re-allocate more and more of his time and land to cabbage production.

A portion of the farmer's cabbage supply schedule might, therefore, be as follows:

Price	Quantity Supplied
$0.25	1,000
.35	2,000
.50	3,000
.75	4,000
1.25	5,000

This schedule shows the *minimum price* that induces the farmer to supply each amount in the list. Note that in contrast to demand analysis, price and quantity supplied are directly related. We must postpone the explanation of why price and quantity vary directly until Chapter 8, after we have analyzed cost and production. For the present we assume that the supply schedule shows the minimum price necessary to induce producers voluntarily to offer each possible quantity for sale. We also assume that an increase in price is required to induce an increase in quantity supplied.

2.6.a—Graphing Supply Schedules

First, consider the supply schedule in Table 2.6.1. This table shows the minimum price necessary to induce firms to supply, per unit of time, each

TABLE 2.6.1

Market Supply Schedule

Quantity Supplied (Units of X)	Prices (Dollars)
7,000	6
6,500	5
6,000	4
5,000	3
4,000	2
3,000	1

of the six quantities listed. In order to induce greater quantities, price must rise; or, in other words, if price increases from $4 to $5, firms will increase quantity supplied from 6,000 units to 6,500 units. Remember that we are assuming a large number of noncolluding firms; in case of a single firm supplying the entire market, a different principle applies (as shown in Chapter 9). Figure 2.6.1 shows a graph of the schedule in Table 2.6.1. This supply curve is drawn under the assumption that price and quantity are directly related, so the curve is positively sloped.

2.6.b—Factors Influencing Supply

As in the case of demand, we might ask why the supply schedule in Table 2.6.1 is what it is. Why, for example, does a price of $5 rather than a price of $4 induce a quantity supplied of 6,500? Or why is not a lower quantity supplied at each price in the list? A much more thorough discussion of supply is undertaken in Chapter 8. For now, we will only briefly mention four factors that affect supply. These are the factors generally held constant when drawing a supply curve.

FIGURE 2.6.1

Market Supply Curve

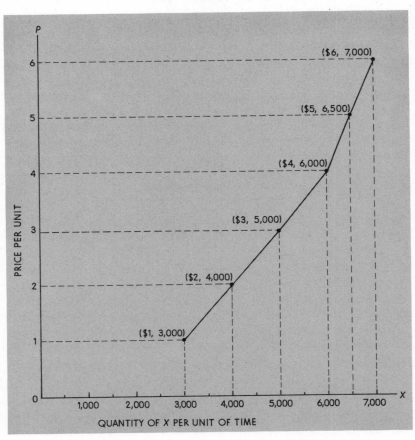

First, technology is assumed to be constant. If a more efficient method of production is discovered, firms generally change the amounts they are willing to supply at each price. Second, the prices of factors of production are usually held constant. For example, a change in wage rates or in the prices of raw materials will change the supply curve. Third, the prices of related goods (in production) are held constant. If the price of corn rises while the price of wheat remains the same, some farmers will switch from growing wheat to growing corn, and less wheat will be supplied. Fourth, the expectations of producers are assumed not to change.

2.6.c—Changes in Supply

When price rises and firms are induced to offer a greater quantity of a good for sale, we say *quantity supplied* increases. When one or more of the factors mentioned in Section 2.6.b change, firms are induced to offer more or less at each price in the schedule; in this case we say supply changes. Consider Figure 2.6.2 in which $S_0 S_0'$ is the initial supply curve.

FIGURE 2.6.2

Shifts in Supply

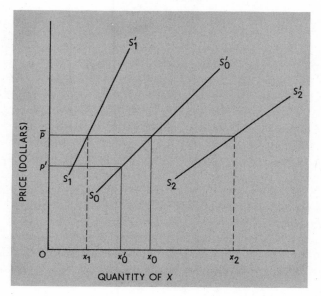

If price falls from $O\bar{p}$ to Op', the quantity of X supplied decreases from Ox_0 to Ox_0', other things remaining the same. If technology changes and supply consequently changes from $S_0 S_0'$ to $S_2 S_2'$, we say supply increases. Firms now wish to offer Ox_2 at price $O\bar{p}$, and they wish to offer more units for sale at each price in the entire range of prices. A movement from

S_0S_0' to S_1S_1' is a decrease in supply. Firms then wish to offer less for sale at each price in the range.

These relations may be summarized as follows:

Relations: When price rises (falls), other things remaining the same, quantity supplied rises (falls). When something held constant in deriving supply changes, for example technology, supply increases or decreases. If firms are induced to offer more (less) at each price, supply has increased (decreased).

2.7 SUPPLY ELASTICITY

As is the case for demand, the coefficient of supply elasticity measures the relative responsiveness of quantity supplied to changes in price *along a given supply schedule.* The computation technique is essentially the same as that used for demand elasticity.

2.7.a—Computation

The coefficient of supply elasticity is defined as

$$\eta_s = \frac{\Delta Q/Q}{\Delta P/P} = \frac{\Delta Q}{\Delta P} \cdot \frac{P}{Q},$$

where ΔQ is change in quantity supplied, ΔP is the change in price, and P and Q are price and quantity supplied. Since Q and P are assumed to change in the same direction, the coefficient is positive. One can use an averaging technique like that discussed for demand when the changes are discrete; that is, when differences in the bases used affect η_s.

If the percentage change in quantity supplied exceeds the percentage change in price, supply is elastic and $\eta_s > 1$. If the two percentages are equal, supply has unitary elasticity and $\eta_s = 1$. If the percentage change in price exceeds the percentage change in quantity, supply is inelastic and $\eta_s < 1$. Therefore, the more elastic is supply, the more responsive is quantity supplied to price changes.[10] Note, however, that in contrast to demand we cannot relate supply elasticity to positive or negative changes in total dollar value supplied; that is, changes in price times quantity supplied at that price. Since price and quantity vary directly, an increase in price increases quantity supplied and hence increases the dollar value of

---

[10] Estimating supply elasticity at a point on a supply curve is quite simple. First, draw a tangent to the curve at the point where elasticity is to be calculated. Extend the tangent toward the left until it reaches the origin, the vertical axis, or the horizontal axis. If the tangent crosses the vertical axis, supply is elastic at the point; if it crosses the horizontal axis it is inelastic; if it passes through the origin, supply has unitary elasticity. For a straight line supply, merely check which axis supply crosses and make the same estimation as described for a tangent line.

quantity supplied whether supply is elastic or inelastic. A fall in price likewise decreases the dollar value of quantity supplied.

2.7.b—Determinants of Supply Elasticity

The responsiveness of quantity supplied to increases in price depends in large measure upon the time period of adjustment and upon how easily resources can be adapted to the production of the good in question. Suppose the price of a particular good increases. If the resources used to produce that good are readily accessible without increasing their prices and if production can physically be increased easily, supply is more elastic than if the opposite holds true; that is, supply would be *less* elastic if the additional resources are obtainable only at rapidly increasing prices. For a price decrease, elasticity depends upon how rapidly resources can be released from the production of the good.

Economists frequently distinguish between momentary, short-run, and long-run supply and supply elasticity. As an example, let us consider the supply of people in a particular profession, say lawyers. Three supply curves for lawyers are shown in Figure 2.7.1. $L_M L_M'$ is the momentary supply of lawyers. At a moment of time there are OL_M lawyers, and this number cannot be instantaneously changed. Suppose the average income of lawyers rises from Op_0 to Op_1; at that moment or over a very short

FIGURE 2.7.1

**Effect of Time of Adjustment
on Supply Elasticity**

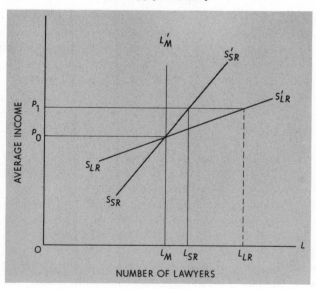

period of time, the number of lawyers cannot be increased. Since quantity does not respond at all, the vertical supply curve $L_M L_M'$ is infinitely inelastic.

Within a reasonably short period of time, however, the rise in the average income of lawyers will induce an increase in the number of lawyers, perhaps from OL_M to OL_{SR}. The increase in income will induce some retired lawyers to begin practice again; some businessmen with law degrees will be induced to leave their companies and enter practice. The resulting short-run supply curve is $S_{SR}S_{SR}'$, the supply curve when a reasonably short period of adjustment is permitted. This curve is more elastic than $L_M L_M'$ because when some adjustment time is permitted, quantity supplied is more responsive to price changes.

The long-run supply curve is $S_{LR}S_{LR}'$, which allows sufficient time for *all* adjustments to be made (we shall define short run and long run more precisely in Chapter 7). In our example, higher average incomes will induce more college graduates to enter law school, and the period of adjustment is long enough to permit them to begin practicing law. Alternatively, if average income declines relative to other professions requiring similar periods of training, the number of lawyers will decline appreciably. Thus, the long-run supply curve $S_{LR}S_{LR}'$ is more elastic than $S_{SR}S_{SR}'$ because quantity is more responsive to price when sufficient adjustment time is permitted.

2.8   MARKET DETERMINATION OF PRICE AND QUANTITY

The purpose of studying supply and demand is to prepare us to analyze their interaction, which determines market price and quantity. A primary reason for separating them is to isolate the factors that determine each so that we can analyze the market effects of changing these factors. Before further analyzing the underlying forces behind the two schedules (in later chapters), we will first examine the interaction of supply and demand in the market.

2.8.a—Equilibrium

Suppose that in the market for X, demanders and suppliers have the schedules set forth in Tables 2.2.1 and 2.6.1 respectively. These schedules are combined in Table 2.8.1. Suppose also that an auctioneer, who does not know the schedules, is assigned the task of finding a price that clears the market; that is, a price at which quantity demanded equals quantity supplied. The auctioneer does not know the market-clearing price, since the schedules change from time to time. Therefore, he begins by picking some price at random and announcing this price to the demanders and suppliers, who then tell him the amounts they wish to purchase or sell at

TABLE 2.8.1

Market Demand and Supply

Price (Dollars)	Quantity Supplied (Units of X)	Quantity Demanded (Units of X)	Excess Supply (+) or Demand (−) (Units of X)
6..........	7,000	2,000	+5,000
5..........	6,500	3,000	+3,500
4..........	6,000	4,000	+2,000
3..........	5,000	5,000	0
2..........	4,000	5,500	−1,500
1..........	3,000	6,000	−3,000

that price. The first price chosen may or may not clear the market. If it does, exchange takes place; if not the auctioneer must choose another price. This time, however, he need not proceed purely at random.

The auctioneer knows from long experience that if quantity demanded exceeds quantity supplied (we call this situation excess demand), he can raise the price and cause quantity demanded to decrease and quantity supplied to increase; that is, excess demand will decrease when price rises. He knows also that if quantity supplied exceeds quantity demanded (called excess supply), he can reduce price and cause a reduction in quantity supplied and an increase in quantity demanded; that is, a price reduction reduces excess supply.

Suppose the first price chosen is $5; 3,000 units are demanded but 6,500 units are offered for sale. There is an excess supply of 3,500 units at that price. To reduce excess supply the auctioneer reduces price, say to $1. Now, since consumers demand 6,000 but producers are willing to supply only 3,000, excess demand is 3,000. The auctioneer raises price to $4 and quantity supplied exceeds quantity demanded by 2,000. He therefore reduces price to $3. Quantity demanded equals quantity supplied and the market is cleared. The equilibrium price and quantity are $3 and 5,000 units.

We can also express the equilibrium solution graphically. In Figure 2.8.1, *DD′* and *SS′* are the market demand and supply curves (these are not graphs of the schedules in Table 2.8.1). It is clear that Op_e and Ox_e are the market-clearing or equilibrium price and quantity. Only at Op_e does quantity demanded equal quantity supplied. In this model we need not make our assumption about the auctioneer. Consumers and producers themselves bid the price up or down if the market is not in equilibrium.

Suppose price happens to be $O\bar{p}$, greater than Op_e. At $O\bar{p}$ producers supply $O\bar{x}_s$ but only $O\bar{x}_d$ is demanded. An excess supply of $\bar{x}_d\bar{x}_s$ develops. This surplus accumulates for the producer. When this happens producers are induced to lower price in order to keep from accumulating unwanted

FIGURE 2.8.1

Market Equilibrium

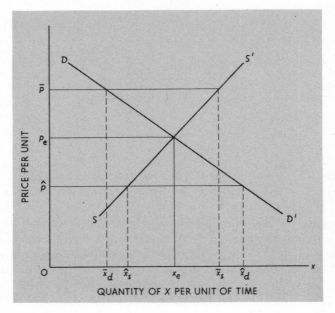

surpluses. (This is the same thing our auctioneer would have done.) Note that at any price above Op_e there is an excess supply, and producers will lower price. On the other hand, suppose price is $O\hat{p}$. Demanders are willing and able to purchase $O\hat{x}_d$, while suppliers are only willing to offer $O\hat{x}_s$ units for sale. Some consumers are not satisfied; there is an excess demand of $\hat{x}_s\hat{x}_d$ in the market. Since their demands are not satisfied, consumers bid the price up (See Chapter 1). Again, this is what our auctioneer would have done if a shortage existed. As consumers continue to bid up the price, quantity demanded decreases and quantity supplied increases until price reaches Op_e and quantity is Ox_e. Any price below Op_e causes a shortage, and the shortage causes consumers to bid up the price. Given no outside influences that prevent price from being bid up or down, an equilibrium price and quantity is attained. This equilibrium price is the price that clears the market; both excess demand and excess supply are zero in equilibrium. Equilibrium is attained in the market because of the following:

Principles: When price is above the equilibrium price, quantity supplied exceeds quantity demanded. The resulting excess supply induces sellers to reduce price in order to sell the surplus. If price is below equilibrium, quantity demanded exceeds quantity supplied. The resulting excess demand causes the unsatisfied consumers to bid up price. Since prices below equilibrium are bid up by consumers and prices above equilibrium are lowered by producers, the market will converge to the equilibrium price-quantity combination.

2.8.b—Demand and Supply Shifts

So long as the determinants of demand and supply do not change, the price-quantity equilibrium described above will not change. Before finishing our study of the market we must see how this equilibrium is disturbed when there are changes in one or more of the factors held constant in deriving demand and supply.

A bit of intuitive reasoning may ease the transition to the somewhat complicated graphical analysis that follows. Consider the career that you plan after graduation. Suppose you plan to become an economist. Suppose also that prior to your graduation Congress passed a law requiring that everyone who buys a share of stock or a bond must, for his own protection, consult with an economist. Would this law please you? Why, or why not? Does it not seem logical that economists' salaries would rise after this law is passed? People now must consult economists where previously they did not. How could they bid away the necessary economists from jobs in academics or government? They would do so simply by offering higher salaries. Before long economists' salaries would have generally risen since universities, government, and so on must meet the increasing bids of potential investors. Or, in terms developed in this chapter, the demand for economists rises. With a given supply of economists, salaries must rise. Of course, after a while the higher salaries may lure others into the profession and drive salaries back down again.

Consider another example. Does a cotton farmer bringing his crop to market want a large or small amount of cotton marketed at the same time? Again, obviously, a small amount because the larger the amount of cotton available, the lower the price of cotton will be. It should thus be intuitively clear that with a given demand the greater the supply, the greater will be the quantity sold but the lower the price will be. In like manner, the greater the demand—for economists, cotton, or anything else—the greater both *quantity* and *price* will be. These relations are intuitively clear; but they can be refined by graphical analysis, to which we now turn.

In panel *a*, Figure 2.8.2, Op_0 and Ox_0 are the equilibrium price and quantity when demand and supply are D_0D_0' and SS'. Suppose income falls and demand decreases to D_1D_1'. At Op_0 quantity supplied exceeds the new quantity demanded by AB; that is, excess supply at Op_0 is AB. Faced with this surplus, sellers reduce price until the new equilibrium is reached at Op_1 and Ox_1. Now suppose the price of some substitute good

FIGURE 2.8.2

Changes in Equilibrium Prices and Quantities

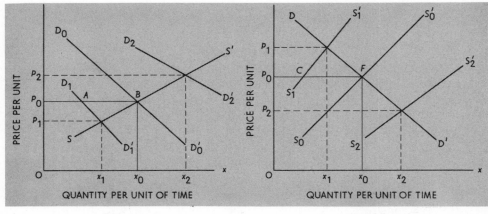

Panel *a*   Panel *b*

increases so that demand increases to D_2D_2'. At price Op_1 quantity demanded far exceeds quantity supplied, and hence a shortage occurs. The
excess demand causes consumers to bid the price up until the new
equilibrium at Op_2 and Ox_2 is reached. We can see that if supply remains
fixed and demand decreases, quantity and price both fall; if demand increases, price and quantity both rise. This direct relation between price
and quantity would be expected when we consider that the movements
take place *along* the supply curve, which is positively sloped.

Panel *b*, Figure 2.8.2, shows what happens to price and quantity when
demand remains constant and supply shifts. Let demand be DD' and
supply S_0S_0'. The original equilibrium thus occurs at price Op_0 and
quantity Ox_0. Now let input prices rise so that supply decreases to S_1S_1'.
The shortage of CF at Op_0 causes consumers to bid up price until equilibrium is reached at Op_1 and Ox_1. Now let technology improve so that
supply increases to S_2S_2'. The surplus at Op_1 causes producers to lower
price. Equilibrium occurs at Op_2 and Ox_2. Thus we see that if demand
remains constant and supply decreases, price rises and quantity falls; if
supply increases, price falls and quantity increases. This inverse relation
is expected since the movement is *along* a negatively sloped demand
curve.

The direction of change is not always immediately apparent when
both supply and demand change simultaneously. In panel *a*, Figure
2.8.3, D_0D_0' and S_0S_0' are the initial demand and supply curves. Their
intersection determines the equilibrium price and quantity, Op_0 and Ox_0.
Now suppose supply increases to S_1S_1' and demand increases to D_1D_1';

FIGURE 2.8.3

Effects of Supply and Demand Shifts

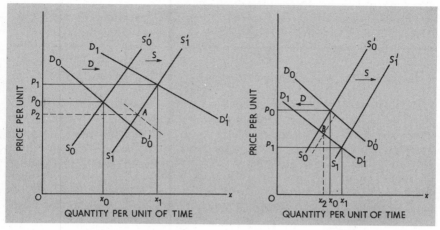

Panel *a*   Panel *b*

price rises to Op_1 and quantity rises to Ox_1. While quantity always increases when both demand and supply increase, price may either increase, decrease, or even remain the same. Suppose supply shifts to S_1S_1' but demand shifts only to the position indicated by the dashed demand curve crossing S_1S_1' at A. With this shift quantity still rises (although by a lesser amount), but price falls to Op_2. Furthermore, by constructing the change in supply or demand still differently, we can cause price to remain at Op_0 while quantity increases.

To see the effect of a decrease in both supply and demand, consider D_1D_1' and S_1S_1' in panel *a* as the original schedules. Next, let them both decrease to D_0D_0' and S_0S_0'. Quantity and price decrease from Ox_1 and Op_1 to Ox_0 and Op_0. While quantity always decreases when both curves decrease, price need not fall.

Exercise: In order to see the point just made, manipulate supply or demand so that price rises above Op_1 as both curves decrease.

Panel *b*, Figure 2.8.3, shows the effect of an increase in one curve accompanied by a decrease in the other. Let supply *increase* from S_0S_0' to S_1S_1' and let demand *decrease* from D_0D_0' to D_1D_1'. Price falls from Op_0 to Op_1 and quantity rises from Ox_0 to Ox_1. While price *must* fall when supply increases and demand decreases, quantity need not increase. Suppose that while demand went to D_1D_1' supply increased only to the position indicated by the dashed line crossing D_1D_1' at B. The new equilibrium entails a price reduction (although not so large as before), but now quantity decreases to Ox_2 rather than rising to Ox_1. To see the effect of a decrease in supply accompanied by an increase in demand, simply assume that demand shifts from D_1D_1' to D_0D_0' and supply from S_1S_1' to S_0S_0'. Price must rise. In this illustration quantity decreases; but quantity may change in either direction.

Exercise: Prove this last point for yourself.

Principles: (1) When demand increases (decreases), supply remaining constant, both price and quantity increase (decrease). (2) When supply increases (decreases), demand remaining constant, price falls (rises) and quantity rises (falls). (3) When both demand and supply increase (decrease) quantity increases (decreases), but price can either increase or decrease, depending upon the relative magnitude of the shifts. (4) When supply and demand shift in opposite directions the change in quantity is indeterminant, but price always changes in the same direction as demand.

2.9 SUPPLY AND DEMAND IN REAL MARKETS: ANALYSIS AND APPLICATION

By this time some students may question the relevance of demand and supply analysis to real world problems. What if sellers do not know the demand or the supply schedules? In fact, do they even know what demand and supply are? It may therefore be profitable to show how demand and supply determine price and allocate output in the absence of perfect knowledge about the schedules. One theoretical model and one example from the real world should help clear up this point.

2.9.a—Theoretical Example

Suppose one day the newspapers all print a scientific report stating that rhubarb makes women more beautiful. Now we know, having gone through the first part of this chapter, that the demand for rhubarb probably increases. But perhaps the grocers, some of whom have not read this chapter, do not know this. How can the market allocate under these conditions?

First, consider what happens to the rhubarb on the grocers' shelves. Assuming that demand in fact increases, grocers find that what had previously been a week's supply of rhubarb at the established price now lasts only until Thursday morning. Customers complain that they cannot get rhubarb. We can use demand analysis to examine the situation *even though buyers and sellers are completely unaware of demand and supply analysis.*

Panel *a*, Figure 2.9.1, shows what happens in the retail market. Price is Op_r, and Ox_r per week is the rate of sales when demand is $D_r{}^0D_r{}^{0\prime}$. Demand increases to $D_r{}^1D_r{}^{1\prime}$. At Op_r consumers now want $Ox_r{}'$ units per week. Grocery stores consequently run out of rhubarb before the week is over. The profitable thing for grocers is to order more rhubarb from wholesalers. When they do, the wholesalers sell more rhubarb and their stocks begin to run low. This is shown in panel b. The original demand is $D_w{}^0D_w{}^{0\prime}$; this is the demand by grocers for wholesale rhubarb. When demand at retail increases, demand at wholesale increases also. Before the shift in demand, retail grocers wanted Ox_w at a wholesale price of Op_w; they now want $Ox_w{}'$.

As their inventories run low, wholesalers instruct their buyers in the commodity market to buy more rhubarb. At any one time, however, there is a limit to the amount of rhubarb available. Therefore, as the buyers try to increase their purchases, they bid against one another and force price up. Panel c indicates what happens in the commodity market. The old demand of wholesalers for rhubarb was $D_c{}^0D_c{}^{0\prime}$ and price was Op_c. Suppose the quantity available is Ox_c (the supply at the moment). When wholesalers' demand rises to $D_c{}^1D_c{}^{1\prime}$, a shortage of $x_cx_c{}'$ develops at price Op_c. Price rises to $Op_c{}'$ to ration the available rhubarb among the competing buyers. (It might be well to note that the scales of the graphs in Figure 2.9.1 are different.)

FIGURE 2.9.1
Supply and Demand Analysis of Real Markets

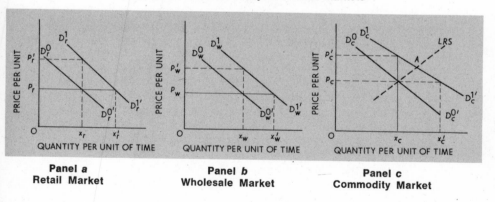

Panel a	Panel b	Panel c
Retail Market	Wholesale Market	Commodity Market

Wholesalers now pay a higher price in the commodity market and consequently raise their price to grocers, to $Op_w{}'$ perhaps. As they tell the grocers, their costs have risen and they are forced to raise prices. The grocers now pay the wholesale price of $Op_w{}'$, so they raise the retail price to $Op_r{}'$. As they tell their complaining customers, costs have risen so they are forced to raise prices. Costs to the grocers and to the wholesalers have, of course, risen, but ultimately it was the increased demand that caused the price rise. And this price must rise until it rations the available rhubarb to those prospective buyers who are both willing and able to pay the price.

Everything that occurs in the transition period occurs not because we draw some curves but because of individual action in the market. We use demand and supply curves only to analyze more clearly what takes place in the market.

We can take the analysis a few steps further. Suppose the higher price in the commodity market induces farmers to increase their rhubarb crop or induces farmers growing other crops to switch to rhubarb. Remember Ox_c and Op_c make up only one point on the long-run supply curve. Assume that there is an upward sloping long-run supply (LRS) passing through point A in panel c. In the commodity market price falls and quantity increases after all adjustments are made (point A, panel c). The increased quantity supplied causes price to fall and quantity sold to rise in the wholesale and in the retail market.

To test his understanding of the analysis, the student should do the following:

Exercises: (1) Complete the graphs in panels *a, b,* and *c* to indicate the new price-quantity relations in the three markets and describe the reason for the changes. (2) Using the three supply curves, L_M, S_{SR}, and S_{LR} in Figure 2.7.1, first draw a demand for lawyers going through the point indicating a price of Op_0 and a quantity of OL_M. Next, draw an increased demand for lawyers. Determine the price and quantity resulting in each of the three periods, describing reasons why each position occurs even though no one actually *knows* the position of the curves. Finally, carry out the same analysis for a decrease in demand.

Exercise: Use the analytical reasoning of this subsection to answer the following problem. Suppose a frost kills a large portion of the orange crop, with a resulting higher price of oranges. It has been said that such an increase in price benefits no one since it cannot elicit a supply response; that is, supply is fixed until the next harvest. The higher price, it is said, simply "lines the pockets of profiteers." Analyze this position (*hint:* be sure to focus on the rationing function of market price).

2.9.b—Demand and Supply of Economists: Some Evidence

We introduced sub-section 2.8.*b* with the hypothetical example of a new law requiring any stock purchaser to consult with an economist before buying. We suggested that the wages of economists would rise but then inserted the *caveat* that as people entered the profession one could not tell exactly what might happen. After World War II, particularly during the late fifties, the relative wages (that is, relative to other professions) of economists and of most university faculty rose significantly. During the same period both business and government at all levels began to think that it would be desirable to consult with economists. People realized that when the large crop of babies born after World War II attained college age the nation's schools would have insufficient faculty to teach them. In short, because society felt it wanted more economists, the demand for economists began to rise.

The increase in demand along with the relatively fixed supply of professional economists caused what was called a "shortage" of economists. As you now realize, in economics a shortage means specifically that market price, for some reason or another, is below equilibrium and that quantity demanded at that price exceeds quantity supplied. In other words there is an excess demand in the market. Figure 2.9.2 helps to illustrate this situation. Assume for simplicity that all economists are alike and received the same wage or possibly just assume some average wage. The short-run supply of economists was SS'. Demand increased from D_0D_0' to D_1D_1'. Equilibrium wage rises from OW_0 to OW_e, but in real-world markets it takes time for prices to rise. People have contracts; lack of information hinders the immediate working of the market. Thus, wages were sticky below OW_e, say at OW_0. Demanders wanted to hire Oq_d at OW_0 while the quantity supplied was only Oq_0. Therefore, an excess demand or shortage of q_0q_d developed. Some demanders went unsatisfied.

FIGURE 2.9.2

**Effect of an Increase in Demand
with Sticky Wages**

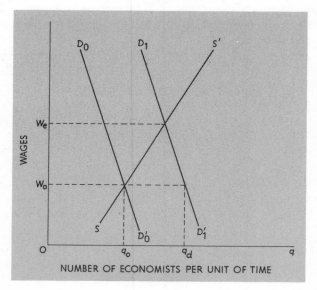

NUMBER OF ECONOMISTS PER UNIT OF TIME

After a while, just as our theory tells us, an upward pressure on wages developed as those unsatisfied demanders attempted to bid away people. For a time, however, demand continued to increase and the equilibrium wage was not attained. To be sure, short-run supply increased also, but not as rapidly as demand. Even as wages were rising, the increase in demand still occasioned excess demand. Government, beginning to worry about the constant shortage of economists and other faculty, attempted to do something about it. Government began to grant massive aid to universities for the training of all types of Ph.D.'s. Also many people were enticed by the rising wage rate to earn advanced degrees and enter academics. Still, equilibrium was not attained immediately.

It takes time to train a Ph.D. in economics or in anything. The influx of new people did not immediately alleviate the shortage because wages were lagging behind the increasing demand. But even as government and others were viewing with alarm the continued shortage of faculty, a few economists were warning that although society was faced with a shortage at that time, it would soon be confronted with an oversupply, sometimes called a surplus.

For example, in 1964 when most people were worried about the grave shortage of Ph.D.'s, Professor Allan M. Cartter predicted the problem of a serious oversupply of new Ph.D.'s by 1969. Cartter noted that in the 1930s only 45 universities were granting as many as ten Ph.D.'s a year contrasted with 106 in 1964. He pointed out that 2,800 doctorates were awarded in 1934 while at the time of his research the figure was 16,000 and rising rapidly. In the 1930s there was almost no federal aid to graduate education; the budget for 1967 allocated $329 million for financial support of graduate students alone.[11] The expansion of graduate education in all areas was fantastic. But it was to take a little time for all of the new Ph.D.'s to enter the market.

Cartter and some others noted this great potential supply. Some noted that the birth rate had fallen since the post-World War II baby boom and that the crowding of colleges would not continue at such a rapid rate. They predicted that the demand for economists would not continue increasing as rapidly and also that when this new increased supply reached the market an excess supply or surplus of Ph.D.'s would result. Figure 2.9.3 illustrates the reason for the prediction of an excess supply. At the time of prediction supply and demand were respectively S_0S_0' and DD'. Wages were still below equilibrium at OW_0. The shortage was q_0q_d. The prediction was that because of the vast increase in graduate training, supply would increase to S_1S_1'.[12] But wages are particularly sticky down-

---

[11] A. M. Cartter, *An Assessment of Quality in Graduate Education.* Washington, D.C.: American Council of Education.

[12] Possibly supply in this analysis should have been momentary supply and drawn as a vertical line. All trained economists need not work as economists, however, so at anytime there may be some elasticity to supply.

FIGURE 2.9.3

**Effect of an Increase in Supply
with Sticky Wages**

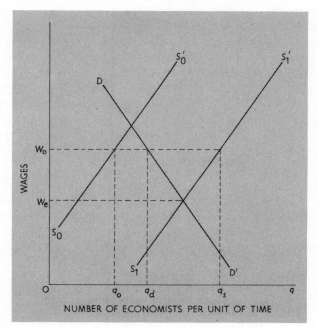

ward. Thus at the wage OW_0, Oq_d would still be demanded but Oq_s would be supplied. An excess supply of q_sq_d would develop. Everyone who wished to be and was qualified to be an economist would not find a job.

What actually happened? In his paper presented to the American Economic Association in 1970, entitled descriptively "Whither the Market for Academic Economists," Cartter pointed out that the market situation was even worse for Ph.D.'s than he had indicated. Many were unable to find jobs. A short-term oversupply had developed. What of the future? One might predict that the increase in supply will slow down, that demand will continue to increase, and that there will be a tendency for the surplus to be relieved. Certainly it appears that graduate enrollment is in fact slowing down its rate of increase.

The purpose of this subsection, however, is not to make predictions but to show how actual markets work. Society wanted more Ph.D.'s. The increased reward increased the supply. Just as sticky wages upward brought about a shortage, sticky wages downward caused a surplus. It is well to remember that markets do not always function instantaneously, but they do function, even though it takes time.

2.10   ANALYTICAL EXERCISES AND EVIDENCE: FLOOR AND CEILING PRICES

Sticky prices after a shift in demand and/or supply are not the only reasons for surpluses or shortages. Excess demand or supply can occur even though neither demand nor supply shifts. For various reasons governments at times interfere with the functioning of demand and supply in the market place. Governments have in the past decided that the price of a particular commodity was either "too high" or "too low." Without evaluating the desirability of the interferences we can use demand and supply curves to analyze the economic effects of two types of interferences, the setting of minimum and maximum prices, and the way in which these interferences cause either a surplus or a shortage of the good.

2.10.a—Theory

If the government imposes a maximum or ceiling price on a good, the effect is to cause a shortage of that good (and frequently to create a black market that rations the quantity available). In Figure 2.10.1 a

FIGURE 2.10.1

Effect of Ceiling Price

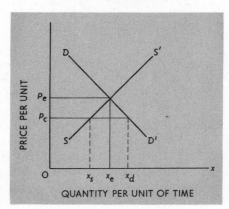

ceiling price Op_c is set on good x. No one can legally sell x for more than Op_c per unit, which is below the equilibrium price, Op_e. At the ceiling price only Ox_e is offered for sale; that is, the *momentary* supply is the vertical line at x_e. Over a period of time the shortage grows worse. After a suitable time period of adjustment, suppliers decrease the quantity supplied still more, to Ox_s. Excess demand is now x_sx_d. Since quantity supplied is less than quantity demanded at the ceiling price, there must be some method of allocating the limited quantity among all those who are willing and able to buy a larger amount. The sellers may devise the method; perhaps consumers queue, with suppliers deciding who comes first in the queue on the basis of under-the-counter offers. On the other hand, the government may devise some system of rationing. But in this case, black markets will develop. In any case the market does the allocating. But when restricted by outside requirements, the allocation is either based upon nonmarket considerations or the market mechanism functions less effectively outside the law.

In contrast the government may feel that the suppliers of x are not earning as much income as they "deserve" and, therefore, set a minimum or floor price. We can see the results of such actions in Figure 2.10.2.

FIGURE 2.10.2

Effect of Floor Price

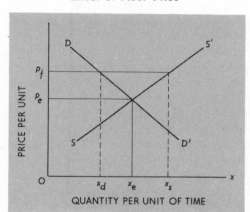

Being dissatisfied with the equilibrium price and quantity, Op_e and Ox_e, the government sets a minimum price of Op_f. Since the law of demand could not concurrently be repealed, consumers demand less (Ox_d) and immediately a surplus of $x_d x_e$ develops. In order to maintain the price Op_f, the government must find some way to limit supply, or it must agree to purchase the surplus. As firms are induced to supply more and as new firms are enticed into the industry by the higher price, the quantity supplied at Op_f increases. If SS' is the long-run supply curve, the increased quantity supplied causes a greater surplus, $x_d x_s$, which the government must now buy or allocate among producers; that is, the government could simply restrict production to Ox_d. The vertical slotted line at that point then becomes the new supply. A price of Op_f now clears the market.

2.10.b—Some Evidence

Our theory leads us to expect that in the case of a governmentally imposed ceiling price, a shortage or excess demand will develop. Over time the supply will decrease and the excess demand will increase. We would expect also that in the case of durables the *quality* will also deteriorate through lack of maintenance. Several well known, frequently cited examples tend to confirm this hypothesis.

The classical example of the effect of a ceiling price is the case of rent controls in large cities, particularly New York. In a study of rent controls it was hypothesized that landlords facing rent controls would react in three ways: (1) they could accept side payments or bribes from those not able to find housing; (2) they could subdivide apartments and charge additional rent on additional units; and (3) they could curtail maintenance.[13] Other studies had shown that the first recourse was widespread while the second, because of governmental controls was not. The Moorhouse study cited here tested the third hypothesis. It was posited that since the landlord could not raise rents after an increase in demand there was no reason to improve the quality of existing facilities. With a fixed quantity and an increased demand the excess demand is manifested by queues. Since the landlord cannot ration the space by increased prices he lowers cost by reducing the maintenance and hence by reducing the quality of existing housing space.

After testing, it was found that the gross income of landlords showed no relation to maintenance, if rent controls are in effect. One can rent out his apartment at the fixed amount whether he continues to maintain it or not within the relevant range. This is expected because of the excess demand. The study found that net income is negatively related to maintenance. Landlords under rent control can increase profit by reducing upkeep.[14] Therefore, when supply cannot be reduced quickly it seems probable that the quality of the existing supply will deteriorate in response to the ceiling. This is one way for suppliers to adjust.

There are many other cases in which governmental price ceilings caused a shortage of something and methods other than price are used to allocate the existing supply. During World War II price ceilings were imposed upon many consumer goods. Government rationed the supply, but the pressure of excess demand increased the expected profits of law violation, and extensive black market operations resulted. The usury laws place a ceiling price on the interest rates that can be charged on a loan. An excess demand for loans results. Who gets the loans? The least risky of course. Who are the least risky? Those with higher incomes. What hap-

---

[13] For the analysis see John C. Moorhouse, "Optimal Housing Under Rent Control," *Southern Economic Journal*, July, 1972, pp. 93–106.

[14] See ibid. for complete results.

pens to those who wish to borrow at the prevailing interest rate? They must go to illegal "loan sharks." Because of the extra costs of breaking the law and because government will not enforce the illegal contract, it is probable that these low income borrowers pay more than they would in the absence of any regulation. Many other examples of ceiling prices can be observed.

Let us turn now to the effect of some floor prices. The typical example of the effect of a price floor, almost a cliché because of its inclusion in almost every elementary economics text, is the support price on many agricultural products. Demand for many of these products is supposedly inelastic. Higher prices would mean higher incomes for farmers (recall the relation between elasticity and revenue). Because of their large numbers it was almost impossible for farmers to get together and fix prices. Government then set a floor price for many agricultural products and, as our theory would predict, excess supply developed. Government had to buy up the resulting surplus from the farmers. In an attempt to lower the surplus, government put acreage controls on many products. Since farmers were certainly not stupid, they obviously put their worst land, not their best, into retirement. Furthermore, they substituted other imputs, like fertilizer, for land and thus increased the productivity of the land being used. For these reasons the excess supply has not been particularly reduced and the problem of persistent surpluses, which our theory predicts, continues. Also the prices to consumers remain higher than they would be in the absence of price controls.

Although the farmer is generally cited when economists mention an example of misallocation from a minimum price set above equilibrium, many other cases of governmentally imposed price floors can be cited.

One case, not generally noted as such, is the price set by the Civil Aeronautics Board on the passenger fare that can be charged by airlines. James Miller III, formerly senior staff economist for the Department of Transportation, said that he believes the regulated fares are on average above equilibrium. Certainly the evidence and theory would lead us to believe that this is in fact the case. First we observe that government regulates the routes that a particular airline can use. As in the case of acreage controls on farmers, this regulation is an attempt to limit the potential excess supply. Secondly, we see airlines discriminating by reducing fares for certain groups, such as wives or students, in an attempt to get around the regulations. Third, we see a good deal of non-price competition. Flights with movies, alcohol, meals, and beautiful stewardesses were all attempts to induce the limited demand at the regulated fare into particular airlines. We also observe a large amount of excess capacity on airplanes. This may indicate a price above equilibrium.[15]

---

[15] A governmentally imposed minimum price is not the only possible cause of non-price competition. As we will see in the chapter on imperfect competition,

Another example of a regulated floor price is the price of checking accounts or demand deposits at banks. Banks sell demand deposits to depositors. The depositors get a good (a checking account) and the banks gain reserves, through which they can make loans at interest. Since the government does not allow banks to pay interest to depositors on demand deposits, in effect, a floor price of zero is imposed upon checking accounts. Banks, unable to compete for deposits through lowering price (that is, paying interest), must compete in other ways. They give away premiums or gifts when one opens an account. They compete in luxurious surroundings, in courteous tellers and officers, and by giving other services to the consumers. If price were fixed below equilibrium we would observe a shortage and would see customers competing to get banks to take their deposits. Many other examples of floor prices could be analyzed.

Exercise: Think of some other examples of floor and ceiling prices. What does our theory predict? What do we observe? Think of some instances in which government sells an item below or above the market clearing price. What do we observe? Begin with camping privileges in popular national parks, water in large cities, governmentally owned housing, admission to state universities.

2.11   CONCLUSION

In this chapter we have analyzed the following principles:

Principle: Demand is a list of prices and of the corresponding quantities that consumers are willing and able to buy at each price in the list per unit of time. Quantity demanded varies inversely with price. Demand (that is, the entire schedule) changes when something held constant in deriving demand changes. Among these are income, tastes, the prices of other goods, and expectations.

Principle: Demand elasticity measures the responsiveness of quantity demanded to price changes. The more (less) responsive quantity demanded is to price, the more elastic (inelastic) is demand. An increase in price causes total revenue to increase if demand is inelastic and to decrease if demand is elastic. The effects are opposite for a price decrease. In case of unitary elasticity there is no change in total revenue for a change in price. Elasticity is affected by the availability of substitutes, the number of uses, and reaction time.

Principle: Supply is the list of prices and the corresponding quantity that will be supplied at each price in the list. Changes in technology, the price of inputs, and the prices of related (in production) goods will shift the entire schedule. Supply elasticity measures the responsiveness of

---

oligopoly (an industry composed of few firms) is characterized by non-price competition. We also observe excess capacity in non-regulated industries. For example, movie theaters are not filled for every performance.

quantity supplied to changes in price. The time period of adjustment is one of the principal determinants of elasticity.

Principle: When price in a market is such that quantity demanded equals quantity supplied the market is in equilibrium. Prices below equilibrium cause excess demand (or shortages). If prices are not artifically fixed, they will be bid up. Prices above equilibrium cause excess supply (or surpluses). If prices are not fixed they will be bid down. When supply and demand change, equilibrium price and quantity will change.

Every day economists use simple demand and supply analysis to solve complex problems and to answer questions dealing with the real world. In fact, demand and supply are probably the most frequently used tools in the economist's bag.

Therefore, much of the remainder of this book is devoted to demand and supply and to the factors that influence demand and supply. As we shall see, however, one must be able to decide *which* demand and *which* supply are relevant for the solution of a particular problem before he can use these tools fruitfully.

In all cases a fundamental concept to remember is that when the price of something falls, more is taken; when the price of something rises less is taken. In the next two chapters we turn to the theory of consumer behavior to see why this is so.

QUESTIONS AND PROBLEMS

1. Make up an inelastic demand schedule (that is, a table). Compute the coefficient of elasticity between two points. Graph the corresponding demand curve. Show what happens when the price of a competitive good falls. Show what happens when consumers' incomes increase. (What assumption must be made to answer the last part of the question?)

2. A decrease in supply raises price, but the higher price causes a decrease in demand, which in turn causes an (at least partially) offsetting fall in price. Comment.

3. The following statement is taken from the *Wall Street Journal,* March 30, 1966: "A retired Atlanta railroad conductor complains that he can no longer visit his neighborhood tavern six times a week. Since the price of his favorite beer went up to 30 cents a glass from 25 cents, he has been dropping in only five times a week." Assuming the man in question consumed the same amount of beer *per visit* before and after the price change, calculate the elasticity of his demand for tavern-dispensed beer.

4. Contrast an individual's "demands" with his "wants."

5. Consider the following table showing income, the quantity of the good demanded, and the price of the good.

Quantity	Income	Price
100	$5,000	$16.00
120	$6,000	$16.00

Compute the income elasticity of the good. Use the averaging method. Next suppose the price of the good changes so that the schedule is now as follows:

Quantity	Income	Price
150.......	$5,000	$10.00
130.......	$6,000	$10.00

Compute again the income elasticity of demand. Note that the sign differs from the first example. Economists call goods whose income elasticity is negative (that is, whose quantity demanded varies inversely with income) "inferior." Note that the income elasticity can change when prices change. We will discuss inferiority much more fully in Chapter 4. Note for now that there is nothing inherent in the good itself that makes it inferior; it is inferior at one price, not inferior at another.

6. Consider the following table showing the quantity of some good X, the price of some other good Y, and income.

Quantity of X	Price of Y	Income
100.........	$2.00	$5,000
120.........	$3.00	$5,000

Compute the cross elasticity of demand, η_{XY}, using the averaging method. Suppose income changes to $10,000 so that the schedule is now

Quantity of X	Price of Y	Income
150.........	$2.00	$10,000
130.........	$3.00	$10,000

Compute again the cross elasticity of demand. Note that the sign changes. Economists frequently, though not always, classify two goods as substitutes when the quantity of one varies directly with the price of the second and as complements when the price of the first varies inversely with the price of the second. Note that cross elasticity can vary with income, so there is nothing inherent in the good itself that makes it a substitute or complement. We will discuss substitutes and complements much more completely in Chapter 4.

7. Begin by graphing straight line demand and supply curves determining equilibrium. Next let demand remain constant and shift supply. Show that the more elastic is demand the greater the change in equilibrium quantity and the less the change in equilibrium price for a given shift in supply. Let supply remain constant while demand changes. Analyze the effect of supply elasticity upon the changes in price and quantity.

8. Consider the following straight-line demand and supply curves:

$$q_d = 50 - 2p$$
$$q_s = 2 + p$$

Define equilibrium as the point where $q_d = q_s$. Find the equilibrium price and quantity (set $q_s = q_d$ and solve for p, then use either demand or supply to solve for q). If a ceiling price of $12.00 is set, what will be the amount of excess demand? (Recall that excess demand is $q_d - q_s$ at $12.00). If a floor price of $20.00 is set, what will be the excess supply?

9. Draw a downsloping demand curve that is concave from below; that is, it is below its tangent at every point. Derive graphically the point elasticity of demand at a point where the curve is quite steep; next show the point elasticity where the curve is not so steep. Find a point of unitary elasticity.

10. Consider an increase in the demand for gasoline in the United States. Describe what would happen in the momentary situation, in the short run, and in the long run.

chapter 3

Theory of Consumer Behavior: Tools of Analysis

3.1 INTRODUCTION

In the discussion of demand and supply in Chapter 2 we postulated certain characteristics of demand curves without analyzing the specific behavioral patterns upon which they are based. Since demand itself is directly related to the way in which consumers are willing and able to act, it is necessary to understand consumer behavior in order to understand the determinants of demand. This chapter and the following describe the modern theory of consumer behavior and the relations between that theory and the theory of demand. First, the tools of analysis are developed; then these tools are used to analyze the way in which consumer behavior affects demand, with particular emphasis upon explaining why market demand curves are negatively sloped.

3.1.a—Example of Marginal Analysis

Before beginning the formal analysis it may be useful to describe a simple hypothetical case in which someone is attempting to maximize something under a fixed constraint. Since the principles developed intuitively here are quite similar to those developed formally later, the analysis should prove instructive.

Imagine a college student cramming for final examinations. He only has six hours of study time remaining and his goal is to get as high an *average* grade as possible in three subjects: economics, mathematics, and statistics (that is, his goal is to maximize the sum of the test scores in the three subjects). His fixed constraint is the remaining time; his goal is to maximize his scores. He must decide how to allocate his time among the subjects.

According to the best estimates he can make, his grade in each subject will depend upon the time allocated to it according to the following schedule:

Economics		Mathematics		Statistics	
Hours of Study	Grade	Hours of Study	Grade	Hours of Study	Grade
0	20	0	40	0	80
1	45	1	52	1	90
2	65	2	62	2	95
3	75	3	71	3	97
4	83	4	78	4	98
5	90	5	83	5	99
6	92	6	86	6	99

What should be his allocation? One method of solving the problem is to add the estimated grades from all possible combinations of study time. We see for example, that if the student allocates three hours to economics, two to mathematics, and one to statistics, his expected total grade is 227 or an average of 75%. By experiment we see also that this grade is higher than any other grade that can be obtained from six hours of study.

Sampling every possible combination of study times can be very complicated. There is a simpler method. First note that the student can obtain grades of 20, 40, and 80 in the three subjects without any study time. Let us now prepare a table showing the *additional* grade points per additional hour spent on each subject. Economists call this the *marginal* return or *marginal* increase.

Now the student can allocate by maximizing the marginal increase from each successive hour of studying up to six. He will allocate the first and the second hours to economics; the return there is highest, 25 and 20 points respectively. The highest return for the third hour is the 12 points he can add by studying mathematics. Each of the remaining three hours are worth 10 points in each of the three areas. As before, we obtain the same allocation three hours in economics, two in mathematics, and one in statistics.

The third method is to allocate time until the ratio of the marginal increases in grade for each pair of subjects equals the ratio of the prices. The price of studying one subject an additional hour is *one hour;* the price ratio is accordingly unity between any two subjects. The allocation of time at which the ratios of all marginal increases are unity is where each marginal increase is ten, the same solution as above. This last method of allocation probably is not at all intuitively obvious to you now. The formal theory must be developed before this approach becomes clear.

The other two approaches should be clear. In any case they should give some indication of the type of analysis used in the theory of consumer behavior.

3.1.b—Utility

The simplest approach to the theory of consumer behavior is based upon a concept called *utility,* which is defined as the satisfaction a person obtains from the goods and services he consumes. Utility is, of course, a subjective phenomenon because each person's physiological and psychological makeup is different from every other's. Yet, if one sought a single criterion to distinguish modern microeconomic theory from its classical antecedents, he would probably find it to be the introduction of *subjective value theory* into economics. Historically, the process of development was a long and involved one. Our discussion of it, however, will be brief; only the most important steps are mentioned.

The earliest psychological approaches to the theory of demand were based upon the notion of subjective utility, as found in the works of Hermann Gossen (1854), William S. Jevons (1871), and Leon Walras (1874). Just as modern theorists do, they assumed that any good or service consumed by a household provides utility. In contrast to most modern theorists, however, they also assumed that utility is cardinally measurable and additive and that the utility derived from one good is independent of the rate of consumption of any other good. We must digress briefly for a definition:

Definition: Cardinal measurability implies that the *difference* between two numbers is itself numerically significant. For example, apples are cardinally measurable; and one may say that four apples are exactly twice as many as two apples. A measurement system is said to be *ordinal* if items can only be ranked as 1st, 2nd, 3rd, and so on. Note: Numerical significance cannot be attached to the difference between 1st and 2nd, 2nd and 3rd, and so on. Each measurement system ranks items. The difference is that in an ordinal system, one can say (for example) that x is greater than y; in a cardinal system, he can say by how much x exceeds y.

Now to return to our train of thought. The more of one good consumed, the greater the total utility associated with it. Each *additional* unit of the good consumed per unit of time adds to total utility, but each adds less than the previous unit. For example, one piece of candy per day might yield a measurable five units of utility. Two pieces per day might yield 9 units of utility; 3 pieces, 11 units; and so on. That is, the second piece of candy adds four units of utility; one less than the first. The third adds two units to the total, two less than the second. Since utility was assumed to be cardinally measurable and additive by these theorists, and since the consumption of one good was assumed to have no effect upon the utility derived from another, a person's total utility is simply the sum of the utilities provided by all the goods he consumes.

Later economists, such as F. Y. Edgeworth (1881), G. B. Antonelli (1886), and Irving Fisher (1892), objected to the additivity assumption. Instead, they assumed that while utility is cardinally measurable, it is not simply the sum of the independent utilities obtained from the consumption of each good. These theorists related the level of total utility to the rates of consumption of all goods simultaneously. In terms of the previous example, the extra or *marginal utility* added by each additional piece of candy depends, among other things, upon the amount of ice cream consumed. Likewise, the extra or marginal utility added by each additional serving of ice cream depends, among other things, upon the amount of pie consumed. Nonetheless, this newer form of the theory rests upon the questionable assumption of *cardinally* measurable utility.

Implicit in the paragraph above is an important definition:

Definition: Marginal utility is the addition to total utility attributable to the addition of one unit of a good to the current rate of its consumption. According to the paragraph above, the marginal utility of good *X* depends not only upon its rate of consumption but upon the rates of consumption of other goods as well.

The last major step in the development of modern utility theory enabled economists to use the concept of utility without resorting to the assumption of cardinal measurability. This final step, which is essentially attributable to Vilfredo Pareto (1906), led to the use of *indifference curves* in analyzing consumer behavior. However, before we use indifference curves, it is essential to examine assumptions underlying this concept.

3.1.c—Assumptions

First, we assume that each consumer has complete information on all matters pertaining to his consumption decisions. A consumer knows the full range of goods available in the market; he knows the technical capacity of each good to satisfy a want. Furthermore, he knows the exact price of each good, and he knows these prices will not be changed by his actions in the market. Finally, the consumer knows what his income will be during his planning period. Given all this information, we also assume that each consumer tries to maximize his satisfaction from consumption *given* his limited income.

Admittedly these assumptions are abstractions from reality. The consumer has only a fairly accurate notion of what his income will be for a reasonable planning period, not perfect knowledge. He only has a notion of the capacity of a good to satisfy a want, not precise knowledge of its capacity to satisfy. No consumer actually succeeds in the task of spending his limited income so as to maximize satisfaction. This failure is attributable to the lack of accurate information. Yet the more or less conscious effort to attain maximum satisfaction from a limited income determines an individual's demand for goods and services. The assumption of complete information does not distort the relevant aspects of the economic world.

Second, we assume that each consumer is able to rank all conceivable bundles of commodities. That is, when confronted with two or more bundles of goods, he is able to determine his order of preference among them. For example, assume that a person is confronted with two choices: (*a*) he can have five candy bars, six pints of ice cream, and one soft drink; or (*b*) he can have four candy bars, five pints of ice cream, and three soft drinks. The person can say one of three things: (*a*) he prefers the first bundle to the second; (*b*) he prefers the second to the first; or (*c*) he would be equally satisfied with either.

Therefore, when evaluating two bundles of goods, an individual either prefers one bundle of goods to the other, or he is indifferent between the two. Since we will use the concept of preference and indifference time and again, it is essential to understand this concept thoroughly now. If a consumer prefers one group of goods to another group, he obviously believes he will get a higher level of satisfaction from the preferred group. The less preferred bundle would, he believes, give less utility than the other. If a person is indifferent between two bundles, he would be perfectly willing to let someone else (or perhaps the flip of a coin) determine his choice. An economist would say that in the consumer's mind either bundle would yield him the same level of utility.

Much of what follows is based upon the consumer's ability to rank groups of commodities; it is important, however, to note what we *did not say* about consumer preference and indifference.

First, we did not say that the consumer estimates *how much* utility or *what level* of satisfaction he will attain from consuming a given bundle of goods. Only the ability to *rank* is fundamental; the ability to measure utility cardinally is not necessary.

Second, we did not imply that an individual can say by *how much* he prefers one bundle of goods to another. Admittedly, a consumer might be able to say he likes one group of goods a great deal more than another group, and perhaps just a little more than still another group. But "great deal" and "just a little" are imprecise; their meanings differ from one person to another. Therefore, at this level of abstraction the theory of consumer behavior is not based upon the assumption that the consumer is able to state the amount by which he prefers one bundle to another.[1]

Third, we did not say *we think he should* choose one bundle over the other, or that we believe he will be better off if he did so. It is only necessary that the consumer be able to rank bundles according to the order of anticipated satisfaction.

Furthermore, we assume that the consumer's preference pattern possesses the following characteristics:

a. Given three bundles of goods (*A, B,* and *C*), if an individual prefers *A* to *B* and *B* to *C*, he must prefer *A* to *C*. Similarly, if an individual is indifferent between *A* and *B* and between *B* and *C*, he must be indifferent between *A* and *C*. Finally, if he is indifferent between *A* and *B* and prefers *B* to *C*, he must prefer *A* to *C*. This assumption obviously can be carried over to four or more different bundles.

b. It therefore follows that if an individual can rank *any pair* of bundles chosen at random from all conceivable bundles, he can rank *all conceivable bundles.*

c. If bundle *A* contains at least as many units of *each commodity* as bundle B, and more units of at least one commodity, A must be preferred to B.

Note, we did not say that if a real world consumer *purchases* one good rather than another he prefers the chosen good. If you drive a Ford rather than a Rolls Royce, we cannot infer that you prefer a Ford to a Rolls. If the Rolls cost less than the Ford at the time of purchase, and you were aware of this, then we could make this inference. If as was probably the case, the Rolls costs more, we can say nothing. If the two goods are presented at equal cost, and you choose one over the other we could say that you prefer that good. Or if two goods are priced differently and you choose the higher price good, we could again deduce that you prefer that good. But if you choose the lower price good, we could say nothing.

Summarizing, the assumptions necessary to analyze consumer behavior can be set out in the following compact form.

Assumptions: (*a*) Each consumer has exact and full knowledge of all information relevant to his consumption decisions—knowledge of the goods and services available and of their technical capacity to satisfy his wants, of market prices, and of his money income.

(*b*) Each consumer has a preference pattern that (*i*) establishes a rank ordering among all bundles of goods; (*ii*) for pairwise comparisons, indicates that *A* is preferred to *B*, *B* preferred to *A*, or that they are indifferent; (*iii*) for three or more way comparisons, indicates that if *A* is

---

[1] It is not quite correct to say that it is impossible to measure the degree of preference. Advanced studies in price theory frequently deal to a greater or lesser extent with the application of probability theory to the problem of ranking budgets. Considerable controversy exists concerning the usefulness of that approach.

preferred (indifferent) to *B* and *B* is preferred (indifferent) to *C*, *A* must be preferred (indifferent) to *C;* (*iv*) states that a greater bundle (in the sense of having at least as much of each good and more of at least one) is always preferred to a smaller one.

3.2 INDIFFERENCE CURVES

Using the assumptions set forth above, we can now analyze two concepts that are fundamental to the theory of consumer behavior, indifference curves and indifference maps.

Definition: An indifference curve is a locus of points—or particular bundles or combinations of goods—each of which yields the same level of total utility or satisfaction.

Definition: An indifference map is a graph that shows a set of indifference curves.

For analytical purposes let us consider a consumer who can use only two different goods, *X* and *Y*, each of which is continuously divisible or infinitesimally variable in quantity.[2] Figure 3.2.1 shows a portion of this consumer's indifference map consisting of four indifference curves labeled I–IV. Our consumer considers all combinations of *X* and *Y* on indifference curve I to be equivalent (for example, 20 *X* and 42 *Y*, and 60 *X* and 10 *Y*); that is, he believes these combinations will yield him the same satisfaction and thus he is indifferent among them. Since he is indifferent between the two specified combinations, he is obviously willing to substitute *X* for *Y* in order to move from point *a* to point *b*. In other words, he is willing to give up 32 units of *Y* to obtain 40 additional units of *X*. Conversely, if he is presently situated at *b* he is willing to forego 40 units of *X* to obtain an additional 32 units of *Y*. Thus he is willing to substitute at the *average* rate of $\frac{4}{5}$ units of *Y* per unit of *X*.

All combinations of goods on indifference curve II (say 30 *Y* and 50 *X*) are superior to *any* combinations of goods on I. Likewise, all combinations on III are superior to any combination on II. Each indifference curve that lies above a given indifference curve represents combinations of *X* and *Y* that are considered superior to, or capable of yielding more utility than, every combination on the lower curve. At every utility level

---

[2] Admittedly, the possibility of continuous variation in quantity *is* perhaps less frequently encountered than "lumpiness," but this assumption permits a great gain in analytical precision at the sacrifice of very little realism. The assumption that bundles consist of no more than two separate goods enables us to analyze the problem of consumer behavior with two dimensional graphs. This assumption is made, therefore, purely for simplicity of exposition. With the use of the differential calculus, bundles of any number of different goods can be handled. But the analytical results based on two goods are exactly the same as those based upon more than two. Here again, the gain in simplicity outweighs the loss of realism.

FIGURE 3.2.1

Indifference Curves

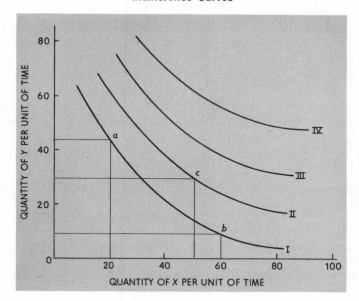

designated by a particular indifference curve, the consumer is willing to substitute X for Y or Y for X at some rate so as to leave him on the same curve (that is, with the same satisfaction or utility level) but consuming different combinations of goods.

Since X and Y are assumed to be continuously divisible, each indifference curve specifies an infinite number of combinations that yield the same amount of satisfaction. Further, it is important to note that the specific utility numbers attached to I, II, III, and IV are immaterial. The numbers might be 5, 7, 12, 32 or 96, 327, 450, 624 or any other set of numbers that *increase*. For the theory of consumer behavior, only the shape of the indifference curves matters. That is to say, only the ordinal ranking of commodity bundles is important. Since a precise measurement of utility is unnecessary, the theory of consumer behavior does not have to be based on the questionable concept of measurable utility. The indifference curves and the concept of preference are all that are required —all bundles of goods situated on the same indifference curve are equivalent; all combinations lying on a higher curve are preferred.

Relations: A consumer regards all bundles yielding the same level of utility as equivalent. The locus of such bundles is called an indifference curve because the consumer is indifferent as to the particular bundle he consumes. The higher, or further to the right, an indifference curve, the greater is the underlying level of utility. Therefore, the higher the indifference curve, the more preferred is each bundle situated on the curve.

To summarize, the essential difference between the older approaches mentioned above and the approach followed here lies in the nature of the measurement scale involved. In the older approaches, utility was assumed to be *cardinally measurable* in some sort of units. The indifference curve approach requires only *ordinal* (ordered or ranking) measurement. Thus the only requirement is that indifference curves rank bundles of goods according to preference. In Figure 3.2.1 all combinations on IV are most preferred; all combinations on III are preferred to those on II and are less desirable than those on IV, and so on.

3.3 CHARACTERISTICS OF INDIFFERENCE CURVES

Indifference curves have four characteristics that are important in our discussion of consumer behavior. The first and fourth properties are assumed ones; the second is based upon our assumptions about consumer behavior; the third is a logical necessity.

For simplicity, assume once more that there are only two continuously divisible goods, X and Y. The X–Y plane is called *commodity space*. The first property is that each point in commodity space lies on one, and only one, indifference curve. This assumption is, of course, derived from the prior assumption that X and Y are continuously divisible. Each point in commodity space represents some specific combination of the two goods and hence some level of utility. As mentioned above, it is possible

FIGURE 3.3.1

Indifference Curves Cannot Intersect

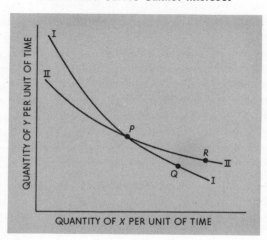

QUANTITY OF X PER UNIT OF TIME

to take away Y and add X or take away X and add Y in an infinite number of ways and leave the consumer with the same level of satisfaction. Thus each point in commodity space lies on an indifference curve (and from the third property, each lies on only one indifference curve). However, for obvious reasons, when graphing an indifference map, only a relatively few curves are used to represent the entire map. But remember: an infinite number of indifference curves lie between any two indifference curves that are drawn.

Second, indifference curves are negatively sloped. This property is based on the assumption that a consumer prefers a greater bundle of goods to a smaller one. An upward sloping indifference curve would indicate that a consumer is indifferent between two combinations of goods, one of which contains more of *both* goods. The fact that a positive amount of one good must be added to the bundle to offset the loss of another good (if the consumer is to remain at the same level of satisfaction) implies negatively sloped indifference curves.

Third, indifference curves cannot intersect. This property is a logical necessity, as illustrated in Figure 3.3.1. In this graph I and II are indifference curves, and the points P, Q, and R represent three different bundles (or combinations of X and Y). R must clearly be preferred to Q because it contains more of both goods. R and P are equivalent because they are situated on the same indifference curve. In like manner, the consumer is indifferent between P and Q. Indifference is a "transitive" relation—that is, if a consumer is indifferent between A and B and between B and C, he must be indifferent between A and C. In our case, R and P are equivalent, as are P and Q. Hence R must be equivalent to Q.

FIGURE 3.3.2

Indifference Curves Are Concave from Above

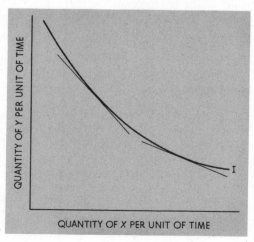

QUANTITY OF Y PER UNIT OF TIME

QUANTITY OF X PER UNIT OF TIME

But as previously mentioned, R is preferred to Q because it contains more of both goods. Hence intersecting indifference curves, such as those shown in Figure 3.3.1, are logically impossible.

The fourth property is that indifference curves are *concave from above* —that is, an indifference curve must lie above its tangent at each point, as illustrated in Figure 3.3.2. The consequences of this property are discussed in the next section dealing with the marginal rate of substitution.

The results of this section may be summarized in the following:

Relations: Indifference curves have the following properties: (*a*) some indifference curve passes through each point in commodity space; (*b*) indifference curves slope downward to the right; (*c*) indifference curves cannot intersect; and (*d*) indifference curves are concave from above.

3.4 MARGINAL RATE OF SUBSTITUTION

As previously emphasized, one essential feature of subjective value theory is that different combinations of commodities can give rise to the same level of utility. In other words, the consumer is indifferent as to the particular combination he obtains. Therefore, as market prices might dictate, one commodity can be substituted for another in the right amount so that the consumer remains just as well off as before. He will, in other words, remain on the same indifference curve. It is of considerable interest to know the rate at which a consumer is willing to substitute one commodity for another in his consumption.

The reason for analyzing this rate of substitution so carefully lies in the concept of utility maximization. As we shall see later in this chapter, a consumer attains maximum satisfaction from his limited money income when he chooses a combination of goods such that the rate at which he is *willing* to substitute goods is the same as the rate at which he is *permitted* to substitute by market prices. Therefore, to understand utility maximization one must understand the rate of substitution in consumption.

3.4.a—Substitution in Consumption

Consider Figure 3.4.1. An indifference curve is represented by I. The consumer is indifferent between bundle R, containing 4 units of X and 18 of Y, and bundle P, containing 11 units of X and 8 of Y. The consumer is willing to substitute 7 units of X for 10 of Y. The *rate* at which he is willing, on average, to substitute X for Y is therefore

$$\frac{\Delta Y}{\Delta X} = \frac{RS}{SP} = \frac{18 - 8}{4 - 11} = -\frac{10}{7},$$

where Δ means "the change in." This ratio measures the average number of units of Y the consumer is willing to forego in order to obtain one

FIGURE 3.4.1

The Marginal Rate of Substitution

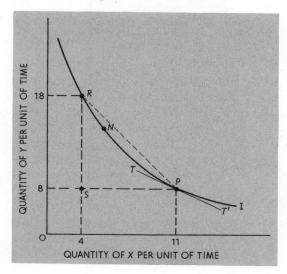

additional unit of X (over the range of consumption pairs under consideration).[3] Thus he is willing to give up $1\frac{3}{7}$ units of Y in order to gain one unit of X. Stated alternatively, the ratio measures the amount of Y that must be sacrificed ($1\frac{3}{7}$ units) per unit of X gained if the consumer is to remain at precisely the same level of satisfaction.

In our subsequent use, we would find it very cumbersome to have the minus sign on the right-hand side of the equation above. Thus we define the rate of substitution as

$$- \frac{\Delta Y}{\Delta X} = \frac{10}{7}.$$

The rate of substitution given by the ratio above is obviously the negative of the slope of the broken straight line joining points R and P. The ratio could be quite different between two alternative points, say N and P. But as the point R moves along I toward P, the ratio RS/SP approaches closer and closer to the slope of the tangent TT' at P. In the limit, for extremely small movements in the neighborhood of P, the negative of the slope of I, which is the negative of the slope of its tangent at P, is called the *marginal rate of substitution of X for Y*.

Definition: The marginal rate of substitution of X for Y measures the number of units of Y that must be sacrificed per unit of X gained so as

---

[3] The ratio is, of course, negative since the change in Y associated with an increase in X is negative. This type of relation results directly from the postulate of negatively sloped indifference curves.

to maintain a constant level of satisfaction. The marginal rate of substitution is given by the negative of the slope of an indifference curve at a point. It is defined only for movements along an indifference curve, never for movements among curves.

Note: Since we wish the marginal rate of substitution to be positive, and since $\Delta Y/\Delta X$ is necessarily negative, the *minus* sign must be attached.

As should be obvious, the term "margin" is again used (as it always is) to denote "the change in" when the change in question is very small.

Note: we shall hereafter use the mnemonic letters *MRS* to denote the marginal rate of substitution of X for Y in consumption or, more generally, the marginal rate of substitution of the variable plotted on the horizontal axis for the variable plotted on the vertical axis.

3.4.b—Interpretation of *MRS*

The meaning of *MRS* may be made clearer if we revert, for the moment, to the older marginal utility approach. First, recall that marginal utility is either (*a*) the increase in utility attributable to a small increase in the rate of consumption of a commodity, holding the level of consumption of all other commodities constant; or (*b*) the decrease in utility attributable to a small decrease in the rate of consumption under the same assumptions.

Now refer to Figure 3.4.2. Suppose the consumer is initially at point *P*, purchasing OY_1 units of Y and OX_1 units of X. He accordingly attains the II level of satisfaction. Suppose his consumption of Y is reduced by a

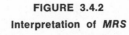

FIGURE 3.4.2

Interpretation of *MRS*

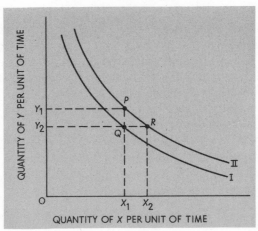

small amount, from OY_1 to OY_2. He moves to point Q on I and suffers a loss of utility represented by the difference between II and I, denoted II–I (for example, if II represents 100 units of utility and I represents 90, he loses 10 units of utility).

The marginal utility of this small reduction in Y consumption is thus the decrease in utility divided by the decrease in Y consumed. If we denote marginal utility by MU, we may represent this change by

$$MU_Y = \frac{\text{II} - \text{I}}{OY_1 - OY_2}.$$

Now let the consumer return to the II level of utility by holding Y consumption at OY_2 and increasing X consumption from OX_1 to OX_2. The marginal utility of X, by our argument above, is

$$MU_X = \frac{\text{II} - \text{I}}{OX_2 - OX_1}.$$

Taking the ratio of the two marginal utilities, one obtains

$$\frac{MU_X}{MU_Y} = \frac{\text{II} - \text{I}}{OX_2 - OX_1} \div \frac{\text{II} - \text{I}}{OY_1 - OY_2} = \frac{OY_1 - OY_2}{OX_2 - OX_1}.$$

But by the figure,

$$\frac{MU_X}{MU_Y} = \frac{OY_1 - OY_2}{OX_2 - OX_1} = \frac{PQ}{QR} = \text{rate of substitution.}$$

Thus for very small movements in the neighborhood of R, the MRS of X for Y is the ratio of the marginal utility of X to the marginal utility of Y. We may thus formulate an alternative

Definition: the MRS of X for Y is equal to the ratio of the marginal utility of X to the marginal utility of Y. In symbols,

$$MRS_{X \text{ for } Y} = \frac{MU_X}{MU_Y}.$$

3.5   DIMINISHING *MRS*

The requirement that indifference curves be concave from above implies that the MRS of X for Y diminishes as X is substituted for Y along an indifference curve. This is illustrated in Figure 3.5.1.

I is an indifference curve; R, N, Q, and P are four bundles situated on this curve. Consider a movement from R to N. In order to maintain the same level of utility, the consumer is willing to sacrifice slightly more than two units of Y to gain one unit of X. Now consider the consumer situated at Q. To move to P and gain one unit of X, the consumer now is willing to give up approximately ½ unit of Y.

This result follows logically from our assumptions that the more of a

FIGURE 3.5.1

Diminishing Marginal Rate of Substitution

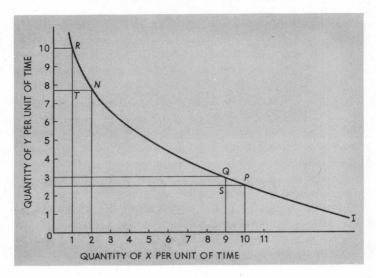

good one consumes, the more of that good he would probably be willing to trade for some other good. For example, if a person at a football game has ten hot dogs and one soft drink, he might be willing to trade three hot dogs for a soft drink. On the other hand, if the same person had only five hot dogs, but three soft drinks, he would perhaps be willing to trade only one hot dog for an additional soft drink.

A marginal utility interpretation of this example might help. First remember that we assume the marginal utility of any commodity is smaller the greater the rate of its consumption. Now picture a graph (or construct one for yourself) in which the number of hot dogs is plotted on the vertical axis, the number of soft drinks on the horizontal.

When the number of hot dogs is great, the marginal utility of hot dogs is relatively low. Similarly, when the number of soft drinks is low, their marginal utility is relatively high. Thus the *MRS*, which is the ratio of the marginal utility of soft drinks to that of hot dogs, is relatively high. Now let the football fan substitute soft drinks for hot dogs (*X* for *Y*, in the previous notation). Increasing the rate of consumption of soft drinks decreases their marginal utility, while reducing the rate of consumption of hot dogs increases theirs. Thus the substitution of soft drinks for hot dogs must lead to a decrease in the *MRS* of soft drinks for hot dogs.

Diminishing *MRS* is further illustrated in Figure 3.5.2. *I* is an indifference curve, and *P*, *Q*, and *R* are three bundles situated on this curve. The horizontal axis is measured so that $OX_1 = X_1X_2 = X_2X_3$. Consider

FIGURE 3.5.2

Diminishing MRS

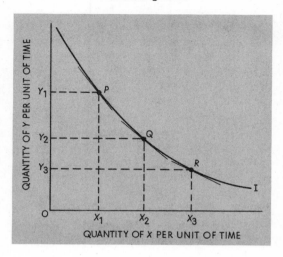

first the movement from P to Q. If P is very close to Q, or the amount X_1X_2 is very small, the MRS at Q is

$$\frac{OY_1 - OY_2}{OX_2 - OX_1} = \frac{Y_1Y_2}{X_1X_2}.$$

Similarly, for a movement from Q to R, the MRS at R is

$$\frac{OY_2 - OY_3}{OX_3 - OX_2} = \frac{Y_2Y_3}{X_2X_3}.$$

By construction $X_1X_2 = X_2X_3$; but very obviously $Y_1Y_2 > Y_2Y_3$. Hence the MRS is less at R than at Q. This is also shown by the absolutely decreasing slopes of the tangents at P, Q, and R.

3.6 THE BUDGET LINE

In Chapter 2 we emphasized that demand indicates what the consumer is willing and able to do. Thus far in this chapter we have concentrated upon what the consumer is *willing* to do; we must now discuss what the consumer is *able* to do.

3.6.a—Limited Money Income

If all consumers had an unlimited money income—in other words, if there were an unlimited pool of resources—there would be no problem of "economizing," nor would there be "economics." But since this utopian state does not exist, even for the richest members of our society, people are compelled to determine their behavior in light of limited financial resources. For the theory of consumer behavior, this means that each consumer has a maximum amount he can spend per period of time. The consumer's problem is to spend this amount in the way that yields him maximum satisfaction.

Continue to assume that there are only two goods, X and Y, bought in quantities x and y. Each individual consumer is confronted with market-determined prices p_x and p_y of X and Y respectively. Finally, the consumer in question has a known and fixed money income (M) for the period under consideration. M is the maximum amount the consumer can spend, and we assume that he spends all of this on X and Y.[4] Thus the amount spent on X (xp_x) plus the amount spent on Y (yp_y) is equal to the stipulated money income. Algebraically,

$$M = xp_x + yp_y. \tag{3.6.1}$$

This equation can be expressed as the equation for a straight line. Solving for y—since y is plotted on the vertical axis—one obtains

$$y = \frac{1}{p_y} M - \frac{p_x}{p_y} x. \tag{3.6.2}$$

Equation (3.6.2) is plotted in Figure 3.6.1. The first term on the right-hand side of equation (3.6.2), $\frac{1}{p_y} M$, shows the amount of Y that can be purchased if no X is purchased at all. This amount is represented by the distance OA in Figure 3.6.1; thus $\frac{1}{p_y} M$ (or point A) is the ordinate intercept of the equation.

In equation (3.6.2) $-\frac{p_x}{p_y}$ is the slope of the line. Consequently, the slope of the budget constraint is the negative of the price ratio. To see this, consider the quantity of X that can be purchased if Y is not bought. This amount is $\frac{1}{p_x} M$, shown by the distance OB in Figure 3.6.1. Since the line obviously has a negative slope, its slope is given by

$$-\frac{OA}{OB} = -\frac{\dfrac{1}{p_y} M}{\dfrac{1}{p_x} M} = -\frac{p_x}{p_y}.$$

---

[4] In more advanced models, saving may be considered as one of the many goods and services available to the consumer. Graphical treatment limits us to two dimensions; thus we ignore saving. This does not mean that the theory of consumer behavior precludes saving—depending upon his preference ordering, a consumer may save much, little, or nothing. Similarly, spending may in fact exceed income in any given period as a result of borrowing or from using assets acquired in the past. The M in question for any period is the total amount of money to be spent during the period.

FIGURE 3.6.1

Budget Line

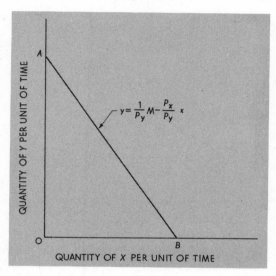

QUANTITY OF X PER UNIT OF TIME

The line in Figure 3.6.1 is called the budget line.

Definition: The budget line is the locus of combinations or bundles of goods that can be purchased if the entire money income is spent. Its slope is the negative of the price ratio.

Note again our assumption that the consumer spends all his money income on X and Y. This implies that the bundle purchased must lie on the budget line.

3.6.b—Shifting the Budget Line

In much of the analysis that follows, we are interested in comparative static changes in quantities purchased resulting from changes in price and money income, both of which are represented graphically by shifts in the budget line.

In Figure 3.6.2, X is a specific good, the quantity of which is measured along the horizontal axis. In contrast, to the preceding discussion, however, Y does not represent another specific good. Let us now call Y "total expenditures on all goods other than X" and measure this amount along the vertical axis. Naturally, the unit of measurement along the horizontal axis is units of X per period of time, and the unit of measurement along the vertical is dollars. We assume that the prices of all goods other than X are fixed.

At the outset, let the price of X be $5 per unit and the consumer's in-

FIGURE 3.6.2

Budget Lines for Changing Income

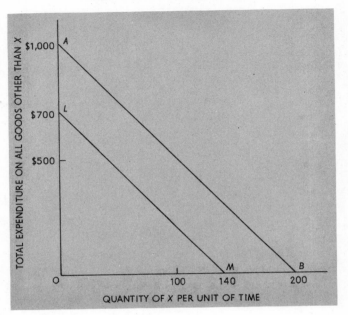

come be $1,000. His budget line (in Figure 3.6.2) is represented by *AB*, a line from $1,000 on the vertical axis to 200 on the horizontal. At a price of $5, the consumer can purchase 200 units of *X* if he spends nothing on other goods (point *B*), he can spend $1,000 on other goods if he buys no *X* (point *A*), or he can consume any other combination represented by a point on *AB*.

As before, the slope of the budget line is the negative of the ratio of the prices. But the price of an additional dollar of expenditure on other goods is obviously one dollar. The negative of the price ratio is, therefore, $-p_x/1 = -p_x$, so the slope of *AB* is -5. To increase his consumption of *X* by one unit, the consumer must give up $5 in expenditures on other goods.

Now let the consumer suffer a $300 decrease in income while all other prices, including the price of *X*, remain the same. The new budget line is *LM*. The consumer can spend $700 (his new income) on other goods, buying no *X*; he can spend the entire $700 on *X*, purchasing 140 units; or he can consume at any other point on the line. The slope of the new budget line *LM* is the same (-5) since the price ratio has not changed. Thus a decrease in money income, prices unchanged, is represented by a parallel shift of the budget line, downward and to the left. It should be easy to see that an *increase* in money income, prices unchanged, is represented by a parallel shift in the other direction.

Figure 3.6.3 shows what happens to the budget line when the price of X increases, money income remaining the same. The axes in this figure are the same as those in Figure 3.6.2. Assume once again that the original money income is $1,000 and the original price of X is $5 per unit. The budget line AB is the same as in Figure 3.6.2. Now assume that the price

FIGURE 3.6.3

Budget Lines for Changing Price of X

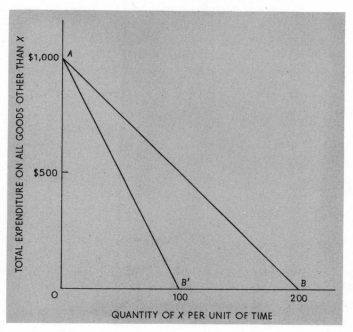

of X increases to $10. As before, the consumer can spend $1,000 on other goods if he purchases no X; the intercept of the budget line on the vertical axis thus remains the same. However, if the consumer spends all his income on X, at the new price of $10 he can buy only 100 units of X with his $1,000 income. The budget line intercepts the horizontal axis at B'. Note that the slope of the budget line (the negative of the price of X) becomes steeper, from −5 to −10. AB' represents the new budget line. An increase in the price of X thus rotates the budget line to the left around point A, the intercept on the vertical axis. It should be easy to see that a decrease in price causes the budget line to rotate to the right.

For an alternative approach, assume that both X and Y are specific goods. In Figure 3.6.4 budget line *AB* is associated with a lower income than budget line *A'B'*. Since the slopes of *AB* and *A'B'* are equal, the price ratio remains constant as the change in money income shifts the budget line. Figure 3.6.5 shows what happens to the budget line when the price of *X* changes, the money price of *Y* (some other good) and money income remaining constant. Since the slope of the budget line is

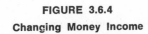

FIGURE 3.6.4

Changing Money Income

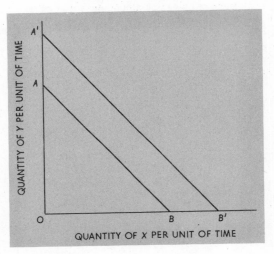

$- p_x/p_y$, the steeper line, *AB'*, is associated with a higher price of *X* than *AB*.

Alternatively, the price change can be explained as follows. At the original price p_x, the maximum purchase of *X* is $\frac{1}{p_x} M$, or the distance *OB*. When the price changes to $p_x{}^*$, the maximum purchase of *X* is $\frac{1}{p_x{}^*} M$, or the distance *OB'*. Thus an increase in the price of *X* is shown by rotating the budget line clockwise around the ordinate intercept. A decrease in the price of *X* is represented by a counterclockwise movement.

Relations: (a) An increase in money income, prices unchanged, is shown by a parallel shift of the budget line—outward and to the right for an increase in money income, and in the direction of the origin for a decrease in money income. (b) A change in the price of *X*, the price of *Y* and money income constant, is shown by rotating the budget line around the ordinate intercept—to the left for a price increase and to the right for a decrease in price.

FIGURE 3.6.5

Changing the Price of X

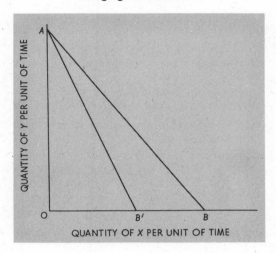

3.7 CONSUMER EQUILIBRIUM

All bundles of goods (combinations of X and Y) designated by the budget line are available to the consumer in the sense that his income allows him to purchase them if he wishes. This line is established by his fixed money income and the given prices of the commodities available. The consumer's indifference map shows his rank ordering of all conceivable bundles of X and Y. The principal assumption upon which the theory of consumer behavior is built is that *a consumer attempts to allocate his limited money income among available goods and services so as to maximize his satisfaction or utility.* Given that assumption and the concepts developed in this chapter, it is a relatively simple matter to determine the way in which a consumer will allocate his income; that is, select the most preferred bundle of goods available to him.

3.7.a—Maximizing Satisfaction Subject to a Limited Money Income

Graphically, the consumer's problem is depicted by Figure 3.7.1. A portion of his indifference map, represented by the four indifference curves drawn in that figure, indicates his preferences among different combinations of goods. Similarly, his budget line, *LM*, specifies the different combinations he can purchase with his limited income, assuming he spends all of his income on X and Y. Thus his choice of combinations is limited by his limited income.

Clearly, the consumer cannot purchase any bundle lying above and to

FIGURE 3.7.1

Consumer Equilibrium

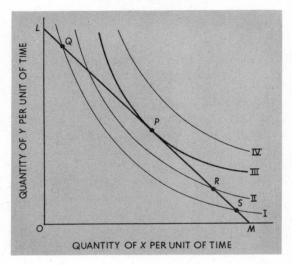

QUANTITY OF X PER UNIT OF TIME

the right of budget line *LM*, and hence he cannot consume any combination lying on indifference curve IV. He can attain some points on curves I, II, and III. Moreover, as already observed, an infinite number of indifference curves lie between curves I and III. Therefore, all points on the budget line between *Q* and *S* are touched by some indifference curve (and, if we extend the map to include curves below I, all points above *Q* and below *S* are touched by some curve). Thus each point on the budget line yields some specific level of utility. Four of the infinite number of attainable combinations on *LM* are represented by points *Q*, *P*, *R*, and *S*.

Suppose the consumer is located at *Q*. Without experimenting, he cannot know for certain whether *Q* represents a maximum position or not. Thus let him experimentally move to combinations just to the left and right of *Q*, along *LM*. Moving to the left lowers his level of satisfaction to some indifference curve below I. But moving to the right brings him to a higher indifference curve; and continued experimentation will lead him to move at least as far as *P*, because each successive movement to the right brings the consumer to a higher indifference curve. If he continued to experiment, however, by moving to the right of *P*, the consumer would find himself upon a lower indifference curve with its lower level of satisfaction. He would accordingly return to the point *P*.

Similarly, if a consumer were situated at *R*, experimentation would lead him to substitute *Y* for *X*, thereby moving in the direction of *P*. He would not stop short of P because each successive substitution of Y for X brings the consumer to a higher indifference curve. Hence the position of maximum satisfaction—*or the point of consumer equilibrium*—is attained at P, where an indifference curve is just tangent to the budget line.

As you will recall, the slope of the budget line is the negative of the price ratio, the ratio of the price of X to the price of Y. As you will also recall, the slope of an indifference curve at any point is called the *MRS* of X for Y. Hence the point of consumer equilibrium is defined by the condition that the *MRS* must equal the price ratio.

The interpretation of this proposition is very straightforward. The *MRS* shows the rate at which the consumer *is willing to substitute* X for Y. The price ratio shows the rate at which he *can substitute* X for Y. Unless these two are equal, it is possible to change the combination of X and Y purchased so as to attain a higher level of satisfaction. For example, suppose the *MRS* is two—meaning the consumer is willing to give up two units of Y in order to obtain one unit of X. Let the price ratio be unity, meaning that one unit of Y can be exchanged for one unit of X. Clearly, the consumer will benefit by trading Y for X, since he is willing to give two Y for one X but only has to give one Y for one X in the market. Generalizing, unless the *MRS* and the price ratio are equal, some exchange can be made so as to push the consumer to a higher level of satisfaction.

Principle: The point of consumer equilibrium—or the maximization of satisfaction subject to a limited money income—is defined by the condition that the *MRS* of *X* for *Y* must equal the ratio of the price of *X* to the price of *Y*.

3.7.b—Marginal Utility Interpretation of Equilibrium

Let us write the condition for consumer equilibrium symbolically:

$$MRS_{x \text{ for } y} = \frac{p_x}{p_y}.$$

Now in section 3.4.b we found that

$$MRS_{x \text{ for } y} = \frac{MU_x}{MU_y}.$$

Thus we may write

$$\frac{MU_x}{MU_y} = \frac{p_x}{p_y},$$

or

$$\frac{MU_x}{p_x} = \frac{MU_y}{p_y}.$$

The relation just above provides an alternative view of the condition for consumer equilibrium. Dividing the marginal utility of a commodity by its price gives the marginal utility per dollar's worth of the commodity bought. In this light we can restate the condition for consumer equilibrium as the following

Principle: To attain equilibrium, a consumer must allocate his money income so that the marginal utility per dollar spent on each commodity is the same for all commodities purchased.

This principle is certainly plausible; and explaining why it is plausible illustrates a method of analysis that is used pervasively in economic theory. Suppose at the current allocation of income, the marginal dollar spent on X yields a greater marginal utility than the marginal dollar spent on Y. That is, suppose

$$\frac{MU_x}{p_x} > \frac{MU_y}{p_y} .$$

Reallocating one dollar of expenditure from Y to X will therefore increase total utility; and it must do so until the marginal utility per dollar's worth is the same for both commodities.

Exercise: Carry out the same line of reasoning for the case in which

$$\frac{MU_x}{p_x} < \frac{MU_y}{p_y} .$$

3.7.c—Corner Solutions

To this point, the discussion implies that in equilibrium the consumer will choose to consume some positive amount of both X and Y, regardless of relative prices. This circumstance obviously need not be the case. A consumer might choose to spend all of his income on one good and purchase none of the other. More particularly, in the next chapter we frequently analyze consumer behavior when X is one good and Y is taken to represent expenditure on all goods other than X. In this case, it would certainly not be uncommon for a consumer to purchase no X, especially if its relative price is high.

One set of theoretical circumstances under which a consumer would choose to spend all of his income on (say) good Y and none on X is depicted in Figure 3.7.2 panel a. Given the budget line LM and the indifference map represented by curves I, II, III, and IV, the highest level of satisfaction attainable from the given money income lies at point L on indifference curve III. The consumer chooses to purchase OL units of Y and no X. This point need not be a point of tangency at which the MRS equals the price ratio (although it could be such a point). Note that an

FIGURE 3.7.2

Corner Solutions

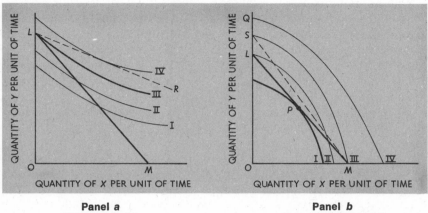

Panel a	Panel b
X Not Bought	X or Y Not Bought

equilibrium situation exists even though there is no point (at both nonnegative X and nonnegative Y) where the MRS equals the price ratio. Economists call such a situation a *corner solution*. Note also, however, that for a sufficiently large decrease in the price of X relative to the price of Y (say to a price ratio depicted by budget line LR), the budget line could become tangent to some indifference curve above III (curve IV) at a point where both X and Y are bought. Hence the consumer will purchase some positive amount of X if its relative price decreases sufficiently.

In other words a corner solution, in which the consumer purchases none of some good X, results when

$$\frac{MU_x}{p_x} < \frac{MU_i}{p_i} = \cdots = \frac{MU_j}{p_j}$$

for all goods i, j, etc. where the ith and jth goods are purchased in finite amounts. The consumer spends all of his income yet the marginal utility per dollar of X is less than the marginal utility per dollar spent on any other good that is purchased. This is generally what we mean when we say that "we cannot afford something." Perhaps you do not own a Cadillac. You say you cannot afford one. Conceivably you could buy one (perhaps by borrowing). So if you do not own one it must be that the alternative expenditure on goods that you consume gives more utility *per dollar* than would a Cadillac, even though a Cadillac would give *more* total utility than your present automobile. Stated differently, one does not consume some good X when the MRS$_{x \text{ for } y}$ (where Y is any other good that is consumed) is less than the price ratio, p_x/p_y, and total income is exhausted.

One last point concerns indifference curves that are not concave from above but are concave from below, as depicted in panel b, Figure 3.7.2. Here the point at which the budget line LM is tangent to an indifference curve, point p, lies not on the highest indifference curve attainable on LM, but on the lowest. The highest level of satisfaction that can be attained, given the budget line LM, lies at point M at the end of indifference curve III. The consumer purchases OM units of X and no Y. Furthermore, there is no price ratio that would induce him to consume at a noncorner or interior point. Suppose the price of Y declines so that the budget line is SM. Now the consumer is indifferent between spending all of his money on Y or all on X; but any other combination would give less satisfaction. A further decrease in the price of Y, say a budget line drawn from Q to M, would cause the consumer to choose OQ units of Y and no X. Therefore, consumer equilibrium for two goods in which finite quantities are chosen requires not only that the MRS equals the price ratio but also that the MRS diminishes along the relevant indifference curve. This last condition is called the second order condition.

3.8   ANALYSES AND APPLICATIONS

3.8.a—Price Search and the Wage Rate

It may well be that you are thinking that people do not in fact react to fixed, market-determined prices. People "shop around" for bargains, for lower prices. Stores advertise their lower prices. Because of the prevalence of price search it may be thought that non-fixed prices refute our theory. No such thing. For many, many economic problems the assumption of given prices is a useful one, which does not affect the theory's ability to make accurate predictions. For other problems the assumption of price search is useful, and this assumption enables one to solve many problems. We can use the simplified theory developed here to analyze the problem of the way in which price search affects consumer behavior.

Assume a consumer with a fixed wage rate. For some goods he is faced with fixed prices. For others the consumer feels that by searching (that is, shopping around) he can find lower prices. For example, he knows that he can buy some good, say X, at p_{xo} (perhaps some catalogue price). He also knows that stores often reduce the price of X, and that prices differ among stores from time to time. He believes that the more time he spends in price search, up to a point, the lower the price he will have to pay for a unit of X; that is, for the consumer $\Delta p_x/\Delta S_x < 0$, where S_x is the time spent in price search for X and, once again, Δ is "the change in." The problem is to determine the amount of time spent shopping for X.

To begin, note that searching for lower prices is not without cost. The total time available is certainly limited; 24 hours in a day, seven days in a week, and so on. The consumer can do three things during this given time: he can work and earn income; he can search and gain reduced prices; he can enjoy leisure (a catchall term that includes consuming goods, sleeping, anything but work and search). He gains utility from leisure just as in the case of a good. Therefore, the cost of a unit of search is the wage that the consumer could have earned had he chosen to work rather than to search.[5] We call this the *opportunity cost* of time.

The expected return from a unit of search is the amount that the consumer believes he will save on a particular purchase by shopping around for a lower price. The expected reduction in price depends upon two things: (1) the efficiency of the consumer in searching and (2) the known price of the product before any search is undertaken. In general, one would feel that the higher the initial price of a good the greater the possible saving from price search. No matter how much you search, you would not reduce the price of a ten cent candy bar more than ten cents. For a higher price item, say a car or a household appliance, the dollar saving may be considerable.

If the consumer values his additional time more (in leisure or in work) than the value of the income he expects to save by additional price search, he will do no more searching. If he values time less, he will search more. Our theory tells us then that consumers will engage in more price search for a good the higher the average price of that good, and the more efficient he is in searching (that is, the higher the return to search). He will engage in less price search for a specific good the higher the wage rate (that is, the higher the cost of search).

The problem is, how do we test this theory? To be operationally meaningful a theory must be susceptible of empirical refutation.[6] For example, a theory that says, "If demand is elastic, an increase in price will decrease total revenue" is not operationally meaningful. It is true by the definition of elasticity and could never be refuted empirically. Our theory of search could be and has been tested. In one study it was shown that a higher price item, an automobile, had less relative price variation than a lower price item, an appliance.[7] One would expect that the more price search undertaken by consumers, the less price variation there would be. Higher price dealers would lose sales and be forced to lower price. If people searched relatively less there would be opportunity for more price variation.

In another study it was shown that the amount of price search people

---

[5] As we shall see in the next chapter, the cost of a unit of leisure is also the wage rate.

[6] For a full discussion see P. A. Samuelson, *Foundations of Economic Analysis* (Cambridge, Mass.: Harvard University Press, 1947) Chapter 1.

[7] See G. J. Stigler, *The Theory of Price,* third edition (New York, The Macmillan Company, 1966) pp. 1–4.

undertake is directly related to their education.[8] If education is directly related to search efficiency, as we would suppose it is, the statement that increased efficiency increases price search is not refuted. The data on wages and price search do not refute the theory that higher wages lead to a higher cost of search time and hence to less search. Neither do they verify it. Over a certain range of incomes, higher incomes are associated with less search; over another range they are associated with more.[9] The problem is that in addition to causing the cost of search to rise, higher wages cause higher incomes also. The higher incomes lead to more purchases, to higher price goods purchased, and thus to more search. The two influences might tend to offset each other. Thus we simply note that the assumption of variable prices can easily be handled in our theory, but we often omit this assumption in the interest of convenience and simplicity, when we are interested in other problems in economics.

3.8.b—Application: The Economics of Philanthropy

It would be a serious mistake if you have acquired the impression, as some people have, that economic theory necessarily assumes humans are coldly calculating individuals concerned only with their personal well-being and therefore are totally uninterested in the welfare of others. This is by no means the case. In fact, we can use the simple analytical techniques developed in this chapter to examine the causes of charitable contributions.[10]

Begin by assuming that an individual's utility depends upon both the amount of his own consumption and the level of consumption enjoyed by other people. Let us assume, for simplicity, only two individuals, A and B. A's utility is a function of his own consumption and of B's. Assume also that it is costless for A to transfer income to B. We need not worry *why* A's utility depends partly upon B's consumption, our only interest is that it does.

Equilibrium for A is depicted by Figure 3.8.1. I_A is one of the family of A's indifference curves between A's own consumption and B's consumption, where B's consumption is measured along the vertical axis and A's along the horizontal. This curve is drawn to reflect A's diminishing marginal rate of substitution between his consumption and B's in the neighborhood of N. That is, around N, the smaller A's consumption be-

---

[8] For several tests, see the unpublished doctoral dissertation by Joel Thomas Kelly, *A Model of Price Search and Allocation of Time in the Theory of Consumer Behavior*, Texas A & M University, 1972, Chapter V.

[9] Ibid.

[10] The remainder of this section is based upon the article by Robert A. Schwartz, "Personal Philanthropic Contributions," *Journal of Political Economy*, Nov./Dec. 1970, pp. 1264–1291.

FIGURE 3.8.1

Philanthopy

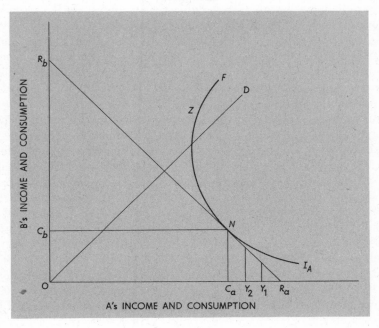

comes relative to B's, the less consumption A is willing to give up to B and remain at the same level of utility. There comes a point at Z where B's consumption is so large relative to A's that the indifference curve bends backwards. That is, A gets *disutility* from any further increases in B's consumption relative to his own. If A's utility increases when B's consumption increases, A feels philanthropic toward B. If A's utility falls from increases in B's consumption, A feels discriminatory. Our curve has been drawn to show that A's feeling toward B depends upon their relative consumption level.

The budget line of A is $R_b R_a$. The distance $OR_b = OR_a$ is the sum of A's and B's income. This is what they both could consume together. Since we assume that transfers are costless, the slope of $R_b R_a$ is unity; that is, a dollar of income transferred from A to B costs A one dollar. The 45° line OD is the line showing equal incomes. Assume that initially A's income is OY_1. Thus B's income is $Y_1 R_a$. A can reach a higher level of utility by transferring $C_a Y_1$ to B, to attain equilibrium at point N. B now consumes OC_b and A consumes OC_a. If A's initial income were less, say OY_2, and B's were larger, A would now transfer less income to B in order to arrive at N, the point of A's highest utility level. Our theory says that the larger one's income relative to another's, the more that will be transferred.

There is, however, another variable that would affect A's willingness to contribute to B. Recall from Chapter 2 that when the price of something falls individuals will demand more. It should be the same for philanthropy. In our model the price was one. A one dollar gift costs the giver one dollar. We observe in the world that a one dollar gift costs less than one dollar when the tax deduction for contributions is considered. The price of a gift is $(1 - T_m)$, where T_m is the marginal tax rate the individual would have paid on the amount that he donated to charity. For example, if someone in the 50% tax bracket makes a deductable $100 donation (we assume he has not reached the deduction ceiling), the cost to him is only $50. He would have been able to keep only $50 of the $100 had he not given the $100 to charity. Thus, our theory predicts that philanthropy depends directly upon one's own income and the marginal tax rate, and indirectly upon the income of others.

This theory has been tested by Robert A. Schwartz for the period 1929–1966.[11] Schwartz aggregated the tax returns of those claiming contributions into three income groups: 0–$10,000; $10,000–$100,000; and greater than $100,000. From the time series he derived elasticities for three variables, price (that is, one minus the tax rate), own income, and income of others. The coefficients of the elasticities had the predicted sign in all income groups over the entire period 1926–1966 and the elasticities were statistically significant.[12] All elasticities were inelastic. For the 0–$10,000 class, price elasticity was −0.85, own income elasticity was 0.19, and income-of-others elasticity was −0.53. For the $10,000–$100,000 group, the respective elasticities were −0.79, +0.76, and −0.43. For the greater than $100,000 group, they were −0.37, +0.40, and −0.38. Schwartz noted that the price elasticity of the highest income group may have been biased downward because some in this group reached the ceiling of deductable contributions.

Many other estimates were made in this same study. The results given here should give some idea about what can be done. We hope that it shows how simple economic theory can be used to analyze relatively complex problems and that we need not assume man is unmotivated by the well-being of others.

3.9 CONCLUSION

Now we are prepared to examine some of the interesting aspects of consumer behavior—how the consumer behaves when confronted with

---

[11] Ibid.

[12] For one sub-period the signs were not as predicted for one group.

changes in his income and in the price ratio. We also have the tools to analyze certain additional economic problems; for example, the relation between an indifference map and demand and the choice between leisure and work.

Among these tools are the following:

Concepts: Marginal utility is the addition to total utility attributable to the addition of one unit of a good to the current rate of consumption. The consumer can rank bundles of goods according to his preferences. He can prefer one bundle to another or he can be indifferent between two bundles. An indifference curve shows combinations of bundles among which a consumer is indifferent. Several indifference curves make an indifference map. The slope of an indifference curve shows the rate at which a consumer is willing to substitute one good for another to remain at a constant level of utility. This slope is called the marginal rate of substitution. The budget line indicates the combinations that the consumer is able to purchase with his limited money income. The market-given price ratio is the slope of the budget line. An increase in income moves the budget line outward, parallel to the old line. A change in a commodity price pivots the budget line. The consumer is in constrained utility-maximizing equilibrium when the budget line is tangent to an indifference curve; that is, when the *MRS* equals the commodity price ratio.

QUESTIONS AND PROBLEMS

1. Comment on the following pair of statements (*a*) consumer preferences are measured by relative prices; (*b*) consumer preferences are independent of relative prices.

2. There are three commodities *X*, *Y*, and *Z*. The table contains a list of bundles composed of different combinations of these three goods. Determine the rank order of the bundles (in this problem, there are no bundles among which the consumer is indifferent).

Bundle	Amount of X	Amount of Y	Amount of Z	Rank Order
A...................	86	88	77	
B...................	86	87	76	
C...................	100	90	80	
D...................	79	80	69	
E...................	85	87	76	
F...................	79	79	68	
G...................	95	89	79	
H...................	80	80	70	
I...................	79	79	69	
J...................	86	87	77	

3. Assume that an individual consumes three goods, *X*, *Y*, and *Z*. The marginal utility (assumed measurable) of each good is independent of the rate

of consumption of the other goods. The prices of the X, Y, and Z are respectively $1, $3, and $5. The total income of the consumer is $65 and his marginal utility schedule is as follows:

Units of Good	Marginal Utility of X (units)	Marginal Utility of Y (units)	Marginal Utility of Z (units)
1...............	12	60	70
2...............	11	55	60
3...............	10	48	50
4...............	9	40	40
5...............	8	32	30
6...............	7	24	25
7...............	6	21	18
8...............	5	18	10
9...............	4	15	3
10...............	3	12	1

    a. How should the consumer allocate his $65 income so as to maximize utility?

    b. Suppose income falls to $43 with the same set of prices; what combination will the consumer choose?

    c. Let income fall to $38; let the price of X rise to $5 while the prices of Y and Z remain at $3 and $5. How does the consumer allocate his income? What would you say if the consumer maintained that he now does not buy X because he can no longer afford it?

4. What does it mean if an indifference curve between goods X and Y *(a)* becomes parallel to the Y axis; *(b)* is positively sloped and has higher indifference curves to its right; *(c)* is positively sloped and has higher indifference curves to its left?

5. In Figure E.3.1, suppose a consumer has the indicated indifference map and the budget line designated *LM*. You know the price of Y is $5 per unit.

    a. What is the consumer's income?

    b. What is the price of X?

    c. Write the equation for the budget line *LM*.

    d. What is the value of the slope of *LM*?

    e. What combination of X and Y will the consumer choose? Why?

    f. What is his marginal rate of substitution in equilibrium?

    g. Explain precisely in terms of *MRS* why the consumer would not choose combinations designated by B or C.

Suppose the budget line shifts to *L'M'*.

    h. At the same prices, what has happened to money income?

    i. What combination does he now choose?

    j. Draw the relevant budget line if money income remains at the original level (designated by *LM*), the price of Y remains at $5, but the price of X rises to $10.

FIGURE E.3.1

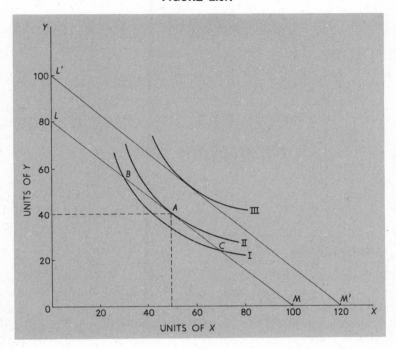

k.   Draw in an indifference curve showing the new equilibrium.

l.   What are the new equilibrium quantities?

6.   Suppose a consumer chooses a combination such that he would be willing to trade four units of X for one unit of Y. Suppose that the price of Y is $10 and the price of X is $5. What should the consumer do to reach equilibrium? If the price of X falls to $2, what should the consumer do?

chapter 4

Theory of Consumer Behavior: Comparative Statics

4.1 INTRODUCTION

Having examined the conditions that determine consumer equilibrium, we are now prepared to analyze some interesting problems concerning consumers' responses to *changes* in income and prices. This analysis involves the technique of comparative statics. Recall from Chapter 1 that through the use of comparative statics it is possible to examine the impact of changes in an independent variable upon certain dependent variables. One first sets up the equilibrium conditions and then changes one of the parameters. This change leads to a different equilibrium. The theorist then *compares* the two equilibria to determine the effect of such a change on the variables. For example, we might set up the equilibrium conditions in a market, then impose a sales tax to determine the effect upon price. The term "statics" means that the theorist compares two equilibria, but he is not interested in the *path* between the two. He is not interested in any values taken by the variables *during the time* required to move from one equilibrium to another. In other words, he abstracts from the time dimension. In this chapter we analyze thoroughly the comparative-statics effects of changing two variables, income and commodity price. Some real-world applications are included.

4.2 CHANGES IN MONEY INCOME

Changes in money income, prices remaining constant, affect the quantities of commodities bought. As explained in Chapter 3, an increase in money income shifts the budget line upward and to the right; since nominal prices remain constant, the movement is a parallel shift. We now analyze the precise way in which a change in money income affects

98

consumption. At the outset, it may be well to emphasize that throughout this section we assume that the prices of all goods remain constant. That is, our comparative static analysis is restricted to a change in money income only.

4.2.a—Income-Consumption Curve: Normal Goods

In Figure 4.2.1 the quantity of *X*, some specific good, is measured along the horizontal axis; "Expenditure on All Goods Other than *X*" is

FIGURE 4.2.1

Income-Consumption Curve

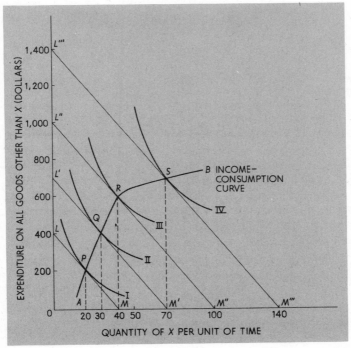

measured in dollars along the vertical axis. Each indifference curve, I–IV, indicates the various combinations of *X* and expenditures on other goods that yield the same level of utility. Higher levels of utility are indicated by the higher numbered indifference curves. Assume that the price of *X* is fixed at $10 per unit and that initially the consumer has an income of $1,000, indicated by budget line *L"M"*. He can spend all of his income on *X* and purchase 100 units, he can buy no *X* and spend all of his income on other goods, or he can purchase any combination on *L"M"*. We know from Chapter 3 that he attains equilibrium at R on indifference curve III, indicating the highest level of utility available to him. He purchases 40 units of X and spends $600 on other goods.

When we decrease his income to $700 the new budget line is $L'M'$. Equilibrium is now at Q, with 30 units of X and $400 spent on other goods. An income of $400 causes the consumer to purchase 20 units of X and spend $200 on other goods. Finally, if income is increased to $1,400, $L'''M'''$ is tangent to IV at 70 and $700. As income changes the point of consumer equilibrium changes as well. The line connecting the successive equilibria is called the income-consumption curve, indicated by AB in Figure 4.2.1. This curve shows the *equilibrium combinations* of X and expenditures on goods other than X at various levels of money income, nominal prices remaining constant throughout. That is, it shows the various static equilibria corresponding to various income levels; it thus shows the comparative static effects of changes in money income at constant commodity prices.

Definition: The locus of points showing consumer equilibria at various levels of money income at constant prices is called the income-consumption curve.

The fact that the income-consumption curve does not bend backward indicates that good X is a *normal* good at all income levels. That is, more X is purchased as money income increases; the income-consumption curve is positively sloped in the case of a normal good.

Definition: A *normal* good is one whose consumption varies *directly* with money income at a specific set of constant prices for specified levels of money income.

4.2.b—Engel Curves

The income-consumption curve may be used to derive an Engel curve for a commodity.

Definition: An Engel curve is a locus of points relating equilibrium quantity to the level of money income. The name is taken from Christian Lorenz Ernst Engel, a 19th-century German statistician.

Engel curves are important for applied studies of economic welfare and for the analysis of family expenditure patterns.

An Engel curve derived from the income-consumption curve in Figure 4.2.1 is constructed in Figure 4.2.2. The four points LM, $L'M'$, $L''M''$, and $L'''M'''$ designate the amounts of good X consumed at each of the four similarly labeled budget lines in Figure 4.2.1. As we shall see, not all Engel curves have the same general slope as the one in Figure 4.2.2.

FIGURE 4.2.2

Engel Curve

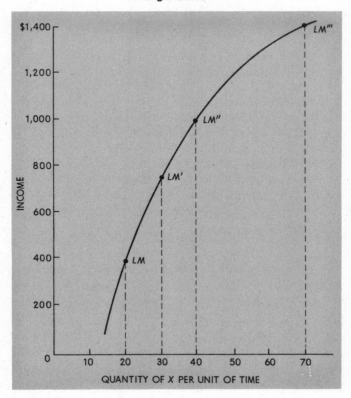

4.2.c—Alternative Approach

Consider Figure 4.2.3. Here X is a good and Y is some other good (not expenditure on all goods other than X). The scales on both axes are the number of units of X and Y. The price ratio is given by the negative of the slope of LM, the original budget line, and remains constant throughout.

With money income represented by LM, the consumer is in equilibrium at point P on indifference curve I, consuming Ox_1 units of X. Now let money income rise to the level represented by $L'M'$. The consumer shifts to a new equilibrium point Q on indifference curve II. He has clearly gained. He also gains when money income shifts to the level corresponding to $L''M''$. The new equilibrium is at point R on indifference curve III. The income-consumption curve now shows the equilibrium combinations of X and Y purchased at various levels of money income, nominal prices remaining the same.

FIGURE 4.2.3

Income-Consumption Curve

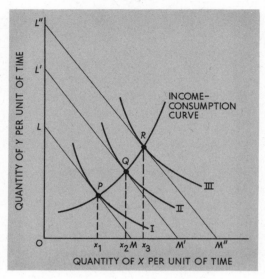

QUANTITY OF X PER UNIT OF TIME

Engel curves relating the consumption of commodity X to income are constructed in Figure 4.2.4. Neither panel a nor panel b is directly based upon the particular income-consumption curve in Figure 4.2.3, but the process should be clear.

At the original equilibrium point P in Figure 4.2.3, money income is $p_x \cdot OM$ (or $p_y \cdot OL$). At income $p_x \cdot OM$, Ox_1 units of X are purchased. This income-consumption point can be plotted on a graph such as panel a, Figure 4.2.4. When the budget line shifts from LM to $L'M'$ (Figure 4.2.3), money income increases to $p_x \cdot OM'$ and consumption to Ox_2 units. This income-consumption pair constitutes another point on the Engel curve graph. Repeating this process for all levels of money income generates a series of points on a graph such as panel a, Figure 4.2.4. The Engel curve is formed by connecting these points by a line.

Two basically different types of Engel curves are shown in panels a and b, Figure 4.2.4. In panel a, the Engel curve slopes upward rather steeply, implying that changes in money income do not have a substantial effect upon the consumption of the good in question. An Engel curve with this property indicates that the good is bought when income is low but that the quantity purchased does not expand rapidly as income increases. However, the gentle upward slope of the Engel curve in panel b indicates that the quantity purchased changes markedly with income.

It would be a serious mistake to attribute the shapes of Engel and income-consumption curves completely to the properties of the goods

FIGURE 4.2.4

Engel Curves

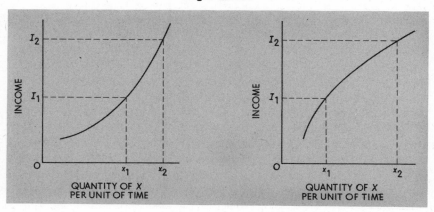

Panel *a*	Panel *b*
Low Income Elasticity	High Income Elasticity

themselves. Engel curves reflect the properties of indifference maps. It may well be true that, as some have said, food, taken as a whole, has an Engel curve shaped like the one in Figure 4.2.4, panel *a*. It may also be true that goods like steaks and fine wines have curves like that in panel *b*. But income-consumption curves, and hence Engel curves, are derived under specific price ratios and under specific preference functions. It certainly could be the case that with one price ratio the derived curves could have one shape, while another ratio could give rise to Engel curves with totally different shapes, even though indifference maps do not change. Or, the introduction of some new goods into the possible consumer's bundle could markedly change the shape of an Engel curve. It would be quite surprising, for example, if the introduction of television did not change the Engel curve for radios.

Exercise: To see how a change in the price ratio can change the shape of an income-consumption curve, construct the I-C curve in Figure 4.2.3 with budget lines much flatter than those in the graph; that is, lines with a lower price of *X* relative to *Y*. Note how the shape changes when the new points of tangency are connected.

4.2.d—Income Elasticity: Graphical Estimation

Just as in the case of demand elasticity, one cannot estimate income elasticity simply by looking at the slope of an Engel curve; that is, by noting whether the curve is concave from below or above.

FIGURE 4.2.5

Derivation of Income Elasticity

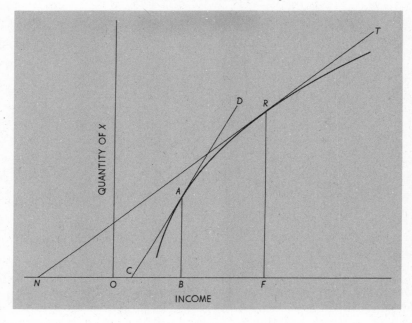

Recall from Chapter 2 that income elasticity is the proportional change in the consumption of a commodity divided by the proportional change in income. $(\Delta x/x)/(\Delta I/I) = (\Delta x/\Delta I)/(I/x)$. Consider the Engel curve in Figure 4.2.5. For analytical convenience, X is now plotted on the vertical axis and income on the horizontal. Assume a very small change in income and in good X in the neighborhood of point A. The rate of change $\Delta x/\Delta I$ in this neighborhood is given by the slope of the tangent, CD, to the curve at A. The rate of change, $\Delta x/\Delta I$ is therefore AB/CB. The income elasticity, η_I, is

$$\eta_I = \frac{\Delta x}{\Delta I} \cdot \frac{I}{x} = \frac{AB}{CB} \cdot \frac{OB}{AB} = \frac{OB}{CB} > 1.$$

Next consider a very small change in the neighborhood of R. In this case income elasticity is given by

$$\eta_I = \frac{\Delta x}{\Delta I} \cdot \frac{I}{x} = \frac{RF}{NF} \cdot \frac{OF}{RF} = \frac{OF}{NF} < 1.$$

It should be clear that if the tangent line intersects the horizontal axis to the right of the origin, the income elasticity of demand is greater than unity. If the tangent line intersects the vertical axis above the origin, the income elasticity of demand is less than unity.

Exercise: Derive the income elasticities of demand at some points on an Engel curve that is concave from above (that is, lies everywhere above its tangent). Use your graph and Figure 4.2.5 to show that the income elasticity of a good decreases (increases) with increased income when the Engel curve is concave from below (above).

4.2.e—Inferior Goods

"Normal" goods are given that name because economists believe that in most cases an increase in income causes an increase in the consumption of a good; they believe that this is the "normal" situation. However, an increase in income may cause a decrease in the consumption of certain commodities at certain price ratios. These commodities are called inferior goods. In other words, an inferior good is a commodity whose income elasticity is negative over the range of income for which it is inferior.

Definition: A good is normal or inferior as its income elasticity is positive or negative. A normal good's Engel curve is positively sloped. The Engel curve for an inferior good is negatively sloped over its range of inferiority.

Figure 4.2.6 shows an increase in income from the level given by the budget line *LM* to that given by *L'M'*. The two budget lines are parallel, so no change in relative price occurs; income increases from *LM* to *L'M'* because of an increase in money income, prices constant. In the change, the position of consumer equilibrium shifts from point *P* on indifference

FIGURE 4.2.6

Illustration of an Inferior Good

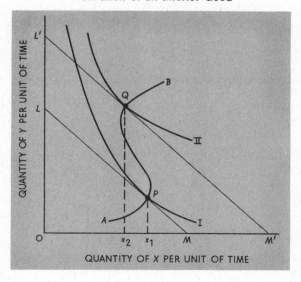

curve I to point Q on indifference curve II. As a result of the increase in real income at the constant relative prices, the quantity demanded of good X falls from Ox_1 to Ox_2. The income-consumption curve, over this range of real income values, rises backward from P to Q; and the entire income-consumption curve might resemble the curve $APQB$. Thus, over the range PQ the Engel curve would be a negatively sloped line. Since the slope of the tangent to the negatively drawn Engel curve is less than zero, the income elasticity of demand is negative.

One brief warning may be in order before we take up changes in price. Economists frequently point out examples such as margarine, hamburger, Volkswagons, dried fruit, etc. and call these goods inferior. Certainly many people, and even society as a whole, may have reduced consumption of some of these goods as income increases. But, since income elasticity varies with income, a good may be inferior over a certain range for some people but have a high income elasticity over another range. Also, in line with the discussion above, the classification of goods as inferior or normal depends upon the price ratio. At one ratio a good may be inferior over a range, while at another ratio it may be normal over the same range. Remember that inferiority and normality are not inherent properties of the goods themselves.

4.3 CHANGES IN PRICE

The reaction of quantity purchased to changes in price is perhaps even more important than the reaction to changes in money income. In this section we assume that money income and the nominal prices of all goods other than X remain constant while the nominal price of X changes. We are thus able to analyze the effect of price upon quantity purchased without simultaneously considering the effect of changes in money income.

4.3.a—Price-Consumption Curves

Figure 4.3.1 contains a portion of an indifference map for a consumer who can consume X (measured in units along the horizontal axis) and goods other than X (the total expenditure on which is measured in dollars along the vertical axis). The consumer has money income of $1,000. When X is priced at $25 per unit the consumer's budget line is LM. He can spend the entire $1,000 on other goods; he can spend the entire $1,000 on 40 units of X at $25 per unit; or he can purchase at some point along LM. By the analysis developed above he chooses to consume at point P, where LM is tangent to indifference curve I. He consumes 24 units of X, thereby spending $600 on this commodity. The remaining $400 is spent on other goods.

Assume that the price of X falls to $10. Now if the consumer wishes to spend all of his income on X, he can purchase 100 units. His budget line at the new price is LM', with a slope of -10 rather than -25. The new equilibrium point of tangency is designated by Q, at which he consumes 70 units of X at a total expense of $700 and spends the remaining $300 on other goods. If price falls to $8 per unit, other things remaining the same, his new budget line is LM'', with a slope of -8. At equilibrium point R he purchases 87.5 units of X. Note that he still spends $700 on X and $300 on all other goods. Finally the price of X falls to $5. The new budget line LM''' is tangent to indifference curve IV at point S. The maximum utility level is attained by spending $550 on 110 units of X and

FIGURE 4.3.1

Price-Consumption Curve

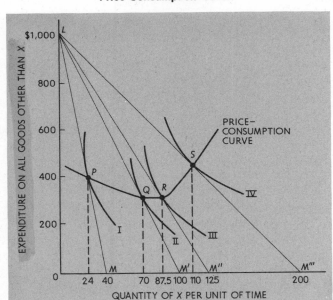

$450 on goods other than X. Thus, each price decrease causes the consumer to purchase more units of X. The line joining points P, Q, R, and S (and all other equilibria) is called the *price-consumption curve*. For a given money income it shows the amount of X consumed as its price changes, other prices remaining the same.

Definition: The price-consumption curve is a locus of equilibrium points relating the quantity of X purchased to its price, money income and all other prices remaining constant. In the case treated above, the price-consumption curve also shows how expenditure on all goods other than X changes as the price of X changes.

4.3.b—Demand Curves

The individual's demand curve for a commodity can be derived from the price-consumption curve, just as an Engel curve is derivable from the income-consumption curve. The price-quantity relations for good X at points *P, Q, R,* and *S,* and presumably for all other points on the price-consumption curve in Figure 4.3.1, are plotted in Figure 4.3.2. The horizontal axis is the same (units of X), but the vertical axis now shows the price of X. When the price of X is given by the slope of *LM* ($25), 24 units of X are purchased; this is indicated by point *P'* in Figure 4.3.2.

FIGURE 4.3.2

Demand Curve

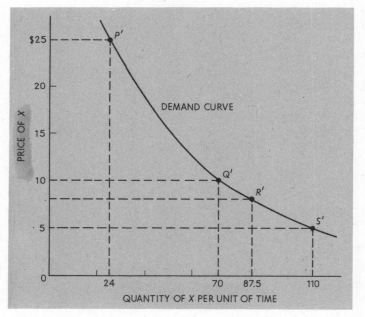

If the price is $10, 70 units are purchased (point *Q'*), and so forth. All other points on the curve are derived similarly. The locus of these points is called the demand curve for X.

Definition: The demand curve of an individual for a specific commodity relates equilibrium quantities bought to market price, money income and nominal prices of all other commodities held constant. The slope of the demand curve illustrates the law of demand: quantity demanded varies inversely with price, income and the prices of other commodities held constant.

Relation: As mentioned in Chapter 2, market demand for a specific commodity is the horizontal sum of all individual demand curves.

4.3.c—Demand Elasticity

Recall from Chapter 2 that the elasticity of demand is the relative responsiveness of quantity demanded to changes in price. It may be determined from the changes in price and in the money income spent on the good.

At this point it may be helpful to review briefly the relation between price elasticity of demand and changes in the total expenditure upon the good in question. First, suppose the nominal price of good X declines by 1 percent. The demand for X is said to be price elastic, of unitary price elasticity, or price inelastic according as the quantity of X demanded expands by more than 1 percent, by exactly 1 percent, or by less than 1 percent.

Next, recall that the total expenditure upon a good is the product of price per unit and the number of units purchased. Given an initial price and quantity bought, a unique initial total expenditure is determined. Now let price fall by 1 percent. If demand is price elastic, quantity demanded expands by more than 1 percent. Thus total expenditure must expand when price falls and demand is price elastic. By the same argument, one finds (a) that total expenditure remains constant when price falls and demand has unitary price elasticity and (b) that total expenditure declines when price falls and demand is price inelastic.

Let us now reexamine the relation between the price-consumption curve in Figure 4.3.1 and the demand curve in Figure 4.3.2. Note in Figure 4.3.1 that when price falls from $25 to $10 (from P to Q on the price-consumption curve), total expenditure on all goods other than X decreases from $400 to $300. If total expenditure on goods other than X declines, with the same money income, total expenditure on X must necessarily rise (from $600 to $700). Therefore demand is elastic between $25 and $10 inasmuch as an increase in total expenditure in response to a price decline implies elastic demand. When the price-consumption curve is negatively sloped between two points (P and Q in Figure 4.3.1), demand is elastic between those points (P' and Q' in Figure 4.3.2).

Consider now the price decline from $10 to $8 (from Q to R). Expenditure on other goods remains the same; with a fixed money income, expenditure on X therefore remains the same. The price-consumption curve neither declines nor rises and thus demand must be, on average, of unitary elasticity between Q' and R' on the demand curve. The student should now work out for himself that demand must be inelastic between R' and S' on the demand curve.

Relations: Demand has unitary price elasticity, is price elastic, or is price inelastic accordingly as the price-consumption curve is horizontal, negatively sloped, or positively sloped. *This relation holds for a price-consumption curve only when total expenditures on all other goods are plotted on the vertical axis.* Thus, the price-consumption curve in Figure 4.3.1 reflects commodity demand that is first (at higher prices) elastic, becomes unitary, and is inelastic thereafter.

4.3.d—Demand and Price-Consumption Curves: Alternative Approach

As in the case of income-consumption curves, we can drop the assumption that the vertical axis denotes total expenditures on all goods other

FIGURE 4.3.3

Price-Consumption Curve

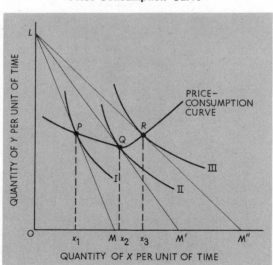

than *X* and assume an indifference map between two goods, *X* and *Y*. In Figure 4.3.3 a consumer's indifference map is represented by indifference curves I, II, and III. Given the price ratio designated by budget line *LM*, equilibrium is attained at point *P*. A fall in the price of *X*, the price of *Y* remaining the same, leads to the new budget line *LM'*.[1] At

---

[1] The student should realize that if the nominal price of *Y* and money income remain constant while the nominal price of *X* declines, the real price of *Y* increases, the real price of *X* decreases, and real money income increases. Our discussion refers almost exclusively to nominal prices and income. Note also that a proportional decrease in both prices would be equivalent to an increase in money income. The budget line would shift outward.

equilibrium point Q the consumer purchases more X and less Y. Finally when the price of X falls again, to the level indicated by LM'', the consumer buys more of both goods. The line connecting these points is, as before, the price-consumption curve.

The demand curve can be drived from the price-consumption curve just as before. When the price of X is given by the slope of LM in Figure 4.3.3, Ox_1 units of X are purchased. This price-consumption pair constitutes one point on the graph in Figure 4.3.4. Similarly, when the price of X falls to the level indicated by the slope of LM', quantity purchased increases to Ox_2. This price-consumption pair is another point that can be plotted on Figure 4.3.4. Plotting all points so obtained and connecting

FIGURE 4.3.4

Demand Curve

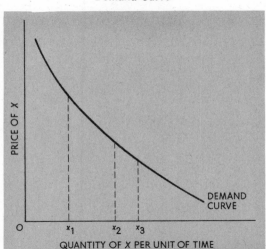

them with a line generates the consumer demand curve, as shown in Figure 4.3.4.

Principle: Quantity demanded varies inversely with price, money income and nominal prices of other commodities remaining constant.

4.4 ESTIMATION OF DEMAND

While theoretical or graphical derivation of consumer demand is simple, empirical estimation of actual demand functions is quite difficult. Statisticians simply do not have available the indifference curves of individuals. In theory we hold everything but price and quantity constant when deriving demand while in actual investigations statisticians may have strong reason to believe that other things have changed during the time over which they have collected their data. It is not enough to go out into the world and gather data, plot these data, and from those plotted points estimate a demand curve. A series of price-quantity observations collected over time may give the series of points plotted in Figure 4.4.1. The line drawn through the points appears to fit the data rather well. Its positive slope, however, is not evidence that the market demand for X is upward sloping. The points plotted in the figure may well designate dif-

FIGURE 4.4.1

**Price-Quantity Observations
From a Time Series**

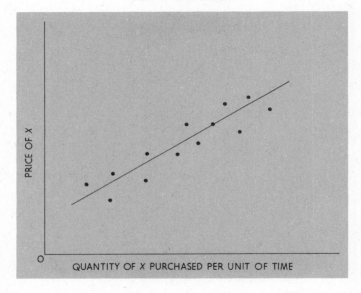

ferent points of equilibrium. Supply and demand could have shifted many times during the period of observation because of changes in other variables. Each indicated point would then be a point of equilibrium. Without knowledge of the way that these other variables change and the way that they affect supply and demand one cannot really say what the line indicates. For example, supply and demand may have shifted over time in the way illustrated by Figure 4.4.2. S_1 and D_1 determine equilibrium point A, S_2 and D_2 determine B, and so forth. From five observations we observe only points A through E. We cannot tell simply from the observations how these points were generated. But economists, businessmen, and governmental agencies are often extremely interested in actually obtaining demand curves for real products. There are several methods of approach that have been used.

FIGURE 4.4.2

Changing Equilibria Over Time

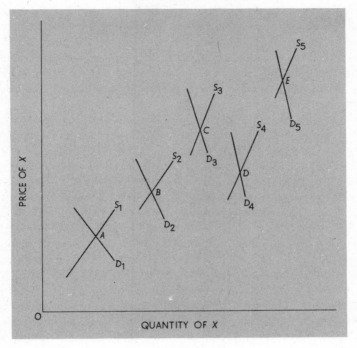

4.4.a—Statistical Techniques

One obvious extension of the technique of estimating demand solely from price-quantity data is to consider statistically those variables that would have been held constant in a controlled experiment. This technique is called multiple regression (the student may wish to re-read the statistical section of Chapter 1). The economist or statistician sets up a model of equations with two or more independent variables. He solves the model to obtain estimating equations. One example of this type is

$$Q_D = b_0 + b_1 P + b_2 W + b_3 P_0,$$

where Q_D is the total quantity demanded, P is per-unit price price of a good, W is an average wage rate, and P_0 is some index of related prices. The bs are the parameters to be estimated by multiple regression techniques. In this way the effect of changes in W and P_0 can be isolated while one attempts to analyse the effect of P on Q_D. Of course, the effect of any other variables that affect supply and demand is not isolated. This omission could cause misleading interpretation. Another problem is the difficulty of obtaining sufficient and correct data so that meaningful results can be generated.

An interesting, though expensive and difficult technique for estimating demand and demand elasticity is the controlled market experiment. One recent experiment involved estimating the demand for farm-raised, fresh channel catfish in supermarkets.[2] This experiment was designed as a service to the agricultural sector of the economy; it was intended to provide information as to the market potential and profitability of increasing catfish production on farms.

The technique of simple regression was used, but the effect of changes in other variables was rigidedly controlled. Supermarkets were chosen to reflect a cross section of urban, suburban, and rural consumers in Atlanta, Georgia. Over a period of several weeks, prices of catfish were varied from $0.79 to $1.29 per pound in ten cent increments in the supermarkets. The cooperating stores held the location and size of the display constant. The quantity supplied was sufficient to satisfy demand at each price, and there was no advertising. Quantity purchased was measured in pounds per 1,000 customers to offset the effect of changes in consumer flow. Atlanta was chosen for the experiment because it was felt that consumers there had prior knowledge of the product. Since supply was theoretically unlimited over the relevant range, the observed points were on the demand curve. The linear demands were estimated in natural numbers, log-linear, and log-log, with extremely high correlation (.93 to .97) in each case. At the approximate midpoint of the data all three forms produced similar elasticities in the range −2.5 to −3.0. Demand was rather elastic, and at high prices there was considerable substitution of other seafood. The current retail price at the time of the experiment was about $1.19 per pound. The experiment indicated that a substantial (70 percent) sales gain would result from a price decrease to $.99 a pound. Costs, however, were above this figure, indicating that considerable sales and profit would result from the development of new cost-saving production techniques. If demand had been shown to be quite inelastic there would have been little use for the agricultural sector to attempt cost reduction in catfish production, and research would be more fruitful elsewhere.

There have been many other similar market experiments designed to estimate the demand for a product without supply changes affecting the experiment. According to marketing experts the technique is quite expensive, and it is difficult to obtain the cooperation of merchants. Thus, this technique is not widely used.

An alternative method of derivation, the questionnaire or survey ap-

---

[2] See "The Demand for Farm-Raised Channel Catfish in Supermarkets: Analysis of a Selected Market," Marketing Research Report No. 993, U.S. Department of Agriculture, Economic Research Service.

proach, is a much cheaper method but far less reliable. Potential or actual consumers are simply questioned about how much of certain goods they *would* buy at several prices. Or what do they consider a "reasonable" price. These surveys may provide some useful indirect information, but the imprecision and ambiguity is, as you probably would expect, extremely high. What consumers say they would do or would buy differs from how they would actually act. In fact, consumers may not even know their future reactions. What a person being questioned says may also depend upon the image he wishes to convey to the questioner. That is, he may not wish to appear miserly and, therefore, says price would not affect his purchases. According to marketing experts, these techniques are not very reliable.

4.4.b—Laboratory Experiments

Laboratory experiments are a compromise between the market experiment and the survey. Volunteers are paid to simulate actual buying conditions without going through markets. In one series of experiments by Edgar A. Pessemier, a large group of university students volunteered to carry out a series of simulated shopping trips for toothpaste, cigarettes, soap, and headache remedies.[3] In the experiment all important factors that affect quantity demanded, except price, were held constant. The volunteer "consumers" were given specified amounts of money to go on shopping trips for particular items, of which several brands were available. Prices were varied for the different trips. Since the subjects had some probability of keeping their purchases and their change (i.e., drawings were held after the experiments in order to determine who kept the merchandise and change) they acted as if they were actually shopping. After many "shopping trips" by many "consumers" an approximation to demand was obtained. The subjects, of course, may not be a particularly accurate cross section of society. All derived demands in the Pessemier experiments were, as expected, downward sloping. Again, as would be expected, the demands for brands of cigarettes was much less elastic than the demands for brands of toothpaste. Other results are reported in the article cited above. The point important for our purposes is that experiments can be made to test the theories that we derive deductively from a given set of assumptions.

Some colleagues of ours have recently been conducting experiments on consumer behavior at an even simpler level. They have set up token economies in mental institutions. In these token economies, which incidentally are supposed to have great therapeutic value, the patients are given tokens in payment for jobs performed. They can exchange these

---

[3] The results are contained in Edgar A. Pessemier, "An Experimental Method for Estimating Demand," *The Journal of Business,* Oct. 1960.

tokens for goods and services in the "store" at the hospital. The experimenters can change prices, incomes, or the reward for jobs and observe the behavior. The researchers feel that these types of tests give them good control of their subjects, a simple institutional structure, and a small number of goods. Having complete control over the supply, so any points generated are on the demand curve, they have generated demand curves and Engel curves, which were tested and compared with the predictions of economic theory. These curves have similar properties to those postulated by the theory of consumer behavior.

Wishing to work at an even simpler level with more control over the experiments, these economists have also begun conducting economic experiments on rats. One can do things with rats, which, because of humanitarian considerations, one would not do with humans. For example, they put a rat on two goods, food and water. Two keys in the rat's chamber give him the two goods. In the beginning the rat could push key one 20 times to receive five pellets of food and key two 20 times for .1 cc of water. The rat was allowed to allocate 4,000 presses in a 24 hour period in any way he wished. The rat was very consistent in his behavior. When the price of one good (the number of presses required) was raised relative to the other, the rat substituted away from the more expensive to the relatively cheaper good. When income and prices were changed in the same proportions the rat continued consuming at approximately the same rate, as economic theory predicts. In short, the rat's demand for food and water exhibits many of the same properties as our theoretical demands. They are now adding "luxury" goods such as Coke, 7-Up, beer, and pretzels in order to observe how these luxuries affect the rat's demand curve.

It is hard to predict how much these controlled experiments will expand our knowledge of consumer behavior, since they are in such early stages. It is interesting that the results thus far do not generally contradict the theory of consumer behavior.[4]

4.4.c—Advertising Restrictions and the Demand for Cigarettes

Sometimes economists estimate certain demand functions not so much because they are interested in these demands per se, but because of the information that can be obtained about policy problems. For example,

[4] For further information about experimental economics see the following papers: John H. Kagel and Robin C. Winkler, "Behavioral Economics: Areas of Cooperative Research between Economics and Applied Behavioral Analysis," *Journal of Applied Behavior Analysis,* Fall 1972, pp. 335–42. J. H. Kagel, "Token Economies and Experimental Economics," *Journal of Political Economy,* July/August 1972, pp. 779–85. J. H. Kagel, et al., *An Experimented Test of Consumer Demand Theory in a Token Economy,* NSF Project #GS 32057, Technical Report No. 2. R. L. Basmann, et al., "Interpretation Systems for Empirical Economic Theories with Application to Theories of Factor and Consumer Demand," Interim Report to the National Science Foundation.

one may have to estimate a demand equation in order to analyze. the economic effect of a specific governmental policy. Such was the case in a recent paper by James L. Hamilton, who wished to estimate the degree to which cigarette consumption in the United States was affected by the Congressional ban of broadcast advertising of cigarettes.[5] To make this estimate he first had to derive the demand for cigarettes.

Hamilton regressed the following independent variables upon annual per capita cigarette consumption by persons 14 years and above: (1) per capita income; (2) a cigarette price index; (3) annual per capita and aggregate cigarette advertising expenditure; and (4) several variables representing the cigarette health scare. The demand was estimated both linearly and log-linearly for several time periods. Estimated advertising elasticities were extremely small and quite far from showing statistical significance.[6] This result was in close agreement with most previous studies in the area.

On the other hand, the variables for the health scare were very significant. Further statistical tests indicated that the health scare was several times more powerful as a deterrent to smoking than was advertising as a sales stimulant. From a linear estimate it appeared that advertising tended to raise cigarette consumption 95 cigarettes a year while cigarette consumption was depressed 253 per year by the Surgeon General's report and 531 per year by the antismoking commercials. Other regression estimates are consistent with this pattern. In most cases, the difference in effects was substantial.

When Congress, to reduce cigarette smoking, banned broadcast advertising of cigarettes, it also ended the free broadcast time for antismoking advertising required by the FCC under its fairness doctrine for controversial issues. Antismoking groups now had to pay for advertising and, of course, did not or could not continue to advertise close to the level attained before the ban. In 1970 the free antismoking advertising was about one-third of total cigarette advertising, a subsidy of about $75

---

[5] This subsection is based upon, James L. Hamilton, "The Demand for Cigarettes: Advertising, The Health Scare, and the Cigarette Advertising Ban," *The Review of Economics and Statistics,* Nov. 1972, pp. 401–11.

[6] You may be wondering why cigarette manufacturers advertise at all if advertising does not affect sales significantly, unless the manufacturers are dumb. Economists generally think that cigarette advertising is used competitively by the different firms to expand (or hold on to) their share of the market. Any firm that stopped advertising would soon experience a substantial loss in sales to the other firms. On the other hand, all firms together could increase or decrease total advertising without much change in sales. It appears that while *total* smoking may not be connected with *total* advertising, the sales of any one manufacturer are related to *its own* advertising. Quite possibly the ban on some cigarette advertising could have increased profits for most of the established firms. The firms' expenses fell while total sales dropped very little. This result is a peculiarity of the market structure called oligopoly, discussed in Chapter 10.

million. Antismoking advertising is now a small fraction of what it was before.

Although no substantive results are in as yet, Hamilton points out that cigarette advertising fell 20–30 per cent in 1971 while per capita consumption increased noticeably after being sluggish for several years. The statistics seem to predict that the ban will increase consumption above what it would have been with both broadcast cigarette advertising and subsidized health scare advertising. Furthermore, the ban seems to strengthen the present manufacturers, since the easiest way for a new company to enter the market was through large-scale broadcast advertising.[7]

Whatever the case, these results point to the value of careful theoretical and empirical analysis of policy changes prior to those changes. They also show another use of demand analysis and estimation.

4.5 SUBSTITUTION AND INCOME EFFECTS

A change in the nominal price of a commodity actually exerts two influences on quantity demanded. In the first place, there is a change in relative price—a change in the terms at which a consumer can exchange one good for another. The change in relative price alone leads to a substitution effect. Second, a change in the nominal price of a good (nominal income remaining constant) causes a change in real income, or in the size of the bundle of goods and services a consumer can buy. If the nominal price of one good falls, all other nominal prices remaining constant, the consumer's real income rises because he can now buy more, either of the good whose price declined or of other goods. The change in price leads to a change in real income and thus to an income effect upon quantity demanded.

4.5.a—Total Effect of a Price Decrease

When the price of one good changes, the prices of other goods and money income remaining constant, the consumer moves from one equilibrium point to another. In normal circumstances, if the price of a good diminishes, more of it is bought; if its price increases, fewer units are taken. The overall change in quantity demanded from one equilibrium position to another is referred to as the total effect.

---

[7] It seems that the cigarette manufacturers knew that the advertising ban could probably benefit them. According to Hamilton the cigarette companies previously *volunteered* to end the private broadcast advertising in exchange for antitrust immunity and the dropping of all proposals for stronger health warnings.

Definition: The total effect of a price change is the total change in quantity demanded as the consumer moves from one equilibrium position to another.

The total effect of a price change is illustrated in Figure 4.5.1. As before, units of X are plotted along the horizontal axis and total expenditures on all goods other than X are measured in dollars along the vertical axis. Assume again that the consumer originally has money income of $1,000 and that the original price of X is $10. Since the consumer can

FIGURE 4.5.1

Substitution and Income Effects for a Decrease in the Price of *X*

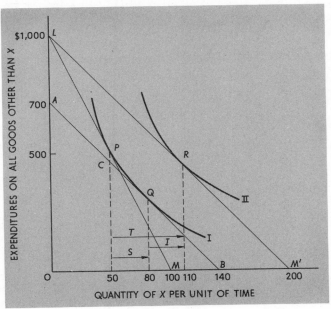

buy 100 units of X if he spends his entire income on X, the original budget line is given by LM. In equilibrium the consumer purchases 50 units of X, spending $500 on X and $500 on all other goods.

When the price of X falls to $5, the relevant budget line becomes LM'. Equilibrium consumption, designated by R, is now 110 units of X, $450 being spent on other goods and $550 on X. Since P is on indifference curve I and R is on II, and since II denotes a higher level of utility than I, the consumer is clearly at a higher level of satisfaction after the price decreases even though his money income has not changed. An economist would say that *real* income is greater. Put alternatively, at the new price of $5 the consumer could spend at the level indicated by P (that is, he could buy 50 units of X and spend $500 on other goods) and still have $250 left to spend on X, on other goods, or on both. The consumer is clearly better off.

The total effect of the decrease in the price of X is the 60-unit increase in the consumption of X (from 50 to 110 units, or the distance T in Figure 4.5.1). This total effect can be broken down into an income and a substitution effect. The substitution effect results from X being relatively cheaper than before the price decline. The consumer substitutes the cheaper good for relatively more expensive ones. The income effect results from the consumer's having more *real* income and hence being able to buy more of both X and of all other goods (even though nominal income is the same before and after the price change).

4.5.b—Income and Substitution Effects for a Normal Good

Assume that when the price of X decreases, the consumer is taxed exactly the amount of *money* that will cause his *real* income to remain constant. That is, he is taxed the amount that makes him continue to consume a bundle on the original indifference curve I. Since he is on the same indifference curve as before, he has the same real income. Thus, after the price reduction he is taxed the amount AL in Figure 4.5.1.

The tax must be the amount that causes the consumer to attain equilibrium on indifference curve I at the *new* price ratio. The gain in real income (that is, the increase in utility) is, therefore, taken away. Graphically, this is illustrated by constructing the fictitious budget line AB, which is tangent to indifference curve I but has a slope that represents the new price of X. Budget line AB, whose slope is -5 (the new price ratio), is tangent to I at point Q. Under these circumstances the consumer would purchase 80 units of X at a cost of $400 and spend $300 on other goods. The necessary tax is obviously $300, reflected by the distance from point L to point A. The consumer is no better off at Q than he was at P; but he substitutes 30 units of X ($80 - 50$) for $200 expenditure on other goods ($500 - $300). This change in the consumption of X is called the *substitution effect* (distance S in Figure 4.5.1). It is easy to see that given the price change and the fictitious reduction in real income, the consumer substitutes X for expenditures on other goods in order not to be made worse off. If he continued to consume 50 units of X, with the new budget line AB he would be at point C, where the level of satisfaction is clearly below that represented by indifference curve I. The consumer must substitute in order to remain as well off as he was before the price change.

Definition: The substitution effect is the change in quantity demanded resulting from a change in relative price holding *real income* constant. In other words, the substitution effect is the change in quantity demanded resulting from a change in price when the change is restricted to a movement along the original indifference curve.

The substitution effect involves a movement along the original indifference curve from P to the imaginary equilibrium Q. The remainder of the total effect, from Q to R or the distance I in Figure 4.5.1, results from the increase in real income; that is, from the shift from indifference curve I to curve II. Since AB and LM' are parallel, the movement does not involve a change in relative prices. It is a real income phenomenon.

Definition: The income effect is the change in quantity demanded resulting from the change in real income incident to the change in the price of X.

From the graph one may easily see that the total effect of the decrease in the price of X upon quantity demanded is the sum of the substitution effect and the income effect. In algebraic terms

Total Effect = Substitution Effect (utility constant) + Income
Effect (price ratio constant).

Or in our example:

60 units = 30 units + 30 units.

In this case the income effect reinforces the substitution effect in that both effects cause an increase in the consumption of X. The income effect for a normal good is positive: an increase in real income leads to an increase in quantity demanded and vice versa.

Principle: For a normal good the income effect reinforces the substitution effect. Thus for a normal good, quantity demanded always varies inversely with price. The law of demand applies to all normal goods.

The result of this section may be summarized as follows.

Relations: The total effect of a price change may be decomposed into a substitution effect and an income effect. The substitution effect is the change in quantity demanded attributable exclusively to a change in the price ratio. The substitution effect is always negative; that is, a fall (increase) in price always causes quantity to rise (fall) when the movement is restricted along an indifference curve. The income effect is the change in quantity demanded attributable exclusively to a change in real income. For normal goods, the income effect is positive. A positive income effect reinforces the negative substitution effect. Thus for normal goods, the demand curve always slopes downward to the right.

4.5.c—Inferior Goods

Our analysis of price changes has thus far been restricted to the case of a normal good. Returning the $300 imaginary tax (increasing real income) caused the consumption of X to increase. As we know from subsection 4.2.*e*, an increase in income need not occasion an increase in the consumption of a particular good. In the case of an inferior good the effect is the opposite.

Consider Figure 4.5.2 in which X is now another good. The consumer has money income of $1,000, the original price of X is $10 (budget line *LM*), and the original point of equilibrium is P (50 units of X and $500 expenditure on other goods). The price of X falls to $5, indicated by the budget line *LM';* in equilibrium the consumer purchases 70 units of X

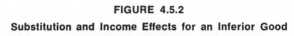

FIGURE 4.5.2

Substitution and Income Effects for an Inferior Good

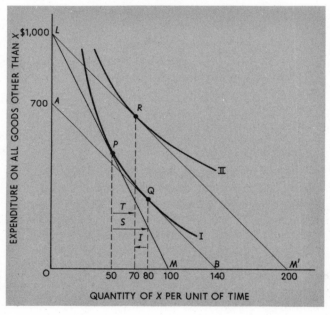

QUANTITY OF X PER UNIT OF TIME

and spends $650 on other goods (R). The total effect (the distance T) is an increase of 20 units.

Budget line *AB* indicates the imaginary tax of $300 that causes the consumer to choose point Q on the original indifference curve I. The substitution effect is therefore an increase in consumption by 30 units, or the distance S. Note that the substitution effect is *greater* than the total effect. Now we return the consumer's gain in real income and the consumer moves from Q to R. In this case the income effect (indicated by the distance I) is negative and to some extent *offsets* the substitution effect rather than reinforcing it. This offsetting effect is to be expected since good X is an inferior good.

Thus for all goods *the change in relative prices* (real income constant) that results from a decrease in price tends to cause an increase in consumption. But in the case of inferior goods, the *increase in real income* that results from the price decrease causes an offsetting decrease in consumption of the good. The law of demand, however, still holds in this case; the total effect of the decrease in price is an increase in quantity demanded.

4.5.d—Giffen's Paradox

Economists believe that in general, in fact almost always, the substitution effect is great enough to offset a negative income effect (if the good is inferior). But in one case, called *Giffen's Paradox* (named for Sir Robert Giffen, a nineteenth century British civil servant who collected data on the effect of price changes), the negative income effect is so strong that it more than offsets the substitution effect. Thus a decline in price leads to a decline in quantity demanded, a rise in price to a rise in quantity demanded.

Figure 4.5.3 illustrates Giffen's Paradox. The budget line *LM* indicates the consumption possibilities for a consumer with $1,000 income at a price of $10 per unit of X. Point *P* is the equilibrium (50 units of X and an expenditure of $500 on other goods). When the price of X decreases

FIGURE 4.5.3

Substitution and Income Effects for a Giffen Good

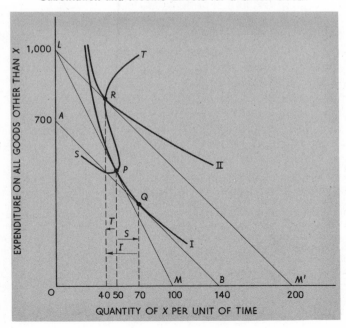

to $5 per unit, equilibrium is reached at point *R* on indifference curve II (40 units of *X* and $800 expenditure on other goods).

The consumer thus chooses to decrease his consumption of *X* by 10 units after a decrease in the price of *X*. The price-consumption curve between *P* and *R* obviously slopes backwards. Throughout a larger range it might look like curve *SPRT*. In the case of Giffen's Paradox the price-consumption curve is *backward rising* over a certain range.

We can analyze Giffen's Paradox more satisfactorily by separating the total effect into its component parts. In Figure 4.5.3 the line *AB* indicates the consumer's budget line at the new price of *X* after his gain in real income has been taken away. Under these conditions he would consume at *Q* (70 units of *X*). Following the analysis described above, the substitution effect causes him to *increase* his consumption of *X* after a decrease in the price of *X* (from 50 to 70 units). The substitution effect is, as always, negative. The income effect causes him to change his consumption from *Q* to *R* or from 70 to 40 units and is more than sufficient to offset the negative substitution effect. Adding the substitution and income effects together, the total effect of the price decline is a decrease in quantity demanded from 50 units at $10 to 40 units at $5. For a commodity such as this, the law of demand is not valid over the specified range.[8]

Definition: Giffen's Paradox refers to a good whose quantity demanded varies directly with price. A good must be an inferior good to be in this category; but not all inferior goods conform to the conditions of Giffen's Paradox. The class of goods for which Giffen's Paradox holds constitutes the only exception to the law of demand.

Whether a commodity is an inferior good or not has nothing to do with the substitution effect of a price change. It is strictly an income phenomenon. Giffen's Paradox relates only to certain inferior goods that violate the law of demand.

As an example, oleomargarine may be an inferior good, but it certainly does not belong in the Giffen's Paradox category. Possibly a reduction in the price of oleomargarine leads to a substitution of margarine for butter. However, an increase in the real income of a family may cause a switch

---

[8] In this text, and in almost all other usages, demand and the Law of Demand are defined in terms of constant money income. Thus real income changes as one moves along a demand curve; Griffen's Paradox can occur, and the law of demand is not universally valid. For certain uses, however, it is convenient to construct a demand curve based on constant real income (and, therefore, varying money income). Such demand curves are called income-compensated demand curves. The "income effect" is, in effect, subtracted out, leaving only the substitution effect. Such demand curves always slope downward to the right, irrespective of the type of good. For a thorough discussion of income-compensated demand curves, see Milton Friedman. "The Marshallian Demand Curve," *Journal of Political Economy*, Vol. LVII (1949), pp. 463–95.

from margarine to butter. But in this case the income effect probably is not great enough to offset the substitution effect.

In all probability there are very few households in the United States or other industrial nations for which Giffen's Paradox obtains. A negative income effect is not all that is required—the good must also be very important in the entire family budget. The classic example is potatoes in 19th-century Ireland. The typical Irish peasant was so poor, it was said, that he spent almost all his cash income for the least expensive means of subsistence, potatoes.

Now suppose the price of potatoes falls. The same number of calories can now be bought for less expenditure on potatoes, so some money is available for green vegetables and perhaps meat. But these items also contain calories, so the consumption of potatoes can actually be reduced. Thus Giffen's Paradox is obtained—a reduction in price leads to a reduction in quantity demanded.

Giffen's Paradox is a bona fide exception to the law of demand. However, in the type of society with which we are presently concerned, Giffen's Paradox is a rare phenomenon. It occurs in few consumer units and, within these units, for very few commodities. Thus when all individual demand curves are aggregated to obtain market demand, it is safe to assume that market quantity demanded varies inversely with price for every commodity.

4.5.e—Alternative Approach

Just as we analyzed the price-consumption and the income-consumption curves by considering both X and Y as specific goods (rather than Y as expenditure on all goods other than X), so also can we isolate the income and substitution effects in this manner.

The effect of an *increase* in the price of X when X and Y are both goods is illustrated in Figure 4.5.4. The original price ratio is indicated by the slope of LM. The consumer attains equilibrium at point P on indifference curve II, purchasing Ox_1 units of X. When the price of X rises, as indicated by shifting the budget line from LM to LM', the consumer moves to a new equilibrium position at R on indifference curve I. At this point he purchases Ox_3 units of X. The total effect of the price change is indicated by the movement from P to R, or by the reduction in quantity demanded from Ox_1 to Ox_3. In other words, the total effect is $Ox_1 - Ox_3 = x_1x_3$. This is a negative total effect because quantity demanded is reduced by x_1x_3 units when price increases.

When the price of X increases the consumer obviously suffers a decline in real income as indicated by the movement from indifference curve II to indifference curve I. Suppose that coincident with the price rise the consumer is given an amount of additional money just sufficient to com-

FIGURE 4.5.4

Substitution and Income Effects for a Normal Good in Case of a Price Rise

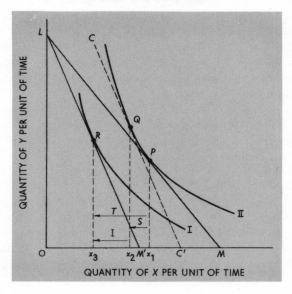

pensate him for the loss in real income he would otherwise sustain. That is, he is given a compensatory payment just sufficient to make him choose to consume on indifference curve II under the new price regime. This new imaginary budget line is CC'; it is tangent to the original indifference curve II at point Q, but it reflects the new price ratio.

The substitution effect is shown by the movement from P to Q, or by the reduction in quantity demanded from Ox_1 to Ox_2. Now let the consumer's real income *fall* from the level represented by the fictitious budget line CC'. The movement from Q to R (the decrease in consumption from Ox_2 to Ox_3) indicates the income effect. Since CC' and LM' are parallel, the movement does not involve a change in relative prices. It is once more a real income phenomenon since the reduction in quantity demanded measures the change in purchases attributable exclusively to the decline in real income, the change in relative prices already have been accounted for by the substitution effect. Note that X is a normal good: the decrease in real income causes a decrease in consumption.

Figures 4.5.5 and 4.5.6 show the effects of an increase in the price of X under the same assumptions as those of Figure 4.5.4, except that X is an inferior good. In fact, in Figure 4.5.6, X is a Giffen good.

Figure 4.5.5 illustrates the effects of an increase in the price of X, which changes the budget line from LM to LM'. Following the now fa-

FIGURE 4.5.5

**Substitution and Income Effects for an Inferior
Good Not Subject to Giffen's Paradox**

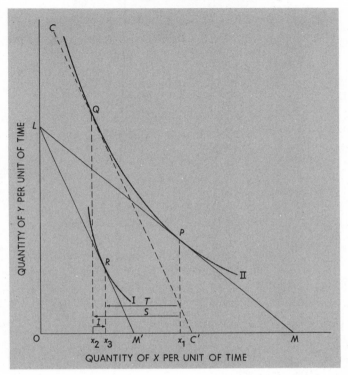

miliar analysis, the consumer changes from point P to point R; he decreases his consumption of X from Ox_1 to Ox_3 (the total effect). The substitution effect, derived by giving the consumer just enough additional money income to compensate him for the decrease in real income occasioned by the price rise, is $P - Q$ (from Ox_1 to Ox_2). The income effect is from Q to R (an *increase* in consumption from Ox_2 to Ox_3). This partial offset to the substitution effect is to be expected since X is an inferior good; a decrease in income causes an increase in the consumption of X.

Exercise: The student should follow the same type of analysis in the case of a price increase for the good subject to Giffen's Paradox, illustrated in Figure 4.5.6.

4.6 CONSUMER'S SURPLUS

One important concept of demand theory that we will use later is consumer's surplus. To illustrate, assume that you would be willing to pay up

FIGURE 4.5.6

Substitution and Income Effects for Giffen's Paradox

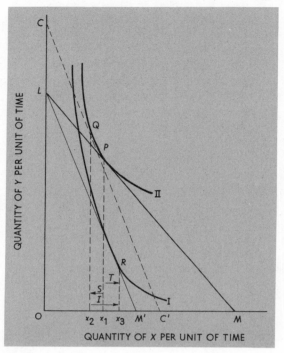

QUANTITY OF X PER UNIT OF TIME

to $1,000 for a weekend vacation in Bermuda. If the market price for this vacation is $700, the $300 difference between what you must pay and what you are willing to pay is called consumer's surplus. Or, consider the following demand schedule for units of X:

Quantity	Price
400	$7
600	5
900	3
1,500	1

Now, if someone is selling X and if he is able to discriminate, that is segregate his market, to those willing to pay $7 each, he would sell 400 units at $7; to those willing to pay $5, he would sell 200 more units at $5 each, 300 more at $3 each, and so forth, as long as he could make a profit. Alternatively, assume the competitive price is $3. Assume also that the down sloping demand is caused by new consumers entering the market. Those willing to pay up to $7 (400 units) save $4 each, and those willing to pay up to $5 rather than do without, save $2 each. The consumer's surplus is (400 × $4 = $1,600) + (200 × $2 = $400) = $2,000.

For a continuous demand curve consumer's surplus can be represented

FIGURE 4.6.1

Consumer's Surplus

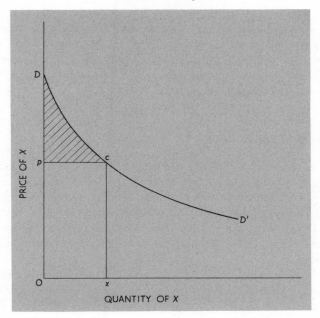

by Figure 4.6.1. DD' is the demand for X, Op is the price, Ox is the quantity sold at Op, and the rectangle $Opcx$ is total revenue. The shaded area pDc represents consumer's surplus. This is the amount that consumers would pay rather than do without X, if the sellers could discriminate and sell to each consumer at the maximum price he would pay rather than do without.

The concept of consumer's surplus is often used in welfare economics. Sometimes the area pDc is used to indicate the welfare gain from having a price Op. This area measures dollars, not utility. Since we cannot compare the added utility from a dollar saved for different individuals, we cannot say that the area pDc measures the satisfaction gained by consumers.

Definition: Consumer's surplus is the area below a demand curve and above the market price. It is frequently used to measure the welfare gain or loss of a decrease or increase in market price.[9]

---

[9] The concept of producer's surplus is used much less frequently. Producer's surplus is simply the area below the market price and above an upward sloping supply curve.

4.7 APPLICATION: LABOR SUPPLY AND GUARANTEED MINIMUM INCOME

The tools developed in this chapter can be used to analyze certain theoretical problems not directly related to the demand for a specific commodity. We will analyze two of these problems in this section: (a) an individual's willingness to supply labor and (b) some possible effects of a guaranteed minimum income.

4.7.a—Supply of Labor

Figure 4.7.1, panel a contains a portion of an individual's indifference map between income and leisure. Instead of depending strictly upon the quantity of goods, utility is now regarded as a function of income and leisure. Note from the shape of the indifference curves that we have assumed that both income and leisure are considered desirable by the individual; that is, he does not become satiated with leisure within the relevant range.

Before considering the problem of how the consumer maximizes utility, a word of explanation about the unit of measurement for leisure and the vertical line at L_m is in order. The unit of measurement along the horizontal axis can be hours per day, days per year, or any other period of time. Obviously if the unit is hours per day, the maximum time for leisure is 24 hours. If the unit is days of leisure, the maximum is 7 per week or 365 per year. The line L_m indicates the maximum attainable units of leisure per time period. If the individual chooses OC' units of leisure per period, he also chooses $C'L_m$ for work; or if he chooses OL_m of leisure, he does not work at all. The unit of measurement chosen for the horizontal axis clearly specifies the unit for the vertical. For example, when leisure is designated as hours per day, the vertical axis must measure income per day. Each indifference curve specifies the various combinations of income and leisure that yield the same level of satisfaction. For example, the consumer considers OC' leisure (and hence $C'L_m$ work) and income $C'H$ equivalent to OA' leisure (and hence $A'L_m$ work) and income $A'A$ since both points lie on the same indifference curve. The slopes of the curves indicate the rates at which an individual is willing to trade leisure for income. We assume for analytical convenience that both income and leisure are continuously divisible.

The budget lines are determined by the payment per unit of time. If the unit is hours per day, the budget line is determined by the individual's hourly wage rate; if days per year, by the earnings per day. Consider budget line Y_1L_m. If the individual works the entire time period (say 24 hours per day) and consequently takes no leisure, he could make OY_1 per time period. Assuming he specializes in leisure and does not

FIGURE 4.7.1

Indifference Curve Analysis of Labor Supply

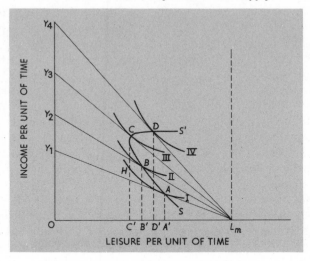

Panel *a*

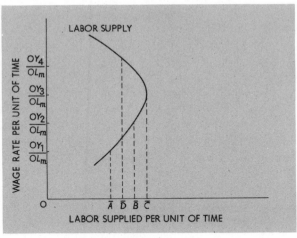

Panel *b*

work, he earns zero income. The slope of the budget line is the relevant wage rate or payment per unit of time. The "cost" of a unit of leisure is the sacrificed earnings for that period of time.[10] Y_2L_m, Y_3L_m, and Y_4L_m are

---

[10] For simplicity we assume a constant wage rate regardless of the amount of time worked. Certainly "overtime" work might be at overtime pay or a second job could be taken at a lower wage than the primary job. We also assume that the individual is free to choose the amount of time he works; sometimes this may not be the case.

the relevant budget lines for higher wage rates, OY_2/OL_m, OY_3/OL_m, and OY_4/OL_m respectively.

With a given wage rate, the highest attainable level of utility is given by the point where the relevant budget line is tangent to the indifference curve. An individual with the wage rate indicated by Y_1L_m achieves his highest attainable level of utility at point A. He chooses OA' leisure, $A'L_m$ work, and receives an income of $A'A$. If the wage rises to that level designated by budget line Y_2L_M, the highest attainable level of utility is at B, where the individual works $B'Lm$ for an income of $B'B$ and enjoys OB' leisure time. Points C and D indicate the equilibria leisure, work and income for the other two budget lines, and SS' connects these and all intermediate equilibria. Thus, SS' indicates the amount of time the individual is willing to work (or the amount of labor he is willing to supply) at each of a series of wages.

Note that at relatively low wages the individual is willing to work more, or to consume less leisure, as the wage rate increases. Since an increase in potential earnings causes leisure to cost more (in lost earnings), he chooses less leisure and more work. After point C, however, further increases in the wage rate induce him to take more leisure and work less. Leisure still costs the individual more as he moves from C to D, but the income effect means that the individual chooses to consume more leisure with the increased earnings (an exercise at the end of this chapter will help clarify this last relation), and the income effect offsets the substitution effect.

Just as we can derive demand and Engel curves from price-consumption and income-consumption curves, we can derive a labor supply curve from curves such as SS'. Figure 4.7.1, panel b, shows the labor supply curve derived from the indifference map in panel a. The distance OA in "b" equals $A'L_M$ in "a" and is the amount of work associated with wage rate OY_I/OL_M, and so on. Since SS' bends backward at C, the labor supply curve bends backward at $O\overline{C}$.

4.7.b—Guaranteed Minimum Income: Theory

Thus far in our analysis we have considered only the effect of market-determined variables (wage rates) upon the individual's choice between leisure and work. Let us now examine the effect of a nonmarket force upon an individual's willingness to supply labor.

Many discussions of guaranteed minimum income ignore the problem of work incentives. In its most familiar form a guaranteed minimum income would allow people to work, but those who are unable to earn the minimum income would receive the difference between what they earn and the designated minimum from the state. It has been asserted that a person who could not make the minimum income would not work, but that anyone who could make more would choose to work. We can analyze the theoretical aspects of the problem rather simply.[11]

Consider an individual with an indifference map for leisure and earnings depicted by curves I, II, and III and earning possibilities shown by budget line $Y_e L_m$ in Figure 4.7.2. Following the type of analysis pre-

FIGURE 4.7.2

Indifference Curve Analysis of a Minimum Guaranteed Income

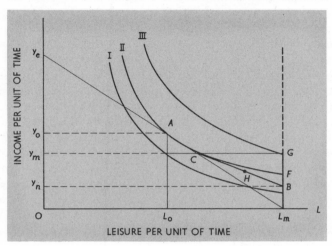

viously developed, we can see that he chooses income OY_0, leisure OL_0, and work time L_0L_m per period of time. Now suppose the government declares that income OY_m per period is a "necessary" income. No one should receive less. The state will make up any difference between what one earns and Y_m assuming, of course, that one earns less than Y_m. Since the individual under consideration is earning more than Y_m, the question is whether the minimum will affect him or not.

Note the way that the guaranteed minimum changes the set of possible incomes. The budget line from C to Y_e remains the same; but since the individual can have at least Y_m no matter how much he works and no matter what his wage rate, the income possibility line changes at point C. The new line becomes Y_eCGL_m. The individual can now attain the highest possible level of utility on indifference curve III by choosing OL_m leisure and no work. Since III is clearly higher than II, the utility maximizing individual will move from A to G even though he could earn more than the guaranteed minimum.

---

[11] The analysis in this and the next subsection is based upon an article by C. T. Brehm and T. R. Saving, "The Demand for General Assistance Payments," *American Economic Review*, December 1964, pp. 1002–18.

Under the circumstances, three factors could change and cause the person to choose to work some portion of the time. First, the minimum income could be decreased to some level below the intersection of indifference curve II with the perpendicular at L_m; for example, OY_n may be the new minimum that causes the person to choose point A. Then the person would choose point A on II. Second, the wage or potential earnings rate could increase enough to induce him to work. A sufficient increase would raise the budget line at least enough for it to become tangent to indifference curve III. Third, the individual might not consider welfare payments as desirable as equal payments for work.

Suppose then that the person attaches some stigma to receiving income from the state. Since he receives less satisfaction from a dollar given him by the state than from an "earned" dollar, he tends to discount state payments by some fraction between zero and one. Say $1 of relief payments is equivalent to $0.50 received for work. The closer to one the discount factor, the less stigma attached. In Figure 4.7.2 let k be the discount factor. Since we assume that the person does not value relief income more than an earned income, $0 < k < 1$. An income of Y_m received from the state would be valued by the individual as equivalent to kY_m "earned" income. Starting from L_m the individual views his income as his earned income plus some fraction k times the difference between the guaranteed minimum and the income he receives from working. His new "budget" line is L_mBCY_e; that is, he views his income as Earned Income $+ k(Y_m -$ Earned Income).

Given the value of his discount factor k (or we might call it his degree of "puritan ethic"), the individual chooses point A on indifference curve II, the highest indifference level attainable by "budget" line L_mBCY_e. If his discount factor k were not as large as that in Figure 4.7.2 and kY_m were raised to (say) above F, the person would choose OL_m leisure and no work in order to reach the highest utility level. With a still different k the highest attainable level could be reached at a point of tangency on segment BC, say at H. The consumer would work some, earn less than OY_m and receive the difference from the state.

The decision concerning whether or not to receive income from the state therefore, theoretically depends upon three factors: (1) the individual's possibility of earning income; (2) the amount at which the state sets the minimum; and (3) the discount factor attached to relief payments.

4.7.c—Guaranteed Minimum Income: Empirical Evidence

The demand for welfare was estimated in the above-cited paper as follows: From the theoretical model the number of assistance recipients out of a specified population is a function of the wage rate, the base income that society sets as a minimum, and the discount factor (k). Those persons receiving assistance because of old age, blindness, or total disability and dependent children were not counted. Neither were social security payments after retirement. Data on average manufacturing wages, population, unemployment, non-agricultural employment, and the average general assistance payments were collected by states over the period 1951–59. The rate of unemployment measures the number of consumers with zero wage alternatives. Non-agricultural employment in a state divided by the state's population gives an index of the degree of urbanization of the state. It was thought that the discount factor (k) would be smaller in rural communities than in urban; that is, rural residents value "unearned" income less than urban. Secondly, as was shown in the study, the degree of urbanization was strongly and positively related to the ease of obtaining assistance payments.

Estimation equations were computed in four ways for each year. Every equation had a significant coefficient (at the one percent level) for at least one variable. In 26 of the 36 equations there were at least two significant coefficients at the ten percent level. Thus, the model seems to explain the observed variation in general assistance payments. The base income variable (that is the average payment) appears to be the most significant variable explaining the number of recipients. It was significant in 16 of 18 cases at the one percent level and in all 18 at the ten percent. The rate of unemployment is next most significant followed closely by the proxy variable for the ease of getting on the rolls. The coefficient of manufacturing wages is least significant.

The authors of the study note that the relation between assistance payments and number of recipients does not imply that society should not give supplements. A working widowed mother may have a greater cost to society than the lost product if she were not working. The social benefit may exceed the social cost. The evidence merely shows that consumers react to costs and benefits when determining whether to go on assistance rolls. The demand for general assistance payments is simply a special case of the traditional demand for leisure theory.

4.8 CONCLUSION

The basic principles of consumer behavior and demand have now been developed. The fundamental point of this chapter is that if consumers behave so as to maximize satisfaction from a limited money income, quantity demanded (with one relatively unimportant exception) will vary inversly with price. Furthermore, an Engel curve is a locus of points relating equilibrium quantity to the level of money income at a specified set of relative prices. The Engel curve slopes upward if the good is normal over that range. If the good is inferior the curve bends backward.

The substitution effect of a price change upon that good is always negative. If the good is normal, the income effect reinforces the substitution effect. If the good is inferior, the income effect to some extent offsets the substitution effect.

QUESTIONS AND PROBLEMS

1. Consider Figure E.4.1. Begin with the consumer in equilibrium with an income of $300 facing the prices $P_X = \$4$ and $P_Y = \$10$.
    a. How much X is consumed in equilibrium? How much Y?
        Let the price of X fall to $2.50, nominal income and P_Y remaining constant.
    b. What is the new equilibrium consumption of X?
    c. How much income must be taken from the consumer to isolate the income and substitution effects?
    d. The total effect of the price decrease is————. The substitution effect is————. The income effect is————.
    e. The good X is————, but not————.
    f. Construct the consumer's demand curve for X with nominal money income constant; with real income (utility) constant.

FIGURE E.4.1

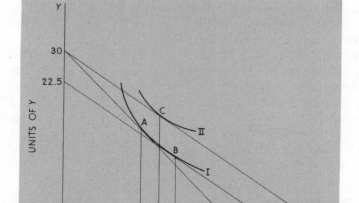

2. Isolate the substitution, income, and total effects for a price decrease in the case of a normal good; for a Giffen good after a price increase.
3. Using an indifference map construct an Engel curve for a normal good. Change the price ratio; do you get a different income-consumption curve and Engel curve?

4. Figure E.4.2 shows an individual's indifference map between leisure and income. Ignore indifference curve III for now and assume that curves I and II make up the map. The unit of time is one day of 24 hours. The wage rate is $3 per hour.

    a. How much does the individual choose to work? How much leisure does he consume?

    Let the wage rate rise to $5 an hour.

    b. Ignoring III, what is his work and leisure time?

    Suppose at the wage rate of $5 the individual was taxed just enough to make him choose a point on the original indifference curve, I.

    c. What is the substitution effect?

    d. Return the taxed income; what is the income effect?

    e. What is the total effect?

    f. In this example leisure is a (normal, inferior) good, and the income effect (offsets, reinforces) the substitution effect.

    g. Derive the associated supply curve for labor.

    Now let the relevant indifference map be I and III.

    h. Derive the new supply of labor curve.

    i. Now the total effect of a wage increase from $3 to $5 is————, the substitution effect is————, and the income effect is————.

    j. Leisure is now a (normal, inferior) good.

    k. What can you say about the classification of leisure and a backward bending supply of labor?

    l. Draw in indifference curve IV tangent to the budget line associated with $5 so that leisure is a normal good but the supply of labor is not backward bending.

FIGURE E.4.2

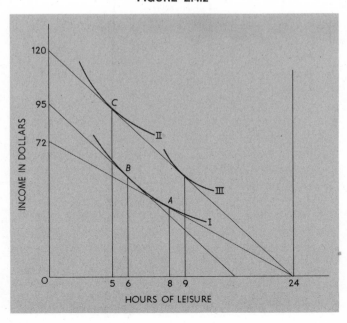

5. Using the tools developed in the analytical exercise and in Problem 4, comment on the following statement: An increase in the income tax causes laborers to work more in order to maintain their present income. (Hint: begin in equilibrium with a laborer earning OY income and enjoying OL leisure at a wage rate of w. Impose an income tax of $k\%$ where $0 < k < 1$. Since the wage rate is now $(1 - k)w$, the budget line pivots downward around the horizontal (leisure) axis. Show that a laborer could increase, decrease, or keep constant his labor time, depending upon his evaluation of leisure).

6. Suppose that you were permitted to experiment (do anything you wished) with a very large group of consumers. How would you attempt to discover the magnitude and size of the substitution effect. (Hint: after a price change, you could change each consumer's income so that he could just purchase the *original* bundle at the new set of input prices. This would be a good approximation of the way in which we kept real income—utility—constant in the text. What would the consumer do?) How could you experiment and find out how a guaranteed minimum income affects labor time? If you were not allowed to experiment how would you answer the last question?

7. The straight line demand function is

$$p = 200 - 5q$$

The price prevailing in the market is $100. What is the total consumers surplus at that price? (Hint: the area of a triangle is ½ [base times height]; solve for q at $p = \$100$ and for h at $q = 0$.) What is the welfare gain from a fall in price to $80?

chapter 5

Some Applications of Supply and Demand Analysis

5.1 INTRODUCTION

Chapters 2 through 4 have introduced the basic points of consumer behavior theory. We have included from time to time some examples of the way in which economic theory has been applied to "real world" economic problems. It seems advisable to pause now, before plunging on into the theories of production and cost, to analyze some additional economic problems. In this way we are continually reminded that one does not study economic theory purely for the sake of knowing economic theory. This body of theory has been designed primarily or even solely to aid us in solving contemporary economic problems and to explain occurrences we observe in the world.

As noted in Chapter 1, the world is too complex for us to consider every aspect of every problem. All that has ever happened to you since you were born *may* affect your purchase of an automobile or a house, but economists disregard most of the less important influences when deriving the demand for automobiles or houses. Economic theory abstracts from the unimportant and throws out the trivial influences to concentrate upon more important influences. Critics of economic theory point out accusingly that people do not always buy the cheapest thing, so the law of downsloping demand does not hold. You do not always order the cheapest dinner in a restaurant or buy the cheapest pair of shoes. But economic theory says no such thing. Downsloping demand simply means that if you raise the price of something, less will be sold, other things held constant. We wish to analyze one thing at a time, and price is one of the important influences upon behavior. We frequently wish to isolate the effect of other things and concentrate upon some other influence. As you will see, we can explain a lot of observed phenomena and answer a lot of economic problems with the simple tools of theory developed thus far. After all, the test of good economic research is the use of simple theory and accurate data to explain complex events.

5.2 THEORY OF JOB CHOICE

One application of theoretical principles that we will use in later analysis is the theory of job choice. The best way to introduce job choice is to begin with a rather old but rather famous joke. It is told that the great Irish humorist George Bernard Shaw was seated next to an attractive, sophisticated lady at an elegant dinner party. After making small talk with the lady for some time, Shaw asked her if she would consider sleeping with him that night for the payment of one million pounds. The lady thought for some time then said that yes she probably would. Shaw then asked her if she would spend the night with him for one pound. The lady answered, indignantly, "Sir, what do you think I am?" Shaw replied, "Madame, we have already settled upon what you are; now we are merely haggling over price."

Shaw may have been quite clever in his retort, but he was exhibiting an utter lack of economic understanding. As an analogy I might ask one of my students if he would haul away my garbage for $55. Probably most students would, although most would not do it for ten cents. This would, by no means, classify those students as garbage collectors. Neither would the lady be classified as whatever Shaw classified her.

Economic theory recognizes that people get different levels of utility from working in different occupations. Economists also observe that people are willing to make a trade-off between less desired occupations and increased incomes. Just as in the case of commodities, supply and demand determine relative wages and relative numbers of employees between different occupations.

The situation can be considered graphically. Assume in Figure 5.2.1 that there are two occupations, a and b. The ratio of those in a to those in b (N_a/N_b) is plotted along the horizontal axis and the relative wage rates (W_a/W_b) along the vertical. As the payment for a work falls relative to the payment for b, society (following the law of demand) will wish to use relatively more a than b.[1] This relation is indicated by DD'. On the other hand, as the relative wage in occupation a rises, people will be induced to leave b and enter a. We assume, for simplicity, that all can perform either job equally well. The supply SS' is upward sloping reflecting different preferences of individuals for the two jobs. At a low relative wage of b only those with strong preferences for b will enter b. A rise in

---

[1] We have simplified the demand for labor a great deal. The demand for any resource, including labor, is a demand *derived* from what that resource can produce. We will take up the more complicated aspects of derived demand in Chapter 11.

b's relative wages will induce those who prefer b less (that is, require a higher return to leave a and enter b) to enter. Equilibrium occurs in Figure 5.2.1 at $(\overline{W}_a/\overline{W}_b)$ and $(\overline{N}_a/\overline{N}_b)$.

If society suddenly values the services of a more, DD' will shift outward to D_1D_1', raising the relative wages in a, overcoming the distaste of some for working in a, and increasing the relative number in a. On the other hand, if people suddenly begin to prefer working in occupation a more, the relative wages in a will fall as the ratio N_a/N_b rises. In this way the wage ratio between occupations can be explained similarly to the price ratio between goods.

You may be thinking that there is an apparent contradiction between the theory and what we observe. Our theory says that higher wages must be offered to induce people to enter less desirable occupations. On the other hand, we observe that the less desirable occupation, like garbage collection, typically pay less than more glamorous occupations, like movie stars. Note, however, that there are differences in the supply offered among occupations, in the qualities employers desire in these occupations, and in the legal ability to enter certain occupations. While garbage collecting may be undesirable, if many people cannot do much else (or are not demanded at the wage rate in other occupations), the supply of applicants will drive down wages. Brain surgery may be a desirable occupation but the training required and the limited number of applicants ac-

FIGURE 5.2.1

**Determination of Relative Wages
and Employment**

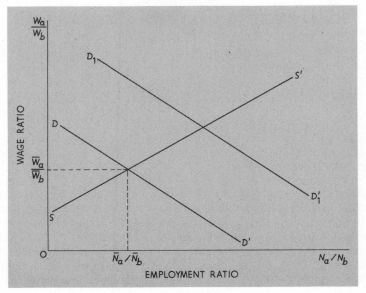

cepted keep wages high. If suddenly the public cared nothing about the talent or looks of actresses, the supply of potential movie stars would rise along with a concomitant fall in wages. In all cases both supply and demand must be considered.

Exercise: Use the model developed here to solve the following problem. Assume the army wishes to hire X number of men. Assume that more than X meet the army's standards. The army has three choices. (1) It can let supply and demand determine the wage which will attract X men (assume an upward sloping supply); (2) it can set wages below equilibrium and draft the number needed; or (3) it can set the wage below equilibrium, draft the number needed, but let people who are drafted pay others to

FIGURE 5.2.2

Economics of the Draft

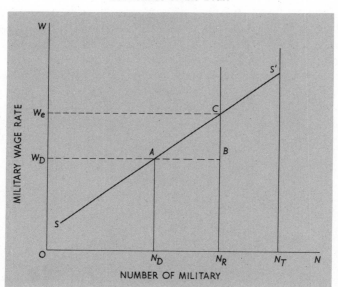

serve for them if they wish and are qualified. Analyze the costs to society, to those drafted, and to the army. Compare the makeup of those who serve under the three cases.

Solution: Let us analyze the problem with the aid of Figure 5.2.2. Assume that from the total number of the population who meet the military's criteria for duty (ON_T), the military desires ON_R. SS' is the supply curve of the ON_T for military duty. The upward slope reflects the difference in taste for military duty and the differences in other opportunities. A free market wage of OW_e would induce the required number ON_R to volunteer. The total cost to society would be OW_eCN_R. If wages are set below OW_e, say at OW_D, ON_D would volunteer and N_DN_R would be drafted. The wage cost to society would be OW_DBN_R. However, those who were drafted from the N_DN_T who did not volunteer would pay (in foregone earnings) the difference between their wage rate and their supply price. The drafted persons would be scattered randomly along N_DN_T if people could not pay others to serve. If draft notices were negotiable the same people would serve as would be induced to enter by the equilibrium wage, OW_e. Anyone who was drafted and had a supply price above OW_e would be induced to pay anyone who was not drafted and had a supply price below OW_e the difference between that supply price and OW_D. Society would still pay OW_DBN_R. Those who were drafted would pay ACB (recall consumer's surplus). Society as a whole thus shifts some of the military costs to those who are chosen by the draft.

5.3 ECONOMICS OF JURY SELECTION

Military conscription has been under widespread attack, not only during the past few years but also throughout recent Western history. Most of the arguments are so well known as to be included in many elementary economic textbooks. In contrast, the procurement of jurors by conscription has been generally accepted. To be sure, the "fairness" of jury trials and alleged biases in jury selection—e.g., discrimination by sex, race, or income—have been heatedly debated. But, the economic implications of conscripting jurors had been largely ignored, until a recent paper by Donald L. Martin analyzed the social costs, the redistribution effect, and the reallocation aspects of juror conscription, and discussed the implications of a volunteer jury system.[2]

Analogous to the military draft, the social cost of a drafted juror consists of the goods and services that society foregoes by having an individual serve on a jury rather than perform his normal occupation. It was estimated in the above cited paper that this cost was $233 million dollars in 1962. The total jury fees in that year were $89 million (in 1958 prices).[3]

The social costs—that is, the lost product—of the procurement of any set of juries depends upon which method of conscription is used. The two methods of conscription most widely used are random selection from a large list (e.g., voter registrations, telephone directories) and the keyman system, in which some "pillars of the community" (keymen) are asked to suggest respected and esteemed persons for the jury list. Since keymen selection draws from occupations with higher opportunity costs (the lost income from serving on a jury) this method would be more costly—estimated at perhaps $48 million higher in 1962.[4]

---

[2] This section is based upon the article by Donald L. Martin, "The Economics of Jury Conscription," *Journal of Political Economy*, July/August 1972, pp. 680–701.

[3] See ibid. for estimation techniques. The year was chosen because it was the only one for which all data were available. Some rather heroic assumptions were made in doing the estimation.

[4] Keymen selection has recently been eliminated in federal courts.

We can compare the costs of random, keyman, and volunteer jury with the use of Figure 5.3.1. Assume there are OJ_2 jurors designated as eligible to serve. OB is the locus of the opportunity cost (foregone earnings) as we increase the number of jurors. For example, the OJ_1th juror foregoes J_1A dollars per day by serving. Assume that all are equally disposed toward serving on juries except for income; thus, if the wage of a juror is above his sacrificed earnings, he would prefer jury service; if below, he would prefer his job. Assume society wishes OJ_1 jurors. If it selected these so as to minimize the cost to society, all with an opportunity cost below AJ_1 would be called.

FIGURE 5.3.1

Conscription of Jurors

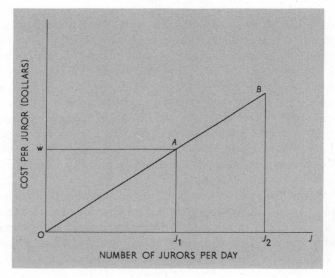

Recall the concept of consumer's surplus from Chapter 4. Following the same type of analysis the total cost to society; that is, foregone product, would be the area OAJ_1 since each juror over the range OJ_1 would sacrifice the product designated by the height of the line $OAB;$ the total product foregone would be the total area. Society could set a wage of OW and all with opportunity costs below this would volunteer, which of course is the same thing.

If selection is random, and the number OJ_1 is chosen from the OJ_2 available, some jurors to the right of OJ_1 with opportunity costs higher than J_1A will be chosen. To the extent that "higher cost" jurors are substituted for "lower cost" jurors, society sacrifices a product greater than the area OAJ_1. Since keyman selection would be biased toward the J_2

end of the horizontal axis, the cost would be even higher using this method. To draw many implications from this approach we would have to assume that productivity as a juror (however defined) is unrelated to occupation.

Other costs noted by Martin result from having jury fees below opportunity costs. Individuals are encouraged by the losses to evade conscription; thus more people are called than will serve, administrative costs will be higher, which adds to the other costs, and resources will be devoted to avoiding duty. Since the cost to the courts will be low under jury conscription, courts will use jurors excessively, resulting in much waiting or idleness by jurors, little idleness of judges, and full use of courtrooms.

Certainly, employers frequently reimburse jurors for their lost earnings. This results in some wealth redistribution and places increased administrative costs upon firms. Furthermore, since reimbursement is an employee benefit, wages are reduced somewhat from what they would have been in the absence of reimbursement. Martin estimates that the total cost of *explicit* taxation for payments to jurors accounts for less than 40 percent of the total cost, lost income of jurors (or firms) making up the other 60 percent. This *implicit* transfer was estimated as $143 million in 1962. After discussing more completely these economic consequences, Martin answers some of the arguments against volunteerism for juries, which you may wish to pursue further in the original article cited above. In any case, the total cost would appear to be less under volunteerism than under the present system. It could, of course, be more costly to taxpayers.

5.4 ECONOMICS OF FERTILITY AND CHILDREN

Recently it has become quite fashionable to worry about the rate of growth of population both in the United States and in the world as a whole. Dire predictions are frequently heard that the United States will be up to the ears in people by the year 2000. This, of course, is in direct contrast to the gloomy predictions made by economists in the 1930s that the rate of population growth had slowed down so much that the United States was doomed for the foreseeable future to economic stagnation. Before analyzing the facts, we can use our elementary theory of consumer behavior to analyze the cyclical variations and the long-term trend in fertility. We will use a theory recently set forth in an excellent paper on population in a recent economic history book to explain the economic influences behind increased and decreased birth rates.[5]

The theory of fertility can be developed within the theory of consumer

[5] This section is based upon portions of Chapter 5 on American population in Lance E. Davis, et al., *American Economic Growth* (New York: Harper and Row, 1972).

choice. Children are considered consumption goods that give various degrees of utility. The cost of a couple's having children is the stream of expenses they devote to raising the children, less any contributions the children make to the family income. The budget constraint and the preference function determine the desired number of children.

This theory does not say that people go through precise calculations about children anymore than the theory of consumer behavior says that people estimate precisely the utility they will gain from any purchase. Just as people have different preferences for other goods, so does the desire for children differ among couples. We observe one couple taking fertility pills while another does everything possible to prevent children. Children do compete with other goods. We observe people substituting a new car or a trip to Europe for an additional child or vice versa. In general, people take cost into consideration when planning their family size. Thus, our theory of consumer behavior predicts that the number of children varies directly with income and with the price of child-competing goods, and inversely with the strength of desires for children and the price of child-related goods.

Two modifications of the theory of consumer behavior must be taken into account in the case of children. First, since we must consider surviving children rather than births, the total depends on mortality rates. Second, the household is a producer as well as a consumer of children, and the production process itself yields satisfaction. Economists call this extra benefit an externality. This external effect in the production of children would lead toward more children than the optimal level. This could be turned around. Children may be an externality from intercourse, so the quantity of intercourse may be non-optimal (sub-optimal?) from the point of view of society. Of course, there are many methods of preventing children, but these are not costless. In any case, a couple's attitude toward birth control determines in some measures its fertility. A more complete theory would include uncertainty.

To interpret recent trends we should analyze influences upon people's tastes for children, and the factors that might change society's taste over a period of time. Three factors seem important. First, the growth of per capita income over time affects fertility in two ways. The budget constraint is pushed outward permitting both more children and more of other goods. Offsetting the budget effect, each generation of young adults comes, on average, from an increasingly prosperous family background and therefore has an increased desire for more goods. Luxuries become necessities from one generation to the other. As the parents' expenditure pattern is passed on to the children, the young adults undergo an increased desire for goods relative to children. It may well be that over the long trend the two child-affecting consequences of increasing per capita income tend to cancel. However, as we shall see, the short-run affects may be significant. The second factor affecting society's taste for children is the increasing level of education, which creates new wants for consumer goods relative to children. Finally, the introduction of new goods affects the utility pattern between goods and children.

We can explain recent trends in fertility with the model. In the 1930s young adults, whose tastes had been developed in the prosperity of the 1920s, experienced a severe depression and decline in income. The enhanced taste for consumption goods passed to them from their parents, along with a decrease in the budget line led to an extremely severe decline in the birth rate. As noted above, economists thought the trend would significantly affect national growth. As you probably know, after World War II society experienced a significant increase in the birth rate; the so-called "war baby boom." The popular explanation is that all the soldiers returned home sex-starved from four years of celibacy. This may offer some explanation, but with the widespread indoctrination of soldiers about birth control, it does not seem to be particularly enlightening, particularly since the trend in births continued almost throughout the 1950s, a period more than long enough for the pressures of celibacy to be relieved.

A better explanation is that the young adults of the late 40s and early 50s grew up during the austerity of depression and the war. Their tastes for consumption goods was not substantially increased by their childhood. The great prosperity after 1946 pushed the budget line outward. Increased income along with relatively stationary consumer wants led to more children. In the 1960s the income of the young declined somewhat. Their tastes for goods were enhanced by the prosperity of their childhoods. Thus society experienced a decline in fertility.

A cyclical fertility effect could be deduced from the model. The relative income of young adults depends, in some measure, on the proportion of young adults in the economy and the state of the economy. When young adults are in short supply, as in post World War II, their relative incomes are high. They have more children leading to an increased supply of young adults in the next generation. This new generation experiences relatively low incomes, which along with their high standard of living during youth causes them to have relatively fewer children. The cycle continues. It is predicted that the fertility decline of the 60s will lead to a new "baby boom" in the late 70s and early 80s.

As noted above, over the long-run secular trend the income effects probably balance out and other factors attain increased importance. In the paper cited it is noted that as the United States grew, regions shifted from frontier, to settled agriculture, to new urban, to old urban. Education generally increased through these stages, causing increased desire for more goods relative to children. More goods were available in each progressive stage, causing a decreased desire for children. Also, outlays upon children become higher and returns from children's production becomes lower through the stages. Statistics show an inverse association between population density and fertility over time. All things considered, however, it is difficult to generalize about the future.

Exercise: What effect would you expect a successful women's liberation movement to have upon fertility in the United States?

Solution: Unknown, because of two possibly offsetting effects. If women's lib is successful one would expect the income of females to increase relative to that of males. The cost of bearing children—the value of the woman's work-time lost while having and tending to children—rises. The substitution effect would cause a decrease in children. On the other hand, as women earn more, family income rises. If children are not an inferior good, the income effect would cause an increase in fertility. We cannot make a clear prediction that either effect will be predominant.

5.5 TIME AND THE DEMAND FOR PASSENGER TRANSPORTATION

Why does one person fly from Washington to New York, another take a train, and yet another drive? Do not say differences in income, or that one person can afford to fly and another cannot. Many rich old ladies take the train, while middle income businessmen and poor students choose to fly. The answer lies in the different valuations of time among people. A paper by Reuben Gronau used simple consumer behavior theory to analyze the problem and to estimate the demand for passenger transportation.[6] Gronau incorporated time into the cost of a trip. In his model the price of a trip, Π, consists of two parts, the money cost and the cost of the time spent traveling:

$$\Pi = P + KT$$

where P is the dollar cost of the trip, T is the time spent traveling and K is the traveler's valuation of a unit of his time, perhaps his wage rate. Assume someone values his time at $10 an hour. A particular trip takes two hours by air and fifteen by rail. If air fare is $150 and rail is $80, the total cost of flying is $170 and of traveling by rail, $230.

The demand for trips is a function of their total cost, and the cost of other inputs, such as hotel, meals, etc. Also, the demand for trips depends upon the demand for visits, which in turn depends upon whether the visit is for business or pleasure, and upon income. For now we will ignore everything except the choice of method of transportation. In the example above the traveler chooses air. We will ignore fear of flying, pleasure

---

[6] This section is based upon Reuben Gronau "The Effect of Traveling Time on the Demand for Passenger Transportation," *Journal of Political Economy*, Mar./Apr. 1970, pp. 377–94. For a general analysis of the importance of time in behavior theory, see G. S. Becker, "A Theory of the Allocation of Time," *Economic Journal*, Sept. 1965, pp. 493–517.

from sightseeing by car, and so on. We will assume that a consumer plans a visit then chooses the cheapest method of travel.

Assume that the money price of a trip varies inversely with the time spent traveling. The theory would predict that those with a high time value would take the most rapid transportation. Gronau notes that statistics show travelers with incomes under $4,000 travel by air less than one-fiftieth of their trips whereas those with incomes above $15,000 go by air in more than one-sixth of the cases. More than seven percent of the trips of the low-income group were by bus; only two percent of the trips of the high-income group were by bus.

Similarly the purpose of a trip would appear to affect the time valuation. A traveler would probably place a higher value on time while on business trips. Since in the short run an individual may not be able to convert his leisure time into work, particularly at the wage of his current job, he would not place so high a value on time spent traveling for pleasure. Again, statistics bear out this prediction. Seventeen percent of business trips and three percent of pleasure trips are by air. Two percent of business trips and five percent of personal trips are by bus. Finally, since the number of passengers does not affect the money price of a trip by automobile, the average money price of a trip by car falls with the number of passengers. Again statistics show that one-half of all auto trips in 1963 involved at least a party of two. Only one-sixth of all air trips involved two or more. Or, less than one-fourth of all car travelers went alone; more than two-thirds of the travelers by public transportation traveled alone.

Gronau attempted to estimate statistically the variables that determined which mode of transportation would be used for a particular trip. First, he estimated the relation of miles traveled to time spent traveling and to the money price of the fare for four different methods of transportation: air, rail, bus, automobile. Using these equations he then found the points at which consumers, who choose the cheapest (total) methods of transportation, would switch from one method to another. For example, if V is the value in dollars per hour of a passenger's time, he would prefer air to rail transportation if

$$V > \frac{1.45 + .01741M}{-3.15 + .02331M},$$

where M is the distance in miles of the trip. He prefers air to bus if

$$V > \frac{3.48 + .02742M}{-2.88 + .02631M},$$

and he prefers rail to bus when

$$V > \frac{2.03 + .01001M}{.27 + .00300M}.$$

(If you assign a value to your time, you can use these inequalities to determine the most economical method of transportation for your next trip.) It was found that an increase in distance increased the time differentials between any two methods of transportation more than the price differentials. Thus, passengers would tend to use the faster method of travel as the distance of a trip increased. The "switching points" between automobile transportation and any other method of transportation depend, of course, upon the number of passengers making the trip. Some examples will show the various relations. Air is cheaper than rail transportation for a trip of 150 miles if the value of one's time exceeds $11.80 an hour. Air is cheaper than bus if the valuation of time exceeds $7.10 an hour. Rail is preferred to bus if the valuation is over $5.30 an hour. Thus, for a 150 mile trip people whose time is worth less than $5.30 an hour go by bus, those whose time valuation is between $5.30 and $11.80 take a train, and if the time valuation exceeds $11.80, they fly. Air saves no time over rail for trips less than 135 miles. Only one who values his time less than $1.00 an hour will always travel by bus. As Gronau points out in conclusion the decision by some railroads to stop passenger services to distances beyond 200 miles and the decline in the passenger share of railroads is quite consistent with the model.

Exercise: Using the methods of this section, answer the following question true or false, and defend your answer. Airlines give discounts to students who fly because they love students, and they believe that students add a lot of class to the flights.

Solution: Probably false. While students may add class to flights, this is probably not the reason for student discounts. The demand of students for flights is probably much more responsive to price changes than the demand of businessmen, when the *total* cost of the trip is considered. An example may explain. Assume a particular flight costs $100 and takes three hours. If a businessman values his time at $100 an hour, the total cost of the trip is $400. If the student's time is worth $20 an hour, his trip costs $160. A decrease of $40 in the price of a ticket reduces the businessman's cost 10 percent while the student's cost falls 25 per cent. Thus, one would expect students to be much more responsive to price cuts in tickets than businessmen. We will discuss price discrimination (charging different people different amounts) in Chapter 9 below.

5.6 ECONOMICS OF CRIME

Judging from the more popular literature in the area, crime or the criminal is essentially a sociological or psychological problem, susceptable only to sociological or psychological analysis. This is not at all correct. Crime and criminal behavior lend themselves easily to basic economic analysis. While there have been many recent economic articles in this area, we will briefly summarize only three of the best to obtain some flavor of the economic approach to crime. We will discuss first the optimum enforcement of laws, second, the economics of heroin, and third, the economics of theft.

One brief warning may be warranted first. While we use basic consumer behavior theory to analyze crime and treat crime as any other economic problem, we do not mean to imply that sociological influences are not important determinants of economic behavior. This is true of many aspects of economic analysis, not just crime. Take certain foods for example. Residents of New York City probably eat more blintzes, lox, and bagels on average than residents of South Texas, whereas residents of South Texas probably eat more enchiladas, chili, and tacos. Residents of Georgia probably eat more grits and turnip greens than the others. Certainly while sociological factors such as childhood habits affect the consumption of these foods, the demands for lox, tacos, and grits are susceptable of economic analysis. These demands can be analyzed like any others. The same is true with crime. People from certain areas and backgrounds are possibly more likely to become criminals than those from others, just as people from certain backgrounds are more likely to become coal miners or doctors. Thus crime resembles other economic activities and can be analyzed using economic theories.

5.6.a—Law Enforcement[7]

A society could probably have zero criminal activity if it were willing to pay the price. A sufficient number of policemen and sufficient severity of sentences could prevent practically all crime. But, law enforcement is costly. Inasmuch as society must give up productive resources to be used in law enforcement, it will choose the amount of enforcement that society (or someone acting for society) believes it can afford. It chooses, by choosing the level of law enforcement, some positive level of crime.

Society can apparently deter crime, at a given level of enforcement, by increasing punishment. The amount of crime is influenced by the probability of getting caught and the assigned value of the punishment if caught. Ignoring the present and future stigma of being a crook (which one should not always ignore in analysis), assume that a person could rob a store and, if successful, gain $1,000. If he attaches a probability of $\frac{1}{2}$ to getting caught, and if the fine were $500, he should rob the store. That is, his expected return is $\frac{1}{2}(\$1,000) - \frac{1}{2}(\$500) = \$250$. Any fine above $1,000 at the same probability of conviction would deter him from the robbery. One would think, therefore, that capital punishment for every crime would be optimal. If a university president wished to keep

---

[7] This subsection is based upon George J. Stigler, "The Optimum Enforcement of Laws," *Journal of Political Economy*, May/June 1970, pp. 526–36.

students and faculty from walking on the grass, he could announce that one, and only one, grasswalker per year would be shot on sight if caught. It seems logical that grass walking would be substantially deterred at very little cost to the university.

For society or a university this may not be the most expedient solution. As always, marginal decisions are important in crime. If the penalty is the same for a minor (in the eyes of society) crime as for a major crime, there is little marginal deterrence to discourage major crimes. If the penalties are the same, one might as well murder if one is going to assault (assuming equal tenacity in attempting to solve the crime). As George Stigler noted in the article cited above, marginal costs (that is, the additional penalties for additional crime) are necessary for marginal deterrence. As Stigler also pointed out along the same line, society must avoid excessive enforcement. If society places no limit on the punishment of innocent persons, crime would be encouraged because of the reduced marginal deterrence. If one is very likely to get locked up whether innocent or guilty, one may as well commit a crime with some possibility of reward. It may well have been in the past that frequent haphazard arrests or general harassment in certain areas actually encouraged increased crime in those areas.

In addition to public expenditure a great deal of private expenditure is undertaken to prevent crime. For example, people hire watchmen and guards, buy locks, and defend themselves from assault. These private expenses should be considered in determining optimal public enforcement. Finally, penalties probably should be related to age, past offenses, and probability of repetition.

The supply of crime for profit (as opposed to crime for recreation) follows from the theory of job choice. One considers the probable reward, the probability of conviction, the probable punishment, the resource costs involved, including the opportunity cost of not being in another occupation, and the capital required, such as burglar tools, and the stigma attached to being a crook. All of these affect the amount of crime. A dropout working part-time in a service station will sacrifice less income by serving a prison term than a plumber or a carpenter. Other things equal, the former is more likely to commit an offense. If I leave 15¢ on my dresser and my maid does not take it, I cannot infer that she is honest. I might try the test by dropping a $10,000 negotiable bond casually out of my pocket in front of her and leave on a four-week vacation. If the probability of detection increases with the number of offenses, criminals are encouraged to commit infrequent crimes that involve large sums of money. Society realizes this, which is why large banks and Fort Knox are guarded more heavily than service stations and drive-in grocery stores. Also larger penalties are put on larger offenses.

To summarize, the demand for and supply of crime depend upon expenditures for enforcement, penalties, and opportunities in non-criminal occupations, among other things. One rule is that the scale of enforcement should be set at a point at which the additional return in preventing crime from any additional expenditure is not less than that additional expenditure. If society specifies a level of enforcement expenditure, it should not spend an additional $100 to prevent $50 worth of crime. On the other hand, if society wishes to spend an additional $100 it should spend it where the return in preventing crime is greatest, as long as the return exceeds $100.[8]

5.6.b—Economics of Heroin

Heroin is quite cheap at the source of supply, relatively cheap as it enters the country, and quite expensive at retail. After it enters the United States it goes through many, many middlemen in its distribution path to the consumer. In most other businesses the overabundance of handlers through the many steps toward retail would be extremely inefficient, and competitors, who would offer to distribute cheaper, would have eliminated many of these steps. As opposed to the distributors of LSD and marijuana, who are essentially amateurs, the distribution of heroin is largely in the hands of professional, organized criminals. In his classic article on the subject Simon Rottenberg explained the "peculiar" structure of the heroin business.[9]

The illegal firm will attempt to maximize security for any given level of activity.[10] The unit of maximization (or in this case, minimization) is the probability of getting caught times the assigned value of the punishment. As noted in 5.6.a above, the probability of detection increases with the number of transactions. The risk of detection is therefore greatest where the average size of the transaction is least. This size becomes smaller at each step as heroin goes from importer to retailers. The number of transactions becomes greater, and the risk of detection increases. Certainly the importer could do his own retailing, and he could choose any number of steps that he wished the distribution to take.

If there is a central authority, possibly the importer, the distribution system will be longer than that which is most efficient, because the organizer wishes to minimize the probability of detection of the organizer. The more steps in the chain of distribution, the less information possessed

---

[8] We might mention, without taking account of the possibility, that a large part of society may not want particular laws enforced. Some that come to mind are prohibition laws and certain laws about sexual behavior.

[9] This subsection is based upon Simon Rottenberg, "The Clandestine Distribution of Heroin, Its Discovery and Suppression," *Journal of Political Economy*, Jan./Feb. 1968, pp. 78–90.

[10] We will look much more closely at the problem of cost minimization or constrained output maximization in Chapter 6.

at any given step, the greater the number of informants that must be gone through to get at the organizer, and the less is his risk. If a single firm is the organizer, it sets prices at each stage just sufficient to attract the required number of people. The differences must be large enough to cover costs, including the cost of conviction and the cost of social stigma. If there are several competing firms the prices are indeterminant and are sensitive to the trading ability of the participants. Participants have an incentive to sell their stock quickly after receipt, since possession of inventories is itself incriminating evidence.

As noted above, heroin is distributed by "organized criminals," and LSD and marijuana largely by amateurs. The rate of return then must be higher in heroin, because traders in heroin are able to enforce a monopoly. A monopoly in LSD and marijuana is more difficult to enforce, possibly for two reasons: more stigma is attached to heroin trade, and amateurs are discouraged from entry; or the cost of being convicted is higher for heroin trade. Thus, far fewer persons wish to enter the heroin trade than the marijuana trade, and monopoly is less easily enforced and protected in marijuana than in heroin. Since many more prospective entrants would have to be excluded from marijuana, the cost of enforcing a monopoly are high.

What would be the consequences of more rigid enforcement of narcotics laws? First, we might note that different crimes affect society differently. Society affects the amount of each type of crime by allocating enforcement. At a given level of total enforcement, society could decrease the costs of committing other crimes while increasing the cost of narcotics' trade by reallocating enforcement toward narcotics. Picture society as having "typical" indifference curves between narcotics and other crime. If the narcotics trade is relatively small the increase in other crimes that it is willing to suffer to reduce narcotics by some unit will be small. If, on the other hand, the narcotics trade is relatively large, society will put up with a much larger increase in other crime for the same diminution of narcotics crime. In a sense we can speak of society as having a "demand" for narcotics crime and for any other crime, because the amount of enforcement society is willing to allocate in any criminal activity determines to a large extent the amount of that activity supplied.[11]

5.6.c—A Cobweb Model of Crime

We can analyze the supply and demand situation in a particular criminal activity with a relatively simple model using somewhat limiting assumptions. Assume, as in any occupation, that when the return per

---

[11] Rottenberg in the remainder of his paper analyzed the economics of police bribery and the way in which society can most efficiently combat this. These aspects will not be discussed here.

FIGURE 5.6.1

Cobweb Model of Crime

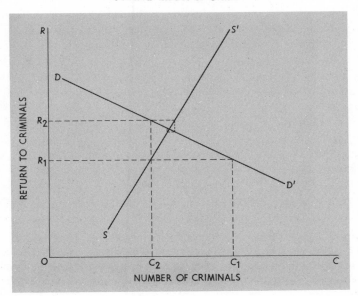

criminal in a particular area of crime rises, more criminals will be induced to enter this activity. The supply of criminals is indicated by SS' in Figure 5.6.1. The supply is affected primarily by the amount of enforcement in this area, the penalty for this crime, and the returns in other areas. Society, therefore, affects supply in these three ways.

Now let us assume that the more people actively engaged in any particular crime, the less the *per unit return* to the individuals engaged in this activity. Using the example in the preceding subsection, if the number of heroin pushers doubles, there may be more total heroin "pushed," but each pusher would find his own return lowered. DD' in Figure 5.6.1 reflects the decreasing returns to increasing numbers of people engaged in a particular crime. Again society affects its "demand" for crime by the amount of resources put into the prevention of this crime. Probably if the number of policemen charged with preventing this crime was doubled, DD' would shift downward, reflecting the diminished returns per criminal at each level of activity. Thus society can affect both the demand for and supply of crime.

Next assume that for some reason OC_1 criminals are engaged in this type of crime. From DD' we see that the return is OR_1. Since the return OR_1 induces only OC_2 into this activity, in the next period the number of criminals is reduced to OC_2. But, with only OC_2 committing this crime, the return rises to OR_2 (from DD') in that period. At a per unit return of OR_2, more criminals are induced in (from SS') during the next period. But with the increased number of criminals the return falls, which, in turn, causes a reduction in number, and so forth. The process continues until the equilibrium number of criminals and the equilibrium return in this crime are given by the intersection of DD' and SS'. Society has the amount of crime it "desires." (Of course, it "desires" less crime, but is unwilling to bear the cost.) Equilibrium continues until something that society does, perhaps increasing enforcement in this or another area, changes the demand, the supply, or both. Then the process begins again.

This type of analysis is called a cobweb model because of the shape of the path toward equilibrium. If the path approaches equilibrium, we say that the model converges. This model converged since supply was drawn steeper than demand. If demand had been steeper than supply, the path would have diverged progressively further away from equilibrium. You will see this by carrying out the following

Exercise: Draw Figure 5.6.1 with demand steeper than supply. Begin with the number of criminals slightly exceeding the equilibrium number. Carry out the analysis as set forth above and show that the number of criminals gets progressively further from equilibrium, alternating between more and fewer than the equilibrium number. Using demand and supply shaped approximately as those in Figure 5.6.1, analyze what happens if the penalty for this crime is decreased; if law enforcement is increased in this area.

5.6.d—Economics of Theft[12]

Theft is a pure transfer payment, and as such involves no economic loss to society. If one person steals from another, society as a whole is no better or no worse off. Some wealth of the victim is transferred to the thief. But, the *existence* of theft does have a large cost of society, even though it involves only a transfer from one person to another.

To analyze, assume first that theft is not illegal. Potential theives would invest their resources (for example, time, burglar tools, getaway cars, and lookouts) up to the point at which any additional resources would cost more than the additional return in stolen assets from using these resources.[13] If an additional tool costs $100 but would add less than

---

[12] This subsection draws upon Gordon Tullock, "The Welfare Costs of Monopolies and Theft," *Western Economic Journal,* June 1967, pp. 224–32. Tullock was primarily interested in the costs of monopoly in this paper. He detoured through the economics of theft as a model to study monopoly. We shall return to this model when we evaluate monopoly later in the book.

[13] We will investigate this idea more rigorously in Chapter 8. Economists would say that the thief invests in resources as long as their marginal returns exceed their marginal cost.

$100 to the take, the thief would not buy it. Similarly, the potential victim wishes to protect his wealh. He would invest in preventive resources (e.g., dogs, locks, guns, and watchmen) up to the point at which any additional resources are expected to prevent a lesser amount of theft than they cost. We should be aware that the return from resources used in theft depends upon the resources used in prevention, just as the protective return from preventive resources depends upon the resources used by thieves. If people begin hiring more guards, the return to thieves from becoming better safecrackers falls.

In time society will attain an equilibrium amount of theft which would probably be positive, since the prevention of all theft would cost too much. But, even though the equilibrium amount of theft involves only transfers, the *existence* of theft costs society considerably. Those resources used to steal and to prevent stealing cost the individuals involved, and they cost society the use of those resources in producing other products. They are *completely wasted* from society's point of view. They are used only to make or to prevent transfers of wealth, not to produce wealth.

Society generally attempts to prevent theft collectively. People find that enforcement of laws by courts and police are sometimes technologically more efficient in preventing theft than individual expenditures on resources. To the extent that collective expenditures are more efficient than private, the returns to theft are reduced, which in turn reduces theft. To be sure, public expenditure does not replace all private preventive expenditure. People still buy locks, hire watchmen, and keep dogs. Both the public and the private preventive expenditure costs society those resources used in prevention. The important point is not how societies allocate between public and private prevention but that the existence of theft costs society resources that could be used to produce wealth.

Although Tullock did not do so we could apply the same model to the analysis of wage and price controls, which are at the time of writing still in existence. According to some of our colleagues who are monetary specialists, wage and price controls have little long-run effect upon inflation other than through their effect upon businessmen's expectations. The primary effect of controls is to alter the wage and price ratios that would have evolved had the market been allowed to function. Consequently, some people benefit and some lose by controls. Those whose prices are distorted in their favor benefit at the expense of those whose prices are adversely affected. With a certain amount of total resources society can produce a certain amount of product. To produce more, society must obtain more resources. Price controls do not augment these resources. As in the case of theft, society is no better or worse off per se, but individuals do experience changes in well-being.

But also as in the case of theft, governments use resources in setting up and in enforcing these controls. Likewise, individuals use resources to avoid the controls and to lobby for favored treatment by the control boards. The economists and lawyers used by firms and government are a cost to society. The time spent by businessmen avoiding controls is a lost resource. To the extent that these resources could be used to produce goods and services, society is worse off.

We have, by no means, exhausted all of the economic analyses of crime. These few examples are only designed as a small sample to show the way in which simple economic techniques can be used to analyze very complex problems.

5.7 DETERIORATION OF SLUM HOUSING

Another complex social problem susceptible of simple economic analysis is the problem of deteriorating slum housing. Stanly Lebergott proposed a partial solution using only the simple tools of supply and demand: if you wish people to supply more of something they have, you must pay them more.[14] Lebergott first pointed out that if half the 10 million housing units in which officially "poor" families live depreciate at 5 percent, then society creates 250,000 slum (or worse) units a year. If the rate of deterioration could be slowed to three percent, the equivalent of 100,000 units a year would be added to acceptable housing—twice the increase in public housing during the year before the publication of Lebergott's paper. Of course, the improvement in housing stock would be even greater.

Lebergott proposed an experiment to be carried out in several housing projects. Pay a reward to any public housing tenant who causes less than average maintenance and repair costs for his apartment during any month. Others would not be charged extra. He rationalizes the proposal as follows. While private landlords reward desirable and punish undesirable behavior (through differences in rents and eviction or noneviction), public housing projects do not. Much of the destruction is done by tenants to their own or to their neighbor's apartments. If it is cold outside, why not leave your garbage in the lobby; there is no cost? A reduction in maintenance and repair costs reduces the generation of slums. In recent years society has added less than three percent a year to the stock of housing, and less than three percent of that is public housing. Thus, if the stock of housing for the poor is to be improved significantly, some way must be found to stop the rapid deterioration of the present stock.

Lebergott proposed some specific points. Each public housing tenant who generates below-average maintenance and repair costs receives

---

[14] For a full exposition see Stanley Lebergott, "Slum Housing: A Proposal," *Journal of Political Economy*, Nov./Dec. 1970, pp. 1362–66.

money equal to the saving. The inspectors and the appraisers would be independent of the housing authority and tenants. Any tenant would be free to participate in the monthly inspection. All children would share in the rewards for saving in the repair of common areas. The project is self financing, since maintenance costs are not trivial. In some projects almost 50 percent of rentals were allocated to maintenance and repair in 1968.

Lebergott made some other points but those mentioned here should serve as examples. The major point is that the more one rewards "good" behavior it is quite likely that more good behavior will be forthcoming. This axiom can be used to analyze many points. This remedy is no panacea, but it is not claimed to be. It is only one suggestion, and is mentioned here merely as an application of simple economic analysis.

5.8 CONCLUSION

All of the applications of analysis described in this chapter are intended only to show how economists have approached real-world problems. The techniques are simple. The solutions may not be perfect, but what solutions are? We only want to show how economists apply their theories, and we do so without criticism. You may wish to read completely some of the articles cited in those papers if you are interested in any particular area. You should find it simple going if you avoid becoming bogged down in complicated statistical techniques. Or you may browse through some of the journals cited, *The Journal of Political Economy, The American Economic Review,* or any your teacher suggests, and find other good but simple applications of economic techniques to other real-world problems. We think you will find the experience rewarding.

ANALYTICAL PROBLEMS

1. People say that governments put taxes on liquor so that people will spend less money on liquor and more on other things. Analyze this position. (Hint: do not neglect elasticity of demand and its effect upon expenditure.)

2. Suppose that charitable contributions are deductable from income taxes. That is, if you donate $100 to charity you do not have to pay taxes on the $100. If you are in the 50 percent tax bracket, the $100 contribution only costs you $50, since you would be able to keep only this amount. How would a decrease in the income tax rate affect charitable contribution. (Hint: a tax change is a price change, and there are two effects from a price change; how will these two effects work?)

3. Assume that a rent freeze is imposed where you go to school.

    a. As a new student what would you think of this?

    b. As a middle age couple already in town?

    c. What would happen to the probability of new construction? to the service of janitors and managers? to the price of homes?

4.   What factors would increase the amount of theft in your city? What factors would decrease it? Do you think an equilibrium amount of theft exists there?

5.   What kind of verdicts would you expect from voluntary the jury system proposed by Martin and described in Section 5.3.

6.   If the government drops all exemptions (including those for children) from federal income taxes, and simply requires each household to pay a certain percentage (say 20 percent) of their income as taxes, regardless of the number of people in the household, what would happen to fertility rates?

chapter 6

Theory of Production

6.1 INTRODUCTION

Demand is only half of the theory of price; supply is the other half. In order to understand supply one must have a thorough understanding of the theory of production. In fact, the theories of cost, distribution, and resource allocation, as well as the theory of supply, are in large part based upon production theory.

Production in a general sense refers to the creation of any *good* or *service* that people will buy. However the concept of production is much clearer when we speak only of goods, since it is simpler to specify the precise inputs and to indentify the quantity and quality of outputs. Therefore, although this discussion is generally restricted to the production of goods by firms that are owned by private entrepreneurs, one should be aware that problems of resource allocation in service trades and government are equally serious even though they are not as fully covered in this text. The principles of production studied here are as applicable to the output of services as to the output of goods, though the application may be more difficult in the former case.

6.2 PRODUCTION FUNCTIONS

Production processes typically require a wide variety of inputs. They are not as simple as "labor," "capital," and "materials"; many qualitatively different types of each are normally used to produce an output. With a given state of technology, the quantity of output depends upon the quantities of the various inputs used. This relation is more formally described by a *production function* associating physical output with physical rates of input.

Definition: A production function is a schedule (or table, or mathematical equation) showing the maximum amount of output that can be produced from any specified set of inputs, given the existing technology or "state of the art." In short, the production function is a catalog of output possibilities.

A hypothetical example of a very simple production function is the production of a student's course grade from study time. This might take the form of a table such as

Expected Grade	*Minimum Study Time (hours)*
A	10
B	6
C	3
D	1
F	0

This table relates the expected grade to the minimum time allocated to study. Note that a student could study more than the required time for a grade but receive no higher grade if he does not advance completely into the next category. Five hours of study still produce only a C. The production function could take the form of a simple equation such as

$$G = 10T,$$

where G is the numerical grade and T is time spent studying. These functions make product (grade) depend only on one input (study time). Other functions relate output or product to two or more inputs. Still more complicated functions relate several different outputs to several different inputs. We will be dealing primarily with one output produced by either one or two inputs. The principles apply to more than two inputs, however.

6.2.a—Fixed and Variable Inputs, the Short and Long Runs

In analyzing the process of physical production it is convenient to introduce an analytical fiction: classification of inputs as fixed and variable. Accordingly, a *fixed input* is defined as one whose quantity cannot readily be changed when market conditions indicate that an immediate change in output is desirable. To be sure, no input is ever *absolutely* fixed, no matter how short the period of time under consideration. But frequently, for the sake of analytical simplicity, we hold some inputs fixed, reasoning perhaps that while these inputs are in fact variable, the cost of immediate variation is so great as to take them out of the range of relevance for the particular decision at hand. Buildings, major pieces of machinery, and managerial personnel are examples of inputs that cannot be rapidly augmented or diminished. A *variable input*, on the other hand, is one whose quantity may be changed almost instantaneously in response to desired changes in output. Many types of labor services and the inputs of raw and processed materials fall in this category.

Corresponding to the fiction of fixed and variable inputs, economists introduce another fiction, the short and long runs. The *short run* refers to that period of time in which the input of one or more productive agents is fixed. Therefore, changes in output must be accomplished exclusively by changes in the usage of variable inputs. Thus if a producer wishes to expand output in the short run, he must usually do so by using more hours of labor service with the existing plant and equipment. Similarly, if he wishes to reduce output in the short run, he may discharge certain types of workers; but he cannot immediately "discharge" a building or a diesel locomotive, even though its usage may fall to zero.

In the long run, however, even this is possible, for the *long run* is defined as that period of time (or planning horizon) in which all inputs are variable. The long run, in other words, refers to that time in the future when output changes can be accomplished in the manner most advantageous to the businessman. For example, in the short run a producer may be able to expand output only by operating his existing plant for more hours per day. This, of course, entails paying overtime rates to workers. In the long run, it may be more economical for him to install additional productive facilities and return to the normal workday.

6.2.b—Fixed or Variable Proportions

Our attention here is restricted mainly to production under conditions of *variable proportions*. The ratio of input quantities may vary; the businessman, therefore, must determine not only the level of output he wishes to produce but also the optimal proportion in which to combine inputs.

There are two different ways of stating the principle of variable proportions. First, variable proportions production implies that output can be changed in the short run by changing the amount of variable inputs used in cooperation with the fixed inputs. Naturally, as the amount of one input is changed, the others remaining constant, the *ratios* change. Second, when production is subject to variable proportions, the *same* output can be produced by various combinations of inputs—that is, by different input ratios. This may apply only to the long run, but it is relevant to the short run when there is more than one variable input.

Most economists regard production under conditions of variable proportions as typical of both the short and long run. There is certainly no doubt that proportions are variable in the long run. When making an investment decision a businessman may choose among a wide variety of different production processes. As polar opposites, an automobile can be almost handmade or it can be made by assembly line techniques. In the short run, however, there may be some cases in which output is subject to fixed proportions.

Fixed-proportions production means that there is one, and only one, ratio of inputs that can be used to produce a good. If output is expanded or contracted, all inputs must be expanded or contracted so as to maintain the fixed input ratio. At first glance this might seem the usual condition: one man and one shovel produce a ditch, two parts hydrogen and one part oxygen produce water. Adding a second shovel or a second part of oxygen will not augment the rate of production.

But in actuality examples of fixed-proportions production are hard to come by. Even the production of most chemical compounds is subject to variable proportions. It is true, for example, that hydrogen and nitrogen must be used in the fixed ratio 3:1 to produce ammonia gas. But if three volumes of hydrogen and one volume of nitrogen are mixed in a glass tube and heated to 400° C., only minute traces of ammonia will be found (and that only after heating for a very long time). However, if finely divided iron is introduced into the tube under the same conditions, almost the entire amount of hydrogen and nitrogen are converted to ammonia gas within minutes. That is to say, the *yield* of ammonia for any given amount of hydrogen and nitrogen depends upon the amount of the catalyst (finely divided iron) used. Proportions are indeed variable from the standpoint of the catalyst not only in this instance but in the production of almost every chemical compound.

The hydrogen-nitrogen-ammonia illustration serves as a convenient introduction to a general view of production processes. One might say that, in the short run, there are three classes of productive inputs. First, there are certain fixed inputs whose quantity cannot be varied. Second, there are variable inputs whose usage may be readily changed. Finally, there are "ingredient" inputs whose quantities may be readily changed but must bear fixed proportions to one another and to output.

It is not difficult to find examples of ingredient inputs. Each brand of cigarettes contains its own special blend of tobaccos. That is, various tobaccos are blended in fixed proportions. And a fixed amount of tobacco blend must be used in each cigarette produced. But the production of cigarettes requires more than the fixed-proportion ingredient inputs. Certain capital equipment—rolling machines, packaging machines, and the like—must be used and human labor services are necessary. In the short run, the building and capital equipment are fixed inputs and most labor services are variable.

In the discussion of production the fixed and variable inputs are stressed. Ingredient inputs are necessary; and they must be used in fixed or relatively fixed proportions or else the quality or character of the product will change. The businessman has little or no choice in this regard. Hence our attention is directed to those aspects of production over which a businessman can exert control.

6.3 PRODUCTION WITH ONE VARIABLE INPUT

To clarify analysis we first introduce some simplifying assumptions whose purpose is to cut through the complexities of dealing with hundreds of different inputs. Thus our attention is focused upon the essential principles of production. More specifically, we assume that there is only one variable input, which can be combined in different proportions with fixed inputs to produce various quantities of output. Note that these assumptions also imply the tacit assumption that inputs may be combined in *various* proportions to produce the commodity in question.

6.3.a—Total, Average, and Marginal Product: Arithmetic Approach

Assume that a firm with a fixed plant can apply different numbers of workers to get output according to columns 1 and 2 of Table 6.3.1. Columns one and two define a production function over a specific range. They specify the product per unit of time for different numbers of workers in that period. The total output rises up to a point (nine workers), then declines. The total output is the *maximum* output obtainable from each number of workers with the given plant.

Average and marginal product are obtained from the production function. The average product of labor (total product/number of workers) rises, reaches a maximum at 15, then declines thereafter. Marginal product is the *additional* output attributable to using one additional worker with a fixed plant (or with the usage of all other inputs fixed). It

TABLE 6.3.1

Total, Average, and Marginal Products of Labor

Number of Workers	Total Output per Unit of Time	Average Product	Marginal Product
1	10	10	10
2	25	12.5	15
3	45	15	20
4	60	15	15
5	70	14	10
6	78	13	8
7	84	12	6
8	88	11	4
9	90	10	2
10	88	8.8	−2

first rises, then falls, becoming negative when an additional worker reduces total product.

Note that we speak of the marginal product of labor, not of the marginal product of a particular laborer. We assume all workers are the same, in the sense that if we reduce the number of workers from eight to seven, total product falls from 88 to 84 regardless of which of the eight workers is released. Thus, the order of hiring makes no difference; the third worker adds 20 units no matter who he is.

Note also from the Table that when average product is rising (falling) marginal product is greater (less) than average. When average reaches its maximum, average equals marginal (at 15). This result is not a peculiarity of this particular table; it occurs for any production function in which the average product peaks. An example should illustrate the point. If you have taken two tests on which you have grades of 70 and 80, your average grade is 75. If your third test grade is higher than 75, say 90, your average rises, to 80 in the example. The 90 is the marginal addition to your total grade. If your third grade is less than 75, the marginal addition is below average and the average falls. This is the relation between all marginal and average schedules. In production theory, if each additional worker adds more (less) than the preceding worker, average product rises (falls).

The short-run production function specified in Table 6.3.1 depicts a form very commonly assumed in production theory. Marginal and average products first increase then decrease with marginal becoming negative after a point. Marginal reaches a peak before the peak of average is attained. At the peak of average, marginal equals average. These relations mean that total product at first increases at an increasing rate, then increases at a decreasing rate, and finally decreases. The graphical exposition in the next sub-section will illustrate these points.

However, while this shape is frequently assumed for a short-run (one variable input) production function, it is not the only shape assumed. We summarize in the following:

Definition: The average product of an input is total product divided by the amount of the input used. Thus, average product is the output-input ratio for each level of output and the corresponding volume of input. The marginal product of an input is the addition to total product attributable to the addition of one unit of the variable input to the production process, the fixed inputs remaining constant.

6.3.b—Total, Average, and Marginal Product: Graphical Approach

The short-run production function in Figure 6.3.1 shows the maximum output per unit of time obtainable from different amounts of the variable input (labor), given a specified amount of the fixed inputs and the re-

FIGURE 6.3.1

Derivation of Average Product from Total Product

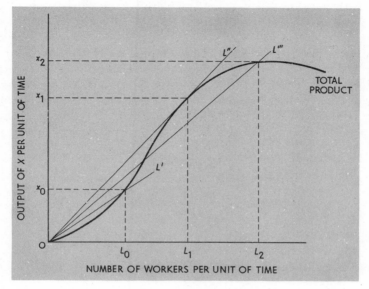

quired amounts of the ingredient inputs. Henceforth, in this section we will assume that both output and the variable input are continuously divisable. This assumption sacrifices little realism yet adds a great deal of analytical convenience.

In the Figure Ox_0 is the *maximum* amount of output obtainable when OL_0 workers are combined with the fixed and ingredient inputs. Likewise, OL_1 workers can produce a maximum of Ox_1, and so forth. Certainly the specified numbers of inputs could produce less than the amount indicated by the total product curve, but not more than that amount. First, total output increases with increases in the variable input up to a point, in this case OL_2 workers. After that so many workers are combined with the fixed inputs that output diminishes when additional workers are employed. Second, production at first increases at an increasing rate, then increases at a decreasing rate until the maximum is reached.

The average product of OL_0 workers is Ox_0/OL_0, the slope of the ray from the origin OL'. In like manner, the average product of any number of workers can be determined by the slope of a ray from the origin to the relevant point on the total product curve; the steeper the slope, the larger the average product. It is easy to see that the slopes of rays from the origin to the total product curve in Figure 6.3.1 increase with additional labor until OL'' becomes tangent at OL_1 workers and Ox_1 output then decrease thereafter (say, to OL''' at OL_2 workers). Hence typical average product curves first increase and then decrease thereafter. This is illustrated by the *AP* curve in Figure 6.3.3.

As with average product, we can derive a marginal product curve from a total product curve. In Figure 6.3.2 OL_0 workers can produce Ox_0 units of output and OL_I can produce Ox_1. L_0L_1 additional workers increase total product by x_0x_1. Marginal product is therefore x_0x_1/L_0L_1 or $\Delta x/\Delta L$, where the symbol Δ denotes "the change in." Let L_1 become very close to L_0; hence x_1 is very close to x_0; $\Delta x/\Delta L$ approaches the tangent T to the total product curve. Therefore, at any point on the total product curve, marginal product, which is the rate of change of total product, can be *estimated* by the slope of the tangent at that point.

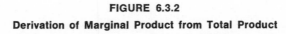

FIGURE 6.3.2

Derivation of Marginal Product from Total Product

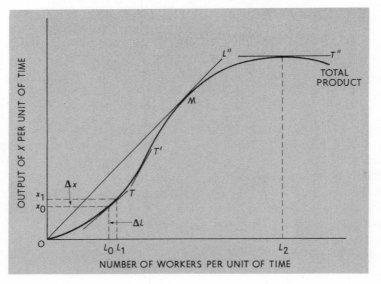

On inspection we see that marginal product first increases; note that T' is steeper than T. It then decreases, OL'' at point M being less steep than T'. Marginal product becomes zero when OL_2 workers are employed (the slope of T'' is zero) and then becomes negative. At point M the slope of the tangent OL'' is also the slope of the ray from the origin to that point. As noted above, average product attains a maximum when a ray from the origin is tangent to the total product curve. Therefore, marginal product equals average product at the latter's maximum point. To repeat, so long as marginal product exceeds average product, the latter must rise; when marginal product is less than average product, the latter must fall. Thus, average product must attain its maximum when it is equal to marginal product.

Figure 6.3.3 illustrates these relations. In this graph one can see not only the relation between marginal and average products but also the relation of these two curves to total product.

Consider first the total product curve. For very small amounts of the variable input, total product rises gradually. But even at a low level of input it begins to rise quite rapidly, reaching its maximum slope (or rate of increase) at point one. Since the slope of the total product curve equals marginal product, the maximum slope (point one) must correspond to the maximum point on the marginal product curve (point four).

FIGURE 6.3.3

Total, Average, and Marginal Products

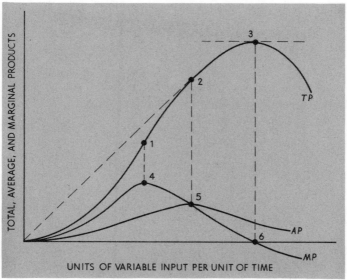

After attaining its maximum slope at point one, the total product curve continues to rise. But output increases at a decreasing rate, so the slope is less steep. Moving outward along the curve from point one, the point is soon reached at which a ray from the origin is just tangent to the curve (point two). Since tangency of the ray to the curve defines the condition for maximum average product, point two lies directly above point five.

As the quantity of variable input is expanded from its value at point two, total product continues to increase. But its rate of increase is progressively slower until point three is finally reached. At this position total product is at a maximum; thereafter it declines until it (conceivably) reaches zero again. Over a tiny range around point three, additional input does not change total output. The slope of the total product curve is zero; thus marginal product must also be zero. This is shown by the fact that points three and six occur at precisely the same input value. And since total product declines beyond point three, marginal product becomes negative.

Most of the important relations have so far been discussed with reference to the total product curve. To emphasize certain relations, however, consider the marginal and average product curves. Marginal product at first increases, reaches a maximum at point four (the point of diminishing marginal physical returns) and declines thereafter. It eventually becomes negative beyond point six, where total product attains its maximum.

Average product also rises at first until it reaches its maximum at point five, where marginal and average products are equal. It subsequently declines, conceivably becoming zero when total product itself becomes zero. Finally, one may observe that marginal product exceeds average product when the latter is increasing and is less than average product when the latter is decreasing.

6.3.c—Law of Diminishing Marginal Physical Returns

The slope of the marginal product curve in Figure 6.3.3 illustrates an important principle, the law of diminishing marginal physical returns. As the number of units of the variable input increases, other inputs held constant, after a point the marginal product of the variable input declines. When the amount of the variable input is small relative to the fixed inputs (the fixed inputs are plentiful relative to the variable input), more intensive utilization of fixed inputs by variable inputs may increase the marginal output of the variable input. Nonetheless a point is quickly reached beyond which an increase in the use of the variable input yields progressively less additional returns. Each additional unit has, on average, fewer units of the fixed inputs with which to work.

Principle (the law of diminishing marginal physical returns): As the amount of a variable input is increased, the amount of other (fixed) inputs held constant, a point is reached beyond which marginal product declines.

This is a simple statement concerning physical relations that have been observed in the real economic world. While it is not susceptible of mathematical proof or refutation, it is of some worth to note that a contrary observation has never been recorded. Psychologists have even found that the law holds true for consecutive study time.[1]

---

[1] Do not make the common mistake, however, of saying that you stopped studying because diminishing returns set in. The term "diminishing returns" is frequently

6.3.d—Three Stages of Production

Economists use the relations among total, average, and marginal products to define three stages of production, illustrated in Figure 6.3.4. Stage I covers that range of variable input usage over which average product increases. In other words, stage I corresponds to increasing *average returns* to the variable inputs. The fixed input is present in uneconomically large proportion relative to the variable input. As we will show in the chapter dealing with wage theory, a rational producer would

FIGURE 6.3.4

Stages of Production

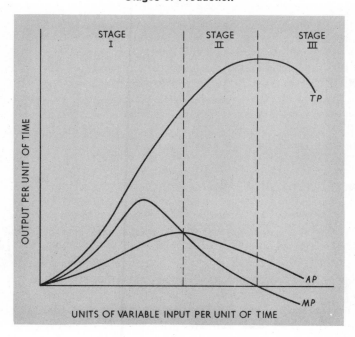

never operate in this range of production: such a small amount of output could be produced by using fewer units of some of the fixed inputs (that is, by allowing some of the fixed input to remain idle, even though payment must be made for all units).

Production would also never occur in stage III, as is more or less obvious from the graph. Stage III is defined as the range of negative

---

heard in noneconomic usage and is almost as frequently misused. Diminishing returns may set in with the first unit of study time, but you may continue studying. You cease studying when the marginal utility of the (expected) increase in grade (or of the pleasure of studying) from an additional unit of study time is less than the expected marginal utility of using that time for something else.

marginal product or declining total product. Additional units of variable input during this stage of production actually cause a decrease in total output. Even if units of the variable input were free, a rational producer would not employ them beyond the point of zero marginal product because their use entails a reduction in total output; additional units of the fixed input must be used if output is to be expanded.

In stage III the variable input is combined with the fixed input in uneconomically large proportions. In terms of agriculture, land is cultivated too intensively. Indeed, the point of zero marginal product of the variable input is called the *intensive margin*. Similarly, in suggestive terminology, at the point of maximum average product the cultivation of land is extensive; and the point of maximum average product is called the *extensive margin*.

We have now eliminated stages I and III. Production must occur in stage II—between the extensive and intensive margins, or over the range of variable input usage from maximum average product to zero marginal product. If output must be produced in quantities not covered by production in stage II, there must be some change in the quantity of fixed input. If a smaller output is desired, the units of fixed input must be reduced; if a larger output is required, it can be achieved only by augmenting fixed input.

6.4 PRODUCTION WITH TWO VARIABLE INPUTS

In our discussion of the fundamental physical relations of production, we have thus far assumed that there is only one variable input. The analysis is continued here for a more general case. Graphically, production is studied under the assumption that there are two variable inputs. One may regard these inputs either as cooperating with one or more fixed inputs or as the only two inputs. The latter situation, of course, is relevant only for the long run. In either case, however, the results of the two-input model are easily extended to cover multiple inputs.

6.4.a—Product Curves for Different Amounts of Fixed Input

When analyzing production with two variable factors, we cannot simply use two sets of average and marginal product curves, such as those discussed in Section 6.3. When the amount of the *now* variable, but *formerly* fixed, factor changes the total, marginal, and average product curves of the variable factor shift. Generally, the greater the amount of fixed input available the greater also are the total, average, and marginal products of a given amount of the variable input. Increasing the fixed input increases the amount of this input per unit of variable input. This

Table 6.4.1

Total, Average, and Marginal Products on One- and Two-Acre Tracts of Land

Product	Size of Tract	Number of Workers					
		1	2	3	4	5	6
Total............	1 acre	20	30	37.5	44	50	55.5
	2 acres	25	40	52.5	64	75	85.5
Average.........	1 acre	20	15	12.5	11	10	9.25
	2 acres	25	20	17.5	16	15	14.25
Marginal........	1 acre	—	10	7.5	6.5	6	5.5
	2 acres	—	15	12.5	11.5	11	10.5

normally results in an increase in the marginal, and hence in the average and total product of the variable input.[2]

This proposition is illustrated in Table 6.4.1 and is shown graphically in Figure 6.4.1. The first row in each part of the Table shows data from a hypothetical agricultural experiment on one-acre tracts of land. The second row shows the corresponding data for experiments on two-acre

FIGURE 6.4.1

Total, Average, and Marginal Products for Two Different Amounts of the Fixed Factor

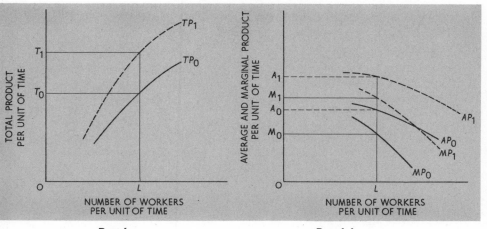

Panel a
Total Product

Panel b
Average and Marginal Products

---

[2] The results of this subsection hold only for the range of production in stage II. Since this is where production takes place, it is of course the stage of greatest interest.

tracts. Comparing each set of rows, the Table shows that for each amount of variable input, the total, average, and marginal products are greater on the two-acre tracts of land. The Table clearly shows that over the relevant range of production augmenting the fixed input augments the productivity of the variable input.

In Figure 6.4.1 TP_0 in panel *a* and AP_0 and MP_0 in panel *b* are the total, average, and marginal curves of labor for a fixed amount of another factor, say capital. If the amount of capital increases, the three curves increase to TP_1, AP_1, and MP_1. This means that for each amount of labor over the relevant range total, average, and marginal products are greater. For example, for OL units of labor, an increase in capital increases total product from OT_0 to OT_1, average product from OA_0 to OA_1, and marginal product from OM_0 to OM_1.

If both labor and capital are variable, each factor has an infinite set of product curves, one for every amount of the other factor. Therefore another tool of analysis is necessary when there is more than one variable factor. This tool is the *production isoquant*.

6.4.b—Production Isoquants

An isoquant in production theory is analogous to an indifference curve in consumer theory. Recall that an indifference curve shows the various combinations of two goods that yield the same level of utility and that an indifference curve above another designates a higher level of utility. Recall also that indifference curves are concave from above, indicating a diminishing marginal rate of substitution.

Definition: An isoquant is a curve showing all possible combinations of inputs physically capable of producing a given level of output. An isoquant lying above another designates a higher level of output. Isoquants are concave from above, indicating a diminishing marginal rate of technical substitution.

Figure 6.4.2 illustrates two typical isoquants. Isoquant I is the locus of combinations of capital and labor yielding 100 units of output. One can product 100 units of output by using 50 units of capital and 15 of labor, by using 10 units of capital and 75 of labor, or by using any other combination on I. Similarly II shows the different combinations of capital and labor that can produce 200 units of output.

Relations: Two isoquants never intersect. There are an infinite number of isoquants between I and II in Figure 6.4.2 because there are an infinite number of production levels between 100 and 200 units, provided the product is infinitesimally divisible.

The isoquants in Figure 6.4.2 are concave from above, as are all isoquants over the range in which production takes place. This concavity

FIGURE 6.4.2

Typical Isoquants

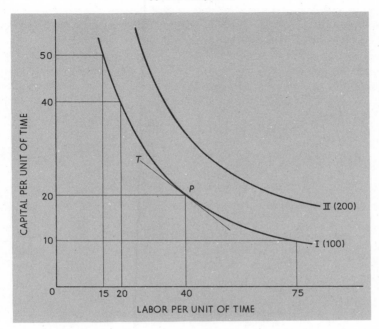

implies that as capital decreases by equal amounts, proportionately more labor must be added in order to maintain the same output level. Either 50 units of capital and 15 units of labor or 40 units of capital and 20 units of labor can be used to produce 100 units of output (Figure 6.4.2). This means that reducing capital by 10 units requires the addition of only 5 units of labor in order to continue producing 100 units of output. On the other hand, moving from 20 to 10 units of capital requires changing from 40 to 75 units of labor. The firm now substitutes 35 units of labor for 10 units of capital.

One of the chief features of production under conditions of variable proportions is that different combinations of inputs can be used to produce a given level of output. In other words, one input can be *substituted* for another in such a way as to maintain a constant level of output. Great theoretical and practical importance attaches to the *rate* at which one input must be substituted for another in order to hold output constant.

Analogous to indifference curve theory, the *rate* at which one input can be substituted for another at a given level of output is measured by the slope of a tangent to the isoquant. In Figure 6.4.2 the slope of the tangent *T* shows the rate at which labor can be substituted for capital in the neighborhood of point P, always maintaining an output of 100 units. For very small movements along an isoquant, the negative of the slope of the tangent is called *the marginal rate of technical substitution,* just as the negative of the slope of a consumer's indifference curve is called the marginal rate of substitution in consumption.

For very small movements along an isoquant the marginal rate of technical substitution of capital for labor is the ratio of the marginal product of labor to the marginal product of capital:

$$MRTS_{K \text{ for } L} = -\frac{\Delta K}{\Delta L} \text{ (output constant)} = \frac{MP_L}{MP_K}.$$

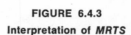

FIGURE 6.4.3

Interpretation of MRTS

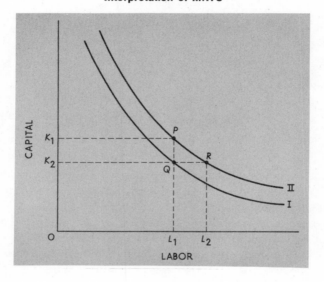

The proof is similar to that in Chapter 3 concerning $MRS_{x \text{ for } y} = \frac{MU_x}{MU_y}$.

Let the producer originally be at point P, Figure 6.4.3. Next let capital be reduced by a small amount from OK_1 to OK_2, labor held constant at OL_1. The reduction in output is represented by the difference between II and I.

The marginal product of capital for this small reduction in output is the decrease in output divided by the decrease in capital:

$$MP_K = \frac{II - I}{OK_1 - OK_2}.$$

Now let the producer return to the II-level of production by holding capital constant at OK_2 and increasing labor from OL_1 to OL_2. The marginal product of labor, by the argument above, is

$$MP_L = \frac{II - I}{OL_1 - OL_2}.$$

Taking the ratio of the two marginal products, we obtain

$$\frac{MP_L}{MP_K} = \frac{II - I}{OL_1 - OL_2} \div \frac{II - I}{OK_2 - OK_2} = \frac{OK_1 - OK_2}{OL_1 - OL_2}.$$

But by the figure,

$$\frac{OK_1 - OK_2}{OL_1 - OL_2} = \frac{PQ}{QR} = MRTS_{K \text{ for } L} = \frac{MP_L}{MP_K},$$

which completes the proof.

Relations: The marginal rate of technical substitution measures the reduction in one input per unit increase in the other that is just sufficient to maintain a constant level of output. The marginal rate of technical substitution of input K for input L at a point on an isoquant is equal to the negative of the slope of the isoquant at that point. It is also equal to the ratio of the marginal product of input L to the marginal product of input K.

6.4.c—Diminishing Marginal Rate of Technical Substitution

The marginal rate of technical substitution of capital for labor diminishes as more and more labor is substituted for capital. This proposition sounds plausible; and it is not difficult to explain.

As additional units of labor are added to a fixed amount of capital the marginal product of labor diminishes. Furthermore, as shown in Figure 6.4.1, if the amount of the fixed input is diminished the marginal product of labor diminishes. Thus two forces are working to diminish the marginal product of labor: (a) less of the fixed input causes a downward *shift* of the marginal product of labor curve; and (b) more units of the variable input (labor) causes a downward movement *along* the marginal product curve. Thus, as labor is substituted for capital the marginal product of labor must decline. For analogous reasons the marginal product of capital increases as less capital and more labor is used. With the quantity of labor fixed, the marginal product of capital rises as fewer units of capital are used. But simultaneously there is an increase in labor input thereby shifting the marginal product of capital curve upward. The same two forces are present in this case: a movement along a marginal product curve and a shift in the location of the curve. In this situation, however, both forces work to increase the marginal product of capital. Thus, as labor is substituted for capital, the marginal product of capital increases.

As already defined, the marginal rate of technical substitution is the ratio of the marginal product of labor to the marginal product of capital. As labor is substituted for capital, the marginal product of labor declines and the marginal product of capital increases. Hence the marginal rate of technical substitution of capital for labor declines as labor is substituted for capital so as to maintain a constant level of output. This may be summarized as follows:

Relation: As labor is substituted for capital along an isoquant (so that output is unchanged), the marginal rate of technical substitution declines.

FIGURE 6.4.4

Diminishing Marginal Rate of Technical Substitution

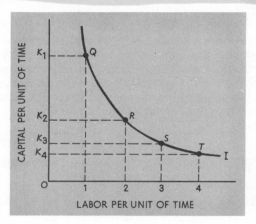

The fact that the marginal rate of technical substitution falls as labor is substituted for capital means that isoquants must be concave from above (that is, in the neighborhood of a point of tangency, the isoquant must lie above the tangent line). This has been mentioned above and is stressed again in Figure 6.4.4.

Q, R, S, and T are four input combinations lying on the isoquant I. Q has the combination OK_1 units of capital and one unit of labor; R has OK_2 units of capital and two units of labor; and so on. For the movement from Q to R, the marginal rate of technical substitution of capital for labor is, by formula,

$$- \frac{OK_1 - OK_2}{1 - 2} = OK_1 - OK_2 .$$

Similarly, for the movements from R to S and S to T, the marginal rates of technical substitution are $OK_2 - OK_3$ and $OK_3 - OK_4$ respectively.

Since the marginal rate of technical substitution of capital for labor diminishes as labor is substituted for capital, it is necessary that $OK_1 - OK_2 > OK_2 - OK_3 > OK_3 - OK_4$. Visually, the amount of capital replaced by successive units of labor will decline if, and only if, the isoquant is concave from above. Since the amount *must* decline, the isoquant must be concave from above.

Relation: Isoquants must be concave from above at every point in order to satisfy the principles of diminishing marginal rate of technical substitution.

6.4.d—Economic Region of Production

Many production functions lead to initial isoquant graphs such as shown in Figure 6.4.2. Others, however, generate an isoquant map such as that shown in Figure 6.4.5. It is like the map in Figure 6.4.2 in that the isoquants do not intersect; the higher the isoquant the greater the level of output; and over a range of input values they are negatively sloped. The only difference lies in the fact that the isoquants in Figure 6.4.5 "bend back upon themselves" or have positively sloped segments.

FIGURE 6.4.5

Full Isoquant Map and the Relevant Range of Production

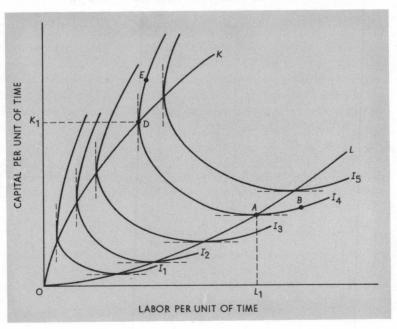

The parallel dashed lines in Figure 6.4.5 indicate the points at which the isoquants bend back upon themselves. The lines OK and OL join these points and form, as we will see, the boundaries of the economic region of production (or the stage II region).

To see why the lines OL and OK form the boundary of production, first consider a movement along I_4 from A to B. An increase in the amount of labor must be accompanied by an *increase* in the amount of capital in order to maintain the same output. On the other hand we could keep the amount of labor constant at OL_1, increase the amount of capital and increase output; that is, reach a higher isoquant. Therefore, labor must have a negative marginal product along I_4 to the right of A, since *additional* capital is required to offset the decreased product from additional labor.

Consider now a movement along I_4 from D to E. Increasing the amount of capital requires an offsetting increase in the amount of labor in order to maintain the same level of production. Keeping capital the same at OK_1 and increasing labor would allow a higher isoquant to be attained and hence a greater output. Therefore, along I_4 above D, capital must have a negative marginal product. By similar argument it is simple to show that along any isoquant in Figure 6.4.5, capital has a negative marginal product above OK and labor has a negative marginal product below OL.

Since an increase in either factor must be accompanied by an offsetting decrease in the other to maintain the same output between OL and OK, both factors must have positive marginal products. Therefore OL is the locus of points for which the marginal product of labor is zero, and OK is the locus of points for which the marginal product of capital is zero. Since no firm would produce where the marginal product of either factor is negative, production occurs within the boundary of OL and OK. These "ridge" lines separate the economic from the uneconomic regions of production. To summarize:

Relations: If the production function is such that intensive and extensive margins for each input exist, the total isoquant map is like the one in Figure 6.4.5. Only those portions of the isoquants lying between the ridge lines (the loci of zero marginal products) are relevant to production.

6.5   OPTIMAL COMBINATION OF RESOURCES

So far the theory of production has been analyzed from the standpoint of an individual entrepreneur. However, nothing has been said about the *optimal* way in which he should combine resources. Any desired level of output can normally be produced by a number of different combinations of inputs. Our task now is to determine the specific combination a producer should select.

Once again we can draw an analogy between production theory and the theory of consumer behavior. Recall that the consumer attains his highest possible level of utility with a fixed income when the budget line is tangent to an indifference curve. Or, consumers maximize utility when the marginal rate of substitution equals the ratio of commodity prices. We shall see in this section that a firm attains its highest possible level of output for any given level of cost (or the lowest cost for any given level of output) when the marginal rate of technical substitution for any two inputs equals the ratio of input prices.

6.5.a—Input Prices and Isocosts

Inputs, as well as outputs, bear specific market prices. In determining his *operating* input combination a producer must pay heed to relative input prices if he is to minimize the cost of producing a given output or maximize output for a given level of cost.

Input prices are determined, as are the prices of goods, by supply and demand in the market. For producers who are not monopsonists or oligopsonists (that is, the sole purchaser or one of a few purchasers of an input), input prices are given by the market and their rates of purchase do not change them. Let us now concentrate upon a producer who is a perfect competitor in the input market, even though he may be a monopolist or an oligopolist (that is, a single seller or one of a few sellers) in his output market.

Let us continue to assume that the two inputs are labor and capital, although the analysis applies equally well to any two productive agents. Denote the quantity of capital and labor by K and L, respectively, and their unit prices by r and w. The total cost $\bar{C}$ of using any volume of K and L is $\bar{C} = rK + wL$, the sum of the cost of K units of capital at r per unit and of L units of labor at w per unit.

To take a more specific example, suppose capital costs $1,000 per unit ($r = \$1,000$) and labor receives a wage of $2,500 per man-year ($w = \$2,500$). If a total of $15,000 is to be spent for inputs, the equation above shows that the following combinations are possible: $\$15,000 = \$1,000\ K + \$2,500\ L$, or $K = 15 - 2.5\ L$. Similarly, if $20,000 is to be spent on inputs, one can purchase the following combinations: $K = 20 - 2.5\ L$. More generally, if the fixed amount $\bar{C}$ is to be spent, the producer can choose among the combinations given by

$$K = \frac{\bar{C}}{r} - \frac{w}{r} L .$$

This is illustrated in Figure 6.5.1. If $15,000 is spent for inputs and no labor is purchased, 15 units of capital may be bought. More generally, if $\bar{C}$ is to be spent and r is the unit cost, $\bar{C}/r$ units of capital may be pur-

FIGURE 6.5.1

Isocost Curves for *r* = $1,000 and *w* = $2,500

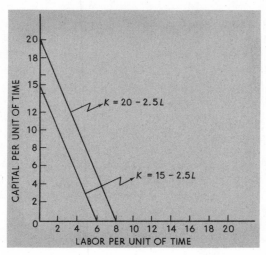

chased. This is the vertical axis *intercept* of the line. If one unit of labor is purchased at $2,500, two and five-tenths units of capital must be sacrificed; if two units of labor are bought, five units of capital must be sacrificed; and so on. Thus as the purchase of labor is increased, the purchase of capital must decrease. For each additional unit of labor, w/r units of capital must be foregone. In Figure 6.5.1, $w/r = 2.5$. Attaching a negative sign, this is the *slope* of the line.

The solid lines in Figure 6.5.1 are called *isocost curves* because they show the various combinations of inputs that may be purchased for a stipulated amount of expenditure. In summary:

Relation: At fixed input prices *r* and *w* for capital and labor, a fixed outlay $\bar{C}$ will purchase any combination of capital and labor given by the following linear equation:

$$K = \frac{\bar{C}}{r} - \frac{w}{r} L .$$

This is the equation for an isocost curve, whose intercept $(\bar{C}/r)$ is the amount of capital that may be purchased if no labor is bought and whose slope is the negative of the input-price ratio (w/r).

6.5.b—Production of a Given Output at Minimum Cost

Whatever output an entrepreneur chooses to produce, he wishes to produce it at the least possible cost. To do this he must organize production in the most efficient way. The basic principles can be illustrated as follows:

Problem: Suppose that Transport Service must produce a certain output of cargo and passenger service per year. The Service is confronted with the following combinations of aircraft and mechanics that can be used to yield this required output over its route pattern.

Combination	Number of Aircraft	Number of Mechanics
No. 1............	60	1,000
2............	61	920
3............	62	850
4............	63	800
5............	64	760
6............	65	730
7............	66	710

If the annual cost resulting from the operation of another aircraft is $250,000, and if mechanics cost them $6,000 each annually, which combination of aircraft and mechanics should Transport Service use to minimize its cost? By trial and error a solution of combination four is obtained. Or, we could use the following method. Begin at combination one. An additional airplane would cost $250,000, but 80 mechanics could be released at a saving of $480,000. A move to two would be beneficial. By moving to three, the firm would save $420,000 in mechanics' salaries and add $250,000 in aircraft expenses. Following the same line of reasoning, the firm could save cost by moving to combination four. It would not move to five since the $240,000 saved is less than the $250,000 added. The similarity to the basic principles of consumer behavior theory should be becoming evident.

Let us analyse the problem graphically. Suppose at given input prices r and w an entrepreneur wishes to produce the output indicated by isoquant I in Figure 6.5.2. Isocost curves KL, $K'L'$, and $K''L''$ represent the infinite number of isocost curves from which the producer can choose at the given input prices. Obviously he chooses the lowest one that enables him to attain output level I. That is, he produces at the cost represented by isocost curve $K'L'$. Any resource expenditure below that, for example, that represented by KL, is not feasible since it is impossible to produce output I with these resource combinations. Any resource combinations above that represented by $K'L'$ are rejected because the entrepreneur wishes to produce the desired output at *least* cost. If he produced at either A or B, at the cost represented by $K''L''$, he can reduce his costs by moving along I to point E. This is the point of optimal resource combination: he uses OK_0 units of capital and OL_0 units of labor.

Equilibrium is reached when the isoquant representing the chosen

FIGURE 6.5.2

**Optimal Input Combination to Minimize Cost
Subject to a Given Level of Output**

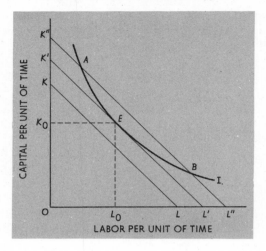

output is just tangent to an isocost curve. Since tangency means that the two slopes are equal, least cost production requires that the marginal rate of technical substitution of capital for labor be equal to the ratio of the price of labor to the price of capital. The market input-price ratio tells the producer the rate at which he *can substitute* one input for another *in purchasing*. The marginal rate of technical substitution tells him the rate at which he *can substitute in production*. So long as the two are not equal, a producer can achieve a lower cost by moving in the direction of equality.

Principle: To minimize cost subject to a given level of output and given input prices, the producer must purchase inputs in quantities such that the marginal rate of technical substitution of captial for labor is equal to the input-price ratio (the price of labor to the price of capital). Thus

$$MRTS_{K \text{ for } L} = \frac{MP_L}{MP_K} = \frac{w}{r}.$$

We can analyze the equilibrium condition in another way. Assume the equilibrium condition did not hold or specifically that

$$\frac{MP_L}{MP_K} < \frac{w}{r}.$$

In other words,

$$\frac{MP_L}{w} < \frac{MP_K}{r}.$$

In this case the marginal product of an additional dollar's worth of labor is less than the marginal product of an additional dollar's worth of capital. The firm could reduce its usage of labor by one dollar, expand its usage of capital by less than one dollar, and remain at the same level of output but with a reduced cost. It could continue to do so so long as the above inequality holds. Eventually MP_L/w would become equal to MP_K/r since MP_L rises with decrease usage of labor and increased usage of capital and MP_K falls with increased capital and decreased labor. By the same reasoning it is easy to see that firms substitute labor for capital until the equality holds if the inequality is reversed.

The most realistic way of examining the problem is to assume that the entrepreneur chooses a level of output and then chooses the input combination that enables him to produce that output at least cost. As an alternative we could assume that the entrepreneur can spend only a fixed amount on production and wishes to attain the highest level of production consistent with that amount of expenditure. Not too surprisingly, the results turn out the same as before. The entrepreneur produces where the isocost curve representing the amount to be spent on production is tangent to an isoquant. This is the highest isoquant attainable. The marginal rate of technical substitution of capital for labor equals the input-price ratio (the price of labor to the price of capital).

Exercise: Draw some isoquants above and below I in Figure 6.5.2. Assume that the producer wishes to obtain the maximum possible output at the cost represented by $K'L'$. Establish that the producer will produce at E, using OL_0 labor and OK_0 capital.

Principle: In order either to maximize output subject to a given cost or to minimize cost subject to a given output, the entrepreneur must employ inputs in such amounts as to equate the marginal rate of technical substitution and the input-price ratio.

We can now examine how factor proportions change when output changes, the factor-price ratio held constant. In Figure 6.5.3 the curves I, II, III are isoquants depicting a representative production function; KL, $K'L'$, and $K''L''$ represent the least cost of producing the three output levels. Since the factor-price ratio does not change, they are parallel.

To summarize: first, factor prices remain constant. Second, each equilibrium point is defined by equality between the marginal rate of technical substitution and the factor-price ratio. Since the latter remains constant, so does the former. Therefore, OS is a locus of points along which the marginal rate of technical substitution is constant. But it is a curve with a special feature. Specifically, it is the locus along which output will expand when factor prices are constant. We may accordingly formulate this result as a

FIGURE 6.5.3

Expansion Path

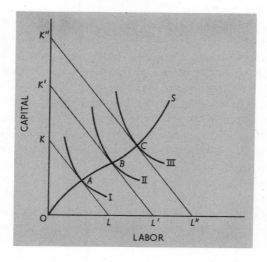

Definition: The expansion path is the curve along which output expands when factor prices remain constant. The expansion path thus shows how factor proportions change when output or expenditure changes, input prices remaining constant throughout. The marginal rate of technical substitution remains constant also since the factor-price ratio is constant.

6.6 ECONOMICS OF POLLUTION: AN APPLICATION OF PRODUCTION THEORY

The 1971 report of the President's Council of Economic Advisors recommended, among other things, that (1) governments should set a price or tax upon pollutors and (2) that local governments should primarily be responsible for the control. Jerome L. Stein, an academic economist, took issue with the second part of the proposal. He combined simple production theory with consumer behavior theory to set forth his arguments. We will summarize some of his analysis in this section.[3]

To begin, assume that we wish to find the optimal amount of pollution for an isolated community. In this community only one output, call it Q, is produced. Assume that the usage of all resources is fixed and that the only way to vary the level of Q is to vary the level of pollution or pollution damage. The more Q is produced the more pollution damage experienced by the community. This "production function" for pollution

---

[3] This section is based upon Jerome L. Stein, "The 1971 Report of the President's Council of Economic Advisers: Micro-Economic Aspects of Public Policy," *American Economic Review*, Sept. 1971, pp. 531–37.

and output is indicated by the line $ORAF$ in Figure 6.6.1. We assume that this function has the "typical" shape. The marginal product of pollution is the slope of the production function, $\Delta Q / \Delta P$. This is the rate at which added pollution can give additional output.

Indifference curves I–IV are the community indifference curves between output, which they consume, and pollution damage. We assume that each household in the community has the same preference structure. These indifference curves have their peculiar shape, because pollution damage is a "bad" to the community rather than a good. Since pollu-

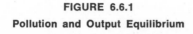

FIGURE 6.6.1

Pollution and Output Equilibrium

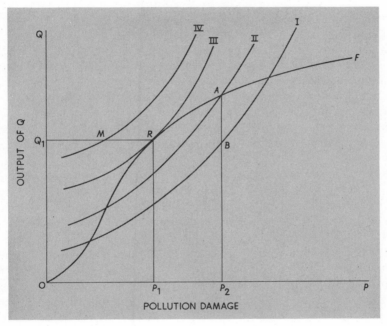

tion gives disutility, people prefer less to more. Higher indifference curves lie above and to the left. For example, the community prefers point A on II to B on I because with the same pollution damage, OP_2, they have more output. Point M on IV is preferred to R on III because with the same output, OQ_1 there is less pollution at M. The marginal rate of substitution is positive (indifference curves slope upward). That is, if output is increased, pollution must be increased also if the community is to remain at the same level of utility.

The production function shows the way in which the community is able to trade off pollution damage for output. The indifference curves show how the community is willing to trade. By the now familiar model of utility maximization the community wishes to be at point R with OQ_1 consumption and OP_1 pollution damage. Note that the community does not opt for zero pollution, notwithstanding what some popular writers say. Remember, pollution abatement has a cost.[4] The cost is reduced output. With zero pollution, consumption would be curtailed below the desired community level. Pollution abatement requires the use of resources that could be used to produce commodities.

The community must set a price for polluting that induces industry to produce at point R. That price in real terms (that is, in terms of output) is given by the slope of the production function at R; that is, if the fine for an additional unit of pollution is equivalent to ten units of output and the firm can produce more than ten units of output it will produce the additional unit of pollution and pay the fine. If it can produce less than ten units, it will choose not to produce the additional output. Thus, if the fine is set equal to the slope at R, which is the marginal product of pollution at R, firms will produce up to OQ_1 because marginal product is greater than the per unit fine.[5] They would not produce beyond OQ_1, because the fine, the marginal product at R, is greater than the marginal product beyond OQ_1. Note that marginal product diminishes because of the way in which the production function is drawn.

Now, suppose that there are two communities in the society. The prices or fines differ, so that the marginal product in community I exceeds the marginal product in community II. If this is the case, society as a whole could have the same amount of pollution and more output by shifting units of pollution (maybe by transferring firms) from the less productive community II to community I where the marginal product of pollution is higher. While society has the same pollution and more output, it is hard to say whether society is better off as a whole, since we cannot compare the utility functions of communities I and II. To the extent that the environment belongs to society as a whole, it obtains more output at zero pollution cost.

An additional problem with local control is that one locality can pollute another locality at zero cost. One town may pump its garbage into the river that flows through another town in the absence of national control. Finally, firms faced with polluting fines may threaten to re-

---

[4] Similar reasoning could be applied to arguments of those who wish us to have perfect products, or perfectly safe products. Commodities can be made closer to perfection, or the risk of using a product can be made lower, but generally, only at a cost. The cost of reducing risk to zero is infinite. This is not to say that society may not prefer less risk, it is only to emphasize that reducing risks, like reducing pollution, costs society something.

[5] We will return to the problem of how much of an input to use in Chapter 11.

locate if the fine is imposed. In the absence of these firms the locality could move to a lower indifference level. Under national control this situation would be less likely to arise.

This brief model is not meant to be the last word in the economics of pollution abatement. In fact, we will return to the subject and set forth a different viewpoint in Chapter 10. This section is meant to show simply the way in which theory can be used to analyze important problems.

6.7 AN APPLICATION: DIFFUSION OF TECHNOLOGY

Historians frequently assert that American technology during the early development of manufacturing was primarily labor-saving. It is said that American industry used much larger amounts of capital relative to the number of workers than equivalent industries in Europe. Because of the supposed labor scarcity in the United States, early manufacturing industry is said to have attempted to substitute capital for labor whenever possible. There is some recent evidence to the contrary. It seems as though this broad historical generality simply is not correct. In an article on the subject, Peter Temin used the theory of production and some data on the demand for steam and water power in manufacturing during the 1840s to analyze this common historical allegation.[6]

The theory of production says that if there are two sources of power and one source becomes relatively cheaper than the other, firms will substitute away from the relatively expensive source toward the cheaper one. In other words, as relative prices change, the slope of the isocost line changes, and at any given level of output firms substitute along the relevant isoquant. Which is labor saving and which is not, is irrelevant.

About 1840 both steam power and water power were used in American industry, and both continued to be used. There were three differences in the two sources of power. First, water power, available only in fixed locations, required transportation charges on material and products; with steam the power could be brought to the material. Second, steam required transport charges on coal or wood if located away from these fuels. Third, in the case of water, the capital cost made up a large portion of the total cost, while the operating cost was quite small. Alternatively, the cost of steam power was primarily operating cost—a large portion of which was labor—and capital was a small portion of the total. One could say that water was labor saving while steam was not. If the historical allegation is correct, the expansion of industry should have been along rivers—the source of water power—and water should have gradually replaced steam. This was not the case. The particular characteristics of

---

[6] This section is based upon a paper by Peter Temin, "Steam and Water Power in the Early 19th Century," *The Journal of Economic History*, June 1966, pp. 187–205.

some industries caused water to continue to be predominant in these cases, while in others under different circumstances steam grew relatively more important. We can examine some evidence to see what happened.

About 1840, in the New England cotton industry, steam power and water power cost approximately the same in the more efficient locations of each. If costs were not about the same, the more expensive source of power would gradually have been eliminated.[7] Both sources, however, continued to be used. The data on steam power came from the records of mills located on the sea coast, and the data on water power, from Lowell, located in the interior. Mills on the coast did not find it necessary to transport coal, the fuel for steam power, overland. Thus steam was less expensive than water in that area. Good sources of water power were available at Lowell and in the interior. The transportation charges for hauling coal overland would have made steam more expensive.

As industry spread to the Midwest coal was nearer at hand. Thus, the transport costs of steam power were reduced. At the same time water power was relatively scarce in that area. Finally, interest rates were higher in the West. The price of capital is the interest that must be paid on the amount that the capital equipment costs. Since capital cost is a significantly larger share of total cost in the case of water power, the higher interest rates caused the price of water power to rise relative to the price of steam. For these reasons, there was some incentive to substitute toward the *less* labor-saving source of power, steam, as industry moved to the West.

On the other hand, the characteristics of particular industries were also quite important in determining the relative usage of each source of power. The cotton industry was an average user of steam. The metals industry, mainly iron, was a larger user of steam than was cotton, but its position was also about average. As ironworks began to be located nearer coal mines there was some transition from water to steam. Previously the iron industry had used charcoal as fuel. Since charcoal could not be transported easily, mills had to be located near large woodlands where they could make their own charcoal. Since water was used for cooling, many chose a water power location for their mill. As coal began to be substituted for charcoal as fuel, mills were relocated toward coal areas. This change made steam relatively less expensive.

The food-products industry, a very heavy user of steam at the time, consisted primarily of sugar, and flour mills. Sugarcane was grown in Louisiana, where there were few water power cites. Since the juice fermented if the cane was not crushed immediately, it could not be transported cheaply to a water power location. Thus, sugar mills used steam

---

[7] We will discuss this point at length in Chapter 8.

power, near the cane fields, extensively. The usage of water in flour mills somewhat offset the effect of sugar on the total steam used in the food product industry, but the effect of sugar was large enough to make food products a heavy user of steam. Sawmills were the largest users of steam. A large number were in the lower Mississippi Valley where there were few good water power cities. Sawmills in isolated locations would have paid higher interest rates making steam cheaper.

While steam was widely used as a source of power around 1840, its importance was concentrated in a few industries. The evidence does show that steam tended to be used when industries had characteristics that made steam cheaper and where high interest rates made water power relatively expensive. This is evidence that the transition of early American industry was not entirely toward labor-saving technology. The choice of technology was made in accordance with our simple theory of production. When relative prices changed firms substituted toward the relatively less expensive input and away from the relatively more expensive inputs.

6.8 CONCLUSION

This chapter contains an explanation of the theory of production and of the optimal combination of inputs when input prices are constant. We turn next to the theory of cost, which relies upon the physical laws of production and upon the prices an entrepreneur must pay for his inputs.

The basic concepts upon which production theory is based are given in the following definitions.

Definition: A production function is a schedule, table, or equation showing the maximum output that can be obtained from any given combination of inputs.

Definition: An isoquant is the locus of points showing combinations of inputs physically capable of producing a given level of output. An isocost line shows all combinations of inputs that can be purchased at some given level of expenditure. The slope of the isoquant, the marginal rate of technical substitution, shows the rate at which one input can be substituted for another while maintaining the same level of output. The slope of the isocost line, the ratio of input prices, shows the rate at which the market allows inputs to be substituted.

The optimal combination of inputs is determined by the following:

Relation: The firm minimizes the cost of producing any given level of output or maximizes the output that can be produced at any given level of cost when the marginal rate of technical substitution equals the ratio of input prices.

QUESTIONS AND PROBLEMS

1. Below are hypothetical data for a manufacturer, possessing a fixed plant, who produces a commodity that requires only one variable input. Total product is given. Compute and graph the average and marginal product curves. Save your basic calculations because they form the basis for a subsequent problem in Chapter 7.

Units of Variable Input	Total Product	Average Product	Marginal Product
1...................	100		
2...................	250		
3...................	410		
4...................	560		
5...................	700		
6...................	830		
7...................	945		
8...................	1,050		
9...................	1,146		
10...................	1,234		
11...................	1,314		
12...................	1,384		
13...................	1,444		
14...................	1,494		
15...................	1,534		
16...................	1,564		
17...................	1,584		
18...................	1,594		

After completing the table and graph, answer the following questions:

a. When marginal product is increasing, what is happening to average product?

b. Does average product begin to fall as soon as marginal product does? That is, which occurs first, the point of diminishing marginal or average returns?

c. When average product is at its maximum, is marginal product less than, equal to, or greater than average product?

d. Does total product increase at a decreasing rate: (i) when average product is rising? (ii) when marginal product is rising? (iii) when average product begins to fall? (iv) when marginal product passes its maximum value?

e. When average product equals zero, what is total product?

f. (i) If average product is to the left of its maximum, which type of input is present in too large proportion? (ii) Which is in too small proportion? (iii) What are two ways of changing the proportion so as to increase average product? (iv) If either of these were done, what would happen to total product? (v) In view of these facts, is it desirable or undesirable, for a social point of view, for a producer to operate with average product below its maximum (to the left)? With marginal product at its maximum? Why is your answer true in each case?

2. Suppose that a product requires two inputs for its production. Then is it correct to say that if the prices of the inputs are equal, optimal behavior on the part of producers will dictate that these inputs be used in equal amounts?

3. Assume that a curve is drawn showing along the abscissa the amounts of a factor *A* employed in combination with a fixed amount of a group of factors called *B*, and along the ordinate the amount of physical product obtainable from these combinations of factors.

   a. How can you find (geometrically) the amount of *A* for which the average physical product per unit of *A* is a maximum?

   b. How can you find (geometrically) the amount of *A* for which the marginal physical product of *A* is a maximum?

   c. Between the two points defined in questions (*a*) and (*b*), will the marginal physical product of *A* increase or decrease as more of *A* is used?

   d. Between these two points, will the average physical product per unit of *A* increase or decrease as more of *A* is used?

   e. At the point defined in (*a*), will the marginal physical product of *A* be higher or lower than the average physical product per unit of *A?* Give reasons.

   f. At the point defined in (*b*), will the marginal physical product of *A* be higher or lower than the average physical product per unit of *A?* Give reasons.

   g. How can you find (geometrically) the amount of *A* for which the marginal physical product of *A* is zero?

4. An expansion path can be derived under the assumption either that firms attempt to produce each output at minimum cost or that they attempt to gain maximum output at each level of cost. The paths are identical in both cases. Explain.

5. Assume two inputs, L and K, then draw an isocost curve tangent to an isoquant. Show the equilibrium quantities of L and K. Next let the price of L rise relative to the price of K. What happens to the slope of the isocost curves? Let the new isocost curve (reflecting the higher price of L) be tangent to the old isoquant. What are the new equilibrium quantities? Let the price of L rise even more, then show the equilibrium quantities of L and K at the level of production given by the original isoquant. Derive a schedule showing the usage of L at each price of L, with output held constant. What can you say about the slope of such an output-constant, substitution-effect-only demand schedule?

6. Fill in the blanks in the following Table:

Usage of the Variable Input	Total Product	Average Product	Marginal Product
4...............		20	—
5...............			15
6...............	102		
7...............			10
8...............		15	
9...............	126		
10...............		12	

7. A charming French lady one told me that she thought American farmers were incredibly wasteful, compared with the French. She pointed out that French farmers planted their vegetables much closer together, weeded by hand many times to keep out all weeds, fertilized much more intensively than Americans, and grew much larger vegetables. Americans on the other hand, planted farther apart, weeded and even harvested by machine (wasting a great deal) and grew smaller vegetables. How would you have suggested I impress the lady with my knowledge of economics?

8. Why would you suspect that India manufactures items that take a lot of labor relative to machinery while the United States produces goods that are more capital intensive?

9. Assume that a firm is producing a good and is also dumping sewage into a river; the more goods it produces the more sewage it dumps. The two are related according to the following schedule:

Production (units)	Sewage in Tons
1,000...............	3
2,000...............	4
3,000...............	6
4,000...............	9
5,000...............	13
6,000...............	18

The firm sells its product at $1 per unit. If you wished to limit sewage to no more than nine tons, what figure per ton of sewage would you set? Assume the firm would not go out of business.

chapter

7

Theory of Cost

7.1 INTRODUCTION

When people speak of the cost of something they generally mean the price that must be paid for the item in question. To a businessman the cost of producing a good usually means the number of dollars that must be paid for enough raw materials, labor, machinery, and other inputs to produce the good. In economics, however, cost means somewhat more.

Consider the cost of attending college for one year. As a first approximation one might say that attending college for one year costs the year's tuition, room, board, book purchases, and incidental expenses. Using that approach it would appear that the cost of attending a particular college is essentially the same for any two students. Under certain circumstances that may not be quite correct. Assume that there are two students at the same school paying approximately the same tuition, board, and so forth. One student, however, is an exceptional baseball player who has been offered a major league contract with a large bonus. The *real* cost to him of attending college is not just the sum of his expenses; it is also what he had to give up to attend college. He must *sacrifice* or *give up* the amount he could have made by playing baseball in order to attend college.

The other student must also sacrifice something in addition to his direct outlays for expenses. Assuming that he is not so athletically inclined, perhaps his best alternative earning possibility might lie in working as a bank teller if he does not attend college. Thus he must sacrifice this amount of potential income. Since bank tellers generally do not receive a large bonus for signing with a bank, the athlete must sacrifice a greater amount; hence the *real* cost of attending college is greater for him than for the nonathlete. The athlete's *best alternative* is greater, so his real total cost is greater.

Or, recall that in previous chapters of this text we included the value of

195

a person's time spent shopping for a good in the price of that good. We included the value of time in the cost to society of having people serve on juries. We use a similar type of analysis when discussing the cost of production. For convenience we speak of two types of cost: (1) the social cost of production, and (2) the private cost of production. Before turning to the mechanics of cost analysis, we must first distinguish between these two costs.

7.1.a—Social Cost of Production

Economists are principally interested in the social cost of production; that is, the cost that society incurs when a resource is used to produce a given commodity. The cost of a productive resource in a particular use (say producing good X) is the amount it could produce in its best alternative (say in producing Y). The foregone Y the resource could have produced had it not been used to produce X is the cost to society. To use a popular wartime example, devoting more resources to the production of guns means using fewer resources to produce butter. The social cost of guns is the amount of butter foregone. Thus, the real cost of fighting a war may exceed the dollar cost specified by government. The social cost of sending a man to the moon is the goods that society gives up by devoting resources to the trip.

Economists speak of this as the alternative or opportunity cost of production.

Definition: The alternative or opportunity cost of producing one unit of commodity X is the amount of commodity Y that must be sacrificed in order to use resources to produce X rather than Y. This is the social cost of production. Therefore, the total cost of production consists of those payments necessary to attract and keep the factors of production attached to the firm, including the resources of the entrepreneur.

7.1.b—Private Cost of Production

There is a close relation between the opportunity cost of producing commodity X and a calculation the producer of X must make. The use of resources to produce X rather than Y entails a social cost; there is a private cost as well because the entrepreneur must pay a price to get the resources he uses. He must pay a certain amount to the resources in order to bid them away from alternative uses. These payments are *explicit* costs to the firm. He incurs some *implicit costs* also, and a complete analysis of costs must take these implicit costs into consideration.

To aid in analyzing the nature of implicit costs, consider two firms that produce good X and are in every way identical, with one exception. Both use identical amounts of the same resources to produce identical amounts of X. The first entrepreneur rents the building he uses. The second inherited his building and therefore pays no rent. Whose costs are higher? An economist would say both are the same, even though the second entrepreneur makes lower payments to outside factors of production. The reason costs are the same is that using his building to produce X costs the second entrepreneur the amount of income he could have received had he leased it at the prevailing rent. Since these two buildings are the same, presumably the market rental would be the same. In other words, a part of the cost incurred by the second entrepreneur is the payment from himself as entrepreneur to himself as the owner of a resource (the building).

Similarly the implicit cost would also include what he could make in the best alternative use of his time and his capital in another occupation had he not been associated with his firm.

Definition: The implicit costs incurred by an entrepreneur in producing a specific commodity consist of the amounts he could earn in the best alternative use of his time and of any other of his resources currently used to produce the commodity in question.

Implicit costs are thus charges that must be added to explicit costs in order to obtain total private costs.

7.2 PLANNING HORIZON

Let us begin our analysis of costs by assuming that an individual considers establishing a firm in a particular industry. The individual is called an entrepreneur. An entrepreneur is one who commits himself to costs (which are known) to produce an output, which he hopes consumers will purchase at a price that covers costs of production. The device for carrying out production is called a firm.

Since the entrepreneur is beginning the firm, he is in the long run. Recall from Chapter 6 that the long run is not some date in the future. The long run means that all inputs are variable to the entrepreneur. Therefore, one of the first things he must decide is the *scale* of operation or the *size* of the firm. To make this decision he must know the cost of producing each level of output. We begin our analysis of cost with the long run rather than the short run because the scale of the firm must be determined before an entrepreneur must decide upon different output levels from a fixed plant.

7.2.a—Derivation of Cost Schedules from a Long-Run Expansion Path

Let us assume for analytical purposes that the individual knows his actions will not affect the price he must pay for the resources he uses. Further, assume that he can estimate the production function for each level of output in the feasible range. Using the methods of Chapter 6, the entrepreneur derives an expansion path. Assuming that the firm uses only two inputs, labor and capital, the characteristics of the derived expansion path are given by columns one–three of Table 7.2.1. Labor costs $5 per unit and capital $10 per unit. Column one gives seven output levels and columns two and three give the optimal combinations of labor and capital for each output level at the prevailing input prices.

Column four gives the total cost of producing each level of output. For example, the least cost method of producing 300 units requires 20 units of labor and 10 of capital. At $5 and $10 respectively the total cost is $200. It should be emphasized that column four is a *least cost schedule* for various rates of production. Obviously the entrepreneur could pay more to produce any output by using less efficient productive processes or by paying some factors of production more than their market prices. He could not, however, produce an output at a cost lower than that given.

As noted above, the total least cost of producing any output consists of two components, the explicit costs and the implicit costs. The explicit costs, given in Table 7.2.1, are the payments the entrepreneur must make

TABLE 7.2.1

Derivation of Long-Run Cost Schedules

1	2	3	4	5	6
	Least Cost Usage of		Total Cost at		Marginal
	Labor	*Capital*	$5 per Unit of Labor $10 per	*Average*	*Cost*
Output	*(Units)*	*(Units)*	*Unit of Capital*	*Cost*	*(per Unit)*
100............	10	7	$120	$1.20	$1.20
200............	12	8	140	.70	.20
300............	20	10	200	.67	.60
400............	30	15	300	.75	1.00
500............	40	22	420	.84	1.20
600............	52	30	560	.93	1.40
700............	60	42	720	1.03	1.60

to the factors of production. The implicit costs are the market values of the resources he owns and uses in production, including the wages he pays himself. We could assume in Table 7.2.1 that the entrepreneur owns the capital. We could assume that implicit costs are zero. Or, we might just ignore them here. In any case, when the entrepreneur plans, he must consider the payments to himself since they cost him what he could receive for the services of these resources had he not chosen to use them himself.

Figure 7.2.1 specifies graphically the least cost schedule for some good X (not the good in Table 7.2.1). For example, the lowest cost of pro-

FIGURE 7.2.1

Long-Run Total Cost Curve

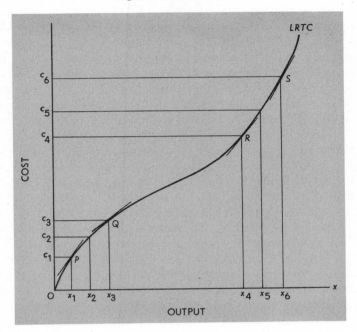

ducing Ox_1 units of X is Oc_1. We assume that the implicit costs of production are included in the curve.[1] It is important to note that the entrepreneur may use different amounts and combinations of resources. Nothing is fixed to him except the set of technological possibilities, or state of the arts, and the prices at which he can purchase resources. Thus completely different production processes may be used to achieve minimum cost at (say) Ox_1 and Ox_2 units of output. This "planning horizon" in which nothing is fixed to the entrepreneur except factor prices and technology is called the long run, and the associated curve that shows the minimum cost of producing each level of output is called the *Long-Run Total Cost Curve.*

Definition: Long-run total cost is the least cost at which each quantity of output can be produced when no resource is fixed in quantity or rate of usage.

---

[1] Note that since the cost curve begins at the origin and not at some positive amount on the vertical axis, we tacitly assume that the entrepreneur can readily vary the amount of his time and other resources he "invests" in the business. That is to say, the implicit costs are as readily variable as the explicit cost when one is considering the long run, or planning horizon. It is only in the short run, as we shall see below, that implicit costs are fixed.

7.2.b—Shape of Long-Run Total Cost Curves

The slope of the long-run total cost ($LRTC$) curve depends exclusively upon the production function and prevailing factor prices. The schedule in Table 7.2.1 and the curve in Figure 7.2.1 reflect some of the commonly assumed characteristics of long-run total costs.

Two characteristics are apparent on inspection. First, costs and output are *directly related;* that is, the curve has a positive slope. It costs more to produce more, which is just another way of saying that resources are scarce or that one never gets "something for nothing" in the real economic world. The second characteristic is that costs first increase at a decreasing rate and then at an increasing rate. For example, in Table 7.2.1 the cost of producing an *additional* 100 units at first decreases and then increases. Producing the first 100 units adds $120 to cost; increasing output from 100 to 200 adds an additional $20 to costs. The next 100 units add $60 to costs, and so forth. Figure 7.2.1 is constructed so that $x_1x_2 = x_2x_3$, whereas c_1c_2 is clearly greater than c_2c_3. This means that the added total cost is greater when the entrepreneur moves from Ox_1 to Ox_2 than when he increases output from Ox_2 to Ox_3. On the other hand, $x_4x_5 = x_5x_6$ but c_4c_5 is less than c_5c_6; over this range the additional cost incurred by producing more output increases. Alternatively stated, the slope at P (indicated by the tangent at that point) is greater than that at the larger ouput corresponding to Q. Incremental costs decrease over this range, even though total costs increase. The slope at R is less steep than that at S, indicating that incremental costs increase over this range.

Let us now summarize graphically and, at the same time, relate long-run total cost to factor prices and the production function. Consider Figure 7.2.2, in which we suppose that output is produced by two inputs, K and L. The known and fixed input prices give us the constant input price ratio, represented by the isocost curves I_1I_1', I_3I_3', etc. Next, the known production function gives us the isoquant map, partially represented by x_1, x_3, etc., in Figure 7.2.2.

As is familiar from Chapter 6, when all inputs are readily variable (that is, the long run), the entrepreneur will choose input combinations that minimize the cost of producing each level of output. This gives us the expansion path $OP'Q'R'S'$. Now let us relate Figures 7.2.1 and 7.2.2. Given the factor-price ratio and the production function, the expansion path shows the combinations of inputs that enable the entrepreneur to produce each level of output at the least possible cost. Given the same production function and factor prices, $LRTC$ also shows the least possible cost of producing each level of output. The points P, Q, R, and S in Figure 7.2.1 correspond exactly to the points P', Q', R', and S', respectively, in Figure 7.2.2. For example, the cost Oc_1 of producing Ox_1 units of output (Figure 7.2.1) is precisely the cost of using OK_1 units of K and

FIGURE 7.2.2

The Expansion Path and Long-Run Cost

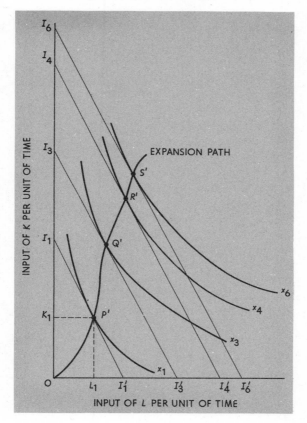

OL_1 units of L to produce the x_1 output at the optimal combination represented by P' (Figure 7.2.2).

7.2.c—Long-Run Average and Long-Run Marginal Costs

The last two columns of Table 7.2.1 specify the long-run average costs and long-run marginal costs associated with the total cost schedule and expansion path.

Definition: Average cost is the total cost of producing a particular quantity of output divided by that quantity.

Definition: Long-run marginal cost is the addition to total cost attributable to an additional unit of output when all inputs are optimally adjusted. It is thus the change in total cost as one moves along the expansion path or the long-run total cost curve.

FIGURE 7.2.3

Derivation of Average Total Cost Curve

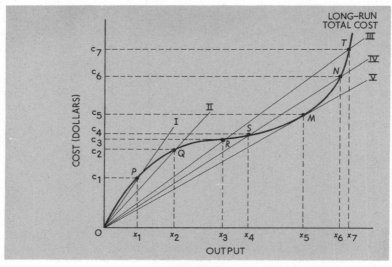

Panel *a*
Long-Run Total Cost

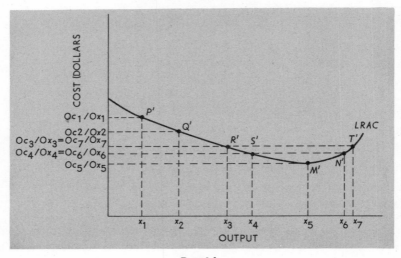

Panel *b*
Long-Run Average Cost

Column five of Table 7.2.1 shows a "typical" average cost that first decreases, reaches a minimum, then increases thereafter. The "typical" marginal cost, as shown in column six, first falls, reaches a minimum before the minimum average cost is attained, then rises thereafter. As is expected, when average cost is falling, marginal cost is below average; when average is rising, marginal cost is above average cost. The explanation given in Chapter 6 of the relation between marginal and average product applies here. Note that the marginal cost in column six is the average marginal cost. Since the table shows production expanding in increments of 100 units, the addition to total cost is given in that way also. Average marginal cost is the change in total cost divided by the change in total output, that is, $\Delta C/\Delta Q$. This is the per-unit marginal cost.

Figure 7.2.3 shows graphically the method of deriving the long-run average cost curve ($LRAC$) from the long-run total cost curve ($LRTC$). Since average cost is total cost divided by the corresponding output, the average cost of a particular quantity is given by the slope of a ray from the origin to the relevant point on $LRTC$. For example, at output Ox_1 in panel a average cost is Oc_1/Ox_1, the slope of the ray I from the origin to point P on the curve. The average cost Oc_1/Ox_1 of Ox_1 units of output is plotted as P' in panel b (the scale of the vertical axis of panel b differs from that of panel a). Point Q' in panel b, showing an average cost of Oc_2/Ox_2 at output Ox_2, is derived similarly. Since the slope of ray II is less than the slope of ray I, average cost is less for Ox_2 units than for Ox_1; this can be seen in panel b.

Note that since ray II is steeper than ray III and ray III steeper than ray IV, average cost is greater at output $Ox_2(Oc_2/Ox_2)$ than at Ox_3 and greater at Ox_3 than at Ox_4. In fact it is clear by inspection that the rays become less and less steep until output Ox_5 is reached, where ray V is tangent to the total cost curve at M. Thus $LRAC$ decreases until, at output Ox_5, it reaches its lowest point (M' in panel b). Further increases in output lead to increases in $LRAC$ since the slopes of the rays begin to increase after output Ox_5. For example, $LRAC$ is the same at $Ox_6(N')$ as at Ox_4; the same is true for Ox_7 and Ox_3. Thus while $LRTC$ continuously increases, $LRAC$ at first decreases (negative slope), reaches a minimum, then rises (positive slope).

The derivation of marginal cost is illustrated in Figure 7.2.4. Panel a contains the same total cost curve $LRTC$ as that in Figure 7.2.3. As output increases from Ox' to Ox'', one moves from point P to point Q and total cost increases from Oc' to Oc''. Marginal cost, the additional cost of producing one more unit of output, is thus

$$MC = \frac{Oc'' - Oc'}{Ox'' - Ox'} = \frac{QR}{PR}.$$

FIGURE 7.2.4
Derivation of Marginal Cost Curve

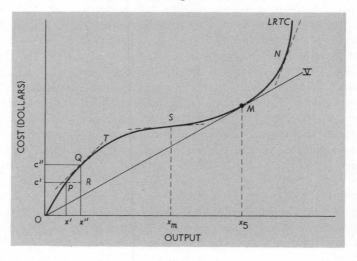

Panel *a*
Long-Run Total Cost

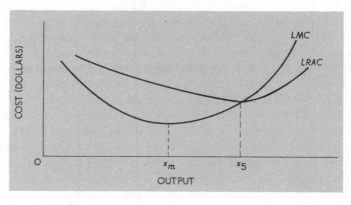

Panel *b*
Long-Run Marginal Cost

As P moves along $LRTC$ toward point Q, the distance between P and Q becomes smaller and the slope of the tangent T at point Q becomes a progressively better estimate of QR/PR. For movements in a tiny neighborhood around point Q, the slope of the tangent is marginal cost at output Ox''.

As one moves along $LRTC$ through points such as P and Q the slope of $LRTC$ diminishes until point S is reached at output Ox_m. Therefore the marginal cost curve (LMC) is constructed in panel b so that it decreases (as the *slope* of $LRTC$ decreases) until output Ox_m is attained and increases thereafter (as the *slope* of $LRTC$ increases).

One point should be noted. As indicated in Figure 7.2.3, the ray V gives minimum $LRAC$. But at this point ray V is tangent to $LRTC$, hence the slope of V also gives LMC at point M. Thus $LMC = LRAC$ when $LRAC$ attains its minimum value. Ray V in Figure 7.2.4, panel a, also illustrates this point. Since the slope of $LRTC$ is less than the slope of a ray from the origin to any point on the curve to the left of M, LMC is less than $LRAC$ from the origin to Ox_5. Since the slope of $LRTC$ is greater than the slope of a ray from the origin to any point on the curve to the right of M, LMC is greater than $LRAC$ at outputs larger than Ox_5.

Exercise: The student should illustrate this point in panel *a* for points *Q* and *N*.

The previously derived $LRAC$ is constructed in Figure 7.2.4 in order to show more clearly the relations between $LRAC$, LMC, and $LRTC$.

Relations: (1) *LRTC* rises continuously, first at a decreasing rate then at an increasing rate. (2) *LRAC* first declines, reaches a minimum, then rises. When *LRAC* reaches its minimum, *LMC* equals *LRAC*. (3) *LMC* first declines, reaches a minimum, and then increases. *LMC* lies below *LRAC* over the range in which *LRAC* declines; it lies above *LRAC* when *LRAC* is rising.

7.2.d—Economies of Scale

We have thus far concentrated exclusively upon describing the typical shapes of the long-run cost curves and have not analyzed the economic forces behind them. These forces are called economies and diseconomies of scale.

Economies of scale cause long-run average cost to decline. As the size of plant and the scale of operation are larger, certain economies of scale are usually realized. That is, after adjusting *all* inputs optimally the unit cost of production is reduced as the size of output is increased.

Adam Smith gave one of the chief reasons for this: specialization and division of labor. When the number of workers is expanded, fixed inputs remaining fixed, the opportunities for specialization and division of labor are rapidly exhausted. The marginal product curve rises, to be sure; but not for long. It very quickly reaches its maximum and declines. When workers and equipment are expanded together, however, very substantial gains may be reaped by division of jobs and the specialization of workers in one job or another.

Proficiency is gained by concentration of effort. If a plant is very small and employs only a small number of workers, each worker will usually have to perform several different jobs in the production process. In doing so he is likely to have to move about the plant, change tools, and so on. Not only are workers not highly specialized but a part of their worktime is consumed in moving about and changing tools. Thus important savings may be realized by expanding the scale of operation. A larger plant with a larger work force may permit each worker to specialize in one job, gaining proficiency and obviating time-consuming interchanges of location and equipment. There naturally will be corresponding reductions in the unit cost of production.

Technological factors constitute a second force contributing to economies of scale. If several different machines, each with a different rate of output, are required in a production process, the operation may have to be quite sizable to permit proper "meshing" of equipment. Suppose only two types of machines are required, one that produces and one that packages the product. If the first machine can produce 30,000 units per day and the second can package 45,000, output will have to be 90,000 per day in order to utilize fully the capacity of each type of machine.

Another technological element is the fact that the cost of purchasing and installing larger machines is usually proportionately less than the cost of smaller machines. For example, a printing press that can run 200,000 papers per day does not cost 10 times as much as one that can run 20,000 per day—nor does it require 10 times as much building space, 10 times as many men to work it, and so forth. Again, expanding size tends to reduce the unit cost of production.

A final technological element is perhaps the most important of all: as the scale of operation expands there is usually a qualitative, as well as a quantitative, change in equipment. Consider ditchdigging. The smallest scale of operation is one man and one shovel. But as the scale expands beyond a certain point one does not simply continue to add men and shovels. Shovels and most workers are replaced by a modern ditchdigging machine. In like manner, expansion of scale normally permits the introduction of various types of automation devices, all of which tend to reduce the unit cost of production.

Thus two broad forces—specialization and division of labor and technological factors—enable producers to reduce unit cost by expanding the scale of operation.[2] These forces give rise to the negatively sloped portion of the long-run average cost curve.

---

[2] This discussion of economies of scale has concentrated upon physical and technological forces. There are financial reasons for economies of scale as well. Large-scale purchasing of raw and processed materials may enable the buyer to obtain more favorable prices (quantity discounts). The same is frequently true of advertising. As another example, financing of large-scale business is normally easier and less expensive; a nationally known business has access to organized security markets, so it may place its bonds and stocks on a more favorable basis. Bank loans also usually come easier and at lower interest rates to large, well-known corporations. These are but examples of many potential economies of scale attributable to financial

But why should it ever rise? After all possible economies of scale have been realized, why doesn't the curve become horizontal?

7.2.e—Diseconomies of Scale

The rising portion of *LRAC* is usually attributed to diseconomies of scale, which means limitations to efficient management. Managing any business entails controlling and coordinating a wide variety of activities— production, transportation, finance, sales, and so on. To perform these managerial functions efficiently the manager must have accurate information; otherwise the essential decision making is done in ignorance.

As the scale of plant expands beyond a certain point, top management necessarily has to delegate responsibility and authority to lower echelon employees. Contact with the daily routine of operation tends to be lost

FIGURE 7.2.5

Various Shapes of *LRAC*

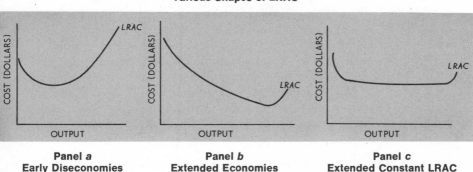

| **Panel *a*** | **Panel *b*** | **Panel *c*** |
| **Early Diseconomies** | **Extended Economies** | **Extended Constant LRAC** |

and efficiency of operation to decline. Red tape and paper work expand; management is generally not as efficient. This increases the cost of the managerial function and, of course, the unit cost of production.

It is very difficult to determine just when diseconomies of scale set in and when they become strong enough to outweigh the economies of scale. In businesses where economies of scale are negligible, diseconomies may soon become of paramount importance, causing *LRAC* to turn up at a relatively small volume of output. Panel *a*, Figure 7.2.5, shows a long-run average cost curve for a firm of this type. In other cases, economies of scale are extremely important. Even after the efficiency of management begins to decline technological economies of scale may offset the dis-

considerations. For a more detailed discussion, see William G. Husband and James C. Dockeray, *Modern Corporation Finance* (6th ed.; Homewood, Ill,: R. D. Irwin, Inc., 1966).

economies over a wide range of output. Thus the *LRAC* curve may not turn upward until a very large volume of output is attained. This case, typified by the so-called natural monopolies, is illustrated in panel *b*, Figure 7.2.5.

In many actual situations, however, neither of these extremes describes the behavior of *LRAC*. A very modest scale of operation may enable a firm to capture all of the economies of scale; however, diseconomies may not be incurred until the volume of output is very great. In this case, *LRAC* would have a long horizontal section as shown in panel *c*. Many economists and businessmen feel that this type of *LRAC* curve describes most production processes in the American economy. For analytical purposes, however, we will assume a "representative" *LRAC*, such as that illustrated in Figure 7.2.4.

7.2.f—Summary

The conventional definition of the long run is "a period of time (not calendar time) of such length that all inputs are variable." Another aspect of the long run has also been stressed, an aspect that is, perhaps, the most important of all. The long run is a *planning horizon*. All production, indeed all economic activity, takes place in the short run. The long run refers to the fact that economic agents, consumers and entrepreneurs, can plan ahead and choose many aspects of the short run in which they will operate in the future. Thus, in a sense the long run consists of all possible short run situations among which an economic agent may choose.

7.3 ESTIMATION OF INDUSTRY LONG-RUN COSTS

When we examine actual industries, we observe that firms in the same industry frequently vary greatly in size. This leads us to believe that the cost curves differ among firms in an industry. Some extremely small firms survive beside veritable giants with many sizes of firms in between. If there is no single scale for firms in an industry, any attempt to measure an industry cost curve must consider the effect of having many sizes in the industry. Once the industry costs have been estimated one can predict what size or range of sizes is optimal—that is, least cost.[3]

Economists have attempted many times to measure industry costs and efficient scale using engineering data. These attempts are usually based

---

[3] In Chapter 8, we will discuss in great detail what is meant by optimal size. The remainder of this section is based upon two related papers: George J. Stigler, "The Economies of Scale" *Journal of Law and Economics,* Oct. 1958, pp. 54–71 and T. R. Saving, "Estimation of Optimum Size of Plant by the Survivor Technique," *Quarterly Journal of Economics,* Nov. 1961, pp. 569–607.

upon the assumption that factors of production are freely available at a constant supply price, and demand conditions are generally not considered when estimating efficient size. One interesting method of estimating costs and optimal scale is the survivor technique, a process developed by G. J. Stigler and T. R. Saving.

7.3.a—Survivor Principle

The survivor principle is based upon the following assumption: all firms in the industry are classified by size, and the share of total industry output is calculated; if the relative share of any class falls, that class is relatively inefficient, and is more inefficient the faster the share is falling.[4] In this way economists can consider not merely the technological composition of firms' costs but also the ability of the firm to solve its other problems—labor relations, innovation, regulation, and so on. In this way one can tell the range over which economies of scale are attainable and points, if any, at which diseconomies are reached.

Examples of this method are Stigler's studies of the steel and automobile industries. In the steel industry during the 1930s and 1940s very small firms and the largest firms experienced a decline in relative share. Intermediate firms, in size classes from two and one-half to twenty-five percent of the industry's capacity grew or retained their share. The smallest sizes lost shares most rapidly. It appears then that over the period of measurement the long-run average cost curve for the part of the steel industry that was measured looked somewhat like the curve in panel *c*, Figure 7.2.5. Of course, this method cannot estimate how much higher than the minimum are the costs of the declining firms.

The analysis was extended from firm size to *plant size*. It was found that the share of the smallest plants—up to almost one percent of industry capacity—declined, with no tendency toward decline for plants above this point, even the very largest. It appears that the diseconomies of large firm size were due to diseconomies of multi-plant operation and not to diseconomies of large plants.

The trend of the passenger automobile industry from 1936 to 1955 differs somewhat from steel. Over this span of time the smallest automobile companies—under five percent of industry capacity—experienced a declining share. During periods of inflation with price control the data revealed diseconomies for the largest class, but substantial economies otherwise. That is, the long-run average cost is shaped like that in panel *c* during inflation, but it does not rise at large size in other times. The petroleum industry from 1947 to 1954 showed essentially the same characteristics as steel in both firm size and plant size. The range of firm

---

[4] Stigler, "Economies of Scale," p. 54.

sizes from one-half of one percent to ten percent of industry capacity contained all classes in the optimal range.

7.3.b—Determinants of Optimal Sizes

After examining these specific industries, Stigler investigated 48 manufacturing industries to isolate the most important determinants of the optimum size firm. In the past, economists had said that influences such as large advertising expenditures, complicated technology, research, and large plant size caused industries to be characterized by large scale firms. After the optimum ranges of sizes for all industries were determined, the average assets of these firms were computed. This average size firm was regressed on advertising, technology and research, and plant size.[5] Advertising expenditure had no significant effect on average optimum size. The other two variables were quite significant. The range of optimal sizes were quite wide indicating strong evidence that many *industry* (but not necessarily firm) cost curves are saucer shaped as in panel *c*.

One frequently hears that very large scale plants are necessary for survival in manufacturing industries today. There are supposedly economies of large scale production in manufacturing that make for large plant size. Evidence based upon the survivor technique does not verify this allegation.

Saving used this technique to investigate the minimum, the average, and the range of optimum sizes for plants in 89 manufacturing industries. The data show wide variation in both mean and minimum optimum sizes. The magnitudes, however, are quite small relative to total industry size. For example, 72 percent of all industries showed minimum optimal plant size—that is, they exhausted all economies of scale—at plant sizes that produced less than one percent of the industry's total output. Ninety-eight percent had a mean optimal size below ten percent of total, and 55 percent showed means at less than one percent. The ranges of optimal size tended to be small compared to the industry's size; 81 percent had ranges that lay below five percent of total. The ranges, however, were large compared to mean optimal size. It appears then that economies of scale in plant size are rapidly exhausted in expansion.

After estimating optimum plant sizes, Saving looked at the causes of large or small average firm size relative to size of the industry. He hypothesized that average firm size is affected by the optimum plant size and the extent of multi-plant operation (as measured by the average number of plants per firm in the industry). Both variables significantly affected average firm size, accounting for about 87 percent of the variation, but the average number of plants was found to be a far more significant determinant. These economies may be more important than plant

---

[5] The ratio of chemists and engineers to total employment was used as a proxy variable for technology.

economies. That is, the optimum size plant is usually not so large as to cause industries to be characterized by a few, very large firms.

Next the determinants of optimum firm size were analyzed to answer why industries differ so greatly in the points at which plant economies of scale end and diseconomies begin. The hypothetical determining variables were (1) industry size, (2) rate of growth of the industry, (3) complexity of the productive process, and (4) the extent of capital intensiveness. These four variables explained approximately 50 percent of the variation in minimum and average plant size in the 89 industries tested. The two most important variables in both regressions were, in order of importance, industry size and capital intensiveness, as measured by the capital to labor ratio. They accounted for about 80 percent of the explained variation. The rate of growth of the industry was not significant at all. The complexity of the productive process, measured by the proportion of chemists and engineers to total labor force, was not highly significant but was more significant in the case of the average optimum plant size than the minimum. The only important variables affecting the range of optimal plant sizes—that is, the length of the horizontal portion of industry long-run average cost—were the mean optimum plant size and the size of the industry.

Certainly there may be biases in the survivor technique from imperfections in data, but other methods of cost estimation must also use imperfect data. In any case this technique gives some interesting insight into the nature of industry costs and the extent of long-run economies and diseconomies of scale.[6]

7.4 THEORY OF COST IN THE SHORT RUN

Once an entrepreneur has investigated all possibilities open to him, he can decide upon a specific scale of output and hence build a plant of such size as to produce this output at the least possible cost. For economic theory, this may be regarded as either *money* cost or *resource* cost because, in the last analysis, they are the same (except in one situation, which is discussed in the last chapter of the book).

7.4.a—Short-Run Total Cost

Prior to investing money resources in buildings, machinery, and so on, the amounts of all resources are variable. That is, the usage of each type of resource can be determined so as to obtain the most efficient (that is, least cost) combination of inputs. But once money resources have been congealed into buildings, machinery, and other *fixed* assets, their amounts

---

[6] For further evidence in this area see Leonard W. Weiss, "The Survival Technique and the Extent of Suboptimal Capacity," *Journal of Political Economy*, June 1964, pp. 246–61.

cannot be readily changed, although their rates of utilization can be decreased by allowing fixed assets to lie idle (note, however, that idle assets cost as much as, perhaps more than, utilized assets). To summarize, in the *short run* there are certain resources whose amounts cannot be changed when the desired rate of output changes, while there are other resources (called variable inputs) whose usage can be changed almost instantaneously.[7]

Suppose an entrepreneur, whose *LRTC* or planning horizon is that indicated in Figure 7.4.1, builds a plant to produce Ox_0 units of output

FIGURE 7.4.1
Short- and Long-Run Total Cost

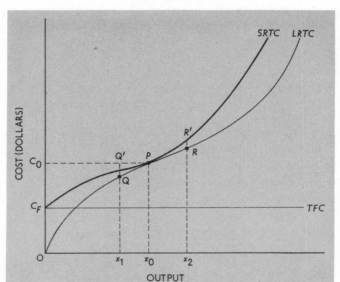

at total cost Oc_0. Since the inputs of certain resources are fixed, the cost to the firm of these resources is fixed also. We can now examine the effect of varying output when the usage of certain resources cannot be changed.

---

[7] It is not quite precise to say that the inputs of some resources cannot be changed. Certainly the firm could scrap a very expensive piece of capital equipment, buy another one twice as large, and have it installed before lunch, *if it is willing to pay the price*. In fact the firm can probably change any input rather rapidly, given, once more, its willingness to pay. The short run is thus a convenient but important analytical device. It is frequently helpful in analyzing problems to suppose some inputs are fixed for a period of time. Moreover, it does not deviate too much from reality to make this assumption since entrepreneurs often consider certain resources as fixed over a period of time. The student should not be overly concerned about the time factor in the short and long run. The fixity of resources is the important element.

The firm operates in the short run—that period of time in which the input of one or more factors of production is fixed, hence the cost of these factors to the firm is fixed also. Since output can be changed in the short run only by changing variable inputs, the cost of these inputs is a variable cost. The sum of the variable and the fixed costs at any level of output is the *total cost* of producing that output.

Definition: Total fixed cost is the sum of the short-run explicit fixed costs and the implicit cost incurred by an entrepreneur.
Definition: Total variable cost is the sum of the amounts spent for each of the variable inputs used.
Definition: Total cost in the short run is the sum of total variable and total fixed cost.

Consider the short-run total cost curve ($SRTC$) in Figure 7.4.1. This is the curve indicating the firm's total cost of production for each level of output when the input of certain resources is fixed. One characteristic of this curve is that $SRTC$ (OC_0) equals $LRTC$ at output level Ox_0. This equality is apparent when we remember that the plant was built (and the input of all resources chosen) so as to produce Ox_0 at the least possible cost. Short-run cost at Ox_0 is therefore also the lowest attainable cost for this output.

A second characteristic is that for any output other than Ox_0, $SRTC$ must be greater than $LRTC$. At output Ox_1 or Ox_2, for example, $SRTC$ could not, by definition, be lower than $LRTC$ because $LRTC$ is defined as the *least cost* for *every* level of output. We should therefore expect that $SRTC$ exceeds $LRTC$ at all rates of output except Ox_0. This point is clearly illustrated in Figure 7.4.2. Again we assume that there are two inputs, K and L. Isoquants x_0, x_1, and x_2 indicate the rates of output corresponding to Ox_0, Ox_1, and Ox_2 in Figure 7.4.1. Given constant input prices, the associated isocost curves are I_0I_0', I_1I_1', and I_2I_2'.

If the entrepreneur believes that x_0 will be the most profitable rate of output, he will hire OL_0 units of labor and invest OK_0 in *fixed* assets. Once his money resources are congealed in the fixed assets OK_0, he operates in the short run. But so long as he produces Ox_0 units of output, he operates at the least possible unit cost; $LRTC$ and $SRTC$ are the same, as indicated by the point of tangency P in Figure 7.4.1.

Now suppose it becomes desirable to change output from x_0 to x_2. In the short run, the entrepreneur cannot move along his expansion path; or to put it differently, with the fixed plant OK_0, K_0K_0' is his *short-run* expansion path. The entrepreneur expands output by expanding labor input operating the same quantity of fixed assets (for example, he expands output by operating overtime in his fixed plant, with the higher overtime pay to his labor force). That is, in the short run he must move to R' instead of R. Cost is higher, as indicated by the dashed line c_2c_2', which lies

FIGURE 7.4.2

Input Combinations and Short-Run Cost

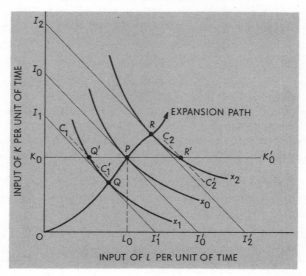

INPUT OF *L* PER UNIT OF TIME

above $I_2 I_2'$. Further, the *reason* for a higher cost in the short run is apparent: at R' the marginal rate of technical substitution is not equal to the input price ratio. The marginal product of a dollar's worth of K exceeds the marginal product of a dollar's worth of L. But in the short run, with K fixed, the entrepreneur can do no better. In the long run, he can; he will expand plant size and reduce labor usage, moving to point R on his expansion path.

Exercise: Using Figures 7.4.1 and 7.4.2, carry out the same argument for a reduction of output to x_1.

A third characteristic of $SRTC$ is the positive cost, OC_F, at zero output. Since we have fixed the input of some resources, the firm must pay these resources the same amount at all outputs. Figure 7.4.1, therefore, shows both components of short-run total costs: (1) total fixed costs (TFC) OC_F, which must be paid regardless of output and (2) total variable costs (TVC), the difference between $SRTC$ and OC_F. TVC changes as output changes since variable costs are the payments to the resources that the firm can vary with output.

7.4.b—Average and Marginal Costs

The short-run total cost of production, including implicit cost, is very important to an enterpreneur. However, one may obtain a deeper understanding of total cost by analyzing the behavior of short-run average cost and marginal cost. The method used in deriving these curves is similar to that used to derive long-run average and marginal costs.

We assume a specific short-run situation such as that developed in subsection 7.4.a. First consider average fixed costs (AFC).

Definition: Average fixed cost is total fixed cost divided by output.

The derivation of AFC, illustrated in Figure 7.4.3, is quite simple. Total fixed cost, OC_F, is shown by the horizontal line TFC in panel a; outputs Ox_1, Ox_2, and Ox_3 are such that $Ox_1 = x_1x_2 = x_2x_3$. Since AFC at a particular output equals TFC divided by that output, average fixed cost is given by the slope of a ray to the relevant point on the TFC curve. For

FIGURE 7.4.3

Derivation of the Average Fixed Cost Curve

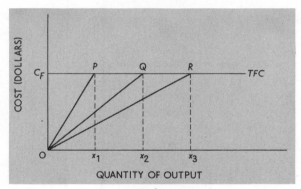

Panel a
Total Fixed Cost

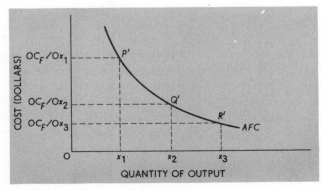

Panel b
Average Fixed Cost

output Ox_1, AFC is the slope of the ray OP, OC_F/Ox_1. Similarly, for output Ox_2, AFC is OC_F/Ox_2, and so on. These values are plotted and connected in panel b. TFC equals AFC times quantity at any point on the curve. Since *TFC* is a constant (OC_F), $x_1P' \times Ox_1 = x_2Q' \times Ox_2 = x_3R' \times Ox_3$, and so on. A curve such as this is called a rectangular hyperbola. It is negatively sloped and approaches, but never reaches, the horizontal axis as output increases. The AFC curve derived from panel a is plotted in panel b.

Now we examine average variable cost (AVC), a concept completely analogous to long-run average costs, since all costs are variable in the long run.

Definition: Average variable cost is total variable cost divided by output.

Having spent considerable time developing the concept of long-run average cost, we need not spend much time deriving the average variable cost curve, since the two techniques are similar.

Figure 7.4.4 shows how AVC is derived from TVC. As is true of all

FIGURE 7.4.4
Derivation of the Average Variable Cost Curve

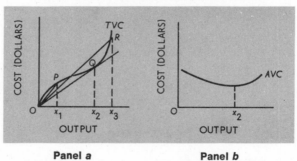

Panel *a*	Panel *b*
Total Variable Cost	Average Variable Cost

"average" curves, the average variable cost associated with any level of output is given by the slope of a ray from the origin to the corresponding point on the TVC curve. As may easily be seen from panel a, the slope of a ray from the origin to the curve steadily diminishes as one passes through points such as P; and it diminishes until the ray is just tangent to the TVC curve at point Q, associated with output Ox_2. Thereafter the slope increases as one moves from Q toward points such as R. This is reflected in panel b by constructing AVC with a negative slope until output Ox_2 is attained. After that point, the slope becomes positive and remains positive.

Although the U-shapes of AVC and long-run average cost are similar, the reasons for their decline and rise are different. The explanation for the curvature of *AVC* lies in the short-run theory of production. Total variable cost at any output consists of the payments to the variable factors of production used to produce that output. *TVC*, therefore, equals the sum of the number of units of each variable input (V) multiplied by unit price (P) of that input. For example, at output Q produced by n variable inputs, $TVC = P_1V_1 + P_2V_2 + P_3V_3 + \ldots + P_nV_n$. For the one-variable case, $TVC = PV$. Average variable cost is *TVC* divided by output (Q), or

$$AVC = \frac{TVC}{Q} = \frac{PV}{Q} = P\left(\frac{V}{Q}\right).$$

The term (V/Q) is the number of units of input divided by the number of units of output. In Chapter 6, we defined the average product (*AP*) of an input as total output (Q) divided by the number of units of input (V). Thus

$$\frac{V}{Q} = \frac{1}{(Q/V)} = \frac{1}{AP},$$

and

$$AVC = P\frac{V}{Q} = P\frac{1}{(Q/V)} = P\left(\frac{1}{AP}\right).$$

Thus average variable cost is the price of the input multiplied by the reciprocal of average product. Since by the law of variable proportions average product normally rises, reaches a maximum, then declines, average variable cost normally falls, reaches a minimum, then rises.

Figure 7.4.5 shows the derivation of short-run average total cost, which may be called average cost or unit cost.

FIGURE 7.4.5
Derivation of the Average Total Cost or Unit Cost Curve

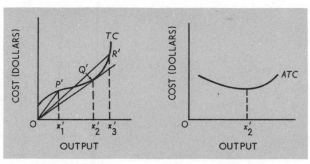

Panel a
Short-Run Total Cost

Panel b
Short-Run Unit Cost

Definition: Average total cost is total cost divided by output.

Exactly the same analysis used for AVC holds for panels a and b, which show the derivation of ATC from TC. The slope of the ray diminishes as one moves along TC until point Q' is reached. At Q' the slope of the ray is least, so minimum ATC is attained at output level Ox_2'. Thereafter the slope of the ray increases continuously, and the ATC curve has a positive slope. (Note: the output level Ox_2' *does not* represent the same quantity as Ox_2 in Figure 7.4.4. As we shall see, AVC reaches its minimum at a lower output than that at which ATC reaches its minimum.)

ATC may also be computed by an alternative method. Since $TC = TFC + TVC$,

$$ATC = \frac{TC}{Q} = \frac{TFC + TVC}{Q} = \frac{TFC}{Q} + \frac{TVC}{Q} = AFC + AVC.$$

Thus one may calculate average cost as the sum of average fixed and average variable cost.

This method of calculation helps to explain the shape of the average total cost curve. Over the range of values for which AFC and AVC both decline, ATC, the sum of AFC and AVC, must obviously decline as well. But even after AVC turns up, the decline in AFC causes ATC to continue to decline. Finally, however, the increase in AVC more than offsets the decline in AFC; ATC therefore reaches its minimum and increases thereafter.

Finally let us examine marginal cost in the short run.

Definition: Marginal cost is the change in total cost attributable to a one-unit change in output.

The definitions of long- and short-run marginal cost that we have given are virtually identical. The concepts are not quite the same, however. Long-run marginal cost refers to the change in cost resulting from a change in output when *all inputs are optimally adjusted.* Short-run marginal cost, on the other hand, refers to the change in cost resulting from a change in output when *only the variable inputs change.* Since the fixed inputs cannot be changed in the short run, input combinations are not optimally adjusted. Thus the short-run marginal cost curve reflects suboptimal adjustment of inputs.

Although the concept of marginal cost differs slightly between the long run and the short run, the process of deriving marginal cost is similar. The marginal cost of, say, the second unit produced is the increase in the total cost caused by changing production from one unit to two units; or, $MC_2 = TC_2 - TC_1$. Since only variable cost changes in the short run, however, the marginal cost of producing an additional unit is the increase in variable cost. Thus the marginal cost of the second unit is also $MC_2 = TVC_2 - TVC_1$.

The derivation of marginal cost is illustrated in Figure 7.4.6. Panel *a* shows the short-run total cost curve *TC*. As output increases from Ox_1 to Ox_2, one moves from point *P* to point *Q*, and total cost increases from Oc_1 to Oc_2. Marginal cost is thus QR/PR. As before, the slope of the tangent *T* at point *Q* becomes a progressively better estimate of *MC* (QR/PR) as the distance between *P* and *Q* becomes smaller and smaller. Thus for small changes, the slope of the total cost curve is marginal cost.

FIGURE 7.4.6

Derivation of the Marginal Cost Curve

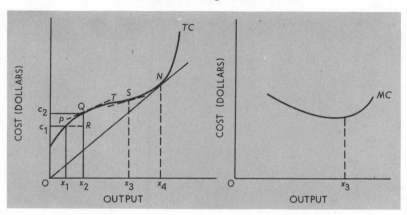

Panel *a*	Panel *b*
Short-Run Total Cost	Short-Run Marginal Cost

As *TC* increases the slope decreases (*MC* decreases) until point S is reached at output Ox_3. Thereafter the slope increases (*MC* increases). The *MC* curve is constructed in panel *b* so that it decreases until output Ox_3 is attained and increases thereafter.

Just as average variable cost is related to average product, marginal cost is related to marginal product. As before, consider the one-variable case in which $TVC = PV$. Thus, if *P* is fixed

$$MC = \frac{\Delta VC}{\Delta Q} = \frac{\Delta(PV)}{\Delta Q} = P\frac{\Delta V}{\Delta Q},$$

where again Δ means "the change in." But, recall that marginal product is $MP = \Delta Q/\Delta V$. Therefore,

$$MC = P\left(\frac{1}{MP}\right).$$

From this relation, as marginal product rises, marginal cost falls; when marginal product declines, marginal cost rises.

One final point concerning the relation of short-run marginal and average cost curves should be noted. As already implied, and as Figure 7.4.7 again illustrates, *TC* and *TVC* have the same slope at each output level. *TC* is simply *TVC* displaced upward by the constant amount *TFC* (see Figure 7.4.7).

At output Ox_0 the tangent (T) to *TVC* has the same slope as the tangent (T') to *TC*. Since the slopes of the two tangents at output Ox_0 are equal, *MC* at Ox_0 is given by the slope of either curve. The same holds true for any other output level. The slope of ray I from the origin gives minimum *AVC*. But at this point (output Ox_1) ray I is just tangent to *TVC*; hence it also gives *MC* at output Ox_1. Thus $MC = AVC$ when

FIGURE 7.4.7

Relation of *MC* to Variable and Total Costs

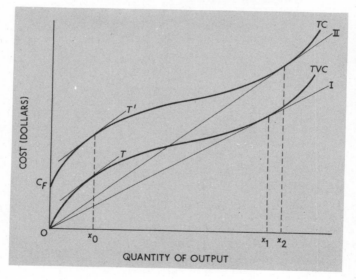

the latter attains its minimum value. Similarly the slope of ray II gives minimum *ATC* (at output Ox_2). At this point the ray is tangent to *TC*; thus its slope also gives *MC* at output Ox_2. Consequently $MC = ATC$ when the latter attains its minimum value. Finally, as is easily seen from Figure 7.4.7, *AVC* attains its minimum at a lower output than the output at which *ATC* attains its minimum.

The properties of the average and marginal cost curves, as derived in this section, are illustrated by the "typical" set of short-run cost curves shown in Figure 7.4.8. The curves indicate the following:

Relations: (a) AFC declines continuously, approaching both axes asymptotically, as shown by points one and two in the figure. AFC is a

FIGURE 7.4.8

Typical Set of Cost Curves

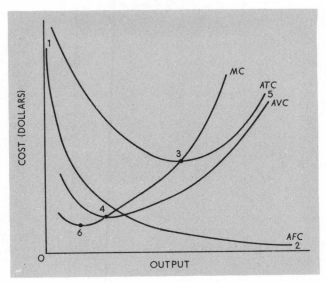

rectangular hyperbola. (*b*) *AVC* first declines, reaches a minimum at point four, and rises thereafter. When *AVC* attains its minimum at point four, *MC* equals *AVC*. As *AFC* approaches asymptotically close to the horizontal axis, *AVC* approaches *ATC* asymptotically, as shown by point five. (*c*) *ATC* first declines, reaches a minimum at point three, and rises thereafter. When *ATC* attains its minimum at point three, *MC* equals *ATC*. (*d*) *MC* first declines, reaches a minimum at point six, and rises thereafter. *MC* equals both *AVC* and *ATC* when these curves attain their minimum values. Furthermore, *MC* lies below both *AVC* and *ATC* over the range in which the curves decline; it lies above them when they are rising.

7.4.c—Numerical Example of Short-Run Cost Schedules

Table 7.4.1 illustrates numerically the characteristics of the cost curves analyzed graphically in subsection 7.4.a and 7.4.b. Average fixed cost decreases over the entire range of output. Both average variable and average total cost first decrease, then increase with average variable cost attaining a minimum at a lower output than that at which average total reaches its minimum. Marginal cost per 100 units is the incremental increase in total cost and variable cost. Marginal cost (average per unit) is below average variable and average total when each is falling and is greater than each when *AVC* and *ATC* are rising.

TABLE 7.4.1

Short-Run Cost Schedules

1 Output	2 Total Cost (Dollars)	3 Fixed Cost (Dollars)	4 Variable Cost (Dollars)	5 Average Fixed Cost	6 Average Variable Cost	7 Average Total Cost	8 Marginal Cost (per 100 Units)	9 Marginal Cost (per Unit)
100	6,000	4,000	2,000	40.00	20.00	60.00	2,000	20.00
200	7,000	4,000	3,000	20.00	15.00	35.00	1,000	10.00
300	7,500	4,000	3,500	13.33	11.67	25.00	500	5.00
400	9,000	4,000	5,000	10.00	12.50	22.50	1,500	15.00
500	11,000	4,000	7,000	8.00	14.00	22.00	2,000	20.00
600	14,000	4,000	10,000	6.67	16.67	23.33	3,000	30.00
700	18,000	4,000	14,000	5.71	20.00	25.71	4,000	40.00
800	24,000	4,000	20,000	5.00	25.00	30.00	6,000	60.00
900	34,000	4,000	30,000	4.44	33.33	37.77	10,000	100.00
1,000	50,000	4,000	46,000	4.00	46.00	50.00	16,000	160.00

7.5 RELATIONS BETWEEN SHORT- AND LONG-RUN AVERAGE AND MARGINAL COSTS

Suppose an entrepreneur has the planning horizon labeled $LRTC$ in all three panels of Figure 7.5.1. By the process developed in Section 7.2 we may derive his long-run average and marginal cost curves and plot these in Figure 7.5.2, the scale of which differs from that of Figure 7.5.1. These curves are labeled $LRAC$ and $LRMC$ respectively. Suppose now that the entrepreneur only considers plants of three different sizes: small, medium, and large.

The three short-run total cost curves ($SRTC_1$, $SRTC_2$, $SRTC_3$) for the three different plants are given in Figure 7.5.1. The total cost curve $SRTC_1$ in panel a is associated with the "small" plant. The fixed resources are fixed to produce output Ox_s at the least possible total cost Oc_1. $SRTC_2$ in panel b is the cost curve for the "medium" plant; the fixed resources are fixed to produce Ox_m at least cost (Oc_2). The cost curve $SRTC_3$ in panel c is associated with the "large" plant, built to produce Ox_l at least cost (Oc_3). LRTC is the same in all three panels.

First consider the small plant. Since $SRTC_1$ lies above $LRTC$ at every output except Ox_s, short-run average cost exceeds long-run average cost at every output except Ox_s.

Exercise: The student should test this assertion by constructing a few rays from the origin to the two total cost curves at the same output level.

At output Ox_s, short- and long-run average costs are equal since the same ray from the origin (II) strikes both total cost curves at this point. Or $SRAC_1 = LRAC = Oc_1/Ox_s$ at output Ox_s. The minimum point on $LRAC$ is attained at an output greater than Ox_s (note ray I from the origin).

Exercise: The student should pivot ray II downward around the origin until II is tangent to $SRTC_1$, in order to ascertain that the output of minimum $SRAC_1$ is greater than Ox_s and less than the output at which $LRTC$ reaches its minimum.

In Figure 7.5.2 (which, as noted above, differs in scale) the short-run average cost curve associated with the small plant is plotted. Note that all of the relations described are apparent in this figure. $SRAC_1$ is greater than $LRAC$ everywhere except at point S' (output Ox_s), at which the two are equal. Both curves attain a minimum at outputs greater than Ox_s, but $SRAC_1$ reaches a minimum at a lower output than does $LRAC$.

It should be obvious that since $SRTC_1$ is tangent to $LRTC$ at S (output Ox_s), short-run and long-run marginal costs (given by the slope of the tangent T in Figure 7.5.1, panel a) are equal at output Ox_s. When moving from Ox_s to any greater output (say Ox_2), the *additional* cost of producing the *added* output is greater in the short run than in the long run because the short run is characterized by suboptimal adjustment. $SRTC_1$

FIGURE 7.5.1
Long-Run and Short-Run Cost Curves

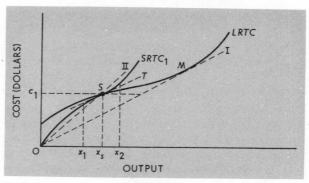

Panel *a*
Small Plant

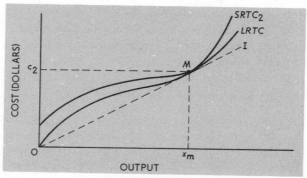

Panel *b*
Medium Plant

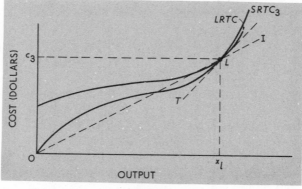

Panel *c*
Large Plant

FIGURE 7.5.2

Long-Run and Short-Run Average and Marginal Costs

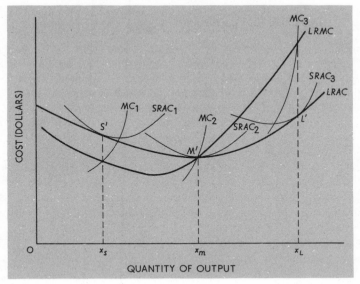

lies further above Oc_1 at Ox_2 than does $LRAC$; thus the *increase* in cost associated with the movement from Ox_s to Ox_2 is greater in the short run. Hence at outputs greater than Ox_s, short-run marginal cost exceeds long-run marginal cost.

When moving from Ox_s to a smaller output (say Ox_1), the reduction in cost associated with that movement is greater in the long run than in the short run because a firm can adjust optimally in the long run. At output Ox_1, $SRTC_1$ exceeds $LRTC$; or $SRTC_1$ is closer to Oc_1 than is $LRTC$ at that output. Since the costs are the same (Oc_1) at Ox_s, the reduction in cost of moving from Ox_s to Ox_1 is less in the short run. Thus short-run marginal cost for the small plant is less than long-run marginal cost at outputs less than Ox_s and greater for outputs larger than Ox_s, the output at which both marginal costs are equal. These relations are shown in Figure 7.5.2.

Turning now to the medium plant in panel *b*, Figure 7.5.1, we see that $SRTC_2$ is tangent to $LRTC$ at output Ox_m with cost Oc_2 (point M). Since the ray from the origin (I) is tangent to both $SRTC_2$ and $LRTC$ at M, $LRAC$, $LRMC$, $SRAC_2$, and $SRMC_2$ are all equal at output Ox_m. Both short- and long-run average costs are at their minima at this point. By the analysis developed for the small plant, we can see that $SRMC_2$ is less (greater) than $LRMC$ at ouputs less (greater) than Ox_m. These relations are shown by $SRAC_2$ and MC_2 in Figure 7.5.2. We see therefore that the medium plant is that which achieves the least long-run average cost.

Using the same methods we can see in panel *c* that for the large plant short-run average cost equals long-run average cost and short-run marginal cost equals long-run marginal cost at output Ox_l (point L).

Exercise: The student should determine for himself from panel *c* that (a) $SRMC_s$ and *LRMC* lie above both average cost curves at output Ox_l; (b) the minimum point on $SRAC_s$ is attained at an output less than Ox_l; (c) $SRMC_s$ is less (greater) than *LRMC* at outputs less (greater) than Ox_l; (d) $SRAC_s$ is greater than *LRAC* at every output except Ox_l.

These relations are shown in Figure 7.5.2 as MC_3 and $SRAC_3$.

In the short run the entrepreneur must operate with one of the three sizes, large, medium, or small. But in the long run, he can build the plant whose size leads to least average cost for any given output. Thus he regards his long-run average cost curve as a planning device, because this curve shows the least cost of producing each possible output. An entrepreneur therefore is normally faced with a choice among quite a wide variety of plants. In Figure 7.5.3 six short-run average and marginal cost curves are shown; but this is really far from enough. Many curves could be drawn between each of those shown. These six curves are only representative of the wide variety that could be constructed.

These many curves generate *LAC* as a planning device. Suppose the entrepreneur thinks the output associated with point *A* in Figure 7.5.3 will be most profitable. He will build the plant represented by SAC_1

FIGURE 7.5.3

Average and Marginal Cost Curves

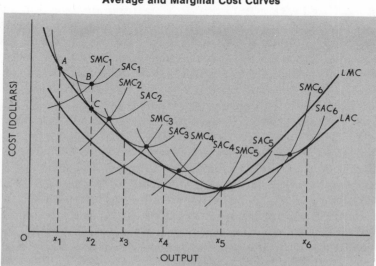

because it will enable him to produce this output at the least possible cost per unit. With the plant whose short-run average cost is given by SAC_1, unit cost could be reduced by expanding output to the amount associated with point B (Ox_2), the minimum point on SAC_1. If demand conditions were suddenly changed so this larger output were desirable, the entrepreneur could easily expand, and he would add to his profitability by reducing unit cost. Nevertheless, when setting his future plans the entrepreneur would decide to construct the plant represented by SAC_2 because he could reduce unit costs even more. He would operate at point C thereby lowering unit cost from the level at point B on SAC_1.

The long-run planning curve, LAC, is a locus of points representing the least unit cost of producing the corresponding output. The entrepreneur determines the size of plant by reference to this curve. He selects that short-run plant which yields the least unit cost of producing the volume of output he anticipates.

Figure 7.5.3 illustrates the following

Relations: (a) *LMC* intersects *LAC* when the latter is at its minimum point. One, and only one, short-run plant has minimum *SAC* that coincides with minimum *LAC* (SAC_s). SMC_s equals *LMC* at this common minimum. (b) At each output where a particular *SAC* is tangent to *LAC,* the relevant *SMC* equals *LMC*. At outputs below (above) the tangency output, the relevant *SMC* is less (greater) than *LMC*. (c) For all *SAC* curves the point of tangency with *LAC* is at an output less (greater) than the output of minimum *SAC* if the tangency is at an output less (greater) than that associated with minimum *LAC*.

7.6 CONCLUSION

The physical conditions of production and resource prices jointly establish the cost of production. If the set of technological possibilities changes, the cost curves change. Or if the prices of some factors of production change, the firm's cost curves change. Therefore, it should be emphasized that cost curves are generally drawn under the assumptions of *constant factor prices* and a *constant technology.*

While the cost of production is important to business firms and to the economy as a whole, it is only half the story. Cost gives one aspect of economic activity; to the individual businessman it comprises his obligation to pay out funds; to the society as a whole it represents the resources that must be sacrificed to obtain a given commodity. The other aspect is revenue or demand. To the individual businessman revenue constitutes the flow of funds from which his obligation may be met. To society, demand represents the social valuation placed on a commodity.

Thus both demand and cost must be taken into consideration. It is to this combination of demand and cost that we turn in Chapter 8.

7.7 ANALYTICAL EXERCISE

Consider an entrepreneur who, for simplicity, we shall assume produces a commodity by means of a fixed asset (capital) and one particular type of labor. At present, he has a fixed plant and he hires the labor he wants at a fixed market wage. The given technology and the given factor prices establish a set of short-run cost curves such, for example, as those shown in Figure 7.4.8.

FIGURE 7.7.1

Some Effects of Featherbedding

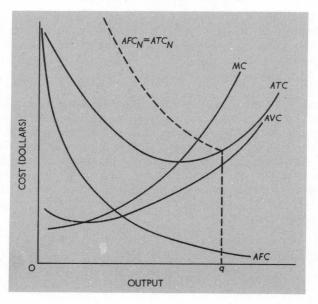

Now suppose the workers organize a labor union. They do not attempt to raise wages, but they are successful in obtaining an effective "featherbedding" contract; that is, the entrepreneur is required to *hire* at least x workers whether he *uses* them or not. What is the effect of the featherbedding contract on the short-run cost curves of this entrepreneur?

To get an answer, let us first note that to be effective featherbedding, the required x workers must equal or exceed the number of workers the entrepreneur would voluntarily choose to employ. Under these conditions, the entrepreneur has no *variable* cost and hence no *marginal* cost at all (that is, until more than x workers are employed). The *AVC* and *MC* curves are coincident with the horizontal axis until output exceeds the output producible in this plant by x workers.

Yet while variable and marginal cost decline to zero, average cost and average fixed cost must rise. Until $x + 1$ workers are hired, all the entrepreneur's costs are fixed costs. Thus the new AFC and ATC curves are identical over that range of output for which used labor is equal to or less than x workers.

The situation is illustrated schematically by means of Figure 7.7.1. The solid curves represent the short-run cost situation prior to featherbedding, where we assume that Oq units of output are produced by the full utilization of x workers. After featherbedding, MC and AVC simply become the line segment Oq. The new average fixed cost (AFC_N) equals the new average total cost (ATC_N) over the output range from zero to Oq. These new curves are represented by the dashed line, whose upward displacement from both AFC and ATC indicates that total cost has risen even though variable cost has declined.

QUESTIONS AND PROBLEMS

1. Return to Problem 1 at the end of Chapter 6. Total product is given; and you have computed average and marginal product. You are also given the following information:

    Total fixed cost (total price of fixed inputs) is $220 per period.
    Units of the variable input cost $100 per unit per period.
    Using this information, complete the following table:

Units of Variable Input	Product			Cost			Average Cost			Marginal Cost
	Total	Aver- age	Mar- ginal	Fixed	Vari- able	Total	Fixed	Vari- able	Total	
1...........	100									
2...........	250									
3...........	410									
4...........	560									
5...........	700									
6...........	830									
7...........	945									
8...........	1,050									
9...........	1,146									
10.........	1,234									
11.........	1,314									
12.........	1,384									
13.........	1,444									
14.........	1,494									
15.........	1,534									
16.........	1,564									
17.........	1,584									
18.........	1,594									

A. Graph the total cost curves on one sheet and the average and marginal curves on another.
B. By reference to table and graph, answer the following questions.
    1. When marginal product is increasing, what is happening to:
        a. Marginal cost?
        b. Average variable cost?
    2. When marginal cost first begins to fall, does average variable cost begin to rise?
    3. What is the relation between marginal cost and average variable cost when marginal and average product are equal?
    4. What is happening to average variable cost while average product is increasing?
    5. Where is average variable cost when average product is at its maximum? What happens to average variable cost after this point?
    6. What happens to marginal cost after the point it equals average variable cost?
        a. How does it compare with average variable cost thereafter?
        b. What is happening to marginal product thereafter?
        c. How does marginal product compare with average product thereafter?
    7. What happens to total fixed cost as output is increased?
    8. What happens to average fixed cost as:
        a. Marginal product increases?
        b. Marginal cost decreases?
        c. Marginal product decreases?
        d. Marginal cost increases?
        e. Average variable cost increases?
    9. How long does average fixed cost decrease?
    10. What happens to average total cost as:
        a. Marginal product increases?
        b. Marginal cost decreases?
        c. Average product increases?
        d. Average variable cost decreases?
    11. Does average cost increase:
        a. As soon as the point of diminishing marginal returns is passed?
        b. As soon as the point of diminishing average returns is passed?
    12. When does average cost increase? Answer this in terms of:
        a. The relation of average cost to marginal cost.
        b. The relation between the increase in average variable cost and the decrease in average fixed cost.

2. A student once was asked to show a cost schedule for a firm where "increasing returns" prevail. He gave the following schedule of average total cost:

Output	ATC
60 units	$15
70 units	12
80 units	8

What would you say to the student?

3. Explain why $SMC = LMC$ at the output where SAC is tangent to LAC, why $LMC > SMC$ at lower outputs, and why $LMC < SMC$ at greater outputs.

4. Is the recognition by entrepreneurs of implicit costs merely a theoretical abstraction, or do real-world businessmen actually take these costs into consideration?

5. In Figure E.7.1, LAC and LMC make up a firm's planning horizon. SAC_1, SAC_2, and SAC_3 are the only three plant sizes available. These are called Plant 1, Plant 2, and Plant 3.

FIGURE E.7.1

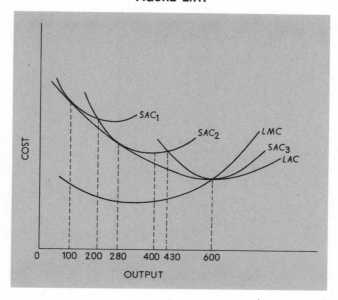

a. Draw accurately the short-run marginal cost curves associated with each plant. Recall the relation between short- and long-run marginal costs.

b. Plant 1 is designed to produce _____ units optimally, Plant 2 is designed to produce _____ units optimally, and Plant 3 is designed to produce _____ units optimally.

c. The firm would produce in Plant 1 any output below _____. It would produce any output between _____ and _____ in Plant 2.

d. SAC_2 attains its minimum at 400 units. Suppose there was another plant (say 4) that could produce 400 optimally. Would the average cost curve associated with this plant attain its minimum above, below or at 400 units?

e. The lowest possible per unit cost is attained at _____ units in

Plant _____. Why would the firm not use this plant to produce every other output, since this is least cost?

6. Fill in the blanks in the following Table:

Units of Output	Total Cost	Fixed Cost	Variable Cost	Average Fixed Cost	Average Variable Cost	Average Total Cost	Marginal Cost
1..........		$100	$ 900				
2..........					$850		
3..........							$ 700
4..........					$800		
5..........						$ 900	
6..........							$1,500
7..........			$7,900				
8..........						$1,300	
9..........	$14,000						

chapter

8

Theory of Price in Perfectly Competitive Markets

8.1 INTRODUCTION

In Chapter 2 we emphasized that supply and demand are the basic determinants of the price of goods. Since goods are produced by firms, an understanding of price theory requires an understanding of the firm's behavior. The two broad general topics covered in Chapters 3–7 supply the framework upon which the theory of the firm is based. *Demand* establishes the revenue side of business operation. *Production and cost* establish the supply conditions. Brought together, revenue and cost for the individual business firm and demand and supply for the entire market determine the market price and output of the firm and industry. Furthermore, as we shall see in this and subsequent chapters, these forces also determine the allocation of resources among industries.

Our analysis is based upon two fundamental assumptions:

8.1.a—Free Markets

First, we assume that each market is free and operates freely in the sense that no external control of market forces exists. One form of external control is governmental intervention—for example, farm crop controls, public utility regulations, or presidential threats to manufacturers. All such controls establish artificial market conditions to which business firms must adjust. Another type of control is collective behavior or collusion of firms in a market. Such behavior limits the free exercise of market forces.

While many markets are not free in the sense used here, a large number are. The object is to analyze the efficiency of resource allocation in free markets. In cases in which the market is not free, one may draw inferences concerning the relative efficiency of free as against controlled

233

markets. Thus the perfectly competitive market serves as a yardstick to measure the performance of other types of market structures.

8.1.b—Profit Maximization

The second fundamental assumption is that entrepreneurs try to maximize profits. This does not mean that businessmen may not be seekers after other goals. Nonetheless, a business cannot remain in business very long unless some profits are earned. It would be a very unusual businessman who treats profits in a cavalier fashion or who, other things remaining the same, prefers less profit to more. Notwithstanding several criticisms of the profit-maximization assumption, this assumption is the only one providing a general theory of firms, markets, and resource allocation that is successful both in explaining and predicting business behavior.

8.2   PERFECT COMPETITION

The theory of the firm set forth in this chapter is based upon the exacting concept of *perfectly competitive markets*. Perfect competition forms the basis of the most important and widely used model of economic behavior. The essence of perfect competition is that neither buyers nor producers recognize any competitiveness among themselves; no *direct* competition among economic agents exists.

The theoretical concept of competition is diametrically opposed to the businessman's concept of competition. For example, a businessman might maintain that the automobile industry or the cigarette industry is quite competitive since each firm in these industries must consider what its rivals will do before it makes a decision about advertising campaigns, design changes, quality improvements, and so forth.

That type of market is far removed from what the economist means when he speaks of perfect competition.[1] Perfect competition permits no personal rivalry (that is, personal in the sense that the firm considers the reaction of competitive firms in determining its own policy). All relevant economic magnitudes are determined by impersonal market forces.

Four important conditions define perfect competition. Taken together, these conditions guarantee a free, impersonal market in which the forces of demand and supply, or of revenue and cost, determine the allocation of resources and the distribution of income.

---

[1] This does not imply that the model of perfect competition is not relevant in predicting the consequences of a disturbance in an economy containing industries that are comprised of a few interdependent firms (economists call such industries oligopolistic). The competitive model is a useful approach to many problems in which the conditions differ from the assumptions set forth here.

8.2.a—Small Size, Large Numbers

First, perfect competition requires that every economic agent be so small, relative to the market as a whole, that it cannot exert a perceptible influence on price. From the standpoint of buyers this means that each consumer taken individually must be so unimportant he cannot obtain special considerations from the sellers. Perhaps the most familiar special consideration is the rebate, especially in the area of transportation services. But there can be many others, such as special credit terms to large buyers, or free additional services. None of these can prevail if the market is perfectly competitive.

From the seller's standpoint, perfect competition requires that each producer be so small he cannot affect market price by changes in his output. If all producers act collectively, changes in quantity will definitely affect market price. But if perfect competition prevails, each producer is so small that individual changes will go unnoticed. In other words, the actions of any individual firm do not affect market supply.

8.2.b—Homogeneous Product

A closely related provision is that the product of each seller in a perfectly competitive market must be identical to the product of every other seller. This ensures that buyers are indifferent as to the firm from which they purchase. Product differences, whether real or imaginary, are precluded by the existence of perfect competition.

In this context the word "product" has a much more detailed meaning than it does in ordinary conversation, where one might regard an automobile or a haircut as a product. For us, this is not adequate to describe a product: every changeable feature of the good must be included. When this is done it is possible to determine whether the market is characterized by a homogeneous, or perfectly standardized, commodity. If it is not, the producer who has a slightly differentiated product has a degree of control over the market and, therefore, over the price of his specific variety; he can thus affect market price by changes in his output. This condition is incompatible with perfect competition.

8.2.c—Free Mobility of Resources

A third precondition for perfect competition is that all resources are perfectly mobile—that each resource required can move in and out of the market very readily in response to pecuniary signals.

The condition of perfect mobility is an exacting one. First, it means that labor must be mobile, not only geographically but among jobs. The latter, in turn, implies that the requisite labor skills are few, simple, and easily learned. Next, free mobility means that the ingredient inputs are not monopolized by an owner or producer. Finally, free mobility means that new firms (or new capital) can enter and leave an industry without extraordinary difficulty. If patents or copyrights are required, entry is not free. Similarly, if vast investment outlays are required, entry certainly is not easy. If average cost declines over an appreciable range of output, established producers will have cost advantages that make entry difficult. In short, free mobility of resources requires free and easy entry and exit of firms into and out of an industry—a condition very difficult to realize in practice.

8.2.d—Perfect Knowledge

Consumers, producers, and resource owners must possess perfect knowledge if a market is to be perfectly competitive. If consumers are not fully cognizant of prices, they might buy at higher prices when lower ones are available. Then there will not be a uniform price in the market. Similarly, if laborers are not aware of the wage rates offered, they may not sell their labor services to the highest bidder. Finally, producers must know costs as well as price in order to attain the most profitable rate of output.

But this is only the beginning. In its fullest sense, perfect knowledge requires complete knowledge of the future as well as the present. In the absence of this omniscience, perfect competition cannot prevail.

The discussion to this point can be summarized by the following:

Characteristics: Perfect competition is an economic model of a market possessing the following characteristics: each economic agent is so small relative to the market that it can exert no perceptible influence on price; the product is homogeneous; there is free mobility of all resources, including free and easy entry and exit of business firms into and out of an industry; and all economic agents in the market possess complete and perfect knowledge.

8.2.e—Conclusion

Glancing at the four requirements above should immediately convince one that no market has been or can be perfectly competitive. Even in basic agricultural markets, where the first three requirements are frequently satisfied, the fourth is obviated by vagaries of weather conditions. One might therefore reasonably ask why such a palpably unrealistic model should be considered at all.

The answer can be given in as much or as little detail as desired. For our present purposes, it is brief. First, generality can be achieved only by means of abstraction. Hence no theory can be perfectly descriptive of real world phenomena. Furthermore, the more accurately a theory describes one specific real-world case the less accurately it describes all others. In any area of thought a theoretician does not select his assumptions on the basis of their presumed correspondence to reality; the conclusions, not the assumptions, are tested against reality.

This leads to a second point of great, if somewhat pragmatic, importance. The conclusions derived from the model of perfect competition have, by and large, permitted accurate explanation and prediction of real world phenomena. That is, perfect competition frequently works as a theoretical model of economic processes even though it does not accurately describe any specific industry. The most persuasive evidence supporting this assertion is the fact that despite the proliferation of more sophisticated models of economic behavior, economists today probably use the model of perfect competition in their research more than ever before.

8.3 PLANNING THE FIRM

At the beginning of Chapter 7 we assumed that a prospective entrepreneur was considering entry into an industry. We assumed that "demand conditions are such that he builds his plant to operate at a particular scale of production, and after the plant is built he operates in the short run." Assuming the industry is perfectly competitive, we can now examine the long-run conditions that determine the size plant he should build. We do this first because operating *plans* are based upon the long run, or planning horizon. It is only after these plans have congealed that a short-run situation exists. We therefore postpone analysis of the short run, in which the firm actually operates, until we analyze the long run, in which the entrepreneur chooses the specific short-run situation that is to be applicable.

8.3.a—Demand of a Firm in Perfect Competition

Suppose that panel *a*, Figure 8.3.1, depicts the equilibrium of the market for the perfectly competitive industry our prospective entrepreneur is planning to enter. Equilibrium price is Op_0 and quantity demanded and supplied Ox_0.

Let us say there are 50,000 firms of approximately the same size in the market. The entrepreneur recognizes that if he enters the industry at approximately the same size as existing firms, sales will rise by only $\frac{1}{500}$ of 1 percent. Such a change would be both graphically and *economically* so small as to have an imperceptible influence on price. The entrepreneur may assume with confidence that any variation in his own output and sales will have a negligible effect upon market price. Concerted action by a large number of sellers can influence market price; but one seller acting alone cannot. The individual firm may therefore assume that the demand curve facing *him* is a horizontal line at the level of price established by demand and supply equilibrium in the market.

The demand curve for any firm in this perfectly competitive industry is shown in panel *b*, Figure 8.3.1. Each producer knows that changes in

FIGURE 8.3.1

Derivation of Demand for a Perfectly Competitive Firm

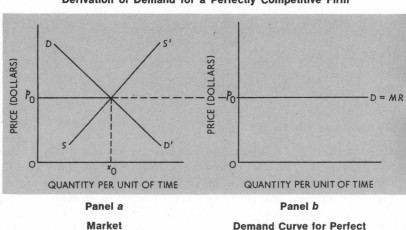

Panel *a*	Panel *b*
Market	Demand Curve for Perfect Competitor

his volume of output will have no perceptible effect upon market price. A change in his rate of sales per period of time will change his revenue, but it will not affect market price.

The producer in a perfectly competitive market, therefore, does not have to reduce his price in order to expand his rate of sales. Any number of units per period of time can be sold at the market equilibrium price. If he were to charge a higher price, he could sell nothing. A lower price would result in a needless loss of revenue. He thus charges the market price for whatever quantity he wishes to produce and sell.

Since price remains constant, each additional unit sold increases total revenue by its (constant) price. In this special case, therefore, price and marginal revenue are equal at every level of sales. Therefore, the demand curve and the marginal revenue curve are identical for a producer in a perfectly competitive market. For this reason, the curve in panel *b* is labeled $D = MR$. When the demand curve is horizontal, demand is said to be perfectly elastic.

Alternatively, recall from Chapter 2 that demand elasticity depends upon the number and closeness of substitutes. The product of a perfectly competitive firm has perfect substitutes—the products of all other firms in the industry. We would expect then that the demand elasticity for a firm's output would be infinite.

The results of this section may be summarized as follows:

Relations: The demand curve (also called the average revenue curve) for a producer in a perfectly competitive market is a horizontal line at the level of the market equilibrium price. The output decisions of the seller do not affect market price. In this case, the demand and marginal revenue curves are identical (that is, $D = AR = MR$); demand is perfectly elastic and the coefficient of price elasticity approaches infinity.[2]

8.3.b—Total Revenue, Total Cost, and Profit

In deciding the size plant to build, the entrepreneur attempts to achieve maximum profit, which is the difference between his total receipts from

TABLE 8.3.1

Revenue, Cost, and Profit

Market Price	Rate of Output and Sales	Total Revenue	Total Cost	Profit (TR − TC)
$5	1	$ 5	$17.00	$ −12.00
5	2	10	18.50	− 8.50
5	3	15	19.50	− 4.50
5	4	20	20.75	− 0.75
5	5	25	22.25	+ 2.75
5	6	30	24.25	+ 5.75
5	7	35	27.50	+ 7.50
5	8	40	32.50	+ 7.50
5	9	45	40.50	+ 4.50
5	10	50	52.50	− 2.50

selling the product (total revenue) and his total cost of producing it. Columns 3 and 4 of Table 8.3.1 show the long-run revenue and cost

---

[2] A perfectly elastic demand means that the coefficient of price elasticity increases without bound as the percentage change in price becomes smaller and smaller. Let us take a numerical example. Suppose the market equilibrium price is $5 and a particular producer is selling 1,000 units at that price. If he increased his price to $5.01, his sales would fall to zero. Thus

$$\frac{\Delta q}{q} = \frac{-1,000}{1,000} \text{ and } \frac{\Delta p}{p} = \frac{1}{500} \text{ ; so } \eta = 500.$$

If he increased the price to only $5.001, his sales would also fall to zero, and η would be 5,000. Thus one generalizes by saying that for infinitesimally small price changes the coefficient of price elasticity approaches infinity under conditions of perfect competition.

schedules of a hypothetical firm planning to enter an industry. Columns one and two show the market price and the attainable rates of output from which total revenue (price times output) is derived. Clearly maximum profit is $7.50, attained at an output of either seven or eight units. The entrepreneur would build his plant to produce either output. The seeming indeterminancy of the rate of output is attributable to the discrete data used in this hypothetical example.

Figure 8.3.2 (not related to Table 8.3.1) shows graphically the long-

FIGURE 8.3.2

Long-Run Cost, Total Revenue, and Profit

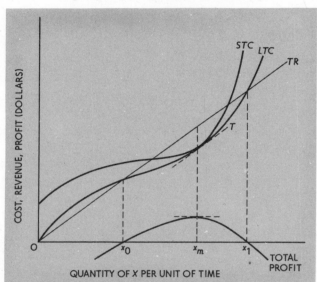

run total cost curve (or planning curve), the total revenue curve (at the prevailing market price), and the profit at each rate of output. The long-run cost curve is essentially the same as those discussed in Chapter 7. The slope of this curve at any point is marginal cost; the slope of a ray from the origin to the curve is average cost.

Total revenue is the price per unit of output (given supply and demand in the market) times the quantity of output. The *TR* line in Figure 8.3.2 indicates total revenue at each level of output. This curve begins at the origin (since at zero units sold, revenue is zero regardless of price), and it is a straight line (since under perfect competition price does not change regardless of the firm's output). The slope of the total revenue curve is, therefore, both price and marginal revenue.

Relations: Total revenue is price times quantity sold; $TR = px$. Average revenue is total revenue divided by output; $AR = \dfrac{TR}{x} = \dfrac{px}{x} = p$. Marginal revenue is the additional revenue from selling one more unit, or the slope of the total revenue curve; $MR = p$ since the additional revenue from one more unit is the market price of that unit.

In Figure 8.3.2 total profit $(TR - TC)$ is represented by the curve so labeled or by the vertical distance between the cost and revenue curves. Since total cost exceeds total revenue at outputs greater than Ox_1 and less than Ox_0, profit is negative over these ranges. At Ox_0 and Ox_1 total revenue equals total cost, and profit is zero. These are called break-even points; but remember that the entrepreneur's opportunity cost is included in total cost, so at the break-even points he makes the potential income of the next best use of his resources. From Ox_0 to Ox_1 profit is positive since total revenue exceeds total cost. This "pure profit" is in addition to his opportunity cost.

Profit is at a maximum when the total profit curve reaches its peak, when the vertical distance between TR and TC is the greatest (at output Ox_m). The maximum profit output occurs when the slope of a tangent (labeled T) to the total cost curve is equal to the slope of the total revenue curve; the vertical distance between total revenue and total cost is maximized.[3] The slope of total revenue being marginal revenue or price and the slope of total cost being marginal cost, maximum profit occurs where marginal cost equals marginal revenue (price).

This is a most important proposition for the theory of the firm under perfect competition. Any time an additional unit of output adds more to receipts than to the cost of production, the entrepreneur will increase his profit by producing it. For example, if producing one more unit adds $6 to cost and the firm can sell it for $7, the extra unit adds $1 to profit. It follows that the entrepreneur increases production so long as price exceeds marginal cost. On the other hand, if producing an additional unit adds more to cost than the price at which it can be sold, that unit would decrease profit and thus would not be produced. It follows, therefore, that the entrepreneur will not increase production when marginal cost exceeds price. At the output where marginal cost equals price, profit is a maximum and the entrepreneur has no incentive to change his level of production. The firm is in equilibrium; the entrepreneur would therefore choose to build a plant of such size as to produce Ox_m at minimum cost. This plant is represented by STC in Figure 8.3.2.

---

[3] Note that the slope of TC equals the slope of TR also at some output between zero and Ox_0. This output, however, would give a loss or negative profit (actually it would give the *largest* loss of any output less than Ox_0). With the assumption of perfect knowledge and profit maximization, no entrepreneur would choose this loss position when positive profits could be made at any output between Ox_0 and Ox_1.

8.3.c—Alternative Approach to Long-Run Planning

We can examine these relations using demand, long-run average cost, and long-run marginal cost. Table 8.3.2 shows the relevant schedules for

TABLE 8.3.2

Marginal Revenue, Marginal Cost, and Profit

Output and Sales	Marginal Revenue or Price	Marginal Cost	Average Cost	Unit Profit	Total Profit
1	$5.00	$17.00	$17.00	$ −12.00	$ −12.00
2	5.00	1.50	9.25	− 4.25	− 8.50
3	5.00	1.00	6.50	− 1.50	− 4.50
4	5.00	1.25	5.19	− 0.19	− 0.75
5	5.00	1.50	4.45	+ 0.55	+ 2.75
6	5.00	2.00	4.04	+ 0.96	+ 5.75
7	5.00	3.25	3.93	+ 1.07	+ 7.50
8	5.00	5.00	4.06	+ 0.94	+ 7.50
9	5.00	8.00	4.50	+ 0.50	+ 4.50
10	5.00	12.00	5.25	− 0.25	− 2.50

the situation set forth in Table 8.3.1; it indicates the same profit maximizing condition as before (any differences are because of rounding errors). Maximum profit again corresponds to seven or eight units of output. Unit profit is maximized at seven units of output, but this is immaterial inasmuch as the entrepreneur is concerned with total profit. Equilibrium is clearly where marginal cost equals price.

So long as the firm can sell an additional unit for more than the marginal cost of producing that unit, it can increase profit by producing one more. If the price is less than marginal cost the firm should not produce that unit, because it costs more to produce than would be gained from its sales.

Let us examine these relations graphically. Figure 8.3.3 specifies the same conditions as Figure 8.3.2 but using marginal and average curves rather than total curves. *LAC* and *LMC* are the long-run average and marginal cost curves. The vertical axes differ in scale, but the horizontal scales are the same. The demand curve indicates the market price (p_0) used in the preceding subsection.

The break-even outputs are Ox_0 and Ox_1. These occur where *LAC* equals price and are at the same break-even outputs shown in Figure 8.3.2. This is apparent when we note that $LAC = \dfrac{LTC}{x}$ and $p_0 = \dfrac{TR}{x}$, when $TR = LTC$, $LAC = p_0$.

Since the profit maximizing output Ox_m is that at which the slope of the total cost curve (marginal cost) equals the slope of the revenue curve

FIGURE 8.3.3

Profit Maximization by the Marginal Approach

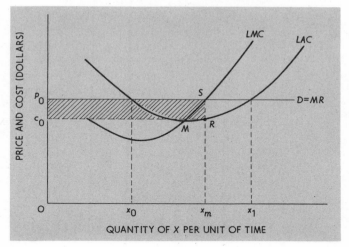

(price), $LMC = p_0$ at Ox_m in Figure 8.3.3. Note that the firm would not attempt to produce at the least unit cost (point M). At M price exceeds LMC; the firm can gain by producing more output. In Figure 8.3.3 total revenue (price times quantity) is given by the area of rectangle $O\,p_0\,S\,x_m$. Total cost (average cost times quantity) is given by the area of $O\,c_0\,R\,x_m$. Thus profit $(TR - TC)$ is given by the area of $c_0\,p_0\,S\,R$.

To summarize, the firm will plan to build its plant of such size that long-run marginal cost equals price. It will be the plant, of course, in which the desired rate of output can be produced for the least unit cost.

8.3.d—Zero and Negative Profit Solutions

Before developing the theory of the firm in the short run (after the entrepreneur builds his plant), let us analyze some alternative situations that may confront an entrepreneur planning to enter the industry. While our prospective entrepreneur was drawing his graphs and deciding upon the scale of operation, suppose other firms, lured by the prospect of profits, entered the industry and increased supply so much that market price fell. We assume for simplicity that all firms face the same cost curves and that the entry of new firms or output changes by old firms do not change costs.[4]

Figure 8.3.4 illustrates the planning situation now facing our prospec-

---

[4] We will drop this assumption later in the chapter when analyzing an industry's supply curve.

FIGURE 8.3.4

Zero and Negative Profit Solutions

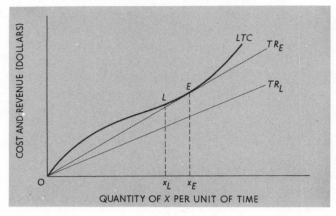

Panel *a*
Total Curves

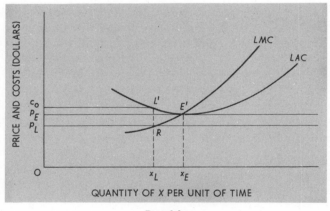

Panel *b*
Average Curves

tive entrepreneur at the new price Op_L, all cost conditions remaining the same as before. In panel *a* the new total revenue curve is TR_L, whose slope reflects the new lower price Op_L. As constructed, it lies below long-run total costs at each nonnegative output. At zero output the two are equal. At each positive output LTC exceeds TR_L and a loss results. The minimum loss *at a positive output* (that is, the least vertical distance between LTC and TR_L) occurs at output Ox_L, where the slope of LTC (MC) equals the slope of TR_L (Op_L). Zero output would lead neither to profit nor to loss; the firm would therefore choose not to enter the industry (that is, to produce zero output).

Panel *b* shows the same situation. Op_L lies below LAC at every output; no positive profit can result. The minimum loss at a positive output occurs at Ox_L, where $LMC = Op_L$. This loss is given by the area of the rectangle $p_L\, c_0\, L'\, R$, the difference between LTC and TR_L. It is once more clear that the firm would not be induced to enter the industry. In fact under the assumption that all firms have the same cost curves, some firms already in the industry would be induced to leave the industry.[5]

If an increase in the number of firms increases supply and lowers price, a decrease in the number of firms decreases supply and raises price. Firms are motivated to leave the industry until market price rises sufficiently to eliminate losses. Let us assume that price rises to Op_E, the slope of TR_E in panel *a*. Since LTC is tangent to TR_E at output Ox_E, total cost equals total revenue, and the firms in the industry make neither profit nor loss at this output. We are assuming, of course, that firms in the industry have sufficient time to make long-run adjustments and attain least cost output. At any other positive output LTC is greater than TR_E and losses would result. Since LTC is tangent to TR_E at Ox_E, $p = MC = $ minimum LAC.

These relations are apparent in panel *b*. Although no profit results, no firm is induced to leave since each makes its opportunity cost; neither is any other firm induced to enter since it would make only its opportunity cost, which presumably it makes already. Each firm is in a profit-maximizing equilibrium, since $LMC = p$; of course, the maximum pure profit is zero. The industry is also in equilibrium since $p = LAC$. Since maximum profit is zero pure profit, no firms leave the industry and none is induced to enter.

We will further analyze the long-run equilibrium of the firm and the industry later in this chapter. Before doing so, however, an analysis of the firm in the short run is in order.

8.4   SHORT-RUN EQUILIBRIUM OF A FIRM

Assume that the entrepreneur, rather than waiting for profits to be competed away, built a plant of optimal size when price was Op_0 and

---

[5] The student might note that we violate our assumption of perfect knowledge by positing that enough firms enter to drive the price down to Op_L. Why would a firm with perfect knowledge enter knowing full well it would make losses? We could assume that demand suddenly falls and drives price to Op_L. The explanation given, however, is more consistent with the model of long-run industry equilibrium to be analyzed later in this chapter.

The reason we know all firms are making losses is that the firms in the industry are operating in the short run and, except for the one point at which they are equal, short-run average cost is everywhere greater than long-run average cost. Thus if price is less than LAC it is also at least as far below SAC, if not further.

when profits were positive. He now operates in the short run, in which the rate of output per period of time can be expanded or diminished only by changing the rate of use of variable inputs. The firm can adjust its rate of output over a wide range subject only to the limitation imposed by its fixed inputs (generally, plant and equipment).

8.4.a—Short-Run Profit Maximization

The analysis of short-run profit maximization is essentially the same as that described for the long run. The firm produces where short-run marginal cost equals price, point E at output Ox_m in Figure 8.4.1. Pro-

FIGURE 8.4.1

Short-Run Equilibrium

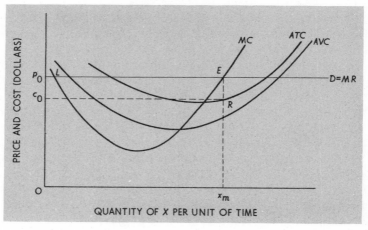

ducing another unit would add more to costs than the firm would receive from the sale of that unit; MC exceeds MR. The firm would not stop short of output Ox_m, however, since at lesser outputs producing another unit adds more to revenue than to cost; MR exceeds MC. Total cost is the area Oc_0Rx_m; total revenue is the area Op_0Ex_m; profit is the difference, the area c_0p_0ER. The firm makes a positive profit.

Note that at point L in Figure 8.4.1 marginal cost also equals price. That is not, however, a point of equilibrium since the firm would not choose to produce this output under the circumstances depicted. In the first place, average cost exceeds price at this output so losses would occur, whereas at some other outputs profits could be realized. Second, the firm could clearly gain by producing an additional unit. Price is greater than marginal cost; thus the firm would be motivated to increase output.[6]

8.4.b—Profit, Loss, and the Firm's Short-Run Supply Curve

The equality of price and short-run marginal cost guarantees either that profit is a maximum or that loss is a minimum. Whether a profit is made or a loss incurred can be determined only by comparing price and average total cost at the equilibrium rate of output. If price exceeds unit cost, the entrepreneur enjoys a short-run profit; on the other hand, if unit cost exceeds price, a loss is suffered.

Figure 8.4.2 illustrates four possible short-run situations for the firm.

FIGURE 8.4.2

Profit, Loss, or Ceasing Production in the Short Run

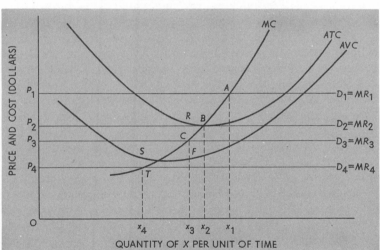

First, the market established price may be Op_1; the firm settles at point A where $MC = Op_1$, produces Ox_1 units, and since ATC is less than price, receives a profit. Second, market price may be Op_2. MC now equals price at point B; the firm produces Ox_2. Since B is the lowest point on ATC, the firm makes neither profit nor loss. Third, if price is Op_3, the

---

[6] Economists say that $MC = P$ is the *necessary* or first order condition for profit maximization and that the second order condition is that where $MC = P$, MC must be positively sloped. The two conditions together are *necessary* and *sufficient* for profit maximization.

firm produces Ox_3; price equals MC at C. Because average cost is greater than price at the optimal output, total cost is greater than total revenue, and the firm suffers a loss. That loss is CR times Ox_3.

When demand is $D_3 = MR_3$, there is simply no way the firm can earn a profit. At every output level average total cost exceeds price. If output were either smaller or greater than Ox_2 units per period of time, the loss would be greater. One might, therefore, ask why the firm does not close down its plant since a loss is incurred at any rate of output.

The basic answer to this question is that an entrepreneur incurring a loss in the short run will continue to produce if, and only if, he loses less by producing than by closing the plant entirely. Remember there are two types of costs in the short run: fixed costs and variable costs. The fixed costs cannot be changed and are incurred whether the plant is operated or not. Fixed costs are unavoidable in the short run and are the same at zero output as at any other.

Therefore, at zero output total revenue would be zero also and total cost would be the total fixed cost. The loss would thus be the amount of total fixed costs. If the firm can produce where $MC = MR$, and if at this output total revenue is greater than total variable cost, a smaller loss is suffered when production takes place. The firm covers all of its variable cost and some revenue is left over to cover a part of fixed cost. The loss is that part of fixed cost not covered and is clearly less than the entire fixed cost.

Returning to Figure 8.4.2 one can see more easily why the firm in the short run would produce at C and not shut down. The firm loses CR dollars per unit produced. However, variable cost is not only covered but there is an excess of CF dollars per unit sold. The excess of price over average variable cost, CF, can be applied to fixed costs. Thus, not all of the fixed costs are lost, as would be the case if production were discontinued. Although a loss is sustained, it is smaller than the loss associated with zero output.

This is not always the case, however. Suppose market price is Op_4, so demand is given by $D_4 = MR_4$. If the firm produced, its equilibrium would be at T where $MC = Op_4$. Output would be Ox_4 units per period of time. Here, however, the average variable cost of production exceeds price. Not only would the firm lose all of its fixed costs, it would also lose ST dollars per unit on its variable costs as well. The firm could improve its earnings situation by producing nothing and losing only fixed cost. Thus when price is below average variable cost, the short-run equilibrium output is zero.

As shown in Chapter 7, average variable cost reaches its minimum at the point at which marginal cost and average variable cost intersect. If price is less than the minimum average variable cost, the loss-minimizing output is zero. For price equal to or greater than minimum average variable cost, equilibrium output is determined by the intersection of marginal cost and the price line.

Principles: (1) Marginal cost tells *how much* to produce, given the choice of a positive output; the firm produces the output for which $MC = P$. (2) Average variable cost tells *whether* to produce; the firm ceases to produce if price falls below minimum *AVC*. (3) Average total cost tells how much profit or loss is made if the firm decides to produce; profit equals the difference between P and *ATC* multiplied by the quantity produced and sold.

Using the principles just discussed, it is possible to derive the short-run supply curve of an individual firm in a perfectly competitive market. The process is illustrated in Figure 8.4.3. Panel *a* shows the marginal cost

FIGURE 8.4.3

Derivation of the Short-Run Supply Curve of an Individual Producer in Perfect Competition

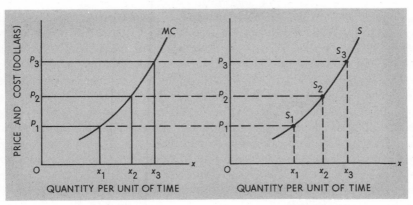

Panel *a*
Positons of Short-Run
Equilibria for the Firm

Panel *b*
Equilibrium Quantities Supplied
by the Firm

curve of a firm for rates of output greater than that associated with minimum average variable cost. Suppose market price is Op_1, the corresponding equilibrium rate of output is Ox_1. Now, find on panel *b* the point associated with the coordinates Op_1, Ox_1. Label this point S_1; it represents the quantity supplied at price Op_1.

Next, suppose price were Op_2. In this case, equilibrium output would be Ox_2. Plot the point associated with the coordinates Op_2, Ox_2 on panel *b*—it is labeled S_2. Similarly, other equilibrium quantities supplied can be determined by postulating other market prices (for example, price Op_3 leads to output Ox_3 and point S_3 on panel *b*). Connecting all the

S-points so generated one obtains the short-run supply curve of the firm, the curve labeled S in panel *b*. But by construction, the S-curve is precisely the same as the *MC* curve. The following is thus established:

Proposition: The short-run supply curve of a firm in perfect competition is precisely its marginal cost curve for all rates of output equal to or greater than the rate of output associated with minimum average variable cost. For market prices lower than minimum average variable cost, equilibrium quantity supplied is zero.

8.4.c—Short-Run Industry Supply Curve

In earlier chapters it was shown that market demand is simply the horizontal sum of the demand curves of all buyers in the market. Deriving the short-run industry supply curve may not be such an easy matter.

As you will recall from Chapter 7, the short-run marginal cost curve of a firm is derived under the assumption that the unit prices of the variable inputs are fixed; no change by the individual firm acting alone can change a factor's unit cost to the firm. This seems a reasonable assumption under perfect competition because one firm is usually so small, relative to all users of the resource, that variations in its rate of purchase will not affect the market price of the resource. In other words, many resource markets are more or less perfectly competitive, at least on the buying side. Thus production, and therefore resource use, can frequently be expanded in one firm without affecting the market price of the resource.

But when *all* producers in an industry *simultaneously* expand output there may be a marked effect upon the resource market. For example, one small cotton textile manufacturer could probably expand his production by 10 percent or even 100 percent without affecting the world price of raw cotton. The few additional bales he might purchase would not have a significant effect on the total demand for raw cotton. If all cotton textile manufacturers in the United States simultaneously attempt to expand output by 10 percent, however, the demand for cotton would probably increase substantially and the resulting increase in the price of cotton would be significant. When all manufacturers attempt to increase output, raw cotton prices are bid up; and the increase in the price of a variable factor of production (raw cotton) causes an increase in all firms' cost curves, including marginal cost.

As a consequence, the industry supply curve usually cannot be obtained by summing horizontally the marginal cost curves of each producer. As industry output expands, input prices normally increase, thereby shifting each marginal cost curve to the left. A great deal of information would be required to obtain the exact supply curve. However, one may generally presume that the industry supply curve is somewhat more steeply sloped and somewhat less elastic when input prices increase in response to an increase in output. In this case, the concept of a competitive industry supply curve is less precise. Nonetheless, doubt is not cast upon the basic fact that in the short run, quantity supplied varies directly with price. The latter is all one needs to draw a positively sloped market supply curve.

8.4.d—Summary of the Short Run

Given the market demand and supply curves, a short-run market price-quantity equilibrium is attained at the price that equates quantity demanded and quantity supplied. The market equilibrium price establishes the horizontal demand or marginal revenue curve for firms in the industry. If the firm produces at all, it attains its profit-maximizing (or loss-minimizing) output where price equals marginal cost. When, at this output, average total cost is greater (less) than price, the firm makes a loss (profit). When average total cost equals price, neither profit nor loss is made. However, when price is below the minimum average variable cost, the firm ceases production in the short run and loses only its fixed costs.

Note: We have now established the process for deriving industry demand and supply curves. The student should return to Chapter 2 to recall how these curves are used in the economic analysis of industry equilibrium and the analysis of comparative static changes.

8.5 LONG-RUN EQUILIBRIUM IN A PERFECTLY COMPETITIVE MARKET

Since all inputs are variable in the long run, an entrepreneur has the option of adjusting his plant size, as well as his output, in order to achieve maximum profit. In the limit, he can liquidate his business entirely and transfer his resources and his command over resources into a more profitable investment alternative. But just as established firms may leave the industry, new firms may enter the industry if profit prospects are brighter than elsewhere. Indeed, adjustment of the number of firms in the industry in response to profit motivation is the key element in establishing long-run equilibrium.

8.5.a—Long-Run Adjustment of an Established Firm

We have already discussed the firm that is contemplating entry into an industry and is deciding what scale plant to build. We have seen that he will build so as to produce at least unit cost the output at which long-run marginal cost equals price. In the long run, an established firm can adjust plant size, and therefore rate of output, in order to attain maximum profit.

Consider a firm in a short-run situation in which it incurs a loss. In looking to the long run, or the planning horizon, the entrepreneur has two options: he can go out of business or he can construct a plant of more suitable size. By the now familiar argument maximum profit is obtained by producing the rate of output in the plant of such size that long-run marginal cost equals price. You will recall that long-run marginal cost shows the addition to total cost attributable to the addition of one unit of output, after plant size has been adjusted so as to produce that rate of output at minimum achievable unit cost.

8.5.b—Long-Run Adjustment of the Industry

The process of attaining long-run equilibrium in a perfectly competitive industry is illustrated in Figure 8.5.1. Suppose each firm in the industry is identical. Its size is represented by SAC_1 and SMC_1 in panel b. The market demand curve is given by DD' in panel a, and the market supply is S_1S_1'. Market equilibrium establishes the price of Op_1 per unit and total output and sales of OX_1 units per period of time. At price Op_1 each plant is built to produce Ox_1 units (the output at which $Op_1 = LMC$) at least possible cost (x_1B). Each firm receives a profit of AB per unit of output. The number of firms multiplied by Ox_1 (each firm's output) equals OX_1 (total output). Although each firm is in equilibrium, the industry itself is not. As we saw earlier in this chapter the appearance of *pure economic profit,* a return in excess of that obtainable elsewhere,

FIGURE 8.5.1

Long-Run Equilibrium Adjustment in a Perfectly Competitive Industry

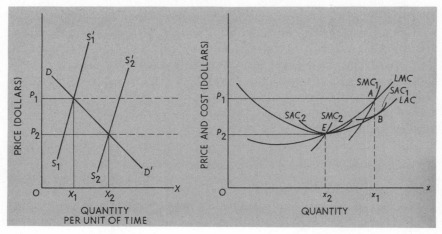

Panel *a*	Panel *b*
Long-Run Market Equilibrium	**Long-Run Equilibrium Adjustment of a Firm**

attracts new firms into the industry, expanding industry supply (say) to S_2S_2' and reducing market price. The process of new entry might be very slow, or it might be very fast. It depends primarily upon the liquid assets in other industries. In any event, as time elapses new firms will enter the industry, thereby shifting the supply curve to the right.

When each firm adjusts optimally to the new market price, the output of each will be smaller. The larger number of firms accounts for the increase in output from OX_1 to OX_2 in panel a. Now all firms produce the output at which Op_2 equals LMC at output Ox_2. The number of old firms plus the number of new entrants times Ox_2 equals OX_2. Since the new price equals LMC and SMC_2 at E, the minimum LAC and the minimum SAC_2, neither profit nor loss is present for any firm. Both the industry and its firms are in long-run equilibrium.

8.5.c—Long-Run Equilibrium in a Perfectly Competitive Firm

This position of long-run equilibrium is inevitable from and is embodied in the assumption of profit maximization and free entry. Each firm strives to achieve the maximum possible profit. In the short run a firm in perfect competition can do nothing more than adjust its output so that marginal cost equals price. In the long run it can adjust the size of its plant and it can select the industry in which it operates, both with an eye to profit.

The long-run equilibrium position of a firm in a perfectly competitive industry is explained by Figure 8.5.2. As we have seen, if price is above Op, each established firm can adjust plant size and earn a pure profit. New firms are attracted into the industry, shifting the supply curve to the right. Price falls, and hence the horizontal demand curve facing each firm, old and new, falls also. All firms readjust. If "too many" firms enter, market price and each firm's horizontal demand curve may fall below Op. Each firm incurs a loss. As their plants and equipment depreciate, some firms will leave the industry, thereby causing the market supply curve to shift to the left. Market price and, accordingly, the horizontal individual demand curves rise.

So long as the cost curves do not change, the only conceivable point of long-run equilibrium occurs at point E in Figure 8.5.2. Each firm in the industry receives neither profit nor loss. There is no incentive for further entry because the rate of return in this industry is the same as in the best alternative. But for the same reason there is no incentive for a firm to leave the industry. The number of firms stabilizes, each firm with a short-run plant represented by SAC and SMC. Note, however, that the entrepreneur is covering his opportunity costs, since these are included in the cost curves. We say the firm earns "normal" profit, but not pure profit.

Firms will enter or leave the industry if there is either pure profit or

FIGURE 8.5.2

Long-Run Equilibrium of a Firm in a Perfectly Competitive Industry

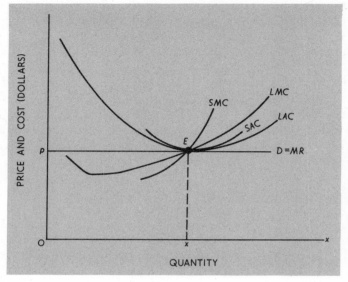

pure loss. Therefore, since the position of long-run equilibrium must be consistent with *zero* profit (and zero loss), it is necessary that price equal average cost. For a firm to attain its individual equilibrium, price must be equal to marginal cost. Therefore, price must equal both marginal and average total cost. This can occur only at the point where average and marginal cost are equal, or at the point of minimum average total cost.[7]

---

[7] Some students may object to the model of long-run equilibrium at the minimum point of each firm's long-run average cost curve on the grounds that the model is based upon the assumption that each firm is exactly like every other firm; that is, each firm's cost curve is the same as that of every other firm. We have made that assumption for simplicity; theory does not require it. To see why the assumption is not necessary, one must understand that any differences in cost are due to differences in the productivity of one or more resources. Assume that all firms except one are alike; that firm, because of (say) a more favorable location, has a lower cost curve. The owner of that location (he might be the owner of the firm) could raise the rent to the firm (if the owner, his opportunity cost would rise) up to the point at which the firm's pure profit disappears. The firm would be motivated to pay the rent since the owner of the firm would still make the equivalent of his best alternative. If he did not pay that rent, some other firm would.

Thus the cost of the previously lower cost firm would tend to rise because of increased rent. It would not, of course, rise above those of other firms because any higher rent would occasion losses; hence no firm would pay it. The same type of argument applies to the superiority of other specialized resources, including the superiority of management. If a superior manager, even a manager-owner, could

The statement, so far, could conceivably apply to any *SAC* and *SMC*. However, unless it applies only to the short-run plant that coincides with minimum long-run average cost, a change in plant size would lead to the appearance of pure profit, and the wheels of adjustment would be set in motion again. These arguments establish the following:

Proposition: Long-run equilibrium for a firm in perfect competition occurs at the point where price equals minimum long-run average cost. At this point minimum short-run average cost equals minimum long-run average cost, and the short- and long-run marginal costs are equal. The position of long-run equilibrium is characterized by a "no profit" situation —the firms have neither a pure profit nor a pure loss, only an accounting profit equal to the rate of return obtainable in other perfectly competitive industries.

8.6 APPLICATION AND EVIDENCE: PROFIT IN DEFENSE INDUSTRIES

The theory developed in this chapter predicts that when profit is "abnormally" high in one sector of the economy, firms will enter that business, drive down prices, and eliminate the above-normal profit, so long as entry is reasonably free. However, we frequently hear about the vast profits being made in some businesses over long periods of time even in the face of free entry. Admittedly no industry exhibits all the characteristics of perfect competition, but the logic of the theory should fit much of the economy. The principal industries in which we hear of "excessive" or "exorbitant" profit over a long period are the defense industries. During times of war or preparation for war the "war profiteers" are allegedly free from competition, otherwise their profits would be competed away. On the other hand, possibly the defense industries do fit our theory. Let us analyze the validity of this point.

When we hear of the profits in the defense establishment we might wonder why investors, induced by these profits, do not change some of their capital from non-defense oriented industry to defense. The resulting increase in capacity, according to our theory, would drive down prices and eliminate the excess profit. The defense industries allegedly have been prospering since World War II. Surely that is sufficient time for entry to have taken place. Only three explanations seem possible. First, government prevents entry. Second, risks are greater in defense industry than elsewhere, and the larger returns are necessary to compensate for

---

lower his firm's costs, he could presumably lower the costs of other firms as well. His hiring price would be bid up, or if he is the owner, his opportunity cost would rise. At equilibrium all firms' long-run average cost curves would, therefore, reach their low points at the same cost (albeit not necessarily at the same output), and no firm would make pure profit or loss (although some might have differing factor payments or rents).

increased risk. Third, the allegation is not correct. It does not seem logical that government, the purchaser, would protect a monopoly position in defense. Therefore, let us examine the evidence to obtain a solution.

In a paper by George J. Stigler and Claire Friedland considerable evidence in this area was presented.[8] The first piece of evidence is the report of 40 major defense contractors on their rates of return from both defense and commercial or non-defense business. From 1958 through 1961, the average return from defense contracts exceeded the average return from non-defense. Furthermore, the average defense oriented return was greater than the average return of the Federal Trade Commission–Securities and Exchange Commission universe of the returns for 3,500 companies. From 1962 through 1968 the average defense rate of return of the 40 defense contractors was less than both the return of these firms from commercial business and the average rate of return of the (FTC–SEC) 3,500 companies. In the last year of the sample, 1968, the defense return averaged 6.8 percent while the 3,500-firm average return was 10.2 percent. Note that the latter years included the period of the vast Viet Nam buildup.

The relative performances of all stocks and the stocks of the major defense contractors point in essentially the same direction. Investments in the defense contractors were almost twice as profitable as the average return from investment in all stocks on the New York Stock Exchange during the 1950s. During the 1960s investments in the major defense contractors did approximately as well as the average investment in all stocks. The correlation of stock market performance with the ratio of defense to total sales shows a positive relation ($r^2 = .295$ for 52 companies) in the 1950s and no relation ($r^2 = .00008$) for the leading defense contractors of 1959 for the 1960s.[9] Recall from the statistical appendix that r^2 is the percentage of variation in the dependent variable associated with variation in the independent variable(s).

From the evidence, it appears that the profitability of defense was higher than normal in the 1950s but that entry (or something) competed away the above normal profits in the 1960s. We do not know if entry into defense is blocked but there is some evidence that the defense industry is riskier than non-defense. Stigler and Friedland found a positive correlation between instability of sales over time for a company and the company's share of business devoted to defense. It seems, however, that defense industry has performed in somewhat the way we would predict: early profits were competed away in the long run.

One might wish to argue that the Renegotiation Board, established by the government in 1951 to keep defense contractors from obtaining "un-

---

[8] George J. Stigler and Claire Friedland, "Profits of Defense Contractors," *American Economic Review*, Sept. 1971, pp. 692–94.

[9] Ibid.

usual" profits from their activities, could have altered the results. However, this board was in effect during almost all the periods examined here, and profits were both high and low during this time. In any case, some evidence obtained by A. M. Agopos and Lowell E. Galloway indicated that the Renegotiation Board, designed to keep down defense profits, may have had little or no effect, and, if there was an effect at all, it was to increase defense profit.[10] Agopos and Galloway tested the hypothesis that the Renegotiation Board had a significant effect upon profit in the aerospace industry over the periods 1942–67. They included a dummy variable in the profit estimating equation for the time in which the board was in operation. The board variable for profit before taxes and renegotiation was *positive and significant* at the five percent level. The board variable for profit after taxes and renegotiation was not significantly different from zero. These results seem to indicate that the presence of the board led to inflated profits by contractors, knowing the board would cut them back.

In addition Agapos and Galloway found that aerospace profits did not respond positively to large increases in defense spending relative to total national product, other than during World War II and the Korean War. In particular the Viet Nam involvement had no significant effect on defense profit in aerospace. This added evidence from one industry reinforces the above evidence for many industries. When large profits exist, firms enter the industry and compete them down to normal, just as our theory predicts.

8.7 CONSTANT AND INCREASING COST INDUSTRIES

The analysis of Section 8.5 was based upon the tacit assumption of "constant cost," in the sense that expanded resource usage does not entail an increase in resource prices. To carry the analysis further, and to make it more explicit, both constant and increasing cost industries are examined in this subsection. The phenomenon of decreasing cost is not examined inasmuch as it is not consistent with all the requirements of perfect competition.

8.7.a—Constant-Cost Industries

Long-run equilibrium and long-run supply price under conditions of constant cost are explained by Figure 8.7.1. Panel *a* shows the long- and short-run conditions of each firm in the industry, while panel *b* depicts the market as a whole. D_1D_1' and S_1S_1' are the original market demand and

---

[10] A. M. Agapos and Lowell E. Galloway, "Defense Profits and the Renegotiation Board in the Aerospace Industry," *Journal of Political Economy*, Sept./Oct. 1970, pp. 1093–1105.

FIGURE 8.7.1

**Long-Run Equilibrium and Supply Price in a Perfectly Competitive
Industry Subject to Constant Cost**

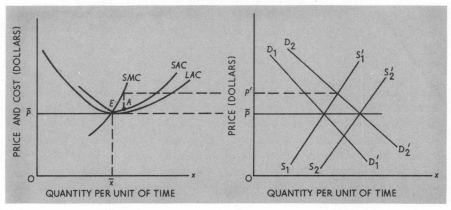

Panel *a*	Panel *b*
Long-Run Equilibrium of the Firm	**Long-Run Market Equilibrium**

supply curves, establishing a market equilibrium price of $O\bar{p}$ dollars per
unit. We assume that the industry has attained a position of long-run
equilibrium, so the position of each firm in the industry is depicted by
panel *a*—the price line is tangent to the long- and short-run average cost
curves at their minimum points.

Now suppose demand increases to $D_2 D_2'$. Instantaneously, with the
number of firms fixed, the price will rise to Op' and each firm will move to
equilibrium at point A. However, at point A each firm earns a pure
economic profit inasmuch as price exceeds average cost. New entrants are
thereby attracted into the industry; the industry supply curve shifts to
the right. In this case we assume that all resources used are so general
that increased usage in this industry does not affect the market price of
resources. As a consequence, the entrance of new firms does not increase
the costs of existing firms; the *LAC* curve of established firms does not
shift and new firms can operate with an identical *LAC* curve. Long-run
equilibrium adjustment to the shift in demand is accomplished when the
number of firms expands to the point at which $S_2 S_2'$ is the industry supply
curve.

In other words, since output can be expanded by expanding the num-
ber of firms producing $O\bar{x}$ units per period of time at average cost $O\bar{p}$,
the industry has a constant long-run supply price equal to $O\bar{p}$ dollars per
unit. If price were above this level, firms of size represented by *SAC*
would continue to enter the industry in order to reap the pure profit
obtainable. If price were less than $O\bar{p}$, some firms would ultimately leave

the industry to avoid the pure economic loss. Hence in the special case in which an expansion of resource usage does not lead to an increase in resource price, the long-run industry supply price is constant. This is precisely the meaning of a constant-cost industry.

Exercise: The student should carry out the same type of analysis for a decrease in demand.

8.7.b—Increasing-Cost Industries

An increasing-cost industry is depicted in Figure 8.7.2. The original situation is the same as in Figure 8.7.1. The industry is in a position of long-run equilibrium. D_1D_1' and S_1S_1' are the market demand and supply curves respectively. Equilibrium price is Op_1. Each firm operates at point E_1, where price equals minimum average cost, both long- and short-run cost. Thus each firm is also in a position of long-run equilibrium.

Let demand shift to D_2D_2' so that price instantaneously rises to a much higher level. The higher price is accompanied by pure economic profit; new firms are consequently attracted into the industry. The usage of resources expands, and now, we assume, resource price expands with resource usage. The cost of inputs therefore increases for the established firms as well as for the new entrants. As a result the entire set of cost curves shifts upward, say to a position represented by LAC_2 in panel a.[11]

Naturally, the process of equilibrium adjustment is not instantaneous. The LAC curve gradually shifts upward as new entrants gradually join the industry. As shown in Figure 8.7.2, the marginal cost curves of all firms shift to the left as new firms enter and bid up factor prices. Thus two forces tend to work in opposite directions upon the industry's supply curve. Shifting marginal cost to the left tends to shift the industry's supply curve to the left. However, new firms enter the industry, and this tends to shift industry supply to the right. The forces causing a shift to the right (entry) must dominate those causing a shift to the left (rise in marginal costs); otherwise total output could not expand as dictated by the increase in market price.

To see why supply must shift to the right after an increase in demand, let us assume that the opposite happens. In Figure 8.7.2 demand, as before, shifts to D_2D_2'. In the short run price and quantity increase along with profits. The profits attract new firms who, upon entering, bid up resource prices. All cost curves rise as indicated in panel a. Suppose, how-

---

[11] As Figure 8.7.2 is constructed, the minimum point on LAC shifts to the left as LAC shifts upward. In fact, minimum LAC can correspond to either a smaller or a larger output. The analysis underlying the exact nature of the shift involves an advanced concept not treated in this text. For a detailed treatment, see C. E. Ferguson and Thomas R. Saving, "Long-Run Scale Adjustments of a Perfectly Competitive Firm and Industry," *American Economic Review*, December 1969, pp. 774–83.

Figure 8.7.2

**Long-Run Euilibrium and Supply Price in a Perfectly Competitive Industry
Subject to Increasing Cost**

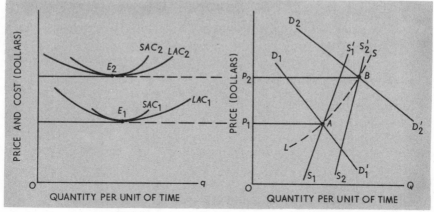

Panel *a*	Panel *b*
Long-Run Equilibrium of the Firm	**Long-Run Market Equilibrium**

ever, that the leftward shift in all marginal cost curves dominates the
tendency for an increase in supply caused by entry. Therefore, the new
supply curve would lie somewhere to the left of S_1S_1'. If demand remains
D_2D_2', price must be greater than Op_2; firms must be making pure profits;
entry must continue. If the same process reoccurs, price will rise further,
costs will rise, profits will continue, and entry will be further encouraged.
Thus a leftward shift in supply is not consistent with equilibrium. At
some point the entry of new firms must dominate the increase in costs,
and supply must shift to the right, though not by as much as it would in
a constant cost industry, since under constant costs no shift in marginal
costs occurs.

The process of adjustment must continue until a position of full long-
run equilibrium is attained. In Figure 8.7.2, this is depicted by the intersection of D_2D_2' and S_2S_2', establishing an equilibrium price of Op_2
dollars per unit. Each firm produces at point E_2, where price equals minimum average cost. The important point to emphasize is that in constant
cost industries new firms enter until price returns to the unchanged level
of minimum, long-run average cost. For industries subject to increasing
cost, new firms enter until minimum long-run average cost shifts upward
to equal the new price.

In the transition from one long-run equilibrium to the other, the long-
run supply price increases from Op_1 to Op_2. This is precisely what is
meant by an increasing-cost industry. In keeping with this, the long-run
industry supply curve is given by a line joining such points as A and B

in panel *b*, *LS*. Thus an increasing cost industry is one with a positively sloped long-run supply curve. Alternatively stated, after all long-run equilibrium adjustments are made, an increasing cost industry is one in which an increase in output requires an increase in long-run supply price.

The result of this section can be summarized as follows:

Relations: Constant or increasing cost in an industry depends entirely upon the way in which resource prices respond to expanded resource usage. If resource prices remain constant, the industry is subject to constant cost; if resource prices increase, the industry is one of increasing cost. The long-run supply curve for a constant-cost industry is a horizontal line at the level of the constant long-run supply price. The long-run industry supply curve under conditions of increasing cost is positively sloped, and the long-run supply price increases as long-run equilibrium quantity supplied expands.

8.8 APPLICATION: TECHNOLOGICAL EXTERNALITIES IN THE NORTHERN LOBSTER INDUSTRY

Some interesting but peculiar examples of increasing cost industries are those industries that use a free but scarce resource. That is, there is no charge made for the resources, but the quantity is limited. Two of these are fishing and lobstering. An interesting paper by Frederick W. Bell analyzed the peculiarities of the Northern Lobster industry.[12] A summary of Bell's findings will serve to explain the way in which free but scarce resources can change the theoretical results set forth above.

The production function of the New England lobster industry is related to the total effort put into fishing. With no fishing there is a maximum lobster population consistant with food, space, and other aspects of the environment. When man intervenes, the natural rate of change in the number of lobsters is affected by the total fishing effort; the more fishing, the smaller the lobster population. But, as the lobster population is decreased, the average catch decreases. Thus, there is a specific quantity of fishing effort associated with a maximum sustainable yield, measured in weight of lobsters caught. Any additional fishing reduces the weight of lobsters caught such that the yield decreases.

Bell estimated an empirical production function for the industry with the total catch dependent upon fishing effort, represented by the total number of traps fished in a year.[13] This production function is graphed in Figure 8.8.1. The catch increases until slightly more than one million

---

[12] Frederick W. Bell, "Technological Externalities and Common-Property Resources: An Empirical Study of the Northern Lobster Industry," *Journal of Political Economy,* Jan./Feb. 1972, pp. 148–58. The remainder of this section is based upon that paper.

[13] He found that average water temperature also affects the catch.

FIGURE 8.8.1

Production Function for Northern Lobster Industry

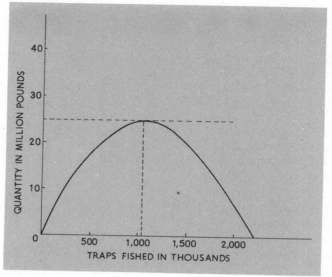

traps are used, and about 25 million pounds of lobster are caught. After that the quantity declines with the number of traps. Thus, 25 million is the maximum sustainable yield (*MSY*).

The empirical long-run marginal and average cost curves for the industry are shown in Figure 8.8.2. Total cost increases with the number of traps fished. Therefore, average cost increases until 25 million pounds, the *MSY* given by the production function. Since quantity falls thereafter with the number of traps, the average cost curve bends backward at 25 million. Marginal cost rises and asymptotically approaches *MSY*.

Since the northern lobster industry accounts for only 14 percent of world lobster sales, lobster prices can be taken as given. The industry will produce where price equals average cost. If at a given price, quantity is such that average cost is below price the profit will entice entry and increase quantity until average cost equals price. *LRAC* is the industry's long-run supply. Bell noted that the model predicted well in the period tested. In 1966, 25 million pounds were produced with 981 thousand traps and lobster sold at about $.76 a pound.

For outputs up to *MSY* (25 million) the marginal cost to the industry exceeds the price of an additional unit of output. For example, at a price of $.70 the output given by *LRAC* is about 21 million. The marginal cost to the industry is much higher than $.70 because of the external effect of increased fishing.

FIGURE 8.8.2

Marginal and Average Cost Curves for Northern Lobster Industry

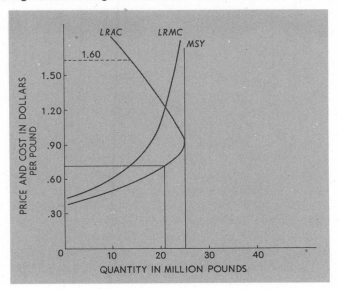

Overfishing is very likely. If, for example, the demand for lobster increases and raises the world price to $1.60, 1.5 million traps would be drawn into the industry and output would fall to 20 million pounds. The industry would be on the downward sloping portion of its production function and the backward bending part of *LRAC*. In this case the higher price would induce fewer rather than more lobsters. Further increases in price from rising consumer demand could destroy the resource unless entry is controlled. Bell's solution, open to some comment, was to set production levels where price equals marginal cost. At high levels of consumer demand and price, this level is the *MSY*.

Most industries do not exhibit the peculiar characteristics that result in the lobster industry because lobster is a free but scarce resource.

8.9 ANALYTICAL EXERCISE

Suppose demand for coal at the retail level is elastic over the relevant price range. Further, suppose the government feels that the price of coal is too high. It therefore places a price ceiling or maximum on coal at the mine. What will happen to the price of coal at the retail level? Will total receipts of retailers increase or decrease?

As a first step let us consider what happens at the mine (or mining area). Assume for analytical purposes that coal mining is a perfectly

competitive, increasing-cost industry. Assume also that before the imposition of the ceiling price, the industry was in long-run equilibrium;
each firm produced the quantity at which $P = LAC$ and therefore enjoyed no pure profit. Figure 8.9.1 shows the market demand and supply

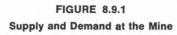

FIGURE 8.9.1

Supply and Demand at the Mine

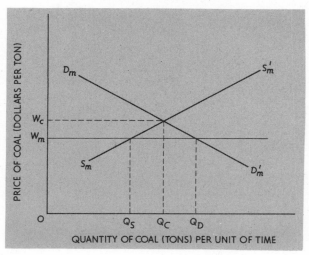

for coal at the mine. Demand $(D_m D_m')$ is the demand curve of retailers
for coal at the mine. It is derived holding the demand for coal from retailers and other factors constant (we assume that individual consumers
cannot purchase coal directly from the mine).

The long-run industry supply curve, $S_m S_m'$, is the type of supply curve
developed in Section 8.7. It is the locus of long-run equilibria for the
mining industry. Since we assume an increasing-cost industry, $S_m S_m'$ is
upward sloping. The equilibrium price at the mine is OW_c and equilibrium quantity is OQ_c.

Figure 8.9.2 shows demand and supply conditions at retail. $D_r D_r'$ is
the consumers' demand for coal. $S_r S_r'$, based upon a given cost of coal at
the mines to retailers (OW_c), is the retailers' supply curve. Since coal is
an input for the retailers, the supply curve for coal at retail should shift
when the price of coal at the mines changes, just as a change in the price
of any factor of production changes the supply of the product produced.
Specifically, when the price at the mine falls, other things remaining the
same, the retail supply curve should shift to the right. That is, if retailers
can buy coal cheaper, they would be willing and able to supply more retail coal at every retail price. Equilibrium in the retail market occurs at a

FIGURE 8.9.2

Demand and Supply at Retail

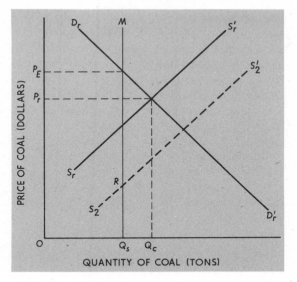

price of OP_r (given a price at the mine of OW_c) and a quantity sold of OQ_c, obviously the same as OQ_c in Figure 8.9.1 because the retailers sell all that they buy.

Returning to Figure 8.9.1, assume that the government sets the ceiling price OW_m. Quantity demanded by retailers at the new price is OQ_D. The new price is below OW_c (the price at which neither profit nor loss occurs); thus firms begin to make losses and some leave the industry. Since we assume that mining is an increasing-cost industry, the exit of firms and the decrease in quantity produced lowers factor prices and hence lowers the long-run average and marginal cost curves of the remaining firms in the industry. Figure 8.9.3 shows the process. Long-run average and marginal costs fall from LAC_1 and LMC_1 to LAC_2 and LMC_2. The minimum point on LAC_2 equals the ceiling price OW_m. Each remaining firm now produces Oq_m (the new equilibrium output) rather than Oq_c, but there are fewer firms, none of which makes pure profit. The new quantity supplied by the industry, indicated in Figure 8.9.1, is OQ_S.[14] Thus a shortage (excess demand) of O_SQ_D occurs at the mines since retailers now wish to purchase OQ_D but the mines are only willing to sell OQ_S. The mining industry must find some method of al-

---

[14] Figure 8.9.3 is drawn under the assumption that the fall in resource prices caused by the exit of firms from the industry shifts the minimum point on LAC to the right. It could just as easily have shifted it to the left (see footnote 11 above). The equilibrium output of each surviving firm is greater, but the output of the industry as a whole is less (see section 8.6.b above).

FIGURE 8.9.3

Cost Curves of an Individual Firm

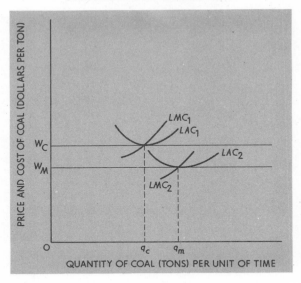

location (rationing, first come first served, favoritism, and so on) in order to determine which retailers get the available supply. In any case only OQ_S is available to the retailers.

Now according to our analysis the lower price of coal at the mine should cause supply at retail to shift to S_2S_2' (Figure 8.9.2). Retail price should fall and the quantity of coal sold should increase as determined by the intersection of D_rD_r' and S_2S_2'. But remember that only OQ_S is produced, so only OQ_S can be sold. The curve S_2S_2' specifies the quantities that retailers are *willing* to sell at the mine price of OW_m; the vertical line MQ_S indicates the maximum amount retailers are *able* to sell at that price. Thus, the curve S_2RM shows the quantities that retailers are *willing and able* to sell at each retail price when the mine price is fixed at OW_m.

The intersection of supply and demand now occurs at the price OP_E, clearly higher than the old price. The quantity sold is OQ_S. After the ceiling price at the mine is imposed, consumers pay a higher price for less coal. Since demand was assumed to be elastic, retailers receive less total revenue.

Exercise: Analyze the problem under the assumption that mining is a constant-cost industry.

8.10   CONCLUSION

Up to this point the salient feature of perfect competition is that, in long-run market equilibrium, market price equals minimum average cost. This means that each unit of output is produced at the lowest possible cost, either from the standpoint of money cost or of resource usage. The product sells for its average (long-run) cost of production; each firm accordingly earns the going rate of return in competitive industries, nothing more or less.

It should be emphasized that firms do not choose to produce the quantity with the lowest possible long-run average cost simply because they believe this level of production is optimal for society and they wish to benefit society. The firms are merely trying to maximize their profits. Given that motivation, the market *forces* firms to produce at that point. If society benefits, it is not through any benevolence of firms but through the functioning of the market. Another point that again warrants emphasis is that the theory of perfect competition is not designed to describe specific real world firms. It is a theoretical model that is frequently useful in explaining real world behavior and in predicting the economic consequences of changes in the different variables contained in the model. The conclusions of the theory, not the assumptions, are the crucial points when analyzing economic problems.

The important points of the theory of perfect competition are summarized in the following

Relation: In the short run the firm produces the quantity at which short-run marginal cost equals price, so long as price exceeds average variable cost. Therefore, marginal cost above average variable cost is the firm's short-run supply. If all input prices are given to the industry, industry short-run supply is the horizontal summation of all marginal cost curves. If the industry's (although not the individual firm's) usage affects the prices of some inputs, industry supply is less elastic than this horizontal summation. In the long run the entry and exit of firms force each firm to produce at minimum *LAC*, where *LAC* = *LMC* = *SAC* = *SMC*. Profit is zero at this output although each entrepreneur earns his opportunity cost. In a constant-cost industry long-run industry supply is a horizontal line at the level of the firm's minimum long-run average cost. If the industry's usage affects the prices of some inputs directly, the industry's long-run supply curve increases with output.

QUESTIONS AND PROBLEMS

1. Use the output-cost data computed from the problem in Chapter 7.
   a. Suppose the price of the commodity is $1.75 per unit.
      i. What would net profit be at each of the following outputs?
         1,314
         1,384
         1,444
         1,494
         1,534
      ii. What is the greatest profit output?

      iii. Is there any output that will yield a greater profit at any price?

      iv. How much more revenue is obtained by selling this number of units than by selling one fewer? What is the relation between marginal revenue and selling price?

      v. If you are given selling price, how can you determine the optimum output by reference to marginal cost?

b. Suppose price is $0.70.

      i. What would net profit be at each of the following outputs?

          410
          560
          700
          830
          945
        1,234
        1,444

      ii. Is there any output that will earn a net profit at this price?

      iii. When price is $0.70, what is the crucial relation between price and average variable cost?

      iv. Consider any price for which the corresponding marginal cost is equal to or less than $0.70. At such a price, what is the relation between marginal cost and average variable cost?

      v. When the relation in (iv) exists, what is the relation between average and marginal product?

      vi. What will the producer do if faced with a permanent price of $0.70?

      vii. Why is it not socially desirable to have a producer operating when price is $0.70?

c. Suppose price is $0.80.

      i. What will the optimum output be?

      ii. Can a profit be made at this price?

      iii. Will the producer operate at all at this price?

      iv. For how long?

d. Determine the supply schedule of this individual producer.

Price	Quantity Supplied
$0.60	
0.70	
0.80	
0.90	
1.00	
1.10	
1.20	
1.30	
1.40	
1.50	
1.60	
1.70	
1.80	
1.90	
2.00	

2. How can we have a constant-cost industry when every firm in the industry operates under conditions of increasing cost?

3. Under what circumstances is the horizontal sum of all firms' marginal cost curves above minimum average variable cost an industry's supply curve? Under what circumstances is it not?

FIGURE E.8.1

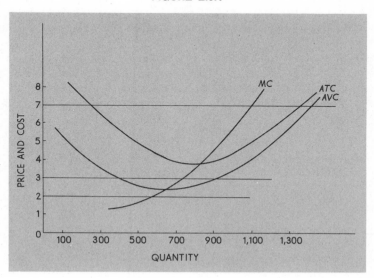

4. Use Figure E.8.1 to answer these questions.
   a. If price is $7 the firm should produce _____ units.
   b. Since average total cost at this profit maximizing output is $_____, total cost is $_____.
   c. Therefore the firm makes a total profit of $_____.
   d. Price then falls to $3. The firm will produce approximately _____ units.
   e. Since average total cost at this output is $_____, total revenue less total cost is $_____.
   f. Total variable cost is $_____; thus, the firm's total revenue covers all of variable cost, leaving approximately $_____ to apply to fixed costs.
   g. If price falls to $2 the firm will produce _____ units. Why?

5. Assume the equation for a perfectly competitive firm's marginal cost curve is $MC = 2 + 2q$. The minimum average variable cost is attained at $6.
   a. What is the lowest output the firm would produce?
   b. If price is $12 the firm would produce _____ units.
   c. If price rises to $24 the firm will produce _____ units.
   d. Assume there are 10,000 firms identical to this one in the industry.

The industry has no effect upon input prices. Derive an industry supply schedule for prices of $14, $16, $18, and $20.

6. Assume that we have an increasing cost industry. Draw market demand and supply curves and show equilibrium. Label the equilibrium price $\bar{p}$. Show a typical firm in the industry in long-run equilibrium. Let market demand fall slightly. Show how market supply must shift so that the industry attains a new long-run equilibrium. Show how the firm's cost curves must change to attain long-run equilibrium. Label long-run industry supply in your market graph. Explain precisely what this supply represents.

7. Assume that the beef industry is a constant-cost industry. Let society's demand for beef increase. Explain precisely the steps that must be taken for society to have more beef at the same price. Suppose that government becomes alarmed at the first sign of rising beef prices, and imposes a ceiling price on beef. What will occur now?

chapter
9

Theory of Price
under Pure Monopoly

9.1 INTRODUCTION

"Perfect competition" provides the economist with a very useful analytical model, even though the exacting conditions of the model never obtain in the real world. The same statement almost applies to the model of pure monopoly, to which we now turn. The conditions of the model are exacting; and it is difficult, if not impossible, to pinpoint a pure monopolist in real world markets. On the other hand, many markets closely approximate monopoly organization, and monopoly analysis often explains observed business behavior quite well.

A pure monopoly exists if there is only *one firm* that produces and sells a particular commodity or service. Since the monopolist is the only seller in the market, he has neither rivals nor direct competitors. Furthermore, no other sellers can enter the market or else a monopoly would not exist. Yet, as we shall see, monopoly does not necessarily guarantee success; it only guarantees that the monopolist can make the best of whatever demand and cost conditions exist without fear of new firms entering the market and competing away his profits.

While the pure monopolist has no *direct competitors* who sell the same product, he does have *indirect competition*. In the first place, all commodities compete for a place in the consumer's budget. Thus, to a certain extent, the monopolist's product competes with all other goods and services in the general struggle for the consumer's dollar. Some goods, however, are closer substitutes for the monopolist's product than others. While there are no perfect or nearly perfect substitutes for a monopoly product (otherwise a monopoly would not exist), a second source of indirect competition lies in the existence of imperfect substitutes.

For example, American Telephone and Telegraph almost has a monopoly in providing long-distance telephone service in the United States. However, there are various substitutes that can be used: mail, railway express, messengers, personal visits, smoke signals. When the Aluminum Company of America (Alcoa) was the only manufacturer of aluminum (prior to World War II) it had no direct competitors, but it did have competition from producers of other metals that were imperfect substitutes. More recently, International Nickel has been in a similar situation. Gas is a fairly good substitute for electricity (usually a regional monopoly) in many cases. Any real world monopolist, therefore, has competition to a greater or lesser degree, which in some measure tends to weaken the monopolist's position. There are, however, no other producers of the monopolist's specific product in the market.

To summarize:

Definition: A pure monopoly exists when there is only one producer in a market. There are no direct competitors or rivals in either the popular or technical sense. However, the policies of a monopolist may be constrained by the indirect competition of all commodities for the consumer's dollar and by reasonably adequate substitute goods.

9.2   DEMAND AND MARGINAL REVENUE UNDER MONOPOLY

The most important object of Chapters 3 and 4 was to show that market demand curves are negatively sloped (except for the truly insignificant case of Giffen's Paradox). Since a monopoly is the only firm selling in the market, the market demand *is* the monopolist's demand curve. As you will recall the market demand curve shows, for each specific price, the quantity of the commodity that buyers will take. Of perhaps equal importance for our analysis of monopoly is the market *marginal revenue,* the variation in total revenue resulting from an additional unit of sales.

Let us consider first why marginal revenue for a monopolist differs from marginal revenue for a perfect competitor. As previously emphasized, a change in the quantity sold by a competitive firm has no noticeable effect upon market price; therefore, marginal revenue to this firm is the market price. On the other hand, a change in the quantity a monopolist sells does effect market price. More specifically, since the monopolist *must lower price* if he wishes to increase his rate of sales, his marginal revenue is not the market price. For example, suppose a monopolist has the demand schedule given in columns one and two of Table 9.2.1. Price times quantity gives the total revenue obtainable from each level of sales. Marginal revenue in column four shows the change in total revenue from an additional unit of sales. The only time marginal revenue equals price is for the first unit sold. That is, at zero sales total revenue is zero; for the first unit sold total revenue is the demand price for one unit. Thus, the change in total revenue is the same as price. Since the monopolist must reduce price to sell additional units, at every other level of output marginal revenue is less than price.

As you will recall from Chapter 7, when average cost decreases, marginal cost is less than average cost. Similarly, since average revenue (price) decreases over the entire range of outputs, marginal revenue is less than average revenue over this range.

Since marginal revenue is the addition to total revenue attributable to an additional unit of sales, total revenue at any level of sales is the summation of all marginal revenues up to that level. This relation is illustrated in column five of Table 9.2.1. Also, Table 9.2.1 shows that marginal

TABLE 9.2.1

Monopoly Demand and Marginal Revenue

Units of Sales	Price	Total Revenue	Marginal Revenue	Sum of MR Entries
1..............	$2.00	$2.00	$2.00	$2.00
2..............	1.80	3.60	1.60	3.60
3..............	1.40	4.20	0.60	4.20
4..............	1.20	4.80	0.40	4.80
5..............	1.00	5.00	0.20	5.00
6..............	0.70	4.20	−0.80	4.20

revenue can be positive or negative, or even zero if output is sufficiently divisible.

Relations: Marginal revenue is the addition to total revenue attributable to the addition of one unit of output to sales per period of time. After the first unit sold, marginal revenue is less than price.

Figure 9.2.1 illustrates the relations between demand, marginal revenue, and total revenue for a monopolist with a linear demand curve. In panels *a* and *b* the scales of the vertical axes differ but the horizontal axes have the same scale. Note the difference between the total revenue curves of a monopolist and a perfect competitor (you will remember that the latter is a monotonically increasing straight line, whose constant slope is the market price). Total revenue (panel *a*) first increases when price is reduced and sales expand; it reaches a maximum at Ox_0 and declines thereafter.

Panel *b* indicates the relations between marginal revenue (MR) and demand. As mentioned above, MR is below price at every output level except the first (since we have assumed continuous data, the two are equal infinitesimally close to the vertical axis). Also, since demand is negatively sloped, MR is as well. Finally, when TR reaches its maximum (at output Ox_0), MR is zero (at output Ox_0, price Op_0). At greater rates of output MR is negative. These relations are clearly indicated when we

FIGURE 9.2.1

Total Revenue, Marginal Revenue, Demand

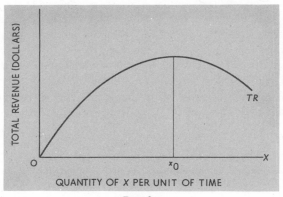

Panel a
Total Revenue

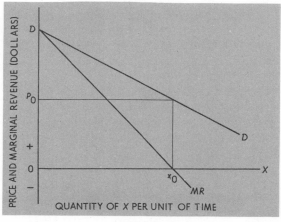

Panel b
Demand and Marginal Revenue

consider the characteristics of marginal revenue: if TR increases, an additional unit of sales per period adds a positive amount to revenue; hence MR is positive. The opposite holds for a decrease in TR.

9.3 GRAPHICAL RELATIONS AMONG DEMAND, MARGINAL REVENUE, AND ELASTICITY

We will first summarize the results of the derivations to be set forth in this section. We will then derive geometrically the relations among demand, marginal revenue, and elasticity. Students in classes not particularly interested in rigorous proofs and derivations may note these relations, skip the actual derivations in subsections *a, b,* and *c,* and go directly on to Section 9.4 without any loss of continuity.

Relations: When demand is linear, *MR* is a negatively sloped straight line that lies exactly halfway between the vertical axis and the demand curve.

Relation: When demand is concave from above (below) marginal revenue is concave from above (below) and lies less (more) than halfway from the vertical axis to demand.

Relation: When marginal revenue is zero, demand has unitary elasticity. When marginal revenue is positive (negative), demand is elastic (inelastic). In terms of the linear demand in panel *b,* Figure 9.2.1, demand is elastic at quantities less than Ox_0 and inelastic at quantities greater than Ox_0. The elasticity is unity at Ox_0. More precisely, the relation can be expressed as $MR = p\left(1 - \dfrac{1}{\eta}\right)$, where η is the absolute value of demand elasticity.

We can now proceed to the derivation of these relations, or the remainder of this section can be omitted.

9.3.a—Graphical Derivation of Marginal Revenue from Linear Demand

We will first show a graphical derivation of the marginal revenue curve. Consider Figure 9.3.1, in which we have a *linear* demand curve *DD′*. Our task is to determine the marginal revenue associated with any (and hence every) point on *DD′*.

Suppose price is *OP;* thus quantity demanded is *OQ* and total revenue is equal to the area of the rectangle *OPRQ*. Recall that from the definition of *MR* the *TR* corresponding to any quantity is the sum of all *MR* figures up to and including *MR* for the quantity under consideration. Graphically, this means that total revenue for each rate of output is equal to the area under the marginal revenue curve.

If we already knew the marginal revenue curve *DM,* total revenue would also equal the area *ODNQ*. At the moment this curve is not known; indeed, our problem is to determine the marginal revenue (*QN*) associated with quantity *OQ* and price *OP = QR*. The only thing we know right now is that there must be an area *ODNQ* which is equal to total revenue, or the area *OPRQ*. Our problem is to locate the point *N*. When the proper *N* is found, we know that area *ODNQ* will equal area *OPRQ*.

These two geometrical shapes have a substantial area in common, namely *OPENQ*. The triangle *ERN* is unique to *OPRQ* and the triangle *EPD* is unique to *ODNQ*. Since *OPENQ* is common, the area of

ODNQ will equal the area *OPRQ* if the area of *EDP* equals the area of *ERN*.

At this point, we have three pieces of information. First, since the opposite angles formed by two intersecting straight lines are equal, angle *DEP* equals angle *REN*. Second, both figures are right triangles (that is, angles *DPE* and *ERN* are right angles). Since two angles are equal, the third must be as well. The two triangles are, accordingly, similar triangles. Finally, we know that if properly constructed the two triangles have equal area. But similar triangles of equal area are congru-

FIGURE 9.3.1

Derivation of Marginal Revenue When Demand Is Linear

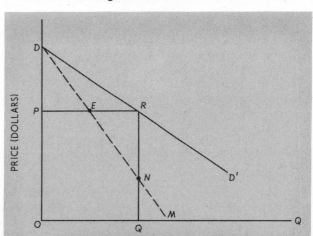

QUANTITY DEMANDED PER UNIT OF TIME

ent, so the corresponding sides must be equal. Hence $PE = ER$ and $DP = RN$.

We have thus obtained a method for finding marginal revenue corresponding to any point on a linear demand curve. Suppose the point in question is *R*. From *R*, drop a perpendicular *RQ* to the quantity axis and a perpendicular *RP* to the price axis. On the perpendicular *RQ* mark off a distance *RN* that is equal to *DP*. When this is done, the distance *NQ* is· the marginal revenue associated with the output *OQ* units. By repeating this process for other points on *DD'*, the *MR* curve is determined.

Another method is equally valid but does not directly follow the logic of locating the point *N*. From the point *R*, drop perpendiculars *RP* and *RQ* to both axes. Find the midpoint *E* of the line *RP*. Draw a straight line from *D* to *E* and extend this line until it intersects *RQ*. The point of intersection is *N*, the point in question.

Relation: When demand is linear, *MR* is a negatively sloped straight line that lies exactly halfway between the vertical axis and the demand curve.

9.3.b—Graphical Derivation of *MR* when Demand is Nonlinear

The derivation of *MR* when demand is nonlinear differs but slightly. The mechanics are explained by means of Figure 9.3.2. *DD'* is the demand curve. The problem is to find marginal revenue corresponding to such points as R_1, R_2, and R_3 on *DD'*. From point R_1, first drop perpendiculars (R_1P_1 and R_1Q_1) to both axes. Next, construct the tangent to *DD'* at R_1 and extend the tangent so that it cuts the vertical axis at point

FIGURE 9.3.2

Derivation of Marginal Revenue from Nonlinear Demand Curve

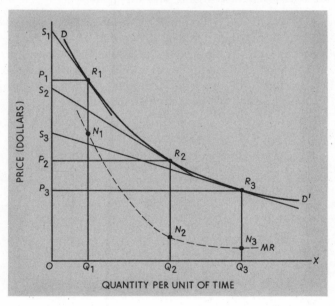

S_1. Since the slope of the curve and of its tangent are the same at the point of tangency, the marginal quantities are also the same. Thus to find marginal revenue at point R_1, mark off a distance $R_1N_1 = S_1P_1$. Then N_1Q_1 is marginal revenue and N_1 is a point on the marginal revenue curve.

Proceeding in the same fashion, select another point R_2 on *DD'* and drop perpendiculars (R_2P_2 and R_2Q_2) to the axes. Next, construct the tangent to *DD'* at R_2 and extend the tangent line to cut the vertical axis at S_2. Finally, mark off the distance $R_2N_2 = S_2P_2$. Marginal revenue is N_2Q_2 and N_2 is another point on the marginal revenue curve. (*Exercise:* carry out the same argument for the point R_3.) Connecting all points so generated—and for accuracy, there must be many of them—establishes the marginal revenue curve corresponding to the given nonlinear demand curve.

Note that when demand is nonlinear, marginal revenue does not lie half the distance from the vertical axis to the demand curve. For demand curves that are concave from above, marginal revenue is less than half the distance from the vertical axis to demand (note where MR crosses P_2R_2 and P_3R_3). For demands concave from below, marginal revenue cuts the perpendicular from the vertical axis to demand to the right of its midpoint.

9.3.c—Marginal Revenue, Demand, and Elasticity

As you will recall from Chapter 2 changes in total expenditure are related to demand elasticity. When demand is elastic, an increase in quantity (decrease in price) causes an increase in total expenditure. Over an inelastic segment of demand, an increase in quantity occasions a decrease in total expenditure, while in the unitary portion, total expenditure remains unchanged. Since total consumer expenditure on a commodity

TABLE 9.3.1

Relations among Marginal Revenue, Elasticity, and Changes in Total Revenue

	1	*2*	*3*
Marginal revenue............	Positive	Negative	Zero
Demand elasticity...........	Elastic	Inelastic	Unitary
Change in total revenue for an increase in quantity.....	Increase	Decrease	No change

is the same as the monopolist's total revenue, the relation of elasticity to marginal revenue follows directly from the above relations. If marginal revenue is positive (negative), a unit increase in sales leads to an increase (decrease) in total revenue. If marginal revenue is zero, a unit change in sales does not change total revenue. Therefore, a positive (negative) marginal revenue indicates that demand is elastic (inelastic) at that quantity. Zero marginal revenue means unitary elasticity. These relations are summarized in Table 9.3.1. They can be seen also in Figure 9.3.3, which shows a straight line demand curve.

FIGURE 9.3.3

Relations among Marginal Revenue, Elasticity, and Demand

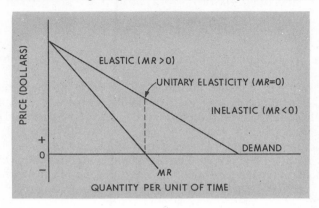

An even more precise relation among price, marginal revenue, and the coefficient of elasticity is given by the equation[1]

$$MR = p\left(1 - \frac{1}{\eta}\right),$$

---

[1] A formal proof of this relation is relegated to a footnote. Consider the accompanying graph.

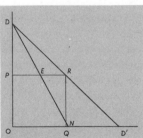

Let DD' be a linear demand curve. This is used merely for convenience because the formula to be developed holds for nonlinear demand curves as well. Consider the point R on DD', corresponding to a price of $OP = QR$ and quantity demanded of $OQ = PR$. NQ is the marginal revenue associated with point R because, by construction, $RN = DP$. Furthermore, at point R the coefficient of price elasticity (η) is RD'/DR.

First note that

$$NQ = RQ - RN. \tag{1}$$

Now since $\dfrac{DP}{PR} = \dfrac{RQ}{QD'}$, and $RN = DP$, it follows that

$$RN = PR\left[\frac{RQ}{QD'}\right] = RQ\left[\frac{PR}{QD'}\right] \tag{2}$$

where η is the absolute value of the price elasticity of demand. Note that when $\eta > 1$ (demand is elastic), $\frac{1}{\eta} < 1$; hence, $\left(1 - \frac{1}{\eta}\right) > 0$. Since $p > 0$, $p\left(1 - \frac{1}{\eta}\right) > 0$. Therefore, $MR > 0$.

Exercise: The student should carry out the same type of analysis for $\eta = 1$ and $\eta < 1$.

Relations: When demand is negatively sloped, marginal revenue is negatively sloped and is less than price at all relevant quantities. The difference between marginal revenue and price depends upon the price elasticity of demand as shown by the formula $MR = p(1 - 1/\eta)$. Total revenue increases at first, reaches a maximum, and declines thereafter. The maximum point on the total revenue curve is attained at precisely that rate of output and sales for which marginal revenue is zero and elasticity is unitary.

9.4 SHORT-RUN EQUILIBRIUM UNDER MONOPOLY

The analysis of perfect competition is based upon two important assumptions: (1) each entrepreneur attempts to maximize profit and (2) the firm operates in an environment free from outside control. Monopoly analysis rests upon the same two assumptions.

9.4.a—Cost under Monopoly

The short-run cost conditions confronting a monopolist are essentially similar to those faced by a perfectly competitive firm. The chief difference lies in the potential impact of output changes on factor prices. In the

---

Substituting equation (2) in equation (1),

$$
\begin{aligned}
NQ &= RQ - RN \\
&= RQ - RQ \left[\frac{PR}{QD'} \right] \\
&= RQ \left[1 - \frac{PR}{QD'} \right].
\end{aligned}
\tag{3}
$$

Next, observe that

$$
\frac{PR}{QD'} = \frac{OQ}{QD'} = \frac{DR}{RD'} = \frac{1}{\eta}.
\tag{4}
$$

Finally, substituting equation (4) in equation (3), one obtains

$$
NQ = RQ \left[1 - \frac{1}{\eta} \right].
\tag{5}
$$

Since NQ is marginal revenue (MR) and RQ is price p, equation (5) can be written to express the relation among marginal revenue, price, and the coefficient of price elasticity as stated in the text:

$$
MR = p\left(1 - \frac{1}{\eta}\right).
$$

theory of perfect competition we assume that each producer is very small relative to the total factor market. He can thereby change *his* rate of output without affecting factor prices (just as a consumer can change his rate of purchases without affecting commodity price).

The assumption just discussed cannot be imposed on the markets for all factors a monopolist hires. To be sure, a monopolist will purchase some unspecialized inputs, such as unskilled labor, whose prices are not affected by his actions. But he will hire certain specialized inputs as well; and since the monopolist *is* the industry, his rates of purchase will have a definite impact upon the prices of these factors. Generally, factor prices will vary directly with the monopolist's use of them.

Notwithstanding the monopolist's possible effect upon factor prices, his cost curves have the same general shape as those described in Chapter 7. The primary implication of rising supply prices of variable inputs is that the average and marginal cost curves rise more rapidly or fall less rapidly than if the input supply prices were constant. Thus, for example, marginal cost rises not only because of diminishing marginal productivity but also because input prices rise with increased use.

9.4.b—Short-Run Equilibrium

A monopolist, just as a perfect competitor, attains maximum profit (or minimum loss) by producing and selling at that rate of output for which the positive (negative) difference between total revenue and total cost is greatest (least). This condition occurs when the slope of the total revenue curve equals the slope of the total cost curve; in other words, when marginal revenue equals marginal cost (even though for the monopolist *MR* does not equal price).

Figure 9.4.1 depicts the marginal cost and marginal revenue curves of a monopolist. Maximum profit or minimum loss occurs at output Ox_0, where *MC* equals *MR*. At any lower output, for example Ox_1, the monopolist can gain additional profit or can reduce his loss by producing and selling an additional unit per period of time. Since *MR* exceeds *MC* at Ox_1, the added revenue from the sale of another unit per period is greater than the additional cost of producing it. He therefore produces additional units until *MR* equals *MC*. Likewise, he would not produce more than Ox_0, for example Ox_2, since at larger outputs the marginal cost of producing another unit per period is greater than the marginal revenue gained from selling it. Thus producing more or less than Ox_0 causes profit (loss) to diminish (increase).

Using the proposition just established, the position of short-run equilibrium is easily described. Figure 9.4.2 shows the relevant cost and revenue curves for a monopolist. Since *AVC* and *AFC* are not necessary for exposition, they are omitted. The profit maximizer produces at *E* where

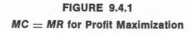

FIGURE 9.4.1

MC = MR for Profit Maximization

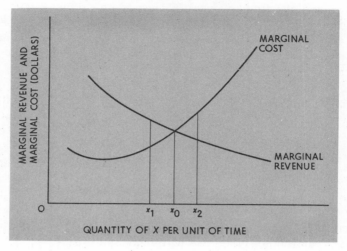

$MC = MR$. Output is Ox, and from the demand curve we see that price must be Op per unit in order to ration the Ox units among those who wish to buy the commodity. Total revenue is $Op \times Ox$, or the area of the rectangle $OpBx$. The unit cost of producing this amount is Oc. Total cost is $Oc \times Ox$, or the area $OcDx$. Profit is $TR - TC$, or the shaded area $cpBD$.

In the example of Figure 9.4.2, the monopolist earns a pure profit in the short run. This need not be the case, however; a monopolistic position does not assure profit. If demand is sufficiently low a monopolist may incur a loss in the short run, just as a pure competitor may. For example, Figure 9.4.3 shows a loss situation. Marginal cost equals marginal revenue at output Ox, which can be sold at price Op. Average cost is Oc. Total cost, $OcDx$ exceeds total revenue $OpBx$; hence the firm makes a loss of $pcDB$.

Note that the monopolist would produce rather than shut down in the short run, since he covers all of his variable cost $(OvNx)$ and still has some revenue $(vpBN)$ left to apply to fixed cost. If demand decreases so that the monopolist cannot cover all of his variable cost at any price, he would shut down and lose only fixed cost. This situation is analogous to that of the perfect competitor, except that we cannot derive a monopoly short-run supply curve.

In the short run the primary difference between monopoly and perfect competition lies in the slope of the demand curve. Either may earn a pure economic profit; either may incur a loss. Of course, another important

FIGURE 9.4.2
Short-Run Equilibrium under Monopoly

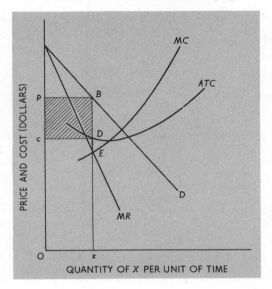

FIGURE 9.4.3
Short-Run Losses under Monopoly

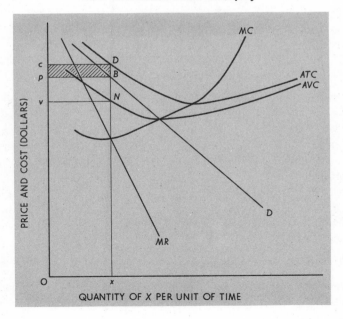

difference is that the monopolist who earns pure profit need not worry about new firms entering the industry and competing his profits away.

Principles: If a monopolist produces a positive output, he maximizes profit or minimizes losses by producing the quantity for which *MC* = *MR*. Since the monopolist's demand is above *MR* at every positive output, equilibrium price exceeds *MC*.

9.4.c—Numerical Illustration

A numerical example can illustrate the principal points of this section. In Table 9.4.1 the demand schedule in columns 1 and 2 yields the total

TABLE 9.4.1

Marginal Revenue–Marginal Cost Approach to Profit Maximization

Output and Sales	Price	Total Revenue	Total Cost	Marginal Revenue	Marginal Cost	Profit
5	$2.00	$10.00	$12.25	—	$0.45	$−2.25
13	1.10	14.30	15.00	$0.54	.34	−0.70
23	0.85	19.55	18.25	.52	.33	+1.30
38	.69	25.92	22.00	.42	.25	+3.92
50	.615	30.75	26.25	.35	.35	+4.50
60	.55	33.00	31.00	.23	.48	+2.00
68	.50	34.00	36.25	.13	.66	−2.25
75	.45	33.75	42.00	−.03	.82	−8.25
81	.40	32.40	48.25	−.23	1.04	−15.85
86	.35	30.10	55.00	−.46	1.35	−25.10

revenue schedule in 3. We can simply subtract the total cost of producing each relevant level of sales from total revenue to obtain the profit from that output. Examination of the profit columns shows that maximum profit ($4.50) occurs at 50 units of output. Marginal revenue and marginal cost, given in columns 5 and 6 give the same result. The monopolist can increase profit by increasing sales so long as marginal revenue exceeds marginal cost. If marginal cost exceeds marginal revenue, profit falls with increased sales. Hence, the monopolist produces and sells 50 units, the level at which marginal cost and marginal revenue are equal.

9.4.d—A Word on Monopoly Supply

A monopolist's marginal cost curve is *not* his supply curve. Recall that supply is the locus of points showing the output forthcoming at each price. Marginal cost is not such a curve for the monopolist. Monopoly price at the quantity where $MC = MR$ is given by the demand curve. Therefore, the price at any given output depends upon the relative position of demand. You can see that many prices are possible (in fact, an infinite number) for a given equilibrium output by working the following

Exercise: In Figure 9.4.2 construct a marginal revenue curve much less steep than *MR* but crossing *MC* at point *E*. Next construct the demand that corresponds to the new *MR*. Note that the new equilibrium price at the equilibrium output (*Ox*) is now lower than the old equilibrium price (*Op*). Thus, *MC* is not supply.

9.5   LONG-RUN EQUILIBRIUM UNDER MONOPOLY

A monopoly exists if there is only one firm in the market. Among other things this statement implies that "entrance" into the market is closed. Thus whether or not a monopolist earns a pure profit in the short run, no other producer can enter the market in the hope of sharing whatever pure profit potential exists. Therefore, pure economic profit is not eliminated in the long run, as in the case of perfect competition. The monopolist will, however, make adjustments in plant size as demand conditions warrant them, even though entry is prohibited.

A monopolist faced with the cost and revenue conditions depicted in Figure 9.5.1 would build his plant to produce the quantity at which long-run marginal cost equals marginal revenue. He produces Ox units per period at a cost of Oc per unit and sells at a price of Op. Long-run profit

FIGURE 9.5.1

Long-Run Equilibrium under Monopoly

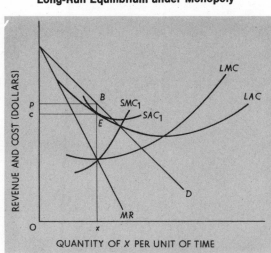

is *cpBE*. By the now familiar argument, this is the maximum profit possible under the given revenue and cost conditions. He operates in the short run with plant size indicated by SAC_1 and SMC_1. New entrants cannot come into the industry and compete away his profits.

But demand or cost conditions can change for reasons other than the entry of new firms; and such changes cause the monopolist to make adjustments. Assume that demand and marginal revenue change. At first the firm will adjust without changing plant size. It will produce the quantity at which the new *MR* equals SMC_1, or it will close down in the short run if it cannot cover variable costs. In the long run the monopolist can change plant size.

Long-run equilibrium adjustment under monopoly must take one of two possible courses. First, if the monopolist incurs a short-run loss, and if there is no plant size that will result in pure profit (or at least, no loss), the monopolist goes out of business. Second, if he suffers a short-run loss or earns a short-run profit with his original plant, he must determine whether a plant of different size (and thus a different price and output) will enable him to earn a larger profit.

The first situation requires no comment. The second is illustrated by Figure 9.5.2. *DD′* and *MR* show the market demand and marginal revenue confronting a monopolist. *LAC* is his long-run average cost curve, and *LMC* is the associated long-run marginal cost curve. Suppose in the

FIGURE 9.5.2

Long-Run Equilibrium for a Monopolist

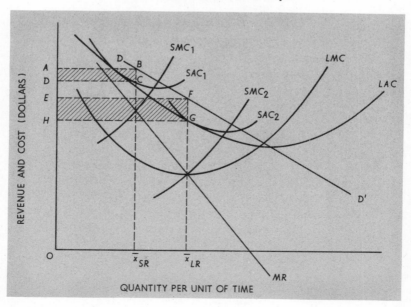

initial period the monopolist built the plant exemplified by SAC_1 and SMC_1. Equality of short-run marginal cost and marginal revenue leads to the sale of $O\bar{x}_{SR}$ units per period at the price OA. At this rate of output unit cost is OD; short-run monopoly profit is represented by the area of the shaded rectangle $ABCD$.

Since a pure economic profit can be reaped, the monopolist would not consider discontinuing production. To this end, long-run marginal cost becomes the relevant consideration. The profit-maximum maximorum is attained when long-run marginal cost equals marginal revenue. The associated rate of output is $O\bar{x}_{LR}$, and price is OE.

By reference to LAC, the plant capable of producing $O\bar{x}_{LR}$ units per period at the least unit cost is the one represented by SAC_2 and SMC_2. Unit cost is accordingly OH, and long-run maximum monopoly profit is given by the area of the shaded rectangle $EFGH$. This profit is obviously (visually) greater than the profit obtainable from the original plant.

Generalizing, we have the following:

Proposition: A monopolist maximizes profit in the long run by producing and marketing that rate of output for which long-run marginal cost equals marginal revenue. The optimal plant is the one whose short-run average cost curve is tangent to the long-run average cost curve at the point corresponding to long-run equilibrium output. At this point short-run marginal cost equals marginal revenue.

The organization described by the proposition above is the best the monopolist can attain; and he *can* attain it because in the long run his plant size is variable and the market is effectively closed to entry.

9.6   COST OF MONOPOLY TO SOCIETY

Economists have done extensive research, both theoretical and empirical, into the welfare effect of monopoly with, as yet, no clear, generally accepted results. On the one hand, we frequently hear of the overwhelming power of monopoly in the economy. Others present an opposing point of view that monopoly poses only a very minor social problem. Let us first attempt to compare theoretically the monopoly equilibrium situation with that of perfect competition. We will then present some empirical evidence concerning the welfare cost of monopoly in the United States.

9.6.a—Comparison with Perfect Competition

Most comparisons between the equilibria of monopoly and perfect competition are tenuous. For example, one sometimes hears that price is lower and output greater under perfect competition than under monopoly. This statement is based upon the following analysis. The monopolist depicted in Figure 9.6.1 produces Ox_M per period of time and sells at a price of Op_M. If we can also assume that MC represents competitive supply, supply equals demand at E. The perfectly competitive industry would sell Ox_C (greater than Ox_M) at a price of Op_E (less than Op_M). There is reason to doubt, however, that MC can represent the supply curve of a perfectly competitive industry. As we have seen, competitive supply is not always the sum of the marginal cost curves. Even if this were so, the sum of n firms' marginal cost curves would not necessarily be the marginal cost curve of a single much larger firm. One can only say

FIGURE 9.6.1

Price and Output Comparisons

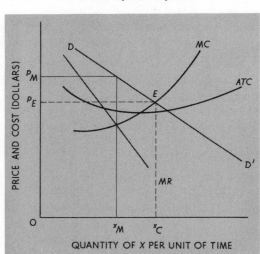

that a monopolist is more likely to earn a pure profit because he can effectively exercise some market control.

We can also say that in long-run industry equilibrium under perfect competition production occurs at the point of minimum long- and short-run average cost. The monopolist utilizes the plant capable of producing his long-run equilibrium output at the least unit cost. Only under the extremely rare circumstances in which marginal revenue intersects marginal cost at minimum long-run average cost would this plant be the one associated with the absolute minimum unit cost. In any case the slightest change in demand would upset this equilibrium.

We should also note that while the perfect competitor produces at the point where marginal cost and price are equal, the monopolist's price *exceeds* marginal cost. Under certain conditions, demand represents the social valuation of the commodity. Similarly, long-run marginal cost, with some exceptions, represents the marginal social cost of production. Under monopoly the marginal value of a commodity to a society exceeds the marginal social cost of its production. Society as a whole would, therefore, benefit by having more of its resources used in producing the commodity in question. The profit-maximizing monopolist will not do this, however, for producing at the point where price equals marginal cost would decrease his profit. Alternatively, the perfect competitor in long-run equilibrium produces the quantity at which the marginal social cost of production equals the marginal social valuation; he does so, however, not because of any innate social consciousness but because the market forces him to do so.

9.6.b—Welfare Loss from Monopoly: An Empirical Estimation

Assume that *DD'* in Figure 9.6.2 represents the demand for a particular commodity. The industry has constant marginal and average costs, at

FIGURE 9.6.2

Welfare Loss from Monopoly

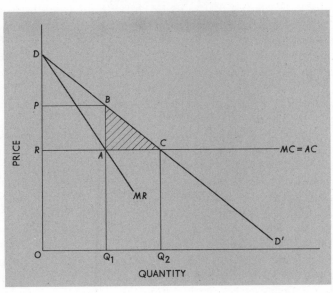

the level $MC = AC = OR$. Under perfect competition, in which marginal cost equals price, the industry would produce OQ_2, and price would be OR. If the industry is taken over by a monopolist, who is faced with the same costs, output would fall to OQ_1 where $MC = MR$; price would rise to OP. The monopolist's "excess" profit is *RPBA*. This is not a net loss to society, however. The profit is simply a transfer from one sector of the economy to the monopolist with no net loss to society—aside from the possible feeling that the monopolist should not have this profit. (Recall the economics of theft in Chapter 5.)

The loss to society is the lost consumer's surplus, represented by the shaded triangle *ABC*. (Recall the discussion of consumer's surplus in Chapter 4.) If society wishes to retain its consumer's surplus by changing output to OQ_2 and price to OR_1 it must transfer resources valued at CAQ_2Q_1 from other industries into this industry.

In 1954, Arnold C. Harberger attempted to measure both the total welfare loss (consumer's surplus) from all monopoly in the United States and the value of the resources that society would have to transfer from competitive industries to the monopolized industries to eliminate this welfare loss.[2] He assumed constant marginal costs, as in the model presented here. He assumed also that those industries with higher than average returns on capital have too few resources and those yielding lower than average returns have too many. Because of the relative tranquility of the period and the availability of good data, Harberger used the years 1924–28 for his estimation.

The value of resources that must be shifted into an industry to eliminate any specific amount of excess profit from the industry clearly depends upon the elasticity of commodity demand for that industry. The more elastic commodity demand, the more output must be increased to eliminate excess profit, and hence the more resources that must be transferred into that industry. Harberger believed that unity was the upper bound of the elasticities of the industries tested and, therefore, used that figure. If he was correct, his estimates would be somewhat biased upward.

If unit elasticity is assumed, the amount of excess profit measures the value of resources that must be transferred into the industry to eliminate the profit. In Figure 9.6.2 let us assume that normal profit is incorporated into $MC = AC$. When price is Op excess profit is the area $RpBA$. Assume that demand has unitary elasticity over the range BC (obviously this is impossible since MR is positive over this range). Thus $OpBQ_1 = ORCQ_2$ and $RpBA$, the excess profit, equals Q_1ACQ_2, the value of resources that must be brought in to eliminate the profit.

Harberger found from his data that 550 million dollars in resources would have to have been transferred from low return to high return industries to eliminate excess profit during this period. Since only 45 percent of all companies were included in the sample, the estimate was raised to 1.2 billion. This transfer would have involved about four percent of all resources in manufacturing or $1\frac{1}{2}$ percent of total resources.

He then estimated how much better off society would have been had

---

[2] See Arnold C. Harberger, "The Welfare Loss from Monopoly," *American Economic Review,* May 1954, pp. 77–87.

the transfer taken place. That is he estimated the total consumer's surplus that would have been gained. The total figure based upon the data was 59 million dollars, less than one-tenth of one percent of national income. In terms of 1954 income this averaged less than $1.50 per person in the United States. When Harberger included certain intangibles in the data, the necessary transfer rose from $1\frac{1}{2}$ percent to $1\frac{3}{4}$ percent of national income, and the welfare loss rose to 81 million dollars.[3]

In all the estimates the total welfare loss came to less than one-tenth of one percent of national income, and in most instances, Harberger used assumptions that biased the estimates upward. This extremely low estimate was startling at the time. It appeared that the United States was not totally in the grasp of ubiquitous monopoly.

These estimates did not go unchallenged. Others attempted to estimate the welfare loss from monopoly, and, perhaps surprisingly, most of the estimates were also rather low. Gordon Tullock, however, added a new dimension to the discussion.[4] Recall from Chapter 5 the economics of theft. Theft involves only a transfer of resources from the victim to the thief. But, because of theft, society uses resources, which could be used productivity, to prevent and to carry out stealing. According to Tullock, monopoly is subject to the same type of analysis.

Monopoly involves only a transfer of resources from the public to the monopolists plus an empirically insignificant welfare loss. Aside from the redistribution question, monopoly, therefore, is an insignificant problem. "Perhaps not," said Tullock. According to his analysis, the welfare losses estimated using Harberger's technique, underestimated the true welfare loss from monopoly. Because the return from establishing a *successful* monopoly is so great, one would expect potential monopolists to expend considerable resources in attempting to form monopolies. In fact, entrepreneurs should be willing to invest resources in attempts to form monopolies until the marginal cost equals the anticipated discounted return. After a monopoly is formed, others will invest resources toward trying to break the monopoly, which in turn means that the monopolist must use additional resources trying to prevent the break. Just as successful theft encourages additional theft, successful monopoly encourages additional attempts to monopolize.

As Tullock noted, identifying and measuring the resources used to gain, break, and hold monopoly are quite difficult. But, it appears that a large amount of the very scarce resource, skilled management, is used toward this end. In any case, the welfare triangle measurement ignores this cost

---

[3] Again note that the welfare loss does not consider the reallocation of income from the rest of society to the monopolists.

[4] See Gordon Tullock, "The Welfare Costs of Monopolies and Theft," *Western Economic Journal,* June 1967, pp. 224–32.

and underestimates the social cost of monopoly. The monopoly question is still far from being settled.

9.7 PRICE DISCRIMINATION UNDER MONOPOLY

Earlier in this chapter we stated that a pure monopoly exists if a commodity has only one seller in a well-defined market. Price discrimination can exist under monopoly if the monopolist is the only seller of a commodity in two or more well-defined, separable markets. Price discrimination means that a monopolist charges different prices for the same commodity in different markets. Price discrimination can occur when a monopolist charges different prices domestically and abroad or perhaps when a doctor charges one fee for an operation to low-income patients and another fee for the same operation to high-income patients.

9.7.a—Price Discrimination in Theory

Certain conditions are necessary for the monopolist to be able to discriminate. First, the markets must be *separable*. If purchasers in the lower price market are able themselves to sell the commodity to buyers in the higher price market, discrimination will not exist for long. For example, a lower price patient cannot resell his operation to a higher price patient, but a lower price buyer of some raw material could perhaps resell it to someone in the higher price market. Discrimination would not be practiced in the latter case. Second, as we shall soon see, demand elasticities must be different in the different markets.

The analysis of discriminatory pricing is a straightforward application of the $MC = MR$ rule. As a first step in that analysis, let us assume that a monopolist has two separate markets for his product. Demand conditions in each market are such that the marginal revenues from selling specified quantities are as given in Table 9.7.1. Assume also that for some reason the monopolist decides to produce 12 units. How should he allocate sales between the two markets?

Consider the first unit; he can gain $45 by selling it in the first market or $34 by selling in the second market. Obviously, if he sells only one unit per period, he will sell it in market I. The second unit per period is also sold in the first market since its sale there increases revenue by $36, whereas it would only bring $34 in market II. Since $34 can be gained in II but only $30 in I, unit three per period is sold in market II. Similar analysis shows that the fourth unit goes to I and the fifth to II. Since unit six adds $22 to revenue in either market, it makes no difference where it is sold; six and seven go to each market. Eight and nine are sold in I because they yield higher marginal revenue there; ten goes to II for the same reason. Unit 11 can go to either market, since the additional revenues are the same, and unit 12 goes to the other. Thus we see that the 12 units

TABLE 9.7.1

Allocation of Sales between Two Markets

Quantity	Marginal Revenue Market I		Marginal Revenue Market II	
1............................	$45	(1)	$34	(3)
2............................	36	(2)	28	(5)
3............................	30	(4)	22	(7)
4............................	22	(6)	13	(10)
5............................	17	(8)	[10]	(12)
6............................	15	(9)	8	
7............................	[10]	(11)	7	
8............................	7		4	
9............................	4		2	
10............................	0		1	

should be divided so that the marginal revenues are the same for the last unit sold in each market; the monopolist sells seven units in market I and five in market II.

Exercise: The student should establish that any further reallocation of the 12 units diminishes total revenue. He should also establish that 17 units should be divided 8 in II and 9 in I.

Principle: The discriminating monopolist allocates a given output such that the marginal revenues in each market are equal. He sells any additional unit in the market with the higher marginal revenue.

This argument establishes the basis for allocating a given output between two markets. It also permits an easy explanation of the condition that different demand elasticities in the two markets are necessary for price discrimination to exist. Recall that marginal revenue may be expressed in the following way:

$$MR = p\left(1 - \frac{1}{\eta}\right),$$

where p is price and η is the elasticity of demand. As just shown, MR must be the same in each market. Therefore, if $MR_I = MR_{II}$, it is necessary that

$$p_I\left(1 - \frac{1}{\eta_I}\right) = p_{II}\left(1 - \frac{1}{\eta_{II}}\right).$$

Thus

$$\frac{p_I}{p_{II}} = \frac{\left(1 - \frac{1}{\eta_{II}}\right)}{\left(1 - \frac{1}{\eta_I}\right)}.$$

Consequently, if the elasticities are equal $(\eta_I = \eta_{II})$, $(1 - \frac{1}{\eta_I}) =$
$(1 - \frac{1}{\eta_{II}})$. Therefore, p_I must equal p_{II}, and price discrimination does not
exist. For $p_I \neq p_{II}$, $\eta_I \neq \eta_{II}$. Price will be lower in the more elastic market.

As we have seen, the first problem confronting a price discriminating
monopolist is to allocate a given level of sales between his markets. The
second problem is to determine the optimal level of sales and, therefore,
the level of price in each of the submarkets. For this calculation both
revenue and cost data are required.

Assume that a monopolist can separate his market into two markets.
The demands and marginal revenues of each are shown in panel *a*,
Figure 9.7.1. D_1D_1' and MR_1 are demand and marginal revenue in the
first market; D_2D_2' and MR_2 are demand and marginal revenue in the
second. Panel *b* shows the horizontal summation of the two demand and
marginal revenue curves. For example, at a price of $O\bar{p}$ consumers in
market I would take Ox_0 and consumers in market II would take Ox_1.
The total quantity demanded at $O\bar{p}$ is accordingly $Ox_0 + Ox_1 = OX_0$,
shown in panel *b*. All other points on D_mD_m' are derived similarly.
$MR_1 = O\bar{p}$ at output Ox_2; $MR_2 = O\bar{p}$ at Ox_3. Therefore, in panel *b*,
$MR_m = O\bar{p}$ at a quantity of $Ox_2 + Ox_3 = OX_1$. Other points on MR_m,
the total market MR curve, are derived similarly.

The demand and marginal revenue conditions depicted in panel *a*,
Figure 9.7.1, are reproduced in Figure 9.7.2, along with average and
marginal costs of production. The profit maximizing output is $O\bar{X}$, the

FIGURE 9.7.1
Submarket and Total Market Demands and Marginal Revenues

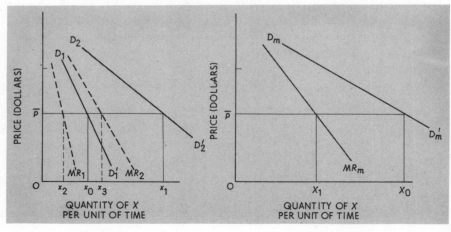

Panel *a*	Panel *b*
Demand and Marginal	Monopoly Demand and
Revenue in Submarkets	Marginal Revenue

quantity at which the total market marginal revenue equals marginal cost. The marginal revenue (equals marginal cost) associated with this output is Om.

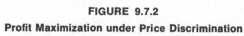

FIGURE 9.7.2

Profit Maximization under Price Discrimination

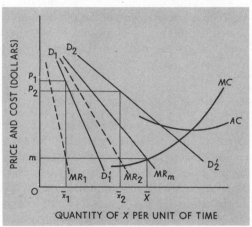

QUANTITY OF X PER UNIT OF TIME

The market allocation rule, previously determined, requires that marginal revenue be the same in each submarket. Since the total market marginal revenue is the added revenue from selling the last unit in either submarket, $MR_1 = MR_2 = Om$. At a marginal revenue of Om, the quantity sold in submarket one is $O\bar{x}_1$; in submarket two, $O\bar{x}_2$. Since MR_m is the horizontal summation of MR_1 and MR_2, $O\bar{x} + O\bar{x}_2 = O\bar{X}$, the total output. Furthermore, from the relevant demand curves the price associated with output $O\bar{x}_1$ in market one is Op_1, the price associated with $O\bar{x}_2$ in market two is Op_2. Because these clearly differ, discrimination can exist.

Summarizing these results:

Proposition: If the aggregate market for a monopolist's product can be divided into submarkets with different price elasticities, the monopolist can profitably practice price discrimination. Total output is determined by equating marginal cost with aggregate monopoly marginal revenue. The output is allocated among the submarkets so as to equate marginal revenue in each submarket with aggregate marginal revenue at the $MC = MR$ point. Finally, price in each submarket is determined directly from the submarket demand curve, given the submarket allocation of sales.

A final relation is worth noting. Since marginal revenue must be the same in each submarket, our $MR—p—\eta$ formula reduces to

$$p_\mathrm{I} \left(1 - \frac{1}{\eta_\mathrm{I}}\right) = p_\mathrm{II} \left(1 - \frac{1}{\eta_\mathrm{II}}\right).$$

Thus if $\eta_\mathrm{I} < \eta_\mathrm{II}$, p_I must necessarily be greater than p_II to preserve the equality. That is, the discriminatory price is greater in the market with the less elastic demand. This helps to explain why students pay more for books and less for airline tickets than professors do. But it explains much more than this. Whenever groups with different demand elasticities exist and there cannot be arbitrage between groups, those who are least willing to substitute other commodities (that is, those with the least elastic demand) will always pay the highest price.

9.7.b—Price Discrimination in Medicine: An Application

The medical profession has become the textbook example of a discriminating monopolist. The discrimination takes the form of scaling fees according to income. Most economists say that doctors discriminate in order to maximize income. The medical profession argues that doctors price discriminate to act as a collection agency for medical charities. That is, they charge high income patients a high fee to finance the low-fee treatment of low income patients. In a classic paper on the subject, Reuben A. Kessel analyzed the motives for medical price discrimination.[5] From the evidence Kessel concluded that doctors discriminate to increase their incomes; that is, the model set forth in 9.7.a explains medical price discrimination. Kessel also analyzed why competition among doctors does not eliminate discrimination and lead to uniform prices. As we shall see in Chapter 10, whenever a reasonably large group of firms joins together to fix prices, some firms, believing they will be unnoticed, always cut prices to maximize their own income. Price fixing generally ends in this way. Given the historical pattern of even very small groups of price fixers breaking up because of price cutting within the group, why can the extremely large number of doctors continue price discrimination? Seemingly many doctors could benefit economically by lowering fees for high income patients and raising them for the poor. This should break the price fixing, but, in contrast with other groups, doctors seldom "cheat" on the cartel. In this sub-section we will summarize Kessel's analysis and evidence.

Kessel first tested the hypothesis that doctors price discriminate because of charitable motives rather than income maximization. He asked why we do not observe parallel behavior in nursing and dentistry, or even by grocery stores. Food is as "necessary" as medical care. The argument

---

[5] Reuben A. Kessel, "Price Discrimination in Medicine," *Journal of Law and Economics,* Oct. 1958, pp. 20–53. The remainder of this subsection is based upon that paper.

is that the state supplies food and shelter but not medical care; therefore, this type of charity is up to the medical profession. But competition is consistent with charitable behavior.

According to Kessel, if the charity hypothesis is in fact correct, there should be no price discrimination between those who have medical insurance and those who do not. If maximization is the reason for discrimination, those who have insurance should pay, on average, higher fees than the uninsured. Insurance affects the *demand* for doctors but does not change the income of an individual. Those with insurance would have a more inelastic demand than those without, and would pay higher fees. The evidence cited by Kessel does show that medical fees are higher for the insured than for the uninsured. This evidence comes from unions and from the insurance industry. Kessel pointed out that the effect of insurance upon fees, abstracting out variations in income, suggests that fees are determined by "what the traffic will bear."

A second bit of evidence that profit rather than charity motivates price discrimination in medicine is the stand of the American Medical Association (AMA) on different types of insurance. The first type of insurance, cash indemnity plans, has not been opposed at all by the AMA or by local medical societies. Cash indemnity plans such as Blue Cross and Blue Shield allow doctors and patients to determine fees just as though there were no insurance. Doctors are, therefore, able to discriminate, and under such plans the demand for medical care is increased.

In contrast, the AMA and local medical societies have strongly opposed prepaid plans that supply medical services directly to patients. Costs of such cooperative plans are independent of income, and as such, represent a threat to doctors' ability to discriminate. These plans provide the means for extensive price cutting to high income patients. The opposition of organized medicine to these types of plans is in strong support of the profit-maximizing discriminating monopolist hypothesis.

According to Kessel, the reasons doctors do not attempt to cut prices individually is the extensive control of the AMA over medical education. Every doctor must undergo an internship administered by hospitals and only hospitals approved by the AMA are sanctioned for internship and residency. Hospitals value intern and residency training, because they can provide medical care more cheaply with interns and residents than without them. Thus, the AMA controls an important resource for hospitals, and its "advice" that hospitals use only doctors who are members of their local medical society is almost always adhered to. Doctors who are "price cutters" can be removed from the local medical societies, and thus are denied access to hospitals. It would be supposed that any doctor who is denied hospital services finds the demand for his services substantially weakened. It, therefore, pays doctors not to lower prices.

Kessel goes on to use the model of price discrimination to explain other aspects of the medical profession; for example, (1) why doctors, in contrast to other professions, are reluctant to criticize other members of the profession; (2) why doctors treat other doctors and their families free; (3) why individual doctors cannot advertise; (4) why some minorities have been discriminated against in admission to medical school. We will not, however, examine these and other implications here. The article itself is quite easy reading, and, we believe, you would find it rather interesting and perhaps shocking.

9.8   MONOPOLISTIC PRICE CUTTING

In general, monopolies or near monopolies are accused of setting price "too high." However, some monopolies have been accused of having cut prices to drive out competitors to attain their monopoly positions. In fact, federal law is quite strict on this point. On the other hand, some economists maintain that established monopolies price below the profit-maximizing price in order to prevent entry. Let us analyze briefly these two cases.

9.8.a—Predatory Price Cutting: An Application

Apparently, many people still believe that monopolists frequently obtain their monopoly position by lowering prices—sometimes below cost—to drive competitors out of business in a particular area. After the rivals have failed, the predatory price cutter, who then has a monopoly, raises prices and reaps the benefit of his monopoly power. A&P among others, has been accused of these tactics. The most famous of all such cases involves the government's case against the Standard Oil Company in 1911. Everyone "knew" that Standard obtained its monopoly power by predatory price cutting to drive out rivals and Standard still remains the typical example of the predator. The evidence that came out in the trial was largely responsible for the emphasis in anti-trust upon "unfair" business practices and for the general feeling about the small firms that face large competitors.

In 1958 John S. McGee, who at the time held the popular belief that Standard Oil obtained a monopoly by predatory price cutting, examined the theoretical implications of the case and the evidence.[6] Both the theory and the evidence indicate that Standard Oil did not obtain monopoly power by predatory price cutting and that it would have been foolish even to attempt this method. McGee found that the story of Standard

---

[6] John S. McGee, "Predatory Price Cutting: The Standard Oil (N.J.) Case," *Journal of Law and Economics,* Oct. 1958, pp. 137–69. The remainder of this subsection is based upon that paper.

Oil's predatory tactics to obtain and hold a monopoly was logically deficient, and he could find no evidence to support it.

In its early stages, the oil refining business was competitive. As late as 1870 Standard Oil had only ten percent of the business, and the industry. was quite easy to enter. Then how did Standard obtain a monopoly? The predatory pricing hypothesis assumes that the predator already has significant monopoly power. To cut prices locally and drive out rivals a firm must have considerable resources elsewhere to survive the period of losses. Standard did not begin with this power. It attained its size and power simply through mergers and acquisitions, paying for the acquisitions by allowing the former owners to share the monopoly gains. Profits increased and everyone (except the consumers) could be better off. Since competitive firms make only a normal return in the long run, they can be purchased for anything above the market value of their assets.

McGee noted that Standard Oil could have attained a large part of its size by merger and acquisition then used predatory tactics to gain full monopoly power. Possibly Standard had complete monopoly power in many areas and was earning substantial profits in these areas. In other areas where competition existed it could have lowered prices. All firms, including Standard, would make losses until the competitors went out of business, leaving monopoly in a formerly competitive area. But it would have been much cheaper for the potential monopolist to buy out the competitors at anything above the competitive value of the assets. Monopoly profits would begin immediately without first suffering the losses from prolonged price wars.

To gain customers from rivals by lower prices the predator must serve them himself. It then begins to suffer increased losses. Competitors could shut down temporarily, letting the potential monopolist get the sales and take the losses. When prices were raised, the competitors would simply re-enter. The cycle could last indefinitely. In those areas where Standard Oil had a substantial share of the market, its losses during a price war would have been considerable. It is simpler to buy out competitors or merge with them. Only if predatory tactics lower the purchase price will such tactics be profitable, but the evidence does not show that this occurred.

The reason that price was lower where Standard had competitors and higher where it had a monopoly is simple. Supply is higher where there are more competitors. Given reasonably similar demand elasticities, price falls when supply increases. Different prices are not evidence that the monopolist is preying by price discrimination. High supply causes lower prices.

From the theory McGee reached the following conclusions: (1) A firm must have monopoly power *before* it can begin predatory price cutting; (2) since purchase or merger is cheaper, it would not pay a firm to use predatory tactics; (3) variations in prices among markets may be explained by differences in supply and differences in demand elasticities.

Evidence from Standard Oil's trial preponderantly favors McGee's theoretical implications over the hypothesis that the company was a predatory price cutter. In most cases the price paid by Standard Oil to acquire rivals was quite high. The owners of rival firms made substantial profits by selling out or merging. One individual found the transaction so profitable that he formed three companies, each of which he sold to Standard. There are other similar instances. Standard Oil established a monopoly, but it did so by acquisition and merger not by predatory price cutting. In fact, quite frequently the competitors instigated price cutting. This is not to say that Standard Oil was a public benefactor. It was still a monopoly, but it was more profitable to monopolize by merger than by price cutting, and the consumers did not benefit from lower prices during the monopolizing period, as they would have had Standard used predatory tactics.

9.8.b—Price Cutting as a Barrier to Entry

Under some circumstances, in the face of *potential* competitors, a monopolist might charge a price below that at which *MC* equals *MR*. For this tactic to be economical the monopolist must enjoy a certain cost advantage over his competitors. This case differs significantly from the

FIGURE 9.8.1

Price Cutting as a Barrier to Entry

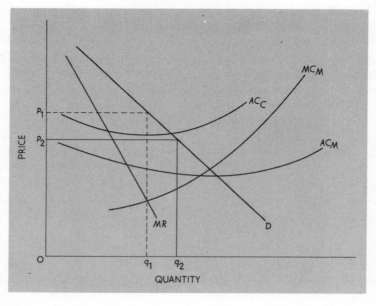

Standard Oil allegation because Standard was not charged with lowering price because of lower costs. Standard supposedly lowered price because it could finance losses out of monopoly profit in other areas.

Figure 9.8.1 illustrates an example in which a monopolist might lower price to prevent entry. A monopolist's long-run average and marginal costs are AC_M and MC_M. Market demand and marginal revenue are D and MR. The profit-maximizing price and quantity are Op_1 and Oq_1. Assume that for technological reasons the most advantaged potential rival has the long-run average cost curve, AC_c. Even though the competitor does suffer a cost disadvantage, he could enter the industry at a price lower than Op_1 but above AC_c and take some of the monopolist's business. The monopolist would then be forced to lower his price.

The monopolist, however, can set a price slightly below the minimum point of his potential competitor's long-run average cost curve. For the competitor to make any profit his price must be above AC_c. If the monopolist sets the price Op_2 and sells Oq_2, the competitor will not be able to make profit and hence will not be induced into competition. The monopolist's profit, of course, will be lower than maximum, but his rival's entry could lower profit even more. If it takes a very long time for a new firm to become established, the monopolist may not wish to sacrifice the stream of higher earnings. But if entry is easy he may well be satisfied with lower profit and the retention of his monopoly situation.

Economists have set forth many other reasons for the emergence and continuation of monopoly. We will postpone an analysis of these until the next chapter.

9.9 ANALYTICAL EXERCISES: MONOPOLY REGULATION

Since some of the social effects of monopoly behavior are thought to be "undesirable," governments from time to time attempt to regulate their behavior by imposing price ceilings and by enacting certain forms of taxation. Without considering social desirability, we can analyze some effects of such regulation upon the price-output behavior of monopolists.

9.9.a—Price Regulation

If government believes a monopolist is making "too much" profit, is charging "too high" a price, or is "restricting" output,[7] it can set a price ceiling on the commodity. As you will recall from Chapter 2, a ceiling price under perfect competition causes a shortage, and some form of

---

[7] "Too much" and "too high" are perhaps undefinable except in the sense that they mean more than or higher than someone wishes them to be. The monopolist "restricts" output only in the sense that $P > MC$.

nonprice allocation of the good must develop. This may or may not be the
case under monopoly.

Consider first the situation in Figure 9.9.1. Under the cost and revenue

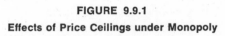

FIGURE 9.9.1

Effects of Price Ceilings under Monopoly

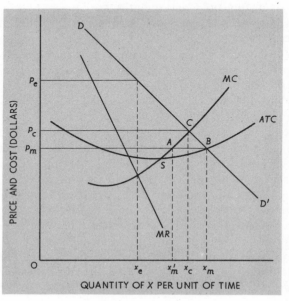

conditions depicted, the nonregulated monopolist sells Ox_e at a price of
Op_e; he obviously makes a substantial pure profit. Now let us assume that
the government imposes a price ceiling (that is, a price less than Op_e).
Suppose Op_c is the maximum price allowed. The segment p_cC becomes
the new demand and marginal revenue up to the output Ox_c. The monopolist can sell any quantity up to Ox_c at a price of Op_c because over this
range actual demand lies above p_cC; he would certainly charge no lower
price. Thus over the segment p_cC, the monopolist's effective demand is a
horizontal line and $P = MR$. After Ox_c the old demand and marginal
revenue curves become effective. The entire new demand is, therefore,
the line p_cCD'. With the new demand curve, marginal revenue now equals
marginal cost at C; the monopolist sells Ox_c units per period at a price of
Op_c. Since C lies on DD', quantity supplied equals quantity demanded
and the market is cleared. Price falls, quantity increases, and marginal
cost now equals price. Further, profit clearly diminishes. Since Ox_e and
Op_e gave *maximum* profit, any other combination, including Op_c and
Ox_c, must give less than maximum profit.

At any ceiling price set between Op_e and Op_c, price would equal MC at an output greater than the quantity the market would demand at that price. Therefore the monopolist sells the quantity given by his demand curve (DD') at the ceiling price. Again price falls from Op_e and quantity increases from Ox_c, but in contrast to Op_c, price exceeds the marginal cost of the last unit sold.

You may think, "If Op_c causes price to fall, quantity to rise, and profit to diminish, why not lower price even farther, possibly to Op_m?" True enough, at Op_m the monopolist could sell Ox_m and still cover costs since $ATC = Op_m$ at Ox_m. Note, however, that the new demand and marginal revenue curve is p_mBD'; therefore, $MR = MC$ at A and the firm would produce Ox_m', which is *less* thanOx_m. Since quantity demanded at Op_m is Ox_m, a shortage of $x_m'\,x_m$ results. In this case the monopolist must allocate by means other than price. In fact, any price below Op_c causes a decrease in quantity from Ox_c and hence a shortage inasmuch as quantity demanded exceeds quantity supplied. The monopolist will produce along his MC curve over the portion SC; but the market demands a greater quantity at each of these prices. If price is set below minimum ATC (point S), the monopolist will go out of business.

Under the conditions assumed in Figure 9.9.1 the greatest quantity is attained by setting the ceiling price so that the monopolist produces where MC intersects actual demand. This result, however, may not always be obtainable by a ceiling price. Figure 9.9.2 depicts such a case. The nonregulated profit-maximizing monopolist in Figure 9.9.2 sells Ox_1 units per period at price Op_1. If the government sets a ceiling price of

FIGURE 9.9.2

Effects of Price Ceilings under Monopoly

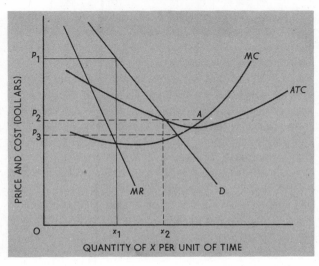

Op_3, the price at which MC crosses demand, the monopolist in the long run would go out of business; at this price he could not cover total costs. In fact, the ceiling could be no lower than Op_2 without forcing the firm to cease production. At Op_2 the firm would sell Ox_2 units per period and make no pure profit. The monopolist would like to produce and sell the quantity at which Op_2 equals MC (point A), but demand conditions would not allow him to sell this quantity. A surplus would occur. Therefore, at any ceiling between Op_1 and Op_2, the firm sells the quantity given by the actual demand curve at that price; at any ceiling below Op_2 the firm eventually shuts down.

8.7.b—Taxation

An alternative method of monopoly regulation is some type of special taxation. We examine here the effects of three common types: the excise or per unit tax, the lump-sum tax, and the percentage of profits tax.

An excise or per unit tax means that for every unit sold, regardless of price, the monopolist must pay a specified amount of money to the government. Assume that the monopolist, whose cost curves ATC_0 and MC_0 are shown in Figure 9.9.3, is charged a tax of k dollars for every unit sold. Total cost after the tax is the total cost of *production* (presumably the

FIGURE 9.9.3

Effects of an Excise Tax under Monopoly

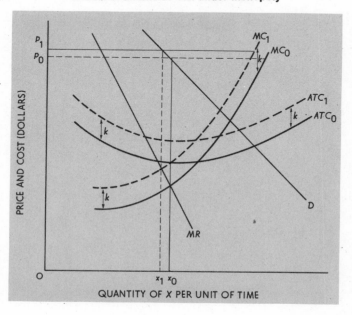

same as before) plus k times output; thus average or unit cost must rise by exactly the amount of the tax, k dollars. The after-tax ATC in Figure 9.9.3 rises from ATC_0 to ATC_1, or by the vertical distance k. MC also rises by k dollars. If it costs MC_0 to produce and sell an additional unit of output before the tax, after the tax it costs $MC_0 + k = MC_1$ to produce and sell that unit. This also is shown in Figure 9.9.3.

Before the tax is imposed the monopolist produces Ox_0 and charges a price of Op_0. After the imposition of the tax, the cost curves shift vertically by the amount k to ATC_1 and MC_1. MC_1 now equals MR at the output Ox_1, so price rises to Op_1. This effect, of course, differs completely from the effect of the ceiling price that causes price to fall and quantity to rise.

Note that the firm absorbs some of the tax and shifts some to the consumers in the form of higher prices. The proportion shifted depends upon the slope of marginal cost and the slope of demand. We can extend the horizontal lines from p_1 and p_0 to the MC curves to see the proportion of k that is shifted. This shows the difference between p_0 and p_1, the amount of the tax shifted, as a fraction of the tax k.

A lump-sum tax has a somewhat different effect upon price and quantity. Assume that instead of imposing an excise tax on the monopolist, the government charges (say) a license fee that remains the same regardless of quantity sold. The license fee is, therefore, a fixed cost to the monopolist. ATC rises after the fee is imposed; at very small outputs ATC rises more than at larger outputs because the larger the output the more units the fee is "spread over." Once the fee is paid, however, no additional tax is charged for an additional unit of production per period. MC, therefore, remains unchanged. Since MC and MR do not change after the lump-sum tax, their point of intersection does not change, and thus price and quantity remain the same after the tax is imposed. The lump-sum tax, which does reduce profits, must not, of course, be so large as to cause a loss and drive the monopolist out of business.

A percentage of profit tax, just as the lump-sum tax, does not affect quantity or price. Assume that a monopolist must pay π percent of his profit (regardless of the profit) as a tax. Since π is presumably between 0 and 100, the monopolist retains $(100 - \pi)$ percent of his profits after paying the tax. Revenue and cost curves remain the same. Before the tax is imposed the monopolist chooses price and quantity so as to maximize profit. After the tax he still chooses the same price and quantity so as to maximize his before tax profit, since he obviously prefers $(100 - \pi)$ percent of the maximum profit to $(100 - \pi)$ percent of some smaller amount.

Tax regulation, therefore, differs from price regulation in several ways even though profits are reduced in all cases. In particular, taxation, in contrast to some price ceilings, cannot force the monopolist to set price equal to marginal cost.

8.6 CONCLUSION

The pure monopolist chooses the output at which $MC = MR$. In contrast to perfect competition, the market does not force the monopolist in the long run to produce the quantity at which long-run ATC is at its minimum and to charge a price equal to minimum long-run ATC and MC. This does not necessarily indicate that price must be higher and quantity lower under monopoly than under perfect competition. Cost conditions may differ between the two forms of organization. We can only say that price under monopoly will not, in the absence of regulation, equal marginal cost and that the entry of competitors will not reduce pure profit to zero. Demand conditions certainly can change so as to eliminate profit, however, since a monopoly position does not guarantee pure profit.

In particular we wish to stress the following definition:

Definition: Marginal revenue is the addition to total revenue obtained from selling an additional unit of output. For a perfect competitor marginal revenue is price. Since a monopolist must lower price to sell more output, his marginal revenue is less than price. In particular the relation is given by $MR = P\left(1 - \dfrac{1}{\eta}\right)$, where η is demand elasticity. If demand is elastic (inelastic), marginal revenue is positive (negative).

For a discriminating monopolist we have the following relations:

Relations: A discriminating monopolist maximizes profit by selling the output at which the market marginal revenue (the horizontal summation of all sub-market marginial revenues) equals marginal cost. He allocates the output so that the marginal revenues in each sub-market are equal. He charges the associated price in each sub-market; the more inelastic the demand, the higher the price. For discrimination to continue there cannot be reselling among sub-markets. Governments can regulate monopoly by taxation or price fixing. Only in certain cases of price fixing can price be made equal to marginal cost.

QUESTIONS AND PROBLEMS

1. We have stated in this chapter that the monopolist does not have a supply curve. Explain! (Hint: What is the definition of supply? Under some circumstances could one price be the minimum necessary to induce him to supply a specific quantity, while under other conditions, not involving cost changes, a lower price would induce him to supply that amount?)

2. Some time ago, most of the major airlines issued student travel cards at a nominal price. These cards permitted college students to fly "space available" (that is, no reservations allowed) at substantial discounts. All but one of these lines wonder if this strategy really paid off; passengers who were not students were found using the cards, and some students insured

themselves available space by reserving seats for fictitious passengers who then did not show up for the flight.

  a. Do the discounts represent price discrimination?

  b. Do the conditions necessary for successful discrimination exist?

3. From 1923 to 1946, Du Pont was virtually the sole American producer of "moistureproof Cellophane," a product for which it held the key patents. In an opinion that exonerated Du Pont of possessing any economically meaningful monopoly, the Supreme Court held "an appraisal of the 'cross-elasticity' of demand in the trade" to be of considerable importance to the decision. Why?

4. Derive the marginal revenue curve for a demand curve concave from above.

FIGURE E.9.1

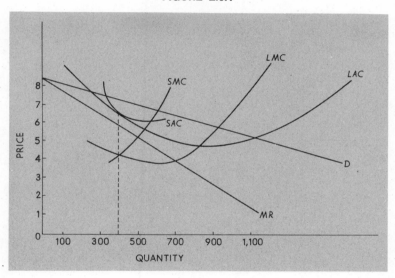

5. Assume a monopolist with the demand and cost curves shown in Figure E.9.1. He is in the short run with the plant designed to produce 400 units optimally.

  a. What output should he produce?

  b. What will be the price?

  c. How much profit is made?

  d. If he can change plant and move into the long run, what will be his output and price?

  e. Will profit increase? How do you know?

  f. Draw the new short-run average and marginal cost curves for the new output.

6. Assume that a monopolist can divide his market into two sub-markets, the

demands and marginal revenues of which are shown in Figure E.9.2, along with marginal cost.

a. Find equilibrium output and price in each market.
b. Which market has the more elastic demand?
c. What would be price and output if the monopolist could not discriminate?

FIGURE E.9.2

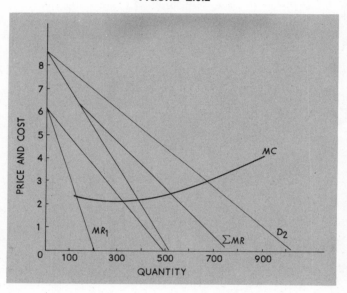

7. A monopolist has a demand curve given by $P = 50 - 2q$ and a marginal revenue of $MR = 50 - 4q$. Marginal cost over the relevant range is $MC = 4 + 2q$.
   a. Find the equilibrium output and price.
   b. Verify graphically that the given marginal revenue is correct for the given demand.

8. Assume a straight line demand curve that cuts the vertical (price) axis at $30 and the horizontal (quantity) axis at 100 units.
   a. Graph the demand and the associated marginal revenue.
   b. Demand has unitary elasticity at _____ units of output and a price of $_____. It is _____ above this price and _____ below this price.

9. A monopolist's revenue and long-run cost curves are shown in Figure E.9.3.
   a. Output and price are _____ and $_____.

b. A ceiling price of $_____ would eliminate profit.
c. Output and price would change to _____ and $_____.
d. An excise tax of $2 per unit would change price to $_____ and output to _____.

FIGURE E.9.3

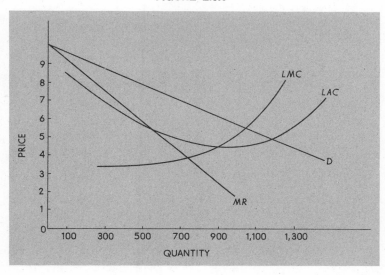

chapter
10

Theories of Price
under Imperfect Competition

10.1 INTRODUCTION

Between the extremes of perfect competition and monopoly come a
large number of theoretical market structures, none of which lends itself
to the rigorous analysis of Chapters 8 and 9. For convenience, we classify
all these "intermediate" market structures into two categories: monopolistic competition and oligopoly. Many of the theories of markets in
these classifications were developed during the late 1920s and early
1930s because of the reaction to the theories of perfect competition and
monopoly. Many economists, after pointing out that the two "extremes"
are not accurate pictures of the real world, turned their attention to the
middle ground between monopoly and perfect competition.

We first present the theory of monopolistic competition; second, discuss some oligopoly models; third, indicate reasons why some industries
are not competitive; and fourth, analyze some effects of attempting to get
more "realism" into the theory of the firm. Although we do not dwell
upon the matter, it should become obvious that most real world problems
can be analyzed within the context of the competition or monopoly model.

10.2 FUNDAMENTALS OF MONOPOLISTIC COMPETITION

One of the most notable achievements of economists who examined
the middle ground between competition and monopoly was that of an
American economist, Edward H. Chamberlin. Our attention is directed
first to his theory of monopolistic competition.[1]

---

[1] E. H. Chamberlin, *The Theory of Monopolistic Competition* (Cambridge, Mass.:
Harvard University Press, 1933).

10.2.a—Heterogeneous Goods and Product Groups

Chamberlin based his theory of monopolistic competition on a solid empirical fact: there are very few monopolies because there are very few commodities for which close substitutes do not exist; similarly there are very few commodities that are entirely homogeneous. Instead, there is a wide range of commodities, some of which have relatively few good substitutes and some of which have many good, but not perfect, substitutes.

For example, one often speaks of an "automobile industry," knowing full well that automobiles are not a homogeneous product. A Ford is a substitute, albeit not a perfect substitute, for a Cadillac. Fords are perhaps better substitutes for Chevrolets; but, in fact, even a Ford Falcon is not a perfect substitute for a "deluxe" Ford, and the latter is not a perfect substitute for a Thunderbird. Each automobile firm has an absolute monopoly over its own brands of cars; but the various brands are, in greater or lesser degree, substitutes. There is intense *personal* competition or rivalry among the firms. Now consider a case at the other extreme. Haircuts from Sam's Barber Shop are closely related to haircuts from Joe's Barber Shop across the street. They are not the same product, however; one shop has a monopoly on "haircuts from Sam's," the other a monopoly on "haircuts from Joe's." At the same price some prefer to get haircuts from Sam, some from Joe.

In these, and in a multitude of other cases, the products are *heterogeneous* rather than homogeneous; hence perfect, and impersonal, competition cannot exist. Second, although heterogeneous, the products are only slightly differentiated. Each is a very close substitute for the other; hence competition exists, but it is a personal competition among rivals who are well aware of each other.

When products are closely related but heterogeneous, one cannot speak of an industry, which is defined as a collection of firms producing a homogeneous good. Nonetheless, it is useful to lump together firms producing very closely related commodities and refer to them as a *product group*. Each producer in the product group has some degree of monopoly power; but not much because other producers market a differentiated but closely related commodity.[2]

10.2.b—Two Demand Curves

In the analysis of perfect competition two demand curves are used: the negatively sloped industry demand curve and the horizontal demand curve confronting each seller. As you will recall, the latter is horizontal

---

[2] At our level of abstraction it is not necessary to specify how closely products must be related in order to be in the same product group.

because each producer of the *homogeneous product* must accept the going price or sell nothing. If he were to raise his price he would forfeit all sales. If he were to lower it, he would needlessly forfeit some revenue.

The two curves required for the theory of monopolistic competition, shown in Figure 10.2.1, are very similar. Suppose the firm in question somehow attains an instantaneous equilibrium at the point E, with output Ox per period and price Op. Suppose further that the entrepreneur contemplates price maneuvering in order to obtain greater profit.

FIGURE 10.2.1

Two Demand Curves

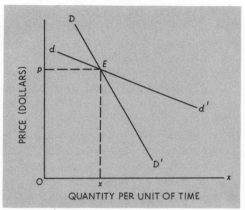

One of Chamberlin's fundamental assumptions is that a large group of monopolistic competitors exists in each product group. Another is that all firms in the group produce closely related and readily substitutable goods. Hence if the entrepreneur contemplates a price reduction from Op, he will expect a substantial expansion in sales. First, sales to his existing clientele will expand. Second, and more important, if other entrepreneurs do not reduce price he will capture a part of their markets. Thus, he can expect an appreciable expansion of sales.

On the other hand, he can expect a substantial loss in sales if he increases his price. Not only will sales to existing customers decline but some of his customers will switch to other producers who have not raised their prices. Consequently, assuming such a large number of sellers in the market that each expects his actions to go unnoticed by his rivals, every entrepreneur will expect his demand curve to be very elastic. The entrepreneur's expected or anticipated demand curve is shown by the relatively elastic curve dd' in Figure 10.2.1. The anticipated demand, dd', is the demand associated with the short-run equilibria to be discussed in Section 10.3.

Anticipating highly elastic demand, each entrepreneur may have an incentive to reduce price; and thus *all* entrepreneurs have this incentive. But if all prices are reduced simultaneously, each entrepreneur will gain only that increment in sales attributable to the general price reduction. He will not capture portions of his rivals' markets. Thus if the actions of one entrepreneur are matched by all other entrepreneurs in the product group, demand will in fact be far less elastic, such as the curve DD' in Figure 10.2.1. In other words, DD' is the curve showing the quantity demanded from any one seller at various prices under the assumption that his competitors' prices are always identical with his.

Relations: The curve dd' shows the increased sales any entrepreneur can expect to enjoy by lowering his price, providing all other entrepreneurs maintain their original prices. DD', on the other hand, shows the actual sales to be gained as a general downward movement of prices takes place.

10.3 SHORT-RUN EQUILIBRIUM: MONOPOLY ASPECT OF MONOPOLISTIC COMPETITION

The theory of monopolistic competition is essentially a long-run theory. In the short run there is virtually no difference between the analysis of monopoly and of monopolistic competition. Each producer of a differentiated product behaves so as to maximize profit. Each producer thinks that his demand is like the anticipated demand dd' in Figue 10.2.1. Each attempts to maximize his profit subject to his anticipated demand. With the anticipated demand and marginal revenue curves, as in Figure 10.3.1, he equates marginal cost with marginal revenue. In the specific example of the figure, this leads to an output of Ox_0 units per period and a price of Op_0 per unit. In the resulting short-run equilibrium, pure profit is represented by the area of the shaded rectangle p_0ABc_0.

So far as the short run is concerned there appears to be very little *competition* in monopolistic competition. But when a longer view is taken one essential element of monopoly is missing. In particular, a monopoly cannot be maintained if there is free entry. Other firms will enter and produce the homogeneous product; and they will continue to enter until all pure profit is eliminated or until the competitive solution is reached.

In the present case the product is differentiated, not homogeneous, so there is no industry to enter. But other firms are free to produce a closely related product; entrance into the product group is not closed. If one or a few firms are obviously enjoying a highly prosperous situation, other firms

FIGURE 10.3.1

**Short-Run Equilibrium of the Firm
under Monopolistic Competition**

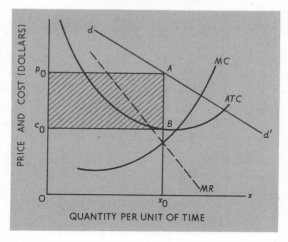

will begin to produce a closely related product. They will "enter" the product group, as it were, and their entrance will have market repercussions not greatly different from the entrance of perfectly competitive firms into an industry.

10.4 LONG-RUN EQUILIBRIUM: COMPETITIVE ASPECTS OF MONOPOLISTIC COMPETITION

All Chamberlin's specializing assumptions have been discussed or implied, yet it may be well to recount them now. First, many firms produce a differentiated product. Each commodity within the product group is a close substitute for every other commodity; and such a large number of sellers is in the product group that each expects his competitive maneuvering to go unnoticed by his rivals. Second, for the present, price is the variable entrepreneurs manipulate in an effort to increase profit. Finally, as Chamberlin puts it, there is the "heroic assumption that both demand and cost curves for all the 'products' are uniform throughout the group. . . . [This only requires] that consumers' preferences be evenly distributed among the different varieties, and that differences between them [the products] be not such as to give rise to differences in cost."[3]

The last assumption merits further comment. In perfect competition all products are homogeneous. Thus it is not unreasonable to assume identical costs of production for all entrepreneurs in the industry—an

---

[3] Chamberlain, *Monopolisitc Competition,* pp. 82–83.

assumption that greatly facilitates analysis because it permits long-run industry equilibrium to be explained by means of a graph pertaining to only one firm. This is precisely the purpose of the assumption under discussion; but it is clearly more restrictive than in perfect competition. Basically one assumes product differences are not so great as to entail cost differences. Different scents for toilet soaps, slightly different tobacco blends, differences in the color of packaging material, and differences in the collar style of men's shirts are but a few examples of product differences that would give rise to little, if any, difference in cost. Yet the assumption is quite restrictive since *marked* quality differences (Volkswagen vis-à-vis Cadillac) are generally precluded.

FIGURE 10.4.1

Long-Run Equilibrium with Entry of Firms

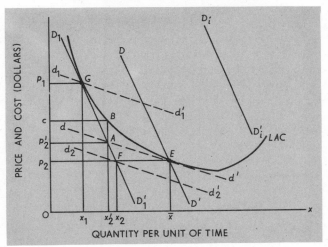

With these assumptions and analytical tools we can proceed immediately to the analysis of long-run equilibrium in the large group case with price competition. Because of easy entry, profits must be competed away to zero in the long run. Only two situations are consistent with zero profit. These are points such as G and E in Figure 10.4.1. At G the firm's actual demand is tangent to LAC; at E the anticipated demand is tangent.

Let D_iD_i' be the initial demand curve. The firm in question, and any other in the product group, reaps a pure profit. Let each firm be in short-run equilibrium. Since entry into the product group is open, new firms selling slightly differentiated products are attracted. The greater variety of available products causes the demand for each seller's product to contract. In the process, DD' shifts to the left. Simultaneously, if entrepreneurs attempt to profit maximize by reducing price, dd' slides down the instantaneously existing DD' and probably becomes somewhat more elastic, because of more substitutes.

The transition from the initial D_iD_i' curve to the ultimate long-run equilibrium at point E could come about in a number of ways. One method is illustrated in Figure 10.4.1, where it is assumed that new firms enter the product group until the proportional demand curve shifts from D_iD_i' to D_1D_1'. It might seem that equilibrium is attained at G, with output of Ox_1 and price Op_1 per unit, inasmuch as pure profit is zero at that point. However, each entrepreneur thinks d_1d_1' is his demand curve. A reduction in price would, in his belief, cause an expansion along d_1d_1'; profit would accordingly expand. But each entrepreneur has the same incentive; so as price is reduced by all, dd' slides down D_1D_1' for each.

The only way that G could be a point of long-run equilibrium is for the market *not* to be characterized by active price competition. A "live and let live" outlook on the part of sellers, tacit agreements, open price associations, price maintenance, customary prices, and professional ethics are a few causes of nonagressive price policies. If price competition is, in fact, lacking, individual entrepreneurs will have no regard for the existence of curves such as d_1d_1'. They will be concerned only with the effects of a general price rise or decline, or with the DD' curve. Pure profit is eliminated when enough firms have entered to push demand to D_1D_1'; the firm, ignoring d_1d_1', produces Ox_1 and sells at Op_1, which is a higher price and lower quantity than those forthcoming under active price competition.

Suppose now that firms do attempt to reduce price and expand along d_1d_1'. However, as all firms attempt to expand, the movement takes place along D_1D_1' and price falls to Op_2', with output per period Ox_2'. Each firm incurs a pure loss represented by the area of the rectangle $cBAp_2'$. It might seem that each firm could eliminate its pure loss by reducing price to Op_2 and moving to point E. Yet with the number of firms giving rise to D_1D_1', a reduction in price to Op_2 would shift the subjective demand curve further down D_1D_1', to the position d_2d_2'. Temporary equilibrium would be attained at F, with sales of Ox_2 rather than $O\bar{x}$ per firm. The situation is necessarily transitory, however, since each firm incurs a pure loss at F. Ultimately some firms must leave the product group; and there is an incentive to do so. As firms leave the group the proportional demand curve shifts to the right, together with the anticipated demand curve; and both probably become somewhat less elastic. The exit of firms must continue until the proportional curve becomes DD' and the anticipated curve dd'. Long-run equilibrium is attained at E. At this point of long-run equilibrium dd' must be tangent to LAC; otherwise each entrepreneur would believe that a change in his price-output policy could augment profit; thus an equilibrium could not exist. Each firm, while having a monopoly of its own "product," is forced to a zero profit position by the competition of rivals producing readily substitutable goods.

Certain questions concerning this equilibrium solution may have been raised in the reader's mind. The first concerns the intersection of anticipated marginal revenue (associated with dashed dd') and marginal cost at the point of tangency between demand and average cost. Would the intersection and the tangency necessarily occur at exactly the same output? If they do not, the profit maximizing entrepreneur would change his output level. This problem can be solved rather easily. As we have shown several times, maximum profit requires $MC = MR$. Since $P = LAC$ at the tangency output, that output gives zero profit. Since LAC is concave from above (it lies above its tangent at all neighborhood points), LAC is greater than demand at all other points and negative profit results. The zero profit solution is the maximum profit solution; hence MC must equal what the entrepreneur *believes* his MR to be at the tangency output. Or we might analyze the problem in another way. Since LAC lies above anticipated demand at every output other than tangency output $O\bar{x}$, total cost lies above total revenue at all outputs except $O\bar{x}$, where they are equal. Thus the two total curves must be tangent (their slopes are equal) at $O\bar{x}$, and marginal cost must equal marginal revenue at the output corresponding to tangency between demand and average cost.

One might also question whether businessmen are so incredibly stupid that they continue to think their price changes will go unnoticed. Time after time they change price, believing the movement will take place along dd'. Each time, however, others do the same and DD' is relevant. Obviously businessmen are not dumb. But when there are large numbers of firms in the groups, each firm changes his price to his own advantage, hoping to get to a more optimal point first, or at least soon enough to capture some of the frictional gains before everyone changes. This hope of being first and capturing frictional gains seems to be a more realistic explanation of the way businessmen act.

Proposition: Large group, long-run equilibrium under price competition and free entry in a monopolistically competitive product group is attained when the anticipated demand is tangent to the long-run unit cost curve. If there is no price competition (collusion) but free entry, equilibrium occurs where actual demand is tangent to *LAC*. When we discuss cartels in this chapter we shall show that the latter is very unstable.

10.5 COMPARISONS OF LONG-RUN EQUILIBRIA

A comparison of long-run equilibria is rather difficult inasmuch as it must rest essentially upon statements pertaining to cost curves. Conditions giving rise to monopoly probably lead to noncomparable differences between competitive and monopolistic costs; for similar reasons, noncomparability is also likely between either of these two and monopolistic competition. However, a few generalizations are possible if one bears in mind that the statements are *relative*, not absolute.

10.5.a—Equilibrium in the Firm

For emphasis, it may be well to recount the "competitive" and "monopolistic" aspects of monopolistic competition. A monopolistically competitive firm is like a monopoly in that it faces anticipated negatively sloped demand and marginal revenue curves; it therefore determines its price-output policy by equating marginal cost with anticipated marginal revenue rather than with price, as in perfect competition. At the same time, the monopolistically competitive firm is like a perfectly competitive one in that it faces impersonal market competition. The long-run result is the absence of pure profit, just as in the competitive case. While all three types may enjoy economic profit in the short run, freedom of entry eliminates it in the long run, except under conditions of pure monopoly. The qualitative nature of rivalry is also different. In perfect competition rivalry is completely impersonal. At the opposite extreme, there is no direct (only indirect and potential) rivalry under monopoly. The case of monopolistic competition is somewhat different, but it lies closer to perfect competition. The monopolistic competitor, at least in abstract, is aware of the slightly differentiated, highly substitutable products of other firms. There would be personal rivalry except for the condition of large numbers—so large that each entrepreneur believes his actions will go unnoticed by his competitors (because they are so numerous that his actions will not have a readily perceptible effect upon any one of them).

10.5.b—Long-Run Equilibria in Industries and Product Groups

In long-run competitive equilibrium, total industry output is produced in a group of plants each of which operates at (long-run) minimum average cost. The product is sold at a price equal to minimum average cost and, it is significant to note, long-run marginal cost equals both price and average cost at this point.

Under monopoly the long-run equilibrium situation is substantially different. The industry output is produced by one firm. The monopolist's plant is unlikely to be of such size as to produce at (long-run) minimum average cost. In any case, price will not equal minimum average cost or marginal cost. Indeed, price will exceed both, so that in long-run equilibrium the marginal social valuation of the commodity exceeds the marginal cost of its production.

In the competitive case, each firm operates a plant to produce the quantity associated with minimum long-run average cost and that size plant and output is called by some "ideal" plant size and "ideal" output. When production of the quantity associated with minimum long-run average cost occurs, the industry's output is sometimes referred to as "ideal." Excess capacity, defined as the difference between actual output and the output associated with minimum long-run average cost, does not exist in long-run equilibrium under perfect competition.

Monopolistic competition is somewhat more difficult to analyze in these terms. In large-group equilibrium with active price competition, price is above marginal cost, although price equals average cost. Since demand is negatively sloped, tangency must occur where average cost is negatively sloped. Therefore, price equals average cost at a point above minimum average cost and at a lower rate of output than that associated with minimum long-run average cost. The difference is excess capacity. In long-run equilibrium under monopolistic competition, each firm has excess capacity.

Some economists, however, argue that the difference is the "cost" society pays for product differentiation and that it is a valid social cost. They then argue that although actual average cost exceeds minimum average cost, when *all* relevant social costs (including the cost of heterogeneity) are included, the firm produces at minimum attainable average cost. Each firm, and the product group as a whole, produces the "sort of ideal" output, and excess capacity does not appear in long-run equilibrium. This argument, however, is *not* universally accepted.

In short, the social welfare aspects of monopolistic competition are ambiguous. From a very microscopic standpoint, each firm produces less than the socially optimal output. On the other hand, if each firm were somehow forced to produce this seemingly desirable level of output at a marginal cost price, private enterprise would no longer represent a viable economic system. Thus the abolition of private enterprise would violate a social welfare criterion (existence of private property rights) that transcends microeconomic considerations, at least in the United States and most industrially advanced western nations. Thus while the theoretical analysis of monopolistic competition is quite clear, the welfare implications of this analysis are not. Micro- and macroeconomic welfare criteria are not consistent or reconcilable. The economist *qua* economist can only indicate the dilemma; establishing definitive social goals and welfare standards is beyond his professional capacity.

10.5.c—Conclusion

During the early stages of its development, the theory of monopolistic competition excited the imaginations of economists, largely because they regarded it as a more *realistic* abstraction from the real world. The anticipated usefulness of the model, however, far exceeded its actual usefulness as an analytical tool or as a framework for developing economic policy.

The assumptions may *in part* be more realistic than those of the competitive and monopoly models. For example, it may be more realistic to assume product heterogeneity with close substitutability than to assume either homogeneity or no close substitutability. On the other hand, some of the assumptions of the theory of monopolistic competition are very unrealistic.

More important, as stressed in Chapter 1, the relevance of the conclusions—not the realism of the assumptions—is what counts. On this score the competitive and monopoly models are clearly superior. The theory of monopolistic competition is much less useful than the competitive and monopolistic models for analyzing real world markets. But even more can be said. The theory of monopolistic competition does not actually provide a particularly realistic description of real world markets. Therefore, one should not take this theory as a prototype of such markets. It is simply an attempt, although not a particularly successful one, to add more realism to the theory of the firm.

Our reason for devoting so much space to the theory of monopolistic competition is to illustrate the problems involved whenever one attempts to gain realism at the expense of rigorous but simple analysis. It is important to understand the theory of monopolistic competition to appreciate more fully the theories of competition and monopoly as analytical devices.

10.6 OLIGOPOLY

Oligopoly, or its limiting form duopoly, is a market situation intermediate between the cases previously studied. In monopoly only one seller is in the market; competition, in either the technical or the popular sense, does not exist. Perfect competition and large-group monopolistic competition represent the opposite. So many firms are in the market that the actions of each are thought to be imperceptible to the others. There is competition in the technical sense, but little or none in the popular sense. The reverse tends to be true in oligopoly; technically, competition is lacking but sometimes there is intense rivalry or competition in the popular sense.

Oligopoly is said to exist when more than one seller is in the market, but when the number is not so large as to render negligible the contribution of each. A market has few enough sellers to be considered oligopolistic if the firms recognize their *mutual interdependence*. In monopoly and competition, firms make decisions and take action without considering how these actions will affect other firms and how, in turn, other firms' reactions will affect them. Oligopolists must take these reactions into account in their decision-making process.

When contemplating a price change, a design innovation, a new advertising campaign, and so on, Ford Motor Company must anticipate how GM and the Chrysler Corporation will react because, without doubt, Ford's actions will affect the demand for Chevrolets and Plymouths.

This, in short, is the oligopoly problem and the central problem in oligopoly analysis. The oligopolistic firm is large enough to recognize (*a*) the mutual interdependence of the firms in the oligopoly and (*b*) the fact that its decisions will affect the other firms who in turn will react in a way that affects the initial firm. The great uncertainty is *how one's competitors will react.*

Since so many industries meet the general description of oligopoly, it would at first glance seem that a general theory of oligopoly would have been developed. The problem in developing an oligopoly theory, however, is the same as the oligopoly problem itself. Mutual interdependence and the resulting uncertainty about reaction patterns make it necessary for the economist to make specific assumptions about behavioral patterns; that is, specific assumptions about how oligopolists *believe* their competitors will react and about how their competitors actually react.

Therefore, as we shall see, the solution to the oligopoly model (that is, equilibrium price and output) depends critically upon the assumptions the economist makes in regard to the behavioral reaction of rival entrepreneurs. Since many different assumptions can and have been made, many different solutions can and have been reached. Thus there is no "theory of oligopoly" in the sense that there is a theory of perfect competition or of monopoly. There is no unique, general solution but merely many different behavioral models, each of which reaches a different solution. Further, none of these models gives a reasonably realistic account of any *one* oligopolistic industry, so no general result can be expected.

A brief discussion of a few of the classical models of oligopoly should highlight some of the problems involved in the attempt to gain realism at the expense of generality. The discussion of these models is intended simply to illustrate the problem of "realism v. generality," not to present a thorough analysis of the models (or, for that matter, to present all the classical models). Except for game-theory models and the Hotelling Case, little credence is today accorded the solutions set forth in this section. Most of the models described were formulated for duopoly (in which there are only two sellers), but they apply to oligopoly as well.

Formal speculation about the duopoly problem is sometimes dated from the work of a French economist, A. A. Cournot, in 1838. He assumed that two duopolists own two mineral springs; they are situated side by side and furnish identical mineral water. There is a cost of sinking the well, but after sinking the well the added cost of selling a cup of water is zero. Therefore, marginal cost is zero at every level of output. Each duopolist believes that the other will not change the *quantity* he sells regardless of what he himself does. Given these assumptions, after many changes in price and output, each duopolist sells one third the output at which marginal cost (zero) equals price (that is, the output at which demand crosses the horizontal axis). Price is lower, total output greater, and profits lower than under monopoly. Price is higher, total output is lower, and profits higher than under perfect competition. This is one solution, but it is based on a rather naïve assumption: each entrepreneur believes his rival will never change his volume of sales, even though he repeatedly observes such changes.

The next solution was developed by an English economist, F. Y. Edgeworth, in 1897. The two firms in the Edgeworth Case are the same as those posited by Cournot; they sell a homogeneous product, are situated side by side, and have zero marginal costs. The only change is that each entrepreneur believes his competitor's *price* will remain constant. Under this assumption an equilibrium price and quantity cannot result. Both fluctuate continually, and so the solution is indeterminant. The Edgeworth solution improves upon Cournot's analysis because *price* rather than *output* is the relevant decision variable for the entrepreneur. Yet in Edgeworth's model, the result of using price as the decision variable is to introduce indeterminancy. Empirically, duopoly and oligopoly markets tend to be somewhat stable. To explain stability in duopoly and oligopoly markets, Harold Hotelling, in 1929, constructed a model that has become famous for its far-reaching significance.

In Hotelling's model two entrepreneurs produce a physically identical product at zero marginal cost. However, the products of the duopolists are differentiated in the eyes of the buyers because of locational differences. Buyers are located uniformly along a straight road. At the same price each buyer purchases from the closer duopolist. Each duopolist is motivated to move as close as possible to the other. They end up locating side by side at the middle of the road. Price and location are stable; and this tends to explain why theaters locate along Broadway and why the Methodists and Baptists are so much alike.

Somewhat later Chamberlin proposed a stable duopoly solution that depends upon mutual recognition of interdependence. Chamberlin's case is exactly that of Cournot except for one assumption and the final result. Chamberlin assumes that the duopolists mutually recognize that the best they can do is to produce the monopoly output and sell it at the monopoly price; they divide the maximum monopoly profit, perhaps each taking half. In Chamberlin's solution, each entrepreneur understands that his actions affect the other and acts accordingly; Chamberlin obtains a stable solution that may not be too far from reality in homogeneous oligopoly situations. However, this is a case of tacit collusion (see Section 10.8).

The last solution to be examined in this section is the application of game theory to oligopoly behavior developed by John von Neumann and Oskar Morgenstern. Their solution requires oligopolists to behave as though they were participants in some game of chance. Each business strategy is a move in the game. The heart of game theory is the minimax principle; and there is much criticism of application of this principle to decision making in economics and business. Essentially, the minimax principle requires each player with a given set of decision possibilities to maximize his profit under the assumption that his rival always takes the least desirable course of action from the former's standpoint. Slightly less precisely, the minimax principle requires the player (or entrepreneur) to adopt the plan of action that will make the *best* of the *worst* possible situation. But this plan of action will not be the *best* if the *worst* possible situation does not arise. It does not allow the entrepreneur to exploit favorable changes in the market or, in any sense, to be "dynamic."

In the real world, of which this is supposed to be a description, it appears that many entrepreneurs attempt to maximize profit under the assumption that very favorable conditions will prevail. And, of course, they generally expend considerable effort to influence the market so as to make the assumption correct. On a more theoretical level, game theory requires more information than is likely to be available. In theoretical economics it seems that the successful application of game theory must await further refinements if, indeed, it can be achieved at all.

10.7 OLIGOPOLY AND PRICE RIGIDITY: THEORY AND EVIDENCE

A traditional feature of oligopoly stressed by many economists since the 1930s is the prevalence of rigid or sticky prices in industries characterized by oligopoly. It was assumed that competitive industries and monopolistic firms adapted to changes in the environment by changing prices and output. Oligopoly supposedly was not so adaptable, since prices were administered and kept rigid. Certainly this hypothesis would have significant microeconomic implications for resource allocation if prices did not react to changes in costs in the case of oligopoly. Implications were even carried over into macroeconomics in order to explain disequilibrium in the economy as a whole. For example, if prices were not flexible downward in many large industries during a downturn in the business cycle, unemployment could result. In this section we will examine the theory of rigid prices and some evidence concerning whether or not oligopolistic prices are rigid.

10.7a—Kinked Demand Curve

The most frequently cited model set forth to explain the allegedly in-flexible prices under oligopoly is the kinked demand curve hypothesis, developed by Paul Sweezy in 1939.[4] This model has been popular up to the present, although it is probably not as popular now as it was in the 1950s.

The kinked demand curve is illustrated in Figure 10.7.1. Suppose an

FIGURE 10.7.1

Kinked Demand Hypothesis

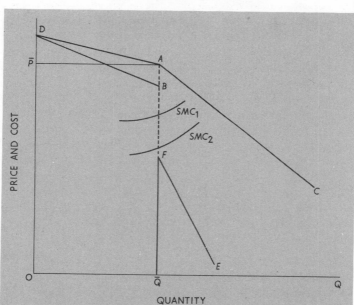

oligopolist's price is somehow set at $O\bar{P}$, and at this price he sells $\overline{OQ}$. He is at point A on his anticipated demand DAC. The kink at A results from the following type of reasoning: the oligopolist believes that if he reduces price below $O\bar{P}$, his competitors will reduce their prices also. Therefore, his own sales will increase very little after the price reduction. Demand at prices below $O\bar{P}$ is AC. This portion is relatively inelastic. The oligopolist thinks also that if he raises his price above $O\bar{P}$, none of his competitors will follow, and sales will decrease substantially. A very elastic demand, such as DA, results for prices above $O\bar{P}$. Thus, a kink

[4] Paul Sweezy, "Demand Under Conditions of Oligopoly," *Journal of Political Economy*, Vol. XLVII (1939), pp. 568–73.

results at A. DB is the marginal revenue curve associated with the more elastic demand, DA, and FE is the marginal revenue associated with the more inelastic demand, AC. The discontinuity is represented by the segment BF.

The principal feature is the absolutely vertical section BF. Marginal cost can intersect the gap in marginal revenue at any point from B to F and nonetheless result in the same market price $O\bar{P}$ and sales $\overline{OQ}$. For example, suppose initial cost conditions give rise to the plant represented by SMC_2. SMC_2 intersects marginal revenue in the vertical segment BF, so price is $O\bar{P}$. If costs rise appreciably, so that SMC_1 now represents the operating costs, price does not change. Or going the other way around, cost could fall from SMC_1 to SMC_2 without affecting market equilibrium price and quantity. Thus, according to the kinked-demand hypothesis, oligopoly prices tend to be very sticky, changing only infrequently and as the result of very significant changes in cost.

This analysis explains *why* a kink occurs but it does not explain *where*. If one knows the equilibrium price he can rationalize it by means of this hypothesis. But the purpose of price theory is to explain how the interaction of demand and cost establishes a unique price-quantity equilibrium. The kinked demand theory does not do this because market equilibrium is consistent with a wide variety of cost situations. This thesis must, accordingly, be regarded as an ex-post rationalization rather than as an ex-ante explanation of market equilibrium.

10.7.b—Sticky Oligopoly Price: Some Empirical Investigations

It may be the case that the kinked demand hypothesis rationalizes a phenomenon that does not occur. The theory appears in most texts in spite of the absence of any empirical evidence to support the theory and even some contradictory evidence.

In 1947 George J. Stigler, using industrial data from the 1930s carried out some tests of the kinked-demand hypothesis.[5] Recall that the theory states that price reductions will be followed but increases will not, when an industry is characterized by oligopoly. As a first piece of evidence Stigler found that in seven highly oligopolistic industries (cigarettes, automobiles, anthracite coal, dynamite, oil, potash, and steel) both price decreases and increases by firms in the industry were rapidly followed by other firms. In none of the seven industries was there any evidence of a kink. In fact, based on experience firms would expect both increases and decreases to be matched rather quickly.

Stigler then compared the stickiness of oligopoly prices in many in-

---

[5] George J. Stigler, "The Kinky Oligopoly Demand Curve and Rigid Prices," *Journal of Political Economy*, Oct. 1947, pp. 432–49. Reprinted in George J. Stigler, *The Organization of Industry*, Richard D. Irwin, Inc., Homewood, Ill., 1968.

dustries with that of prices in industries characterized by pure monopoly. Even though their outputs varied significantly more than that of most of the oligopolistic industries tested, the two monopolies during the period (aluminum and nickel) were characterized by significantly more price rigidity than the oligopolies. Furthermore, the oligopolists, who had periods of known explicit collusion, experienced extreme price rigidity during collusion. The kinked demand hypothesis would predict that collusion would eliminate the kink and lead to greater flexibility. There was much more flexibility during periods of non-collusion.

The kinked demand hypothesis would also predict that the fewer the number of firms in the oligopoly, the more flexible the price. Stigler's data showed the opposite effect; the average number of price changes in the industry during the period of observation varied *directly* with the number of dominant firms in the oligopoly. In summary, Stigler's sample, while small, showed little evidence of a kinked demand or of price rigidity in oligopolies.

Much later, Julian L. Simon tested the oligopolistic kinked-demand hypothesis using changes in advertising rates in business magazines for the period 1955–1964.[6] His data indicated that monopolistic magazines, that is, magazines with no competitors in the same category, do not change rates any more frequently than do magazines with a few close competitors within their classification. In fact, Simon found that with one exception, magazines in one-magazine groups change price less frequently than do magazines in multiple-magazine groups. Also, there was progressively more frequent price changes in going from single-magazine to ten-magazine groups. The main results of the test show no evidence that oligopoly changes price less frequently than does monopoly. This is a contradiction to the kinked demand hypotheses.

10.8 SOME "MARKET" SOLUTIONS TO THE OLIGOPOLY PROBLEM

The classical treatments of duopoly, with the exception of Chamberlin's model and a few others, are based upon the assumption that entrepreneurs act independently of one another even though they are interdependent in the market. We turn now to some theories based upon explicit or implicit collusion among firms. We should note that so far we have excluded the possibility of collusive behavior not only in this chapter but in Chapters 8 and 9 as well. The reason is that collusive behavior is illegal according to the Sherman Act and other legislation and court decisions. However, antitrust litigation still flourishes; so oligopolists must in fact recognize their mutual interdependence.

    [6] Julian L. Simon, "A Further Test of the Kinky Oligopoly Demand Curve," *The American Economic Review,* Dec. 1969, pp. 971–75.

10.8.a—Cartels and Profit Maximization

A *cartel* is a combination of firms whose objective is to limit the competitive forces within a market. It may take the form of open collusion, the member firms entering into an enforceable contract pertaining to price and other market variables. This is perhaps best illustrated by the German *Kartelle;* but the NRA codes of our Great Depression years fall into this category as well. On the other hand, a cartel may be formed by secret collusion among sellers; many examples of this exist in American economic history. Most tend to date to the early years of the 20th century; but at the time of this writing the Federal Trade Commission has pending an action against a group of paperboard manufacturers, charging them with collusive price fixing—that is, with forming an illegal cartel. And in academic administrative circles, the American Economic Associa-

FIGURE 10.8.1

Cartel Profit Maximization

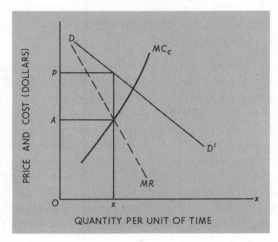

QUANTITY PER UNIT OF TIME

tion is charged with having a cartel that sets exorbitant prices for the services of new Ph.D. recipients.

The cases of open and secret collusion offer the best examples of cartels. However, in a broad sense trade associations, professional organizations, and the like perform many functions usually associated with a cartel. Of the wide variety of services a cartel may perform for its members, two are of central importance: price fixing and market sharing. In this section, we will examine price fixing in an "ideal" cartel.

Suppose a group of firms producing a homogeneous commodity forms a cartel. A central management body is appointed, its function being to determine the uniform cartel price. The task, in theory, is relatively simple, as illustrated in Figure 10.8.1. Market demand for the homogeneous commodity is given by *DD'*, so marginal revenue is given by the dashed line *MR*. The cartel marginal cost curve must be determined by the management body. If all firms in the cartel purchase all inputs in perfectly competitive markets, the cartel marginal cost curve (MC_c) is simply the horizontal sum of the marginal cost curves of the member firms. Otherwise, allowance must be made for the increase in input price accompanying an increase in input usage; MC_c will stand further to the left than it would if all input markets were perfectly competitive.

In either case the management group determines cartel marginal cost MC_c. The problem is the simple one of determining the price that maximizes cartel profit—the monopoly price. From Figure 10.8.1, marginal cost and marginal revenue intersect at the level *OA;* thus the market price *Op* is the one the cartel management will establish. Given the demand curve *DD'*, buyers will purchase *Ox* units from the members of the cartel. The second important problem confronting the cartel management is *how* to distribute the total sales of *Ox* units among the member firms.

10.8.b—Cartels and Market Sharing

Fundamentally there are two methods of sales allocation: nonprice competition and quotas. The former is usually associated with "loose" cartels. A uniform price is fixed and each firm is allowed to sell all it can at that price. The only requirement is that firms do not reduce price below the cartel price. There are many examples of this type of cartel organization in the United States today. For instance, in most localities both medical doctors and lawyers have associations whose code of ethics is frequently the basis of price agreement. The patient market, for example, is divided among the various doctors by nonprice competition: each patient selects the doctor of his choice. Similarly, the generally uniform prices of haircuts, major brands of gasoline, and movie tickets do not result from perfect competition within the market. Rather, they result from tacit, and sometimes open, agreement upon a price; the sellers compete with one another but *not* by price variations.

The so-called fair trade laws of many states establish loose, but very legal, cartels. Under these laws the manufacturer of a commodity may set its retail price. The retail sellers of the commodity (the sometimes reluctant members of the cartel) are forbidden by law to charge a lower price. The various retailers compete for sales by advertising, customer credit policies, repair and maintenance services, delivery, and such. But price is not a variable in the market.

The second method of market sharing is the *quota* system, of which there are several variants. Indeed, there is no uniform principle by which quotas can be determined. In practice, the bargaining ability of a firm's representative and the importance of the firm to the cartel are likely to be the most important elements in determining a quota. Beyond this are two popular methods. The first of these has a statistical base, either the relative sales of the firm in some pre cartel base period or the "productive capacity" of the firm. As a practical matter, the choice of base period or of the measure of capacity is a matter of bargaining among the members. Thus the most skillful bargainer is likely to come out best.

The second popular basis for the quota system is geographical division of the market. Some of the more dramatic illustrations involve international markets. For example, an agreement between Du Pont and Imperial Chemicals divided the market for certain products so that the former had exclusive sales rights in North and Central America (except for British possessions) and the latter had exclusive rights in the British Empire and Egypt. Another example is an agreement between the American company Röhm and Haas and its German counterpart Roehm und Haas. The former was given exclusive rights in North, Central, and South America, and in Australia, New Zealand, and Japan; the latter was given Europe and Asia, except for Japan. These illustrations can be multiplied many times over, but they should serve to indicate the quota by geographical division.

While quota agreement is quite difficult in practice, in theory some guidelines can be laid down. Consider the "ideal" cartel represented in Figure 10.8.1. A reasonable criterion for the management group would be "minimize total cartel cost." Minimum cartel cost is achieved when each firm produces the rate of output for which its marginal cost equals the common cartel marginal cost and marginal revenue. Thus each firm would produce the amount for which its marginal cost is OA (Figure 10.8.1); by the summing process to obtain MC_c total cartel output will be Ox. The difficulty involved with this method is that the lower cost firms obtain the bulk of the market and the bulk of profits. To make this method of allocation acceptable to all members, a profit sharing system more or less independent of sales quota must be devised.

In certain cases the member firms may be able to agree upon the share of the market each is to have. This is illustrated in Figure 10.8.2 for an "ideal" situation. Suppose only two firms are in the market and they decide to divide the market evenly. The market demand curve is DD', so the half-share curve for each firm is Dd. The curve marginal to Dd is the dashed line MR, the half-share marginal revenue for each firm. Suppose each firm has identical costs, represented by SAC and SMC. Each will decide to produce Ox units with price Op corresponding to the intersection of MC and MR. A uniform price of Op is established and $Ox_c = 2\ Ox$ units are supplied. This happens, in our special case, to be a tenable solution because the market demand curve is consistent with the sale of Ox_c units at the price Op.

To see this, let us go the other way around. Suppose a cartel management group is formed and given the task of maximizing cartel profit. With

FIGURE 10.8.2

Ideal Market Sharing in a Cartel

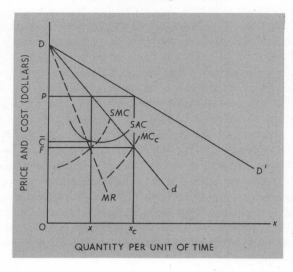

the demand curve *DD'*, the management group views *Dd* as marginal revenue. Next, summing the identical *SMC* curves, it obtains cartel marginal cost *MC*$_c$. The intersection of cartel marginal cost and cartel marginal revenue occurs at the level *OF*, corresponding to output *Ox*$_c$ and price *Op*. The same is true for the individual firms, so the firms' decision to share the market equally is consistent with the objective market conditions. But this is a rare situation; cost differences between the firms would have created a situation inconsistent with market conditions and the voluntary market-sharing agreement would collapse. That, as we shall see, is what is most likely to happen to cartels anyhow.

10.8.c—Short and Turbulent Life of Cartels

Unless backed by strong legal provisions, cartels are very likely to collapse from internal pressure (before being found out by the Federal Trade Commission). A few large, geographically concentrated firms producing a homogeneous commodity may form a very successful cartel and maintain it, at least during periods of prosperity. But the greater the number of firms, the greater the scope of product differentiation, and the greater the geographical dispersion of firms the easier it is to "cheat" on the cartel's policy. In times of marked prosperity profit may be so great that there is little incentive to cheat. But when profits are low or negative there is a marked incentive; and when the incentive exists enterprising entrepreneurs will discover what they believe to be ingenious methods of cheating.

The typical cartel is characterized by high (perhaps monopoly) price, relatively low output, and a distribution of sales among firms such that each firm operates at less than minimum unit cost. In this situation any one firm can profit greatly from secret price concessions. Indeed, with homogeneous product, a firm offering price concessions can capture as much of the market as he desires, providing the other members adhere to the cartel's price policy. Thus secret price concessions do not have to be extensive before the obedient members experience a marked decline in sales. Recognizing that one or more members are cheating, the formerly obedient members must themselves reduce price in order to remain viable. The cartel accordingly collapses. Without effective *legal* sanctions, the life of a cartel is likely to be brief, ending whenever a business recession occurs.

Or, recall the collusion situation in the model of monopolistic competition. Price collusion along with free entry resulted in a zero-profit solution for each firm. *DD'*, the firm's demand when all firms change price together becomes tangent to the firm's long-run average cost curve. The solution is not consistent with short-run equilibrium. Each firm's anticipated demand, *dd'*, crossed the average cost curve. If any firm could cut prices and not be noticed by the others, that firm would make positive profit. Each firm is strongly tempted to move along *dd'* and make profits, at least in the short run until others notice. If one firm is tempted all are tempted, and the cartel, tacit or open, breaks up when a few firms decide to change.

10.8.d—Price Leadership in Oligopoly

Another type of market solution of the oligopoly problem is *price leadership* by one or a few firms. This solution does not require open collusion but the firms must tacitly agree to the solution. Price leadership has in fact been quite common in certain industries. For example, Clair Wilcox lists, among others, the following industries as characterized by price leadership: nonferrous alloys, steel, agricultural implements, and newsprint.[7] Similarly, in their interview study A. D. H. Kaplan, J. B. Dirlam, and R. F. Lanzillotti found that Goodyear Tire and Rubber, National Steel, Gulf Oil, and Kroger Grocery follow the price leadership of other firms in the market.[8]

To introduce the price leadership model, consider the simple illustration in Figure 10.8.3, an extension of the market sharing cartel model of Figure 10.8.2. Two firms produce a homogeneous commodity whose mar-

---

[7] Clair Wilcox, *Competition and Monopoly in American Industry*, Temporary National Economic Committee, Monograph No. 21 (Washington, D.C.: U.S. Government Printing Office, 1940), pp. 121–32.

[8] A. D. H. Kaplan, Joel B. Dirlam, and Robert F. Lanzillotti, *Pricing in Big Business* (Washington, D.C.: Brookings Institution, 1958), pp. 201–7.

FIGURE 10.8.3
Price Leadership by the Lower Cost Firm

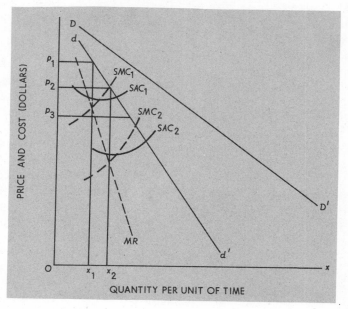

QUANTITY PER UNIT OF TIME

ket demand is given by DD'. By either explicit collusion or tacit agreement the firms decide to split the market evenly. Thus each views dd' as his demand curve and MR as his marginal revenue curve. In this case, however, the costs of the two producers are different; firm one has substantially higher costs than firm two, as shown by $SAC_1 - SMC_1$ and $SAC_2 - SMC_2$ respectively.

Other things equal, firm one would like to charge Op_1 per unit and sell Ox_1 units. This price-output policy would lead to maximum profit for firm one; but firm two can do much better since its marginal cost is substantially below its marginal revenue at this point. In this situation, firm two has an effective control. Being a lower cost producer, entrepreneur two can set the lower price Op_2 that maximizes his profit. Entrepreneur one has no choice but to follow; if he tries to retain Op_1, his sales will be zero. Hence the higher cost firm must be content to accept the price decision of the lower cost firm.

The particular solution shown here is not a very likely one. If this situation existed in a market, entrepreneur two would hardly agree, tacitly or otherwise, to split the market evenly. But given the antitrust laws in the United States he would not drive entrepreneur one out of the market. He has the power to do so. By setting a price such as Op_3, he can earn a pure profit and ultimately drive firm one out of the market. But then he would face the legal problems of monopoly. A better solution, from the viewpoint of the lower cost firm, is to tolerate a "competitor." Thus while not sharing the market equally, as in this illustration, entrepreneur two would nevertheless set a price high enough for entrepreneur one to remain in the market. This is the opposite case from that discussed in Chapter 9, in which a monopolist set a low enough price to keep competitors out.

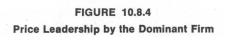

FIGURE 10.8.4

Price Leadership by the Dominant Firm

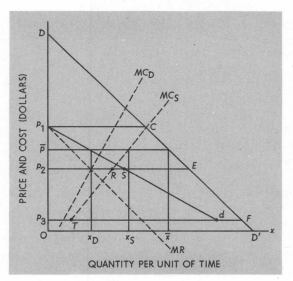

A much more typical example of price leadership is illustrated in Figure 10.8.4. The model is a somewhat exaggerated representation of a situation which, some say, exists in several American industries. There is one (or a small number of) dominant firm(s) and numerous small ones. As shown by the marginal cost curves in Figure 10.8.4, the dominant firm is almost as large as all the small firms combined (MC_D is the marginal cost of the dominant firm and MC_S is the horizontal sum of the marginal cost curves of the small firms).

The dominant firm could possibly eliminate all its rivals by a price war. But in addition to being costly this would establish a monopoly with its attendant legal problems. A more desirable course of action for the dominant firm is to establish the market price and let the small firms sell all they wish at that price. The small firms, recognizing their position, will behave as perfectly competitive firms do. That is, they will regard their demand curve as a horizontal line at the prevailing price and sell that amount for which marginal cost equals price. Notice that this does not entail the long-run zero profit solution because price may be set far above (minimum) unit cost.

The problem confronting the dominant firm is to determine the price that will maximize its profit while allowing the small firms to sell all they wish at that price. To do this it is necessary to find the demand curve for the dominant firm. Suppose DD' is the market demand curve and MC_S is the horizontal summation of the marginal cost curves of the small firms. Since the small firms equate marginal cost and price, MC_S is also the collective supply curve of the small firms.

First, suppose the dominant firm sets the price Op_1. The small firms would sell p_1C units, exactly the market quantity demanded. Hence sales by the dominant firm would be zero, and p_1 would be a point on its demand curve. If price Op_2 were set by the dominant firm, the small firms would sell p_2R units, and the dominant firm would sell $RE = p_2S$ units; thus S is also a point on its demand curve. Finally, suppose the price were set at Op_3. The small firms would sell p_3T units and the dominant firm $TF = p_3d$ units. For a price below Op_3, only the dominant firm would sell. Hence its demand curve is p_1dFD', and its marginal revenue is given by the dashed line MR.

Equating marginal revenue and marginal cost (MC_D), the dominant firm sets the price $O\bar{p}$ and sells Ox_D units. At this price the small firms sell Ox_S units; and by construction of the demand curve p_1dFD', $Ox_D + Ox_S$ must equal $O\bar{x}$, the total quantity sold at price $O\bar{p}$.

Many variations of this basic price leadership model can be constructed by changing the assumptions. One may allow for two or more dominant firms, for product differentiation, for geographically separated sellers and transportation cost, and so on. Nonetheless, the basic results are much the same; and they may help to explain price-output policies in some oligopoly markets.

10.9 COMPETITION IN OLIGOPOLY MARKETS

In general, oligopolists do not like active price competition. To be sure, as noted above, prices do fluctuate under oligopoly, but this is frequently the result of price leadership. Also price wars occasionally erupt; but this really does not indicate price competition. A price war indicates that the (probably implicit) communication channels among firms in the market are temporarily out of repair. In the normal course of events, the pre-price-war situation is quickly restored.

Absence of price competition is the inference to be drawn from almost every model of oligopoly behavior analyzed so far. The alternative forms of nonprice competition are as diverse as the minds of inventive entrepreneurs can make them. Yet there is one central feature: an entrepreneur attempts to attract customers to himself (and, therefore, away from rivals) by some means other than a price differential. Nonprice competition accordingly involves the differentiation of a product that is fundamentally more or less homogeneous. The ways of differentiating are diverse, but three principal methods deserve mention.

Perhaps the most important technique of nonprice competition is advertising. In the United States, and increasingly in European countries, advertising is the uniformly most accepted method of attracting customers, accepted at least by businessmen if not by economists. The "pros and cons" of advertising expenditure have been argued at length; the argument is likely to continue because the question at stake is a moot one. But for good or not, advertising is an established practice that is presumably considered worthwhile, for otherwise businessmen would not continue to spend billions of dollars annually on this type of nonprice competition.

Another important type of nonprice competition consists of creating bona fide (and sometimes spurious) quality differentials among products. The general effect of quality differentiation is to divide a broad market into a group of submarkets among which there is usually a relatively large price differential. The automobile market offers a good example. There are definite, physically specifiable differences between a Ford Falcon and the Ford Motor Company's Continental. There is also a substantial price difference; no one buyer is likely to be a potential customer in both markets, except perhaps for automobiles to perform two fundamentally different services (family car and business runabout).

Ford is not alone in creating quality differentials, however. General Motors and Chrysler do the same; and they engage in active nonprice competition within each of the submarkets. Further, the automobile market example brings to light a social criticism of quality competition. Quality differentials may be created so that items supposedly in one class overlap with items in another, as do, for example, Pontiac, Oldsmobile, and Buick. Thus within the broad market not only is there competition to create new quality classes and gain the competitive edge of being the first in the market; there is also competition within quality classes.

Finally, a third major technique of nonprice competition is design differences. This type could also be illustrated by the automobile market; but the market for golf clubs serves just as well. MacGregor, Wilson, Spalding, and other producers now change models annually, just as do automobile manufacturers. They also create (possibly spurious) quality differentials as between sporting-goods stores and pro shops. But within, say, the pro-shop market, the competition among companies is strictly a matter of club design.

These three types of nonprice competition far from exhaust the possible methods but they do illustrate the ways in which entrepreneurs can spend resources in an effort to attract customers to their particular "brands."

10.10   WELFARE EFFECTS OF OLIGOPOLY

Since there are many models of oligopoly behavior, each predicting different results, it is impossible to be precise about the welfare effects of oligopolistic market organization. Furthermore, any set of static welfare criteria one applies to the situation may be relatively insignificant in a dynamic context. Nonetheless, a few things may be said.

First, whatever the model, two characteristics common to all oligopoly markets can be isolated. Firms in an oligopoly presumably produce their output at the minimum attainable unit cost. But there is no reason to believe their output uniquely corresponds to minimum long-run average cost. Hence oligopoly requires more units of resources per unit of commodity produced than absolutely necessary. Furthermore, since pure economic profit normally accompanies oligopolistic market organization, price is higher than both average and marginal cost. In whatever equilibrium is reached, the marginal valuation of buyers is greater than the marginal cost of output. If the commodity were priced at either marginal or average cost, buyers would like to purchase more than producers would be willing to sell.

A second consideration is also important. Vast amounts of resources are devoted to advertising and to creating quality and design differentials. The allocation of some resources for these purposes is doubtless justifiable. For example, to the extent that advertising merely reports price and seller location, it helps keep buyers better informed. Similarly, certain quality and design differentials may be socially desirable. Nonetheless, there is a strong presumption (based upon purely empirical grounds) that oligopolists push all forms of nonprice competition beyond the socially desirable limits. In absence of evidence to the contrary, it is reasonable to conclude that buyers in oligopoly markets would be better off if there were more active price competition and less nonprice competition.

As noted, the welfare criteria imposed so far are static; and from the standpoint of these criteria, oligopoly fares rather badly. However, dynamic considerations should not be entirely ignored. Industrial research and development, the now famous R & D, was essential to the development of our modern industrial economy and is essential to its continued viability and growth. Many argue, with considerable persuasiveness, that R & D usually thrives only in oligopolistic markets. Neither perfect competitors nor pure monopolists have the incentive; and perfect competitors are usually not large enough to support research departments. Oligopolistic firms, on the other hand, always have the incentive: improve the product or reduce its cost so as to increase profit. Furthermore, such firms are typically large enough to absorb the short-run cost of R & D in order to reap its long-run payoff. In short, all sorts of static welfare criteria may be violated more or less with impunity if the dynamic rate of growth is *sufficiently rapid. Some economists, and all oligopolists, hold that oligopolistic market organization is essential for the dynamic growth of the economy.

10.11 BARRIERS TO COMPETITION

We have studied four theoretical market structures: perfect competition, pure monopoly, monopolistic competition, and oligopoly. We have examined the behavioral characteristics and some welfare implications of each. Before our study of markets is complete one final task remains: a brief examination of why some industries are oligopolies or even approach monopolies and why others are closer to perfect or monopolistic competition. Or, in some industries why do the few largest firms produce a large percentage of total output while in other industries no firm has a substantial share of the total market? Part of the answer to this question lies in the barriers to entry of new firms. If oligopoly or monopoly is to exist for long, something must prevent new firms from entering the industry or prevent those that do enter from growing. Another part of the answer lies in the reasons why some firms are able to attain an oligopoly or monopoly position in the first place. These factors are called the bases of oligopoly or monopoly.

One of the most important bases of monopoly or oligopoly is the control of raw material supplies. If one firm, or perhaps a few firms, control all of the known supply of a necessary ingredient of a particular product, the firm or firms can refuse to sell that ingredient to other firms at a price low enough for them to compete. Since no others can produce the product, a monopoly or oligopoly results. For example, for many years the Aluminum Company of America (Alcoa) owned almost every source of bauxite, a necessary ingredient in the production of aluminum. The control of resource supply, coupled with certain patent rights, provided Alcoa with an absolute monopoly in aluminum production. Indeed, it was only after World War II that the federal courts effectively broke Alcoa's monopoly of the aluminum market. The International Nickel Company has enjoyed much the same position over a relatively long period.

Nonetheless, a firm's control of the source of raw material supply does not guarantee that it will choose to exploit its opportunity to be a monopolist. If diseconomies of scale set in at a low level of output, relative to demand, the firm may find it more profitable to sell the raw material to other firms. The number of firms that may enter the industry depends in large part on economies of scale. If economies of scale are only attainable at a relatively large level of output (but not the entire market output), few firms will enter and oligopoly will result. If all economies of scale are attainable at low levels of output, more firms will enter. However, the sole owner of the raw material remains a monopolist in the raw material market. Only if it is more profitable will he choose to be a monopolist of the product as well.

Another barrier to competition lies in the patent laws of the United States. These laws make it possible for a person to apply for and obtain the exclusive right to produce a certain commodity or to produce a commodity by means of a specified process that gives it an absolute cost advantage. Obviously, such exclusive rights can easily lead to monopoly or, if a few firms hold the patents, to oligopoly. Alcoa is an example of a monopoly based upon both resource control and patent rights. E. I. Du Pont de Nemours & Co. has enjoyed patent monopolies over many commodities, cellophane being perhaps the most notable. At one time the Eastman Kodak Company enjoyed a similar position (by lease from a German company); more recently the Minnesota Mining and Manufacturing Company ("Three M") has enjoyed patent monopoly or near-monopoly for products such as their Scotch Tape and Thermofax Copier.

Despite these notable examples, holding a patent on a product or on a production process may not be quite what it seems in many instances. In the first place, like the exclusive owner of some necessary raw material, the holder of a product patent may not choose to exploit his monopoly position. If diseconomies of scale set in at a low level of production, the patent holder may find it more profitable to sell production rights to a few firms (in which case oligopoly results) or to many. Second, the owner of a patented lower cost production process may have a cost advantage over competitors, but he may sell only a small part of the industry's total output at his equilibrium position. The new technique will lead to patent monopoly only if his firm can supply the market and still undersell competition. Third, a patent gives one the exclusive right to produce a particular, meticulously specified commodity or to use a particular meticulously specified process to produce a commodity others can produce. But a patent does not preclude the development of closely related substitute goods or closely allied production processes. International Business Machines has the exclusive right to produce IBM machines; but many other millisecond computers are available and there is keen competition in the computer market. The above-mentioned Du Pont patent on cellophane gave Du Pont a monopoly in that product. According to the U.S. Supreme Court, however, the relevant market is not the cellophane market but the market for flexible packaging material, in which Du Pont had an 18 percent share—obviously not a monopoly position. The same is true of production processes. Thus while patents may sometimes establish pure monopolies, at other times they are merely permits to enter highly—but not perfectly—competitive markets.

A third source of oligopoly or monopoly, clearly related to the two sources just discussed, lies in the cost of establishing an efficient production plant, especially in relation to the size of the market. The situation we are now discussing is frequently called "natural" monopoly or "natural" oligopoly. It comes into existence when the minimum average cost of production occurs at a rate of output so large that one or a few firms can supply the entire market at a price covering full cost. If minimum average cost occurs at a rate of output sufficient, or more than sufficient, for just one firm to supply the entire market and cover full cost, a natural monopoly results.

Suppose there exists a situation in which a few firms supply the entire market, and each enjoys a pure profit. Because of the advantages of large size, cost at smaller rates of output is so high that entry is not profitable for small-scale firms. On the other hand, the entry of another large-scale producer is also discouraged because the added production of this firm would increase supply and drive price below the pure profit level for all firms. Therefore, entry is discouraged.

Suppose a similar situation exists, but now only two firms are in the market. Suppose also that the long-run average cost curve of each is such that splitting the market between the two requires each firm necessarily to produce at a relatively high average cost. Each has an incentive to lower price and increase output because average cost will also decline. But if both act in this fashion, price will surely fall more rapidly than average cost. The ultimate result is likely to be the emergence of only one firm in a monopoly position. The term natural monopoly simply designates that the natural result of market forces is the development of a monopoly organization. One may carry the analysis further and describe similar circumstances in which the relations between average cost and market demand can cause an industry to become oligopolistic.

Examples of natural monopoly are not hard to come by. Virtually all public utilities are natural monopolies and vice versa. Municipal waterworks, electrical power companies, sewage disposal systems, telephone companies, and many transportation services are examples of natural monopolies on both local and national levels.

Another frequently cited barrier to competition is the advantages established firms sometimes have over new firms. On the cost side the established firms, perhaps because of a history of good earnings, may be able to secure financing at a more favorable rate than new firms. On the demand side, older firms may have built up over the years the allegiance of a group of buyers. New firms might find this difficult to overcome. For durable goods buyer allegiance can be built by establishing a reputation for service. No one knows what the service or repair policy of a new firm may be. Or the preference of buyers can be built by a long, successful advertising campaign; this type of allegiance is also probably more prevalent for durable goods. Although technical economies or diseconomies of scale may be insignificant, new firms might have considerable difficulty establishing a market organization and overcoming buyer preference for older firms.

The role of advertising in fostering oligopoly has, however, been a source of controversy. Some argue that advertising acts as a barrier to entry by strengthening buyer preferences for the products of established firms. On the other hand, consider the great difficulty of entering an established industry without access to advertising. A good way for entrenched oligopolists to discourage entry would be, in fact, to get the government to prohibit advertising. The reputation of the old firms would enable them to continue their dominance. A new firm would have difficulty informing the public about the availability of a new product unless it advertised. Thus advertising may be a way for a new firm to overcome the advantages of older firms in being established. The effect of advertising on oligopoly remains a point of disagreement among economists.

The final source of monopoly and oligopoly to be discussed here is government. Although the United States does enforce antitrust laws with varying degrees of severity, governments at all levels frequently act to further monopoly and erect barriers to competition. One method is the granting of a market franchise. Use of a market franchise is frequently associated with natural monopolies and public utilities, but it need not be. A market franchise is actually a contract entered into by some governmental body (for instance, a city government) and a business concern. The governmental unit gives a business firm the exclusive right to market a good or service within its jurisdiction. The business firm, in turn, agrees to permit the governmental unit to control certain aspects of its market conduct. For example, the governmental unit may limit, or attempt to limit, the firm to a "fair return on fair market value of assets." In other cases the governmental unit may establish the price and permit the firm to earn whatever it can at that price. There are many other ways in which the governmental unit can exercise control over the firm. The essential feature, however, is that a governmental unit establishes the firm as a monopoly in return for various types of control over the price and output policies of the business.

Another way in which the government inhibits competition, some assert, is by purchasing from the larger firms rather than the smaller firms in many industries. Those who hold this position maintain that government contracts give the larger firms an advantage not only over other firms in the industry but also over prospective entrants. Others posit that tariffs hinder entry into oligopolistic industries. While tariffs do not necessarily prevent competition, they do make it easier for firms in an industry to collude. Another governmentally fostered base of oligopoly and monopoly is the federal tax structure. When this tax structure encourages reinvestment in established corporations at the expense of investment in new entrants, even though the new firms would be more efficient, competition is inhibited.[10]

10.12   OLIGOPOLY AND ECONOMIC ANALYSIS

Writing in 1952, Professor Fritz Machlup commented that "Familiarity with the classical models (of oligopoly) has become a kind of hall-mark of the education of an economic theorist, even if it helps him more in the comprehension of the traditional lingo than in the analysis of current economic problems."[11] And again: "Sliding along a smooth curve until it intersects another curve is a healthy mental exercise; and solving a set of simultaneous equations is too; but neither of these will ensure our understanding of the way a man makes up his mind when he ponders a business decision."[12]

Machlup's statements point up the problem. When the number of sellers is very large, each can confidently and properly expect that *his independent* actions will have an imperceptible effect upon the market. A competitive producer does not have to guess how his rivals will react to his policies because he does not have any *rivals*. Neither does a monopolist; so no guesswork is involved. But oligopoly is a matter of close rivalry among firms; and building a *model* of oligopoly behavior is usually a matter of specifying how one oligopolist tries to second-guess his opponents. Therefore, economic analysis based upon such models is almost bound to be unreliable because neither economists nor psychiatrists are likely to guess how businessmen guess when confronted with a business decision.

This indictment may be a bit strong because there is one guess that is frequently good, namely that intelligent oligopolists will collude, openly if possible, surreptitiously or tacitly otherwise. This is the reason for studying the Chamberlin model, the cartel model, and the price leadership model. But note: all of these could as well have been studied in Chapter 9 as in the present chapter. When any kind of collusion is allowed, monopoly or near-monopoly results emerge. In these cases, it is a matter of taste whether one says his analysis is based upon monopoly or oligopoly models.

In general, one is well prepared for economic analysis if he has a

---

[10] For a more detailed discussion of the bases of monopoly, see George J. Stigler, *The Theory of Price*, 3d ed. (New York: Macmillan & Co., 1966), pp. 220–27.

[11] Fritz Machlup, *The Economics of Sellers' Competition* (Baltimore: The Johns Hopkins Press, 1952), p. 369.

[12] Ibid., p. 370.

thorough understanding of the competitive and monopoly models though, as Machlup said, he will not know all the jargon of the trade unless he studies oligopoly models as well.

10.13   ECONOMIC ANALYSIS: OLIGOPOLY, COMPETITION, AND POLLUTION

It is not altogether correct to say that the theories of oligopoly are totally useless for economic analysis. For example, a colleague of ours, W. P. Gramm, used some theoretical characteristics of oligopoly to make some points and predictions (that later proved reliable) about the capacity of the market system to abate pollution.[13]

As Gramm noted, pollution generally is analyzed as a social cost imposed upon society by the market system with no possibility for self-correction. Supposedly, only government through direct controls, fines, or subsidies can act against pollution. In the absence of governmental intervention no firm is motivated to act alone to decrease its own polluting because of the cost involved. Gramm, however, showed that the standard analysis is relevant only to competition and monopoly; under oligopoly there can exist both the means and motivation to decrease pollution.

As stressed in this chapter, oligopolists do not like price competition; they do attempt to compete among themselves by product differentials. Any oligopolist likes to differentiate his product, in the minds of consumers, from those of his close competitors. Therefore, Gramm suggests that if consumers can be marginally motivated to purchase on the basis of pollution and non-pollution, firms will be motivated to some extent to correct pollution. Non-pollution is a form of product differentiation. Firms gain advantages by advertising and identifying with non-pollution, but the consumers must be aware of pollution and care enough about correction.

Competitors would have no basis for pollution abatement. They produce a homogeneous product, indistinguishable from that of any other competitor. A monopoly may have the resources to act against pollution, but, because of its strong market position, it would have little motivation to do so. A monopolistic competitor would have the motivation to differentiate products but would quite possibly lack resources. Thus, oligopoly appears to be, at least theoretically, the most responsive to consumer pressure to cease polluting, particularly when the oligopolists have large financial resources and a research department. While pollution abatement is a cost to the firm, it does not necessarily follow that product price must rise if oligopolists voluntarily undertake abatement for product differentiation. If the public is motivated to buy on the

[13] W. P. Gramm, "A Theoretical Note on the Capacity of the Market System to Abate Pollution," *Land Economics*, Aug. 1969, pp. 336–38.

basis of non-pollution, the oligopolists may substitute some abatement for advertising. In any case, if consumers are motivated sufficiently to purchase from non-polluting firms, they may be willing to bear some of the costs of abatement in the form of higher prices.

We might note that Gramm's paper admittedly was concerned solely with the theoretical existence of motivation and not with the empirical relevance of that motivation. He did, however, question why oligopolistic firms had not been motivated in the past to seek product differentiation through non-pollution. He answered that this may indicate that the consuming public is uniformed of the problem or is unconcerned; that is, unwilling to pay the price. If either is the case, pollution is not solely attributable to the market system. If people will pay the price, many firms will differentiate by non-pollution. When there is a demand, there is usually someone to fill it, if it can be done at a profit. If a pollutor could not sell his products, he would soon stop polluting or go out of business.

One could argue, as Gramm suggested in closing, that any single individual would feel that he, acting alone, would have little or no effect. Therefore, he would not be motivated to discriminate on the basis of pollution. He points out that the same argument could be made about voting. Voting costs time, but millions vote. Many consumers have boycotted grapes and lettuce with a certain amount of success. Labor boycotts of products are a prime example of consumer power through discriminatory purchasing. Nazi Germany's boycotts of Jewish merchants, racial discrimination in purchasing, the southern blacks' boycotts of public transportation during the early civil rights movement are all examples of discriminatory purchasing. In any case, when a large segment of the public wishes to make a point, it can certainly do so successfully, even if there is a cost involved.

In passing, we might note that Gramm actually predicted a coming trend. Since the paper appeared we have noted an increasing tendency for firms, most of which are oligopolies, to do considerable advertising telling the public that they do not pollute. The oil companies in particular seem to be turning in that direction. It will be interesting to see how successful consumer pressure—if any is forthcoming—will be. In any case, this is one example in which oligopoly theory was used to analyze a problem and make a prediction. However, as noted, the theories of competition and monopoly are used much more frequently. In general, oligopoly theory and the theory of monopolistic competition are not frequently used in analysis. For this reason the analysis and application in this chapter has been slight.

QUESTIONS AND PROBLEMS

1. "The smaller the seller's share in the market, the greater the temptation for him to cut prices in slack time." Discuss.

2. *a.* Draw the necessary curves to show a monopolistic competitor enjoying pure profits.
   b. Show the amount of pure profit.
   c. Now draw demand and marginal revenue curves that, presumably under the influence of newcomers' competition, are so much further downward and to the left that pure profit is zero.

3. Assume that the bituminous coal industry is a competitive industry in long-run equilibrium. Now assume that the firms in the industry form a cartel.
   a. What will happen to the equilibrium output and price of coal and why?
   b. How should the output be distributed among the individual firms?
   c. After the cartel is operating, are there incentives for the individual firm to cheat? Why or why not?

4. Why do we say that there is no general theory of oligopoly?

5. A monopolistic competitor has the cost and revenue curves in Figure E.10.1. The demands *DD′* and *dd′* are those described in the text.
   a. If the market is characterized by intense price cutting and some entry, long-run equilibrium is at _____ units of output and a price of $_____.
   b. Excess capacity is _____ units.
   c. If there is no price competition but free entry, long-run equilibrium is established at _____ units and a price of $_____.
   d. Excess capacity is now _____ units.
   e. What would be the long-run price if the firm were a perfect competitor?

FIGURE E.10.1

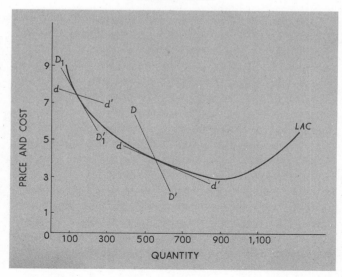

6. An industry is characterized by one dominant firm and many small fringe firms. Industry demand and the long-run supply curve of the fringe firms is given in Figure E.10.2, along with the marginal cost curve of the dominant firm. Assume that the dominant firm sets a price, allows the fringe firms to sell all they wish, and supplies the rest of the market.
    a. Derive the dominant firm's demand and marginal revenue.
    b. What price does the dominant firm choose?
    c. The market is divided with the dominant firm supplying _____ units and the fringe firms supplying _____.

FIGURE E.10.2

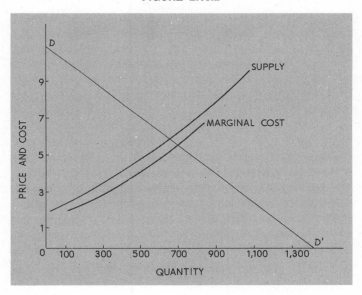

7. Assume two firms in an industry with cost curves given by AC_1–MC_1 and AC_2–MC_2 in Figure E.10.3 on p. 346. Market demand is DD'. The two will divide the market equally.
    a. Derive each firm's demand and marginal revenue.
    b. The higher cost firm would like for price to be $_____.
    c. At that price the higher cost firm could make a profit of $_____ and the lower cost firm a profit of $_____.
    d. The lower cost firm will set a price of $_____. Its profit now becomes $_____, while the high cost firm's profit falls to $_____.
    e. Why will the high cost firm permit this price?
    f. If the lower price firm wished to have the entire market it could set a price of $_____, and have profits of $_____.
    g. Why might it not do this?

FIGURE E.10.3

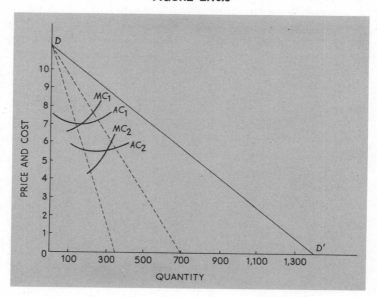

8. If you were attempting to establish a price fixing cartel in an industry,
    a. Would you prefer many or few firms? Why?
    b. How could you prevent cheating (price cutting) by cartel members? Why would they have an incentive to cheat?
    c. Would you keep substantial or very few records? What are the advantages and disadvantages of each?
    d. How could you prevent entry into the industry?
    e. How could government help you prevent entry and even cheating?
    f. How would you try to talk government into helping? Under what conditions might this work?

9. In 1969 an informal price survey was conducted of the prostitutes in a particular four-block area in San Francisco. From the 30 to 40 prostitutes sampled (that is, questioned about prices) it was found that the price of each was identical to the price of every other for equivalent services even though they differed somewhat in certain characteristics.
    a. Give two possible explanations for the uniformity of prices. (Note: prostitution was illegal at the time.)
    b. If one of your explanation was a cartel, how would price cutting or cheating have been discouraged?
    c. Since there was no price competition how do you suspect the firms competed?

chapter
11

Theory of Distribution

11.1 INTRODUCTION

We have now developed the modern or neoclassical theory of value—a theory explaining the origin of demand, supply, and market price. A central part of this theory of value is the marginal cost of production and its possible reflection in the supply curve. Costs and supply, in turn, depend upon the technological conditions of production and the cost of productive services. So far we have assumed that both are given; and we will continue to assume that the physical conditions of production are technologically given and do not change over the time period relevant to our analysis. But now we must determine the prices of productive services, the distribution half of "value and distribution," or modern microeconomic theory.

Broadly speaking, the theory of input pricing does not differ from the theory of pricing goods. Both are fundamentally based upon the interaction of demand and supply. In the present case, demand arises from business firms (rather than consumers) and supply, at least the supply of labor services, arises from individuals who are not only sellers of labor time but also consumers. Furthermore, for the more interesting cases of capital and labor, one determines the price of using the resource for a stipulated period of time, not the price of purchasing the resource. In other respects, however, the theory of distribution is the theory of value of productive services.

The previous level of abstraction is maintained throughout. This is certainly to be expected in the part of the chapter that presents the marginal productivity theory of distribution in perfectly competitive input and output markets. When imperfections appear in either market, however, the situation changes appreciably. This is especially true when large employers bargain directly with representatives of powerful labor organizations. When there are market imperfections, labor unions tend to

347

arise. The theoretical discussion in the latter part may seem far removed from the dramatic world of GM v. UAW. Indeed it is, in a certain sense. Yet the theoretical results obtained do set limits within which collective bargaining agreements are likely to occur.

Our point of view is that collective bargaining between management and union representatives constitutes bilateral monopoly, an indeterminate economic situation. Our analysis sets broad limits within which the solution lies. To push further requires one or more *courses,* not chapters. For example, there is a substantial body of theory concerning the collective bargaining process, but an understanding of labor markets also requires an extensive knowledge of the institutional framework within which labor unions and business management operate. This type of knowledge must be acquired in "applied" courses or contexts, just as applied courses supplement other portions of microeconomic theory.

11.2 DEMAND FOR A PRODUCTIVE SERVICE: PERFECT COMPETITION IN INPUT MARKETS, ONE VARIABLE INPUT

As indicated in the Introduction, this Chapter is not intended to be a practical man's guide to wage determination. Yet marginal productivity theory constitutes a framework in which practical problems can be analyzed; thus it is a useful tool for economic theorists. The theory developed here is applicable to any productive service, although the most natural application refers to the demand for labor. Thus when we speak of the demand for labor, the demand for a productive service of any type is implied. We begin by allowing only one resource to vary. In the next section, we relax this assumption and let many inputs vary.

11.2.a—Demand of a Perfectly Competitive Firm

It is intuitively obvious that a firm would increase the amount of labor used if the additional labor contributes more to the firm's income than to its cost. Assume that the wage rate is $10 a day and that the price of the firm's product is $1. If increasing its labor force by one more worker adds more than 10 units of output per day, the firm would hire the additional worker. The *value of the marginal product* (more than $10) exceeds the wage rate ($10). If an additional worker adds less than 10 units, he would not be hired. The value of the marginal product would be less than the wage.

Definition: The value of the marginal product of a factor of production is the addition to total revenue attributable to the addition of one more unit of the factor. Thus the value of the marginal product is equal to the marginal product multiplied by commodity price.

Let us consider another numerical example. A perfectly competitive firm sells a product for $5 and employs labor at a wage rate of $20 a day. Table 11.2.1 lists the daily total product, marginal product, and value of marginal product (price of the product times marginal product) for zero through nine workers. Under these conditions the firm hires six workers. It would not hire fewer than six, since hiring the sixth adds $25 to revenue but costs only $20. The firm increases net revenue by $5. It would not hire seven workers because revenue would increase by $15 while cost would increase by $20, thereby causing a decrease in net

TABLE 11.2.1

Value of the Marginal Product and Individual Demand for Labor

Units of Variable Input	Total Product	Marginal Product	Value of Marginal Product
0	0	—	—
1	10	10	$ 50
2	30	20	100
3	50	20	100
4	65	15	75
5	75	10	50
6	80	5	25
7	83	3	15
8	84	1	5
9	81	-3	-15

revenue of $5. If, however, the wage rate dropped below $15 (say to $14) the work force would increase to seven (an additional $15 revenue can be gained at a cost of $14). If wages rose above $25 but remained below $50, the firm would reduce the labor force to five.

Exercise: In order to ascertain that hiring six workers is profit maximizing at a wage of $20, assume a fixed cost of $100 and compute the profit rates for all units in stage II (recall from Chapter 6 that stage II is the range from maximum average product to zero marginal product).

To get more directly to the proposition we seek, consider Figure 11.2.1. Suppose the value of the marginal product is given by the curve labeled VMP. The market wage rate is $O\bar{w}$, so the supply of labor to the firm is the horizontal line S_L. First, suppose the firm employed only OL_1 units of labor. At that rate of employment, the value of the marginal product is $L_1C = Ow_1 > O\bar{w}$, the wage rate. At this point of operation an additional unit of labor adds more to total revenue than to total cost (inasmuch as it adds the value of its marginal product to total revenue and its unit wage rate to cost). Hence a profit-maximizing entrepreneur would add

FIGURE 11.2.1

Proof of *VMP* = w̄ Theorem

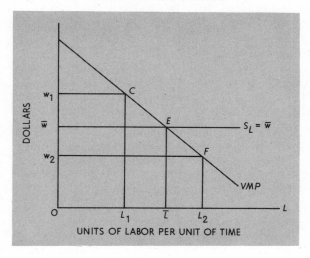

additional units of labor; and indeed, he would continue to add units so long as the value of the marginal product exceeds the wage rate.

Next, suppose OL_2 units of labor were employed. At this point the value of the marginal product $L_2F = Ow_2$ is less than the wage rate. Each unit of labor adds more to total cost than to total revenue. Hence a profit-maximizing entrepreneur would not employ OL_2 units, or any number for which the wage rate exceeds the value of the marginal product. These arguments show that neither more nor fewer than $O\overline{L}$ units of labor would be employed and that to employ $O\overline{L}$ units leads to profit maximization. The statements are summarized as follows:

Proposition: A profit-maximizing entrepreneur will employ units of a variable productive service until the point is reached at which the value of the marginal product of the input is exactly equal to the input price.

In other words, given the market wage rate or the supply of labor curve to the firm, a perfectly competitive producer determines the quantity of labor to hire by equating the value of the marginal product to the wage rate. If the wage rate were Ow_1 (Fig. 11.2.1), the firm would employ OL_1 units of labor to equate the value of the marginal product to the given wage rate. Similarly, if the wage rate were Ow_2, the firm would employ OL_2 units of labor. By definition of a demand curve, therefore, the value of the marginal product curve is established as the firm's demand curve for labor, when only labor is variable.

Definition: The firm's demand curve for a *single* variable productive service is given by the value of the marginal product curve of the productive service in question. This is, of course, limited to production in stage II.

11.2.b—Monopoly in the Commodity Market

The analytical principles underlying the demand for a single variable input are the same for perfectly and imperfectly competitive commodity markets. However, since commodity price and marginal revenue are different in imperfectly competitive markets, the value of the marginal product of a variable resource is not the relevant guide. Since the principle of employment theory is the same for all types of imperfect competition in the selling market, our attention is restricted to monopoly.

When a perfectly competitive seller employs an additional unit of labor, his output is augmented by the marginal product of that unit. In like manner, his total revenue is augmented by the value of its marginal product inasmuch as commodity price remains unchanged. When a monopolist employs additional labor, his output also increases by the marginal product of the additional workers. However, to sell the larger output, commodity price must be reduced; hence total revenue is not augmented by the marginal product of the additional workers.

A numerical example might clarify this point. In Table 11.2.2 columns one and two give the production function when labor is the only variable input. Columns two and three show the demand for the commodity that is produced by labor. Column four is the total revenue (price times quantity) associated with each level of labor usage, and column six is the marginal product of labor. The crucial amounts in the demand for labor are shown in columns five and seven. Column five shows the addition to total revenue (from column four) from increasing labor by one unit. This figure is called the *Marginal Revenue Product* (MRP) of labor. MRP can also be computed by multiplying marginal product times marginal revenue, in this case the average or per-unit-of-output marginal revenue. For example, the average marginal revenue associated with changing from three to four units of labor is $350 (the additional revenue) divided by the change in total product, 15; or $MR = \Delta R/\Delta Q$.

Definition: Marginal Revenue Product is the additional revenue attributable to the addition of one unit of the variable input. It is per-unit marginal revenue times marginal product.

Note that marginal revenue product is less than the value of marginal product, since marginal revenue is less than price. Marginal revenue product is the *net* addition to total revenue. For example, the gross addition to revenue from increasing the variable input from three to four units is 15, the added production, times $30, the selling price, or 15 × $30 = $450. But to sell 15 additional units price must fall by $20. Thus, the "lost" revenue from the price reduction is 5 × $20 = $100, since five units could have been sold for $50. This loss must be subtracted from the gross gain; or, $450 − $100 = $350 = MRP.

Columns five and seven of Table 11.2.2 show the monopolist's demand for a single variable input. For example, if the daily wage is $25, the monopolist would hire eight workers. Each worker up to the ninth adds more than $25 (the additional daily cost per worker) to revenue. The ninth adds $13, and thus would cost the firm $25 − $13 = $12. If wages rise to $50 a day, the firm would reduce labor to six units. Both the seventh and the eighth add less than $50 to total revenue.

To illustrate graphically, consider the marginal revenue product curve in Figure 11.2.2. It must quite obviously slope downward to the right because two forces work to cause marginal revenue product to diminish as the level of employment increases: (*a*) the marginal physical product declines (over the relevant range of production) as additional units of the variable service are added, and (*b*) marginal revenue declines as output expands and commodity price falls.

By assumption, the monopolist purchases the variable service in a perfectly competitive input market. Hence he views his supply of input curve as a horizontal line at the level of the prevailing market price, $O\bar{w}$.

Given the market price $O\bar{w}$, we wish to prove that equilibrium employment is $O\bar{v}$. Suppose the contrary, in particular that Ov_1 units of the variable service are used. At the Ov_1 level of utilization the last unit adds Ow_1 to total revenue but only $O\bar{w}$ to total cost. Since $Ow_1 > O\bar{w}$, profit is augmented by employing that unit. Furthermore, profit increases when additional units are employed so long as marginal revenue product exceeds the market equilibrium price of the input. Thus a profit-maximizing monopolist would never employ fewer than $O\bar{v}$ units of the variable service. The opposite argument holds when more than $O\bar{v}$ units are employed, for then an additional unit of the variable service adds more to total cost than to total revenue. Therefore, a profit-maximizing monopolist will adjust employment so that marginal revenue product equals input price. If only one variable productive service is used, the marginal revenue product curve is, therefore, the monopolist's demand curve for the variable service in question.

Proposition: An imperfectly competitive producer who purchases a variable productive resource in a perfectly competitive input market will employ that amount of the service for which marginal revenue product equals market price. Consequently, the marginal revenue product curve is the monopolist's demand curve for the variable service when only one variable input is used. Marginal revenue product declines with output for two reasons: (1) marginal product declines as more units of the variable

TABLE 11.2.2

(1) Units of Labor	(2) Total Product	(3) Commodity Price	(4) Total Revenue	(5) Additional Total Revenue per Unit Additional Labor	(6) Marginal Product	(7) Marginal Revenue Product MR × MP
3	5	$50.00	$250			
4	20	30.00	600	$350	15	$350
5	30	25.00	750	150	10	150
6	38	22.00	836	86	8	86
7	44	20.00	880	44	6	44
8	48	19.00	912	32	4	32
9	50	18.50	925	13	2	13
10	51	18.00	918	−7	1	−7

FIGURE 11.2.2

Monopoly Demand for a Single Variable Service

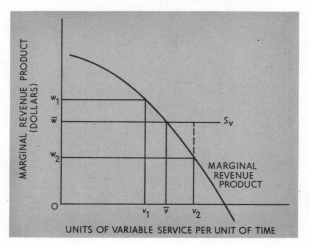

input are added; (2) to sell the additional output the monopolist must lower commodity price.

11.3 DEMAND FOR A PRODUCTIVE SERVICE: PERFECT COMPETITION IN INPUT MARKETS, SEVERAL VARIABLE INPUTS

When a production process involves more than one variable productive service, the derivation of input demand curves is more complicated. The value of the marginal product curve and the marginal revenue product curve are no longer the perfect competitor's and the monopolist's demand for an input. The reason lies in the fact that the various inputs are interdependent in the production process, so a change in the price of one input leads to changes in the rates of utilization of the others. You will recall from Chapter 6, however, that a factor's marginal product curve is derived under the assumption that the amount of other inputs remains constant. Therefore, changes in the rates of utilization of other inputs shift the marginal product curve of the input whose price initially changes.

11.3.a—Perfect Competition in the Commodity Market

Consider Figure 11.3.1. Suppose that equilibrium for a perfectly competitive firm initially exists at point A. The market wage rate is Ow_1, the

FIGURE 11.3.1

Individual Input Demand When Several Variable Inputs Are Used

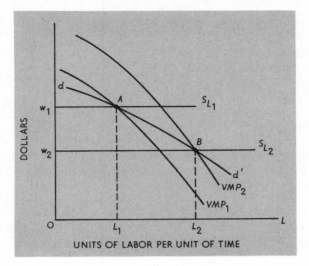

value of the marginal product curve for labor is VMP_1 when labor is the only input varied, and OL_1 units of labor are employed. Now let the equilibrium wage rate fall to Ow_2, so that the perfectly elastic supply curve of labor to the firm is S_{L2}.

When the wage rate falls from Ow_1 to Ow_2, the usage of labor expands. However, the expansion does not take place along VMP_1. When the quantity of labor used and the level of output change, the usage of other variable inputs changes as well. Under these conditions labor's marginal product curve shifts.[1]

Since the value of the marginal product is equal to marginal product multiplied by the constant market price of the commodity, the value of the marginal product of labor curve must shift as well. Suppose it shifts to VMP_2. The new equilibrium is reached at point B. Other points similar to A and B can be generated in the same manner. Thus the demand curve dd' can be determined from successive changes in the market wage rate and the value of the marginal product curve. The input demand curve, while more difficult to derive, is just as determinate in the multiple input case as in the single input situation.

---

[1] Unfortunately this assertion, which is essential for the results of this section, cannot be proved graphically and the mathematical proof is long and tedious. For detailed treatment of the general case, see C. E. Ferguson, *The Neoclassical Theory of Production and Distribution* (London and New York: Cambridge University Press, 1969), Chapters 6 and 9.

11.3.b—Monopoly in the Commodity Market

Analogous to the case of perfect competition, when more than one variable input is used in the production process of a monopolist, the marginal revenue product curve is not the demand curve (for the reasons already discussed in this section). After a change in the wage rate the marginal revenue product curve shifts as all variable inputs are adjusted. The input demand curve is generated exactly as in Figure 11.3.1; the only change is the substitution of MRP for *VMP*.

The results of this section thus far can be summarized in the following important proposition.

Proposition: An entrepreneur's demand curve for a variable productive agent can be derived when more than one variable input is used. This demand curve must be negatively sloped.[2]

The determinants of the demand for a variable productive service by an individual firm, while embodied in our derivation of the demand curve, have not been stated explicitly. It may serve well to enumerate them now.

First, the greater the quantity of cooperating services employed, the greater the demand for a given quantity of the variable service in question. This proposition follows immediately from the fact that the greater the quantity of cooperating inputs the greater the marginal product of the input in question.

Second, the demand price for a variable productive service will be greater the higher the selling price of the commodity it is used to produce. Fixing marginal product, the greater the commodity price the greater the value of the marginal product (or marginal revenue product).

Third, the demand price for a variable productive service will be lower the greater the quantity of the service currently in use. For a given commodity price, this proposition follows immediately from the law of diminishing marginal physical returns.

Finally, the demand for a variable productive service depends upon "the state of the art," or technology. Given the production function, marginal product and the value of the marginal product for each commodity price are known and do not change except for the first point above. However, technology does change; and it should be apparent that technological progress changes the marginal productivity of all inputs. Thus a technological change that makes a variable input more productive also makes the demand for any given quantity of it greater, and vice versa.

---

[2] This proposition requires a mathematical proof; see the citation in footnote 1 (Ferguson, *Production and Distribution*).

11.3.c—Monopolistic Exploitation

The important difference between monopoly and perfect competition is that the monopolist's demand is based upon marginal revenue product rather than the value of marginal product. This gives rise to what is sometimes called monopolistic exploitation.

According to Joan Robinson's definition,[3] a productive service is exploited if it is employed at a price that is less than the value of its marginal product. As we have seen, it is to the advantage of any individual producer (whether monopolist or competitor) to hire a variable service until the point is reached at which an additional unit adds precisely the same amount to total cost and total revenue. This is simply the input market implication of profit maximization.

When a perfectly competitive producer follows this rule a variable service receives the value of its marginal product because price and marginal revenue are the same. This is not true, however, when the commodity market is imperfect. Marginal revenue is less than price and marginal revenue product is correspondingly less than the value of the marginal product. Profit-maximizing behavior of imperfectly competitive producers causes the market price of a productive service to be less than the value of its marginal product.

If the market price of the commodity reflects its social value, the productive service receives less than its contribution to social value. Raising the input price is not a remedy, however, because producers would merely reduce the level of employment until marginal revenue product equaled the higher input price. The trouble initially lies in the fact that imperfectly competitive producers do not use as much of the resource as is socially desirable and do not attain the correspondingly desirable level of output. The fundamental difficulty rests in the difference between price (marginal social valuation) and marginal (social) cost at the profit-maximizing output. Thus so long as imperfectly competitive producers exist there must be some "monopolistic exploitation" of productive agents.

The significance of this exploitation can easily be exaggerated. Furthermore, the alternatives to exploitation are not attractive. Either there must be state ownership and operation of all nonperfectly competitive industries or else there must be rigid price control by the state. For a variety of reasons, either alternative is likely to raise more problems than it solves.

Question: Why would a person work for a monopolist and be exploited, when he could work for a perfect competitor and escape exploitation? Hint: What are workers interested in?

---

[3] This term is apparently attributable to Joan Robinson; see her *Economics of Imperfect Competition* (London: Macmillan & Co., Ltd., 1933), pp. 381–91.

11.4   MARKET DEMAND FOR AN INPUT

The market demand for a variable productive service, just as the market demand for a commodity, is the horizontal summation of the constituent individual demands. In some cases, however, the process of addition for productive services is considerably more complicated, because when all firms expand or contract simultaneously the market price of the commodity changes. Nonetheless, the market demand curve can be obtained.

The situation is analogous to the derivation of a perfectly competitive industry's supply curve from the firms' supply curves. Recall that any firm can change its level of output without affecting input prices. But when all firms attempt to vary output together, input prices change and each firm's supply curve shifts. Therefore, industry supply is the horizontal summation of these "shifted" supplies. In the case of input demand any perfectly competitive firm can vary its inputs and thus its output, without affecting commodity price. When all firms respond to a change in the price of an input, commodity price does change. Since each firm's demand for the input is derived holding commodity price constant, all input demands shift when all firms change simultaneously.

To illustrate the process, assume that a typical employing firm is depicted in Figure 11.4.1, panel *a*. For the going market price of the commodity produced, d_1d_1' is the firm's demand curve for the variable productive service, as derived in Figure 11.3.1. If the market price of the resource is Ow_1, the firm uses Ov_1 units. Aggregating over all em-

FIGURE 11.4.1

Derivation of the Market Demand for a Variable Productive Service

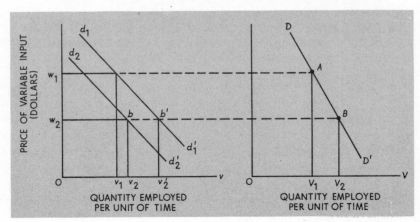

Panel *a*	Panel *b*
The Demand of a Firm for a	**Market Demand for a**
Variable Productive Service	**Variable Productive Service**

ploying firms in the industry, OV_1 units of the service are used. Thus point A in panel b is one point on the industry demand curve for the variable productive service.

Next, suppose the price of the service declines to Ow_2 (because, for example, the supply curve of the variable service shifts to the right). Other things being equal, the firm would move along d_1d_1' to point b', employing Ov_2' units of the service. But other things are not equal. When all firms expand their usage of the input, total output expands. Or stated differently, the market supply curve for the commodity shifts to the right because of the decline in the input's price. For a given commodity demand, commodity price must fall; and when it does the individual demand curves for the variable productive service also fall.

In panel a, the decline in individual input demand attributable to the decline in commodity price is represented by the shift leftward from d_1d_1' to d_2d_2'. At input price Ow_2, b is the equilibrium point, with Ov_2 units employed. Aggregating for all employers, OV_2 units of the productive service are used and point B is obtained in panel b. Any number of points such as A and B can be generated by varying the market price of the productive service. Connecting these points by a line, one obtains DD', the industry demand for the variable productive service.

If an industry is monopolized by a single firm, the monopoly demand for an input is the same as the industry demand. If several industries demand an input, the total market demand is the horizontal summation of every industry's demand, assuming, of course, that we ignore the effect of changes in commodity price in one industry upon commodity prices in other industries that demand the input.[4] There is some minor qualification in case of oligopoly and monopolistic competition. In these cases it must be considered that, like perfect competition, when all firms attempt to expand output, market price falls.

11.5 SUPPLY OF A VARIABLE PRODUCTIVE SERVICE

All variable productive services may be broadly classified into three groups: natural resources, intermediate goods, and labor. Intermediate goods are those produced by one entrepreneur and sold to another, who in turn utilizes them in his productive process. For example, cotton is produced by a farmer and (after middlemen) sold as an intermediate good to a manufacturer of damask; the damask, in turn, becomes an intermediate good in the manufacture of upholstered furniture. The short-run supply curves of intermediate goods are positively sloped because

---

[4] In that branch of theory called general equilibrium analysis, to be mentioned briefly in the next chapter, we assume that the prices of everything are interrelated. For now we are concerned with partial equilibrium analysis and can ignore many of the cross effects.

they are the *commodity outputs* of manufacturers, even if they are variable inputs to others; and, as shown in Chapter 8, short-run commodity supply curves are positively sloped.

Natural resources may be regarded as the commodity outputs (usually of mining operations. As such, they also have positively sloped short-run supply curves. Thus our attention can be restricted to the final category: labor.

11.5.a—General Consideration

As population increases and its age composition changes, as people migrate from one area to another, and as education and reeducation enable people to shift occupations, rather dramatic changes can occur in the supply of various types of labor at various locations throughout the nation. These changes represent *shifts* in the supply curve and are quite independent of its slope. To get at the supply curve for a well-defined market, assume that the following are constants (they are temporarily impounded in *ceteris paribus*): the size of the population, the labor force participation rate, and the occupational and geographic distribution of the labor force. One first asks, what induces a person to forego leisure for work?

11.5.b—Market Supply of Labor

The analytical exercise in Chapter 4 shows how an individual supply of labor is derived from indifference curves between leisure and income (the student should review that exercise before going on). In that section we showed that given a wage increase, an individual might choose to work more (sacrifice leisure) or to work less (take more leisure), depending upon the shape of his indifference map. Therefore, an individual's supply of labor curve may be positively sloped over some range and negatively sloped over other ranges of the wage rate. The crucial question, however, is how their *sum* behaves—what is the shape of the market supply curve of any specified type of labor.

In fact, considerably more can be said about the *sum* than about the constituent parts. First, consider the situation in which one industry exclusively uses a specialized type of labor. In the short run nothing can be said about the slope or shape of the labor supply curve. It may be positive, it may be negative, or it may have segments of positive and negative slope. But now let us relax our assumption concerning occupational immobility; and, in the long run, one must. The master baker can become an apprentice candlestick maker if the financial inducement is sufficient. But more to the point, young people planning their education and career must surely be affected by current returns in various professions. Thus in the long run the supply of specialized labor is likely to have a positive slope.

The other case, in which labor is not specialized to one particular industry, is even more clear. In particular, if more than one industry uses a particular type of labor, the labor supply curve to any one industry must be positively sloped. Suppose any one industry increases its employment; the wage rate must rise for two reasons. First, to expand employment workers must be obtained from other industries, thereby increasing the demand price of labor. Second, the industries that lose labor must reduce output; hence commodity prices in these industries will tend to rise, causing an additional upward pressure on the demand price of labor. Thus the industry attempting to expand employment must face a positively sloped supply of labor curve.[5]

In summary, we have the following:

Relation: The short-run supply curves of raw materials and intermediate goods are positively sloped, as are the supply curves of nonspecialized types of labor. In the very short run the supply of specialized labor may take any shape or slope; but in the long run it too tends to be positively sloped.

11.6 MARKET EQUILIBRIUM AND RETURNS TO INPUTS

11.6.a—Equilibrium in the Input Market

The demand for and supply of a variable productive service jointly determine its market equilibrium price; this is precisely marginal productivity theory. In Figure 11.6.1, DD' and SS' are the demand and supply curves. Their intersection at point E determines the market equilibrium price $O\bar{w}$ and quantity demanded and supplied $O\bar{v}$.

If the price of the variable input (say labor) exceeds $O\bar{w}$ more people wish to work in this occupation than employers are willing to hire at that wage. Since there is a surplus of workers, wages are bid down by the workers until the surplus is eliminated (in the absence, of course, of minimum wages). If the wage rate is below $O\bar{w}$, producers want to employ more workers than are willing to work at that wage. Employers, faced with a "shortage" of labor, bid the wage rate up to $O\bar{w}$. The analysis is similar to that in Chapter 2. The only features unique to this analysis

---

[5] There are two possible exceptions, each of which leads to a horizontal industry supply of labor curve. First, if the industry is exceedingly small or if it uses only very small quantities of labor, its effect upon the market may be negligible. That is, the industry may stand to the market as a perfectly competitive firm does to the industry. Second, if there is unemployment of the particular type of labor under consideration, the supply of labor to all industries may be perfectly elastic up to the point of full employment. Thereafter the supply curve would rise. The latter is a disequilibrium situation not encompassed in the analysis here.

FIGURE 11.6.1

**Market Equilibrium Determination of the Price of a Variable
Productive Servce**

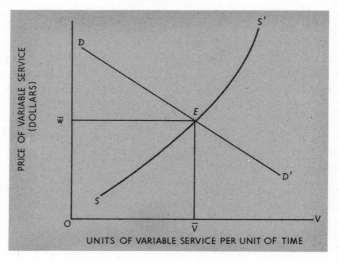

UNITS OF VARIABLE SERVICE PER UNIT OF TIME

are the methods of determining the demand for variable productive services and the supply of labor services. The fact that input demand is based upon the value of the marginal product of the input gives rise to the label "marginal productivity theory."

11.6.b—Short Run and Quasi Rents

Since all resources are variable in the long run, marginal productivity theory covers all resources in the long run. However, in the short run certain inputs are fixed; they cannot be varied and hence a "marginal product" cannot readily be generated. The return to short-run fixed factors, denoted "quasi rent," therefore requires another explanation.

The explanation of quasi rents requires the customary cost curve graph, illustrated in Figure 11.6.2. In that figure, ATC, AVC, and MC denote average cost, average variable cost, and marginal cost respectively. Suppose market price is $O\bar{P}$. The profit-maximizing firm produces $O\bar{Q}$ units of output and incurs variable costs which, on average, amount to $OA = \bar{Q}D$ dollars per unit of output. Thus the total expenditure required to sustain the necessary employment of variable productive services, is represented by $OAD\bar{Q}$. Total revenue is $O\bar{P}E\bar{Q}$; thus the difference between total revenue and total variable cost is $A\bar{P}ED$. Similarly, if market price were OA per unit, the difference between total revenue and total variable cost would be $HAFG$.

This difference *is* quasi rent, which must always be nonnegative (if

FIGURE 11.6.2

Determination of Quasi Rent

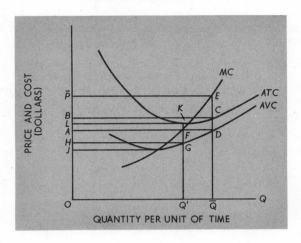

price fell to *OJ*, total revenue and total variable cost would be equal; if price fell below *OJ*, production would cease and total revenue and total variable cost would both equal zero). Notice that quasi rent is the total return ascribable to the fixed inputs. If price is $O\bar{P}$, quasi rent can be divided into two components: the amount *ABCD* representing their opportunity cost, and the amount $B\bar{P}EC$ representing the pure economic profit attributable to their use in this industry rather than in their best alternative use. Similarly, if market price is *OA*, quasi rent (*HAFG*) has two components: the amount *HLKG*, the opportunity cost of using the fixed inputs in this industry; and the (negative) amount *ALKF*, which represents the pure economic loss incurred as a penalty for using the resources in their current employment.

It should be emphasized that quasi rent is strictly a short-run phenomenon. In the long run when all factors are variable, quasi rent is always eliminated.

11.7 EFFECTS OF LABOR UNIONS AND MINIMUM WAGES

A study of labor unions and of the collective bargaining process, even on a theoretical level is beyond the scope of this work. We can only point out very briefly, without discussing collective bargaining, the possible impact of interferences with market equilibrium.

11.7.a—Theoretical Effects

Consider any typical labor market with some kind of supply of labor curve; for simplicity, assume that it is positively sloped. If the workers in this market are unionized, the union bargaining representative fundamentally has one power to exert: he can make the effective supply of labor curve a horizontal line at any wage level he wishes, at least until the horizontal line reaches the existing supply curve. That is to say, the union representative can name a wage rate and guarantee the availability of workers at this price.

Let us suppose the labor market in question is perfectly competitive (large number of purchasers of this type of labor) and unorganized. The situation is depicted in panel *a*, Figure 11.7.1, where D_L and S_L are the

FIGURE 11.7.1

Effects of a Labor Union in a Perfectly Competitive Labor Market

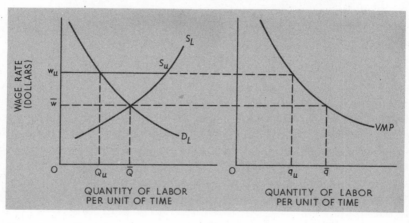

Panel *a*	Panel *b*
The Market	The Firm

demand for and supply of labor respectively. The market equilibrium wage rate is $O\overline{w}$ and $O\overline{Q}$ units of labor are employed. Each individual firm (panel *b*) accordingly employs $O\overline{q}$ units. Next, suppose the labor market is unionized. If the union does not attempt to raise wages the situation might remain as it is. However, scoring wage increases or other benefits is the *raison d'être* of unions. Thus suppose the bargaining agency sets Ow_u as the wage rate; in other words, the union supply of labor curve $w_u S_u S_L$ is established. OQ_u units of labor are employed, each firm taking Oq_u units. The result is a rise in wages and a decline in employment. In perfectly competitive input markets this is *all* unions can do.

This does not necessarily mean a union cannot benefit its members. If the demand for labor is inelastic, an increase in the wage rate will result in an increase in total wages paid to the workers, even though the number of workers employed is less. If the union can somehow equitably divide the proceeds of OQ_u employed workers among the $O\overline{Q}$ potential workers, all will benefit. Such a division is easy to achieve. Suppose $OQ_u = \frac{1}{2}\ O\overline{Q}$ and that a 40-hour week characterizes the market. Then OQ_u units of labor can be furnished by having $O\overline{Q}$ units work a 20-hour week.

The other side of the coin is worth examining, however. If the demand for labor is elastic, total wage receipts will decline and the union cannot compensate the $Q_u\overline{Q}$ workers who are unemployed because of the increase in wage rates. Thus in perfectly competitive labor markets labor unions are not an unmitigated blessing.[6]

The effect of a minimum wage rate placed above equilibrium is similar. Those who retain their jobs in industries covered by the minimum wages are better off with the higher wage. Those who lose their jobs (that is, the "surplus" labor) are worse off. They must find work in industries not covered by minimum wages. The supply of labor increases in these uncovered industries, and the wage rate there is bid down. Therefore, a minimum wage makes some better off and some worse off. The question is, who benefits and who gains?

If all workers were homogeneous, as in our theory, the impact would be randomly distributed. If, as in the real world, workers differ in productivity and in employers' feelings toward them, the least productive workers and those most disadvantaged in their "reputation" with employers are released. While theory can say no more, we can examine a little empirical evidence for further insight into the problem.

11.7.b—Minimum Wages and Teenage Unemployment: Some Evidence

As noted above, an increase in the minimum wage causes some unemployment or shifting to industries not covered. In addition, there may be some shifting by employers from unskilled to skilled labor in the industries covered. The burden largely falls on those who are least skilled, least productive, or least desirable in the eyes of employers. Economists largely agree on this point. Any major disagreement concerns the magnitude of the unemployment effect. As we emphasized in the case of labor unions, the unemployment effect of an externally imposed wage increase can vary from negligible to substantial, depending upon the elasticity of the demand for labor.

A recent study by Thomas Gale Moore examined the impact of the minimum wage on disadvantaged classes of workers.[7] Moore notes, as we

---

[6] The analysis will differ somewhat when we consider a single buyer of labor (called a monopsonist) in the next section.

[7] Thomas Gale Moore, "The Effect of Minimum Wages on Teenage Unemployment Rates," *Journal of Political Economy*, July/August, 1971, pp. 897–902. The remainder of this section is based upon that paper.

did above, that the unskilled and inexperienced would theoretically be affected most by the minimum wage. He suggested that teenagers, especially non-white teenagers, probably suffer most from a rising minimum wage. Unemployment rates of teenagers relative to those of adults have, in fact, risen since World War II, but some argue that this is the result of an increased relative supply of teenagers. Moore's model tested this hypothesis.

Theoretically, an increase in the minimum wage rate increases the wages of unskilled (those affected by the minimum wage) relative to the wages of the skilled. Recall from Chapter 6 that changes in *relative* input prices cause substitution away from the relatively more expensive input. Since it takes time for employers to substitute capital and skilled labor for unskilled labor, the impact upon the unskilled increases over time. Thereafter, the impact gradually lessens as the *general* level of wages rises. Therefore, the unemployment effect of a specific increase in the minimum wage rate at first increases then decreases over time. Furthermore, the total unemployment effect should be greater the more extensive is the coverage. For example, if all industries were covered, anyone whose productivity was less than the minimum wage would be unemployed. If only a few industries were under the regulation, those unemployed in these industries would seek jobs in the uncovered industries, driving down wages there. But they would not be unemployed. The more extensive the coverage, the more difficult it is for the disadvantaged to find a job.

In Moore's model the unemployment rates of four classes of teenagers (white, non-white, male, and female, 16 to 20 years old) and males 20 to 25 were regressed upon overall market conditions, minimum wages as a proportion of average hourly earnings for nonfarm workers, the coverage of the minimum wage, and the unemployment rate of males 25 and older. The period of coverage was 1954–1968.

Moore obtained the following results. The minimum wage rate as a proportion of hourly earnings was highly significant (at the .01 level) in explaining unemployment in all four categories of teenagers. This variable was not significant in explaining unemployment for males between 20 and 25. The general unemployment level (that is, the unemployment rate for males 25 and older) was highly significant (.01) in explaining unemployment for all categories (except for one test for females 16–19, in which the level was .1). The percentage of workers covered by minimum wages was highly significant in explaining unemployment for males and females 16–19, and for males, 20–24. It was somewhat less significant for the other categories. It appears that the burden of minimum wages is much less by the time a worker becomes 20. By then the workers would have gained experience or undergone training. They would no longer be disadvantaged. Moore points out that his results may understate the impact of the minimum wage. High unemployment can cause potential workers to drop out of the labor force. There is evidence that this has happened in the teenage labor force.

In 1969, the U.S. Secretary of Labor recommended making the minimum wage universal. Using the model, Moore estimated that this would raise non-white teenage unemployment an additional 9.7 percent. He also showed that the Secretary's proposal to increase the minimum wage rate would increase unemployment in all teenage categories.

11.8 MONOPSONY: MONOPOLY IN THE INPUT MARKET

Thus far we have assumed that the price of an input is determined by supply and demand in the resource market. The entrepreneur, whether a perfect competitor or a monopolist, believes he can acquire as many units of the input as he wants at the going market price. In other words no firm, acting alone, has a perceptible effect upon the price of the input. This obviously is not the case in all situations. There are sometimes only a few, and in the limit one, purchasers of a productive service. Clearly when only a few firms purchase an input, each will affect input price by changing input usage. We therefore need new tools to analyze the behavior of such firms.

For analytical simplicity we consider only a single buyer of an input, called a monopsonist. However, the analytical principles are the same when there are a few buyers of an input, called oligopsonists.

11.8.a—Marginal Expense of Input (MEI)

The supply curve for most productive services or productive agents is positively sloped. Since a monopsonist is the sole buyer of a productive service, he faces this positively sloped market supply of input curve. In order to hire more of an input he must raise the price of that input. Each unit of input receives the same price. Therefore, in order to increase his usage of an input the monopsonist must pay *all* units an increased price. Thus he considers not simply the price of an additional unit of input but the *marginal expense* of purchasing additional units.

Table 11.8.1 might clarify this point. Columns one and two indicate the labor supply to the monopsonist. Column three is the *additional* expense of increasing labor by one unit. The firm can hire 5 workers at $10 an hour. To hire an additional worker the wage rate must rise to $12 an hour. With five workers the hourly wage bill is $50 an hour; with six it is $72. Hiring the additional unit costs an additional $22 an hour, even though the wage rate rises by only $2. Hiring the additional unit costs $12; but, increasing the wage of the previous five from $10 to $12 increases expenses an additional ($5 \times $2 =) $10. We can use the same

TABLE 11.8.1

INPUT SUPPLY AND MARGINAL EXPENSE OF INPUT

Price	Quantity Supplied	Marginal Expense of Input	Marginal Revenue Product
$10............	5		
12............	6..........	$22..........	$70
14............	7..........	26..........	50
16............	8..........	30..........	40
18............	9..........	34..........	36
20..........	10..........	38..........	34
22............	11..........	42..........	31

analysis to derive each entry in column three. When we consider the addition of one unit of an input, the addition to total cost is the *marginal expense of input*. It includes the price paid to the additional unit *plus* the increase that must be paid to the units already employed. Therefore, for every unit except the first, the marginal expense of input exceeds price.

The supply curve of a variable input and the marginal expense of input curve are shown graphically in Figure 11.8.1. Since the price per unit rises as employment increases, the marginal expense of input exceeds price at all employment levels; and the marginal expense of input curve is positively sloped, lies to the left of the supply curve, and typically rises more rapidly than the latter.

FIGURE 11.8.1

Marginal Expense of Input

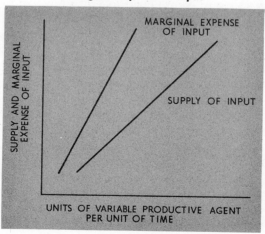

Definition: The marginal expense of input is the increase in total cost (and in total variable cost and in total cost of input) attributable to the addition of one unit of the variable productive agent.

11.8.b—Price and Employment under Monopsony

The relevant curves for price determination under monopsony are the MEI and the value of the marginal product curve (if the firm is a perfect competitor in the commodity market) or the marginal revenue product curve (if it is a monopolist), assuming one variable input. Assume that the firm is a monopolist. The firm is confronted with a positively sloped supply of input curve and the higher marginal expense of input curve. The situation is illustrated in Table 11.8.1 and in Figure 11.8.2. Using this table and graph we will prove the following:

Proposition: A profit-maximizing monopsonist will employ a variable productive service until the point is reached at which the marginal expense of input equals its marginal revenue product. The price of the input is determined by the corresponding point on its supply curve.

The proof of this proposition follows immediately from the definitions of marginal revenue product and marginal expense of input. Marginal revenue product is the addition to total revenue attributable to the addition of one unit of the variable input; the marginal expense of input is the addition to total cost resulting from the employment of an additional unit. Therefore, so long as marginal revenue product exceeds the marginal expense of input, profit can be augmented by expanding input usage. On the other hand, if the marginal expense of input exceeds its marginal revenue product, profit is less or loss greater than if fewer units of the input were employed. Consequently, profit is maximized by employing that quantity of the variable service for which the marginal expense of input equals marginal revenue product.

For example, assume only one variable input in Table 11.8.1. The marginal revenue product schedule for 6 through 11 workers is given in column four. Each worker up through the ninth adds more to hourly revenue (MRP) than is added to hourly cost (MEI). Thereafter the tenth and eleventh add more to cost than to revenue. The firm hires nine units.

In the continuous case the equality of MRP and MEI occurs at point E in Figure 11.8.2, and $O\bar{v}$ units of the service are accordingly employed. At this point the supply of input curve becomes particularly relevant. $O\bar{v}$ units of the variable productive agent are associated with point E' on the supply of input curve. Thus $O\bar{v}$ units will be offered at $O\bar{w}$ per unit. Hence $O\bar{w}$ is the market equilibrium input price corresponding to market equilibrium employment $O\bar{v}$. If the monopsonist is a perfect competitor

FIGURE 11.8.2

Price and Employment under Monopsony

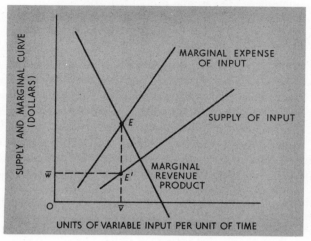

UNITS OF VARIABLE INPUT PER UNIT OF TIME

in the commodity market the situation is similar, except that the demand curve is the value of marginal product curve. It employs the variable input until the value of marginal product equals the marginal expense of input.

11.8.c—Monopsonistic Exploitation and Unions

In subsection 11.3.c it was shown that monopoly in the commodity market leads to monopolistic exploitation in the input market. Each productive service is paid its marginal revenue product, which is less than the value of its marginal product. Monopsonistic exploitation is something, in addition to this, as illustrated by Figure 11.8.3. The monopsonist-monopolist depicted here hires Ov units of the variable input, because at this level $MEI = MRP$, at a price of Ow. Some monopolistic exploitation is involved since marginal revenue product is less than the value of the marginal product of Ov units. Some additional (monopsonistic) exploitation develops also since the variable input receives even less than its marginal revenue product. It receives Ow, and its marginal revenue product is Or, which in turn is less than the value of its marginal product.

In monopsonistic or oligopsonistic markets unions may benefit their members if they employ rational policies. Consider the monopsony labor market represented by Figure 11.8.4. If the labor force is not organized, equilibrium is attained at point c, where marginal revenue product equals the marginal expense of input (based upon the positively sloped supply of input curve S_L). The equilibrium wage is $O\bar{w}$, and equilibrium employment is $O\overline{L}$. Now suppose the workers establish a union that bargains collectively with the monopsonist.

At one extreme the union may attempt to achieve maximum employment for its members. To this end, it establishes the supply of labor curve $w'aS_L$. The associated marginal expense of input curve accordingly becomes $w'abMEI_L$. Marginal revenue product equals the marginal expense of input at point a; OL_m units of labor are therefore employed at the wage Ow'. Consequently, as one alternative, the union can achieve a

FIGURE 11.8.3

Monopsonistic Exploitation

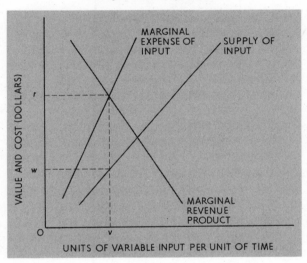

small increase in wages accompanied by an increase in the number of workers employed. Each unit of labor receives its contribution to the firm's total receipts; the exploitation uniquely attributable to monopsony is eliminated.

At another extreme, suppose the union decides to maintain the initial level of employment $O\overline{L}$. It accordingly establishes the supply curve $w_m dS_L$. Marginal revenue product equals the marginal expense of input at point c; hence equilibrium employment is $O\overline{L}$ and the associated equilibrium wage is Ow_m. This wage rate is the maximum attainable without a reduction in employment below the pre-union level. At the wage Ow_m, however, the union can achieve a substantial wage increase without affecting employment. Again, the unique portion of monopsonistic exploitation is removed.

We have considered only two cases. The union can select other

FIGURE 11.8.4

Economic Effects of a Labor Union in a Monopsonistic Labor Market

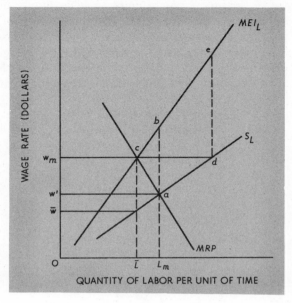

policies, scoring increases in both employment and the wage rate. The union can harm its members only if the demand for labor is elastic and it sets the supply of labor curve so that the equilibrium wage exceeds Ow_m. But even then the unique portion of monopsonistic exploitation would be eliminated. Thus we have a general principle that broadly describes the economic effects of labor unions: labor unions can eliminate the portion of total monopsonistic exploitation that is uniquely attributable to monopsony in the labor market; however, the portion attributable to monopoly can in no way be eliminated by trade union activity.

11.8.d—Empirical Investigation: The Effect of Monopsony on Teacher's Salaries

Our theory has told us nothing about the effect of monopsony upon wages in specific industries. Certainly workers receive less than the value of their marginal product, but that is not what concerns workers. Their primary interest is the amount of salary they can spend, not whether or not they are exploited. In theory we cannot answer whether wages are higher in the absence of monopoly or where it is present. We can form hypotheses, but in effect this is an empirical question.

One investigation of the problem was set forth in a recent paper by

John H. Landon and Robert N. Baird.[8] That paper attempted to demonstrate the effect of monopsony in the market for public school teachers. Their hypothesis was that competition in the market for teachers should result in higher salary levels. They examined the question of whether the salaries of first year teachers were higher where many small districts competed or where there was only one large consolidated district in the region.

According to Landon and Baird, the principal determinants of teacher's salaries in a district are (1) the district's ability to pay; (2) its willingness to pay; (3) the elasticity of the supply of teachers to the district. Ability to pay depends upon the value of local resources (taxable property) and the availability of outside funds. Willingness is reflected in the ratio of taxes to income or assets. Supply elasticity is affected by the availability of alternative opportunities. A large number of competing districts nearby increases teaching options. In a heavily populated area with a single system, the district is in essence a monopsonist. Teachers must move to change assignments. Of course, if formerly competing districts collude, they form a monopsony.

Landon and Baird used multiple regression analysis of 1966–67 data from 136 school districts. Their dependent variable was the salary of beginning teachers with no experience. The independent variables were the number of school districts in the county of the district in question (to reflect monopsony power), per capita income and the proportion of school revenue raised locally (to reflect ability to pay), and property tax rates (to reflect willingness to pay). When all 136 districts were included, every variable had the expected sign (a positive relation) and the relation of monopsony power was highly significant (at the 0.5 percent level). They concluded that the more districts in a county, the less monopsony power possessed by the district and the higher the salaries of beginning teachers. When the districts were subdivided according to size, the monopsony variable was still significant at the 0.5 percent level except in those districts with a school enrollment greater than 100,000. The authors speculated that this is not a contradiction. Because these districts were quite large (the average enrollment was 191,600), they had considerable monopsony power, even when there were many other districts (likely to be much smaller) in the same county. They presented evidence consistent with that hypothesis.

From the results of the investigation it appears that monopsony in the local market for teachers does affect teachers' salaries significantly. As the authors point out, the recent popular proposals for school district decentralization should result in pressures for higher teachers' salaries.

---

[8] John H. Landon and Robert N. Baird, "Monopsony in the Market for Public School Teachers," *American Economic Review*, Dec. 1971, pp. 966–71. The remainder of this subsection is based upon that paper.

Any movement toward consolidation would increase the bargaining position of administrators.

11.9 ANALYSIS AND EVIDENCE: EFFECT OF DISCRIMINATION IN EMPLOYMENT

Like it or not, people do discriminate. Discrimination takes many forms. One discriminates in his friends and associates. Discrimination in housing exists. There is discrimination in school admission and in employment. Likewise, there are many criteria for discrimination: money, looks, race, religion, sex, and so forth. Discrimination in employment occurs when employment decisions are influenced by characteristics other than productivity.

First consider discrimination in employment under monopsony. This type takes two forms. In the first instance the monopsonist uses his power, not to force down wages, but to satisfy his or his employees' preferences for particular types of individuals. If only a segment of his potential labor force meets his criteria for employment, he sets a wage rate high enough to allow him to hire only the "desirable" workers, and he can operate without hiring any of the undesirables.[9] Thus, the monopsonist can take some of his monopsony profit in the form of discrimination. This type of discrimination costs the firm income.

On the other hand, employment discrimination adds to the monopsonist's income. Under employment discrimination the monopsonist can divide his prospective employees into two or more separate markets, each of which has upward sloping supply and MEI curves. Paralleling the case of the discriminating monopolist (from Chapter 9), the discriminating monopsonist hires the total amount of the input at which the horizontal summation of the marginal expense of input curves equals the downward sloping marginal revenue product curve. He equalizes the MEIs in each separate hiring market. The wage in each market is given by the relevant supply curve. The more elastic the supply in any given market the higher the wage rate. This is to be expected since the greater supply elasticity reflects more alternative employment opportunities; thus workers in this market must be paid more. Obviously the firm must find some way to separate markets and keep them separate.

Exercise: Graph the case of the discriminating monopsonist with two markets, each of which has a straight line, upward sloping supply curve. Demonstrate that wage varies directly with supply elasticity. If necessary, review the section on discriminating monopoly in Chapter 9.

---

[9] For an analysis of discrimination under monopsony see Martin Bronfenbrenner, *Income Distribution Theory* (Aldine-Atherton: Chicago and New York, 1971), pp. 199–204. The first part of this section is based upon the material in these pages.

Recently Barbara R. Bergmann used a different approach to analyze the economic effect of racial discrimination in employment upon both employers and employees of all races and to estimate the losses that whites would be expected to take if discrimination ended.[10]

Bergmann's model assumes that the reason that blacks have historically received low pay has been crowding. The crowding hypothesis states that some jobs are open to blacks and some are not. Even allowing for any differences in education the jobs freely open to blacks have generally been of low status, and even these occupations have been relatively few. Bergmann documents this hypothesis by showing the relatively few occupations, among all occupations in which the majority are not high school graduates, that are more than proportionally represented by black workers. These few jobs are predominantly menial. Of the thirty occupations, black workers came within ten percent of expected employment in only four. They were underrepresented in 18, and overrepresented in eight. Service workers and nonfarm laborers accounted for 85 percent of the surplus of black workers.

If the fields are limited, the wages in these fields are driven down by workers who would choose another occupation if it were open. Or, the marginal productivity in the open jobs is driven down by more entry than would occur if all jobs were open. The effect upon whites would be opposite. In jobs reserved for them, their marginal productivity, and thus their wages, would be higher without black competition, but not necessarily proportionally. Furthermore, according to Bergmann, the few blacks who work in occupations largely reserved for whites receive lower wages because of their lower opportunity cost. The only other opportunity is frequently in an "open" occupation at lower wages.

Bergmann made several estimates from equations that used wage and occupation data from 1967. These equations took any educational differences into account. It was found that in the absence of discrimination and crowding, black workers would experience substantial gains in wages. Most white males would experience only trivial losses in income, and most of the remainder would suffer moderate losses. Those whites who did not finish elementary school would be, as expected, the most seriously affected, according to the estimates. The wage loss of this group, 14 percent of all white males over 25 with income, would be between 6 and 9 percent. For white females in the lowest education group (those who did not finish high school) the loss would be in the range of 9–14 percent. This would affect 45 percent of white females over 25 with income. The reason for the larger effect is, according to Bergmann, probably the heavy concentration of black females in domestic occupations.

As Bergmann noted, the rearrangement of the workers toward occupa-

[10] See Barbara R. Bergmann, "The Effect on White Incomes of Discrimination in Employment," *Journal of Political Economy*, March/April 1971, pp. 294–313.

tions with higher marginal productivity might increase society's efficiency. However, the figures showed that the total gain in income would probably be less than 1.5 percent.

Therefore, the major effect of ending race discrimination would be a slight distribution effect. The majority of white workers would be only trivially affected. For the others, the effect would occur slowly over time (if discrimination ends) and would be manifested not as a wage drop but, as a slowing of the trend in white wage increases. As a final note, there would be a decrease in the total number of workers in predominately black occupations. This change would cause a change in relative prices, with some damage, as Bergmann noted, to those who must pay more for domestic service and other services.[11]

In another study of discrimination Bradley R. Schiller performed some statistical tests to see if job and education discrimination (that is, lack of equal opportunities, other things being equal) have been racially oriented, or if discrimination depends more upon the economic status of one's parents.[12] He compared the achievements of blacks and whites raised by families who received public assistance to see if class discrimination is potentially as strong in limiting job and educational achievement as is racial discrimination.

Schiller ran regressions relating education and early achievements of the sampled young adults from families that received aid to dependent children (AFDC) to family background. Regressions on blacks, whites, and all sampled young adults were used. The tests showed that the educational level and occupational status of the parents were related to the son's educational level, and all three were related to the son's occupational attainment. The correlation (that is, the percentage of observed variation in attainment explained by the dependent variables) was low for all regressions, possibly because of the low variance in the sampled group. The whites demonstrated a much higher carry-over from educational attainment to early occupational success. In the sample, additional schooling for AFDC youths had much more effect for whites than for blacks. The economic achievement of the parents apparently had more positive effect upon whites also.

Schiller used the estimation equations to predict the average level of occupational attainment black AFDC children would have achieved, if they had been able to benefit from their parents' status and their own education at the same rate as white AFDC children. Assuming the same

---

[11] As noted, this part of the section on discrimination is from ibid. There are several qualifications and comparisons with other literature in that paper, but these are not discussed here.

[12] Bradley R. Schiller, "Class Discrimination vs. Racial Discrimination," *The Review of Economics and Statistics*, Aug. 1971, pp. 263–69. The remainder of this section is based upon that paper.

opportunity for blacks as for whites, he estimated an increase in the average occupational attainment of black youths of approximately 25 percent. Schiller concluded that equal opportunity is not present even among those from the lowest income position.

On the other hand, there was no evidence of racial differences in educational opportunities for those in the sample. The educational opportunities of the poor are equal for both races.

Finally, Schiller compared the educational and occupational attainments of both black and white AFDC sons with a sample of non-AFDC offspring. Both AFDC groups were lower in each category. Comparing the occupational attainments of poor blacks and whites, he concluded that slightly less than half of the low attainment of poor blacks was attributable to being from a poor family and slightly more than half from being black. Schiller found no direct evidence of racial discrimination per se in education; all discrimination was attributable to class.

The author notes two qualifications to his study. First, any differences in ability are not included; neither are differences in the type of education received. Low income children frequently received inferior schooling.

Schiller concludes, even though the data are incomplete, that many opportunity barriers may be economic in origin, rather than solely racial. As a policy recommendation he suggests that economic obstacles to occupations and educations be emphasized more than previously.

Of course, this is only one suggestion. Other economists may well come up with different solutions from their evidence. This section on discrimination, as presented, merely indicates a very small sample of what economists are doing in one important and interesting problem area. It does show that empirical economists sometimes do things more interesting than estimating the demand for razor blades or the supply of corn.

11.10 SUMMARY

We have covered many topics and developed many theories in this chapter. The more important points are summarized in the following propositions:

Proposition: When only one input is variable to the firm, the demand for that resource is the value of its marginal product in the case of a perfectly competitive firm and its marginal revenue product curve in the case of a monopolist. These curves measure the value of an additional unit of the resource to the firm. When several resources are variable, these curves shift, but the resource still receives its VMP or MRP in equilibrium.

Proposition: The demand for an input by a perfectly competitive industry is not the horizontal summation of each firm's demand. While any firm can change its level of output without changing commodity price, the industry as a whole cannot. Thus, in deriving industry demand, one must take account of the effect upon commodity price. The demand of a monopolist is the industry's demand, since the monopolist is the industry.

Proposition: Input prices are determined in input markets by the interaction of supply and demand. The supply of an input is frequently, though not always upward sloping to an industry.

Proposition: A monopsonist is a firm that faces an upward sloping supply curve for one or more inputs. It hires the quantity at which MRP equals the marginal expense of the input (MEI). The input receives a lower price than its MRP.

Proposition: An input is said to be exploited if it receives less than the value of its marginal product. Unions can in some instances eliminate monopsonistic exploitation; they cannot eliminate monopolistic exploitation.

Proposition: The term "discrimination" is used in many ways. Care must be taken to recognize the sense in which this word is used when interpreting economic studies.

QUESTIONS AND PROBLEMS

1. "A payment system based upon marginal productivity is a just system since everyone gets what he deserves." Comment.

2. Analyze some effects of a federal minimum wage. Do they differ from the effects of a state or local minimum wage?

3. From the point of view of a whole industry, the supply of a certain type of skilled labor may be scarce and, at the same time, of infinite elasticity from the point of view of each single firm within the industry. Explain.

4. You are attempting to get a labor union started in a firm. What conditions would make your job easier? What conditions would make it harder?

5. A monopolist has a commodity demand given by columns 2 and 3. There is one variable input, labor, whose production function (per day) is given by columns 1 and 2.

Units of Labor	Units of Output	Demand Price	Marginal Revenue Product
1	12	$40	
2	30	20	
3	42	16	
4	50	15	
5	56	14	
6	61	13	
7	64	12	
8	65	11	
9	65	11	
10	60	13.50	

a. Derive labor's marginal product schedule.
b. Derive the marginal revenue product schedule.
c. If labor is free, how many units would the firm hire.
d. If the wage rate is $15, how many units would be hired?
e. How much monopolistic exploitation exists?
f. If the fixed cost is $200 how much is profit?

6. Figure E.11.1 shows the short-run cost curves of a competitive firm.

FIGURE E.11.1

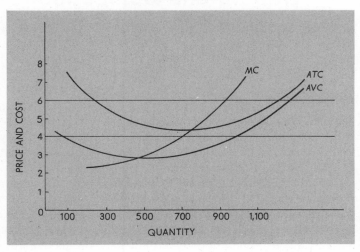

a. If price is $6 what is output?
b. What is the amount of quasi-rent?
c. How much of quasi-rent is attributable to the opportunity cost of the fixed inputs and how much is pure profit?
d. Answer questions b and c in the case of a $4 price.

7. A competitive firm uses two inputs, labor and capital. The marginal product of labor is 10 units per period and the marginal product of capital is 12. Output sells for $2 per unit. The price of labor is $15 per period; the price of capital is $30 per period. What will the firm probably do? Can you answer if the firm is a monopolist?

chapter
12

Welfare and Competition

12.1 INTRODUCTION

In Chapter 1 we emphasized two points that should be reiterated now. First, social welfare is the *dominate quiesitum* of economic theory. Second, the theory of general economic equilibrium is too mathematical to be treated at this level of study. Unfortunately, most of "welfare economics" depends upon general equilibrium theory and is, therefore, too mathematical as well.

Let us go another way around. We now have many pieces of something like a jigsaw puzzle. We have the principles of consumer behavior; we have the technological conditions determined by production functions, and we know how these conditions determine cost; we know how producers equate marginal cost with marginal revenue; and finally, we know how all this affects the factor markets. The question is: can all these pieces be fitted together to form a coherent picture?

The answer is yes if there is competition in all markets. Adam Smith explained this in a very heuristic manner when he talked about his doctrine of the "invisible hand." Each person, acting in his own self-interest, is led by the price system to act in a way that benefits the whole society. If we get much more rigorous than this, we are in the midst of the full mathematical complexities of general equilibrium theory.

In this chapter we cannot try to put the pieces together in a logical order. It can be done, but it can only be done in a more advanced course. But what we can try to do is to indicate why perfect competition can lead to maximum social welfare, and why it sometimes does not.

The chapter is not at all analytical in nature; it is not meant to be. The primary purpose is to allow the student to get a feel for the more complex general equilibrium analysis and welfare theory. Since this is merely an introduction to the theories there are no sections on real-world applications or empirical investigations as there were in the previous chapters. Rather we wish to wrap up the book and your course with a little bit about what comes next in economic theory.

12.2 GENERAL EQUILIBRIUM

Before turning to welfare economics, a few words on general equilibrium are in order. We do this by means of a fanciful example, below, but first we must recount what *general* equilibrium means.

12.2.a—Attaining Equilibrium

Given a set of commodity prices, consumers determine their demands by equating marginal rates of substitution with the corresponding commodity price ratios. Given a set of input prices, producers determine supply by equating the marginal rates of technical substitution with the corresponding input price ratios. Finally, workers determine the supply of labor by equating the marginal rate of substitution of income for leisure with the wage rate.[1] *The problem* of general equilibrium is as follows: can we find a set of prices at which the demands of consumers are voluntarily fulfilled by the supplies of producers who use all productive resources that are voluntarily supplied at the going set of prices? If so, a general equilibrium may exist.

Now to our fanciful example—a highly stylized account of the way in which a general equilibrium might in fact be obtained in a competitive economy. First, suppose that all commodities can be for all practical purposes, instantaneously produced. Next suppose that each morning, all consumers, producers, and resource suppliers in the economy meet in a large forum or marketplace. The society employs an auctioneer, who begins the business by shouting out a set of resource and commodity prices.

Given these prices, each consumer equates his MRS with the price ratios and gives the auctioneer a list of his quantities demanded. Similarly, each producer equates his MRTS with the input-price ratios, determines his cost, and consequently determines the profit-maximizing quantities he is willing to supply. These lists of quantities supplied also go to the auctioneer. Finally, resource suppliers determine the number of hours they are willing to work by equating the MRS of income for leisure with the announced wage rate. Each worker also notifies the auctioneer of his decision.

The auctioneer must now do four things: (*a*) he aggregates all con-

---

[1] Notice that all resources supplied except labor—which includes entrepreneurship, janitorial work, the services of a neurosurgeon, and so on—are *produced* resources and therefore fall into another category. Agricultural land is an exception. It can easily be accommodated within the theory; but at this level of abstraction, it hardly seems necessary to do so.

sumers' lists of quantities demanded to determine the aggregate quantity demanded of each commodity at the announced set of prices; (*b*) he aggregates all producers' lists of quantities supplied to determine the aggregate quantity supplied of each commodity at the announced set of prices; (*c*) by reference to each firm's production function and then by aggregation, he determines the aggregate quantity of labor demanded at the announced set of prices; and (*d*) he aggregates the resource suppliers' lists of quantities of labor offered to determine the aggregate quantity of labor supplied at the announced set of prices.[2]

The auctioneer now knows the aggregate quantities demanded and supplied of both commodities and resources. A general equilibrium will exist if, and only if, quantity demanded equals quantity supplied in *every* market, commodity and resource alike. Otherwise there will be an excess demand for some commodities and an excess supply of others; and there will either be an excess demand for or supply of labor resources. Thus, unless *every market* is in equilibrium (that is, quantity demanded equals quantity supplied), every economic agent cannot be in equilibrium. Finally, there cannot be a general equilibrium unless each economic agent is in equilibrium, for otherwise some individual would take market action to change things.

At the first set of prices announced by the auctioneer, quantities demanded and supplied will doubtless not be equal in all markets. The auctioneer must then announce a new set of prices, raising prices in those markets in which there is excess demand, lowering them when there is excess supply. After the second set of tentative prices becomes available, each consumer, producer, and resource supplier again gives the auctioneer a list of his quantities demanded or supplied. And again, market quantities demanded and supplied probably will not balance.

A third set of prices will be required, and this set also will probably not establish a general equilibrium. However, so long as bidding is competitive, the auctioneer can "zero in" on the general equilibrium set of prices because he has one sure guide to follow: raise price when there is excess demand, lower it when there is excess supply.[3]

As stated initially, this is a fanciful account of the process of attaining a general economic equilibrium—it is not even approximately descriptive of any real world market. However the account is indicative of the way in which competitive bids and counterbids in all markets push the economy *toward* a general equilibrium. Needless to say, it is never in fact at-

---

[2] There is a fine point that we should mention, but upon which we need not dwell. Consumers are also resource suppliers. Thus their labor supply decision determines their expected income, which in turn helps to determine their demand for commodities.

[3] Technically, the procedure just described is called a Walrasian *tatonnement* process.

tained. But there is a tendency toward it; and at times we can profitably analyze the situation that would exist if the general equilibrium existed. This is true for many problems; but it is perhaps most important in analyzing the social welfare results of various forms of market and economic organization.

12.2.b—Edgeworth Box Diagram

The basic general equilibrium can be given a simple graphical treatment. However, while the model is simple, a good bit of insight into the economic process can be obtained.

Assume only two people and only two goods. Each person has an *initial endowment* of each good, but he does not necessarily have the goods in the proportion that yields him greatest satisfaction. If not, some exchange of commodities between individuals will arise. To analyze exchange and other problems as well, we need to develop a graphical device known as the Edgeworth box diagram, named for its originator, F. Y. Edgeworth, a famous British economist of the late nineteenth century. This device is a graphical technique for illustrating the interaction be-

FIGURE 12.2.1

Constructing the Edgeworth Box Diagram for a Consumption Problem

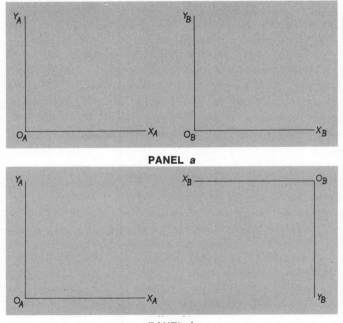

PANEL a

PANEL b

FIGURE 12.2.2
Edgeworth Box Diagram

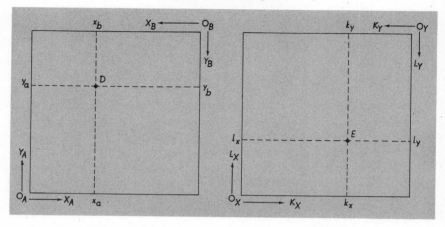

PANEL *a*
**EDGEWORTH BOX DIAGRAM
FOR CONSUMPTION PROBLEM**

PANEL *b*
**EDGEWORTH BOX DIAGRAM
FOR PRODUCTION PROBLEM**

tween two economic activities when their inputs are fixed in quantity. It is thus an ideal instrument for analyzing economic welfare and general equilibrium.

First consider Figure 12.2.1. There are two consumption goods, X and Y; these goods are available in absolutely fixed amounts. In addition, there are only two individuals in the society, A and B; they initially possess an endowment of X and Y, but the endowment ratio is not the one either would choose if he were allowed to specify it. This general equilibrium problem is graphically illustrated by constructing an *origin* for A, labeled O_A, and plotting quantities of the two goods along the abscissa and ordinate. Thus from the origin O_A, the quantity of X held by $A(X_A)$ is plotted on the abscissa and the quantity of $Y(Y_A)$ on the ordinate. A similar graph for B, with origin O_B, may be constructed beside the graph for A. These two basic graphs are illustrated in panel a, Figure 12.2.1.

Next, rotate the B-graph 180° to the left, so that it is actually "upside down" when viewed normally, as shown in panel b. The Edgeworth box diagram is formed by bringing the two graphs together. There could conceivably be a problem involving the lengths of the axes; if the X axes meshed, the Y axes might not. The problem does not in fact exist, however, because of our assumption concerning fixed availabilities of X and Y. $X_A + X_B$ must equal X, and $Y_A + Y_B$ must equal Y. The length of each axis measures the fixed quantity of the good it represents; when the two "halves" in panel b are brought together both axes mesh. One thus obtains panel a, Figure 12.2.2.

The point D in panel a indicates the initial endowment of X and Y possessed by A and B. A begins with $O_A x_A$ units of X and $O_A y_A$ units of Y. Since the aggregates are fixed, B must originally hold $O_B x_B = X - O_A x_A$ units of X and $O_B y_B = Y - O_A y_A$ units of Y.

In a similar fashion, not illustrated in detail, one may construct an Edgeworth diagram for a production problem. The finished product is shown in panel b, Figure 12.2.2. Two goods, X and Y, are produced by means of two inputs, K and L. The two inputs are fixed in aggregate quantity. The origin of coordinates for good X is O_X, for good Y is O_Y. The inputs of K and L used in producing X and Y are plotted along the axes. Accordingly, any point in the box represents a particular allocation of the two inputs between the two production processes. At point E, for example, $O_X k_X$ units of K and $O_X l_X$ units of L are used in producing X. As a consequence, $O_Y k_Y = K - O_X k_X$ units of K, and $O_Y l_Y = L - O_X l_X$ units of L, are allocated to the production of Y.

12.2.c—Equilibrium of Exchange

As a first step toward general equilibrium analysis, consider an economy in which exchange of initial endowments takes place. For the moment, production is ignored. If you like, you may think of the problem in the following context. There exists a small country with only two inhabitants, A and B, each of whom owns one half the land area. A and B neither sow nor reap; they merely gather goods of types X and Y that fall nightly. Each gathers only the goods that fall on his land; but the two types do not fall uniformly. There is a relatively heavy concentration of Y on A's property and, consequently, a relatively heavy concentration of X on B's land.

The problem of exchange is analyzed by means of the Edgeworth box diagram in Figure 12.2.3. To the basic box diagram, whose dimensions represent the nightly precipitation of goods, we add indifference curves for A and B. For example, the curve I_A shows combinations of X and Y that yield A the same level of satisfaction. In ordinary fashion, II_A represents a greater level of satisfaction than I_A; III_A than II_A; and so on. Quite generally, A's well being is enhanced by moving toward the B origin; B, in turn, enjoys greater satisfaction the closer he moves toward the A origin.

Suppose the initial endowment (the nightly fall of goods) is given by point D; A has $O_A x_A$ units of X and $O_A y_A$ units of Y. Similarly, B has $O_B x_B$ and $O_B y_B$ units of X and Y respectively. The initial endowment places A on his indifference curve II_A and B on his curve I_B. At point D, A's marginal rate of substitution of X for Y, given by the slope of

FIGURE 12.2.3

General Equilibrium of Exchange

FIGURE 12.2.3

General Equilibrium of Exchange

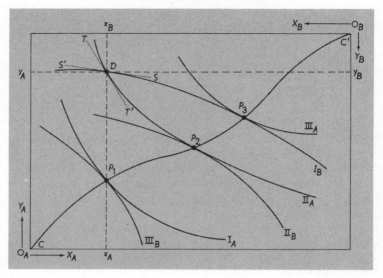

TT', is relatively high; *A* would be willing to sacrifice, say, three units of *Y* in order to obtain one additional unit of *X*. At the same point, *B* has a relatively low marginal rate of substitution, as shown by the slope of *SS'*. Or turning it around, *B* has a relatively high marginal rate of substitution of *Y* for *X*. He may, for example, be willing to forego four units of *X* to obtain one unit of *Y*.

A situation such as this will always lead to exchange if the parties concerned are free to trade. From the point *D*, *A* will trade some *Y* to *B*, receiving *X* in exchange. The exact bargain reached by the two traders cannot be determined. If *B* is the more skillful negotiator, he may induce *A* to move along II_A to the point P_2. All the benefit of trade goes to *B*, who jumps from I_B to II_B. Just oppositely, *A* might steer the bargain to point P_3, thereby increasing his level of satisfaction from II_A to III_A, *B*'s utility level remaining I_B. Starting from point *D*, the ultimate exchange is very likely to lead to some point between P_2 and P_3; but the skill of the bargainers and their initial endowments determine the exact location. In any case one can be made better off without causing the other to become worse off, or both can become better off in the sense of attaining a higher level of utility.

One important thing can be said. Exchange will take place until the marginal rate of substitution of *X* for *Y* is the same for both traders. If the two marginal rates are different, one or both parties can benefit from exchange; neither party need lose. In other words, the exchange equilibrium can occur only at points such as P_1, P_2, and P_3 in Figure 12.2.3. The locus CC', called the *contract* or *conflict curve*, is a curve joining all points of tangency between one of A's indifference curves and one of B's. It is thus the locus along which the marginal rates of substitution are equal for both traders. We accordingly have the following proposition:

Proposition: The general equilibrium of exchange occurs at a point where the marginal rate of substitution between every pair of goods is the same for all parties consuming both goods. The exchange equilibrium is not unique; it may occur at any point along the contract curve (for multiple traders, it is more properly called the contract hypersurface).

The contract curve is an optimal locus in the sense that if the trading parties are located at some point not on the curve, one or both can benefit, and neither suffer a loss, by exchanging goods so as to move to a point on the curve. To be sure, some points not on the curve are preferable to some points on the curve. But for any point not on the curve, one or more attainable points on the curve are preferable.

The chief characteristic of each point on the contract curve is that a movement away from the point must benefit one party and harm the other. More generally, suppose there are n people in a society. This society has attained exchange equilibrium (that is, a point on the contract curve) if, and only if, there is *no reorganization* that will benefit some of the n members without harming at least one. Turning the statement around, an organization does not represent a point on the curve if there is any change that will make some people better off and will not make anyone worse off. Every organization that leads to a point on the contract curve is said to be a *Pareto-optimal organization*.

Definition: A Pareto-optimal organization is one such that any change that makes some people better off makes some others worse off. That is, an organization is Pareto-optimal if, and only if, there is no change that will make one or more better off without making anyone worse off. Thus every point on the contract curve is Pareto optimal, and the contract curve is a locus of Pareto optimality.

12.2.d—General Equilibrium of Production

The analysis of the general equilibrium of production is precisely the same as that of the general equilibrium of exchange. The only difference is terminology (economic jargon). The fixed endowments of inputs K and L determine the dimensions of the Edgeworth box diagram in Figure 12.2.4. Next, the given and unchanging production functions for goods X and Y enable us to construct the isoquant maps for each, illustrated by curves such as II_x and III_y.

Suppose inputs are originally allocated between production of com-

FIGURE 12.2.4

General Equilibrium of Production

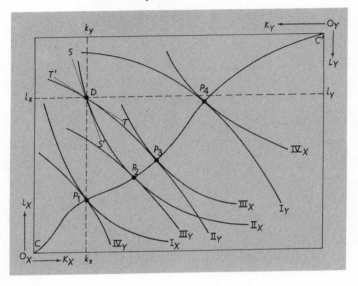

modities X and Y so that $O_X k_X$ units of K and $O_X l_X$ units of L are used in making X; the remainder, $O_Y k_Y$ and $O_Y l_Y$ units of K and L respectively, is used to produce Y. This allocation is represented by point D in the Edgeworth box—the point at which II_X intersects II_Y. At the allocation D, the marginal rate of technical substitution of K for L in producing X, given by the slope of SS', is relatively low. The marginal product of K in producing X is high relative to the marginal product of L. The II_X level of production can be maintained by substituting a relatively small amount of K for a relatively larger amount of L. The opposite situation prevails in Y production, as shown by the slope of TT'. The marginal rate of technical substitution of K for L in producing Y is relatively high; thus a comparatively large amount of K can be released by substituting a relatively small amount of L while maintaining the II_Y level of output.

If the producer of X at point D substitutes one unit of K he can, let us suppose, release two units of L. The producer of Y, by employing the two units of L released from X production, can maintain output and release, let us suppose, four units of K. Thus from a point such as D input substitution by producers will enable the society to move to P_2, P_3, or any point in between. At P_2, the output of X is the same as at D, but the output of Y has been increased to the III_Y level. If the movement is to P_3, the output of X increases with no change in the volume of Y production.

The foregoing discussion establishes a pervasive principle. Whenever the marginal rate of technical substitution between two inputs is different for two producers, one or both outputs may be increased, and neither decreased, by making the appropriate input substitutions. In the example in Figure 12.2.4, the X producer would substitute K for L, decreasing the marginal product of K, increasing that of L, and thereby raising the marginal rate of technical substitution. The producer of Y, on the other hand, should substitute L for K, with the opposite results. Production of one or both goods can always be increased without an aggregate increase in inputs unless the marginal rates of technical substitution between the inputs are the same for both producers.

The locus CC', again called the *contract* or *conflict curve*, is a curve showing all input allocations that equalize the marginal rates of technical substitution—that is, the locus of tangencies between an X isoquant and a Y isoquant. We can accordingly state the following:

Proposition: The general equilibrium of production occurs at a point where the marginal rate of technical substitution between every pair of inputs is the same for all producers who use both inputs. The production equilibrium is not unique; it may occur at any point along the contract curve; but each point represents a Pareto-optimal equilibrium organization.

The contract curve is an optimal locus in the sense that if the producers are located at a point not on the curve, the output of one or both commodities can be increased, and the output of neither decreased, by making input substitutions so as to move to a point on the curve. For any point not on the curve there are one or more attainable points on the curve associated with a greater aggregate output.

12.2.e—General Equilibrium of Production and Exchange

For any input endowment there are an infinite number of potential production equilibria that are Pareto optimal; that is, any point on the contract curve in Figure 12.2.4. Each point represents a particular volume of output of X and of Y, and thereby dictates the dimensions of an Edgeworth box diagram for exchange (such as Figure 12.2.3). Furthermore, each consumption-exchange box leads to an infinite number of potential exchange equilibria that are Pareto optimal; that is, any point on the contract curve associated with the box in question. Accordingly, there are a multiple infinity of potential general equilibria of production and exchange.

The object of any society is to attain that particular general equilibrium which maximizes the economic welfare of its inhabitants. As we shall see below, there are ways by which either a free enterprise system or a decentralized socialist state may attain the optimum.

12.3 SOCIAL WELFARE

12.3.a—The Difficult Concept of Social Welfare

The concept of social welfare is difficult either to define or to describe. This is largely because it encompasses so many conflicting interests. In a full-employment economy, with which we are exclusively concerned,[4] if one person gets more of some good or service, someone else must get less. What benefits one must hurt someone else if things are properly organized (more on this later). When one transfers this idea of conflicting interest to the aggregate level, there is the familiar trade-off between guns and butter, between potatoes and stereo tapes, and so forth. Some people prefer potatoes, some stereo tapes. When more of one of these commodities is produced, it is necessary to produce less of the other. Thus if more potatoes are produced, potato lovers benefit and stereo lovers suffer.

There is a similar type of consideration on the individual level. As a *consumer,* I benefit when I get more and you or someone else gets less. But as a *citizen,* the same may not be true. That is, overall I may feel better off if I give up some of my income or consumption so that others may consume somewhat more. Thus, for example, childless couples may vote in favor of school bond taxes; people contribute to the Salvation Army, the United Fund, and other agencies that redistribute income from better off to less well-off families. This is just to say that each household is confronted with a choice that involves two different roles: as consumers, the more they have the better off they are; but as citizens, they may elect to forego some consumption in order to help others.

This too may be aggregated, as it were, to yield the national counterpart. As a nation of consumers, the more we consume the better off we are. Yet each year we give billions of dollars (and therefore consumption goods) in foreign aid to underdeveloped countries. Again we have two roles: a nation of consumers and a nation that is conscious of the wants of those who are less well off.

12.3.b—Pareto Optimality

For the reasons just given, and for related ones as well, it is virtually impossible to define social welfare accurately; and in particular, it is impossible to define *maximum* social welfare. Yet almost daily, a society must make decisions that affect its welfare: *should* we give foreign aid to underdeveloped countries? *should* we tax the consumption of tobacco, alcohol, gasoline, jewelry, and so on? *should* we give income to those households that cannot earn income? There are many such questions that

---

[4] The effects of unemployment and the resulting underemployment equilibrium are usually treated in courses in macroeconomic theory.

confront a society. Most of them involve economic considerations; so surely economists must be able to say *something* about them.

Actually they can say very little. Economists cannot establish the goals of a society nor can they say what is "good" for one person or for a collection of people. In general, economists can only determine the most efficient way by which to achieve a stipulated goal. Nonetheless, economists can make one prescriptive statement: if a change can be made such that one or more people are better off and *none* worse off, the society's welfare will be increased if the change is made. We must first define "better off":

Definition: A person is said to be better off in organization *A* than in organization *B* if he gets as much of every good and service and more of at least one good or service in *A* than he gets in *B*.

We can now return to the concept of Pareto optimality.

Definition: A social organization is said to be Pareto optimal if there is no change that will benefit some people without making some others worse off.

This is admittedly a very weak concept of social welfare. To illustrate this, suppose a new transcontinental highway is to be constructed. This will benefit millions of travelers. But it also forces the government to condemn (under the right of eminent domain) the homesteads of a few families. These families, of course, are paid a "fair market price" for their property. However, some of the families may be unwilling to sell for a fair market price; yet they must by law, and they are made worse off. Millions may benefit and one be harmed. Economists qua economists cannot say that the new highway increases or decreases social welfare. For this reason economists are primarily interested in Pareto optimality because it expresses efficiency and not because the concept is a social goal. The technical efficiency aspect of welfare economics is a major aspect of the subject to economists.

To summarize the implications of the concept of Pareto optimality:

Principles: (a) if there is a change that will benefit one or more people without making *anyone* worse off, the change is socially desirable; (b) if a change helps some and hurts others—the *numbers* are immaterial—no conclusion can be reached by an economist.

12.3.c—Perfect Competition and Pareto Optimality

While the concept of Pareto optimality is a weak one, it does establish some useful boundaries for the role of economists in making welfare recommendations. In this section we want to indicate why the following important proposition concerning Pareto optimality is true:

Proposition: Assume that there is perfect competition in every market. The set of input and output prices that establishes a general economic equilibrium will also establish a Pareto optimal organization of society.

Let us first consider consumers. If there is perfect competition, all consumers face the same set of commodity prices. Since each consuming unit sets MRS equal to the price ratio, the MRS of any one consumer is equal to the MRS of *any other* consuming unit. Since all consumers are just willing to exchange commodities in the same ratio, it is impossible to make one better off without making another worse off (that is, suppose the *common* MRS of X for Y is 3:1. If someone is allowed to trade 2:1, someone else must be *forced* to trade at a ratio at which he would not voluntarily trade). Thus, a Pareto optimum is established.

Next consider producers. In maximizing profit, entrepreneurs necessarily arrange the combination of inputs so as to minimize the unit cost of production. Under perfect competition, the factor-price ratios are the same to all producers. Since each producer equates his MRTS to the common factor-price ratio, the MRTS is the same for all. Consequently, there is no reallocation of inputs that would increase one producer's output without reducing another's. Again we have a Pareto optimal organization.

Finally, in this competitive general equilibrium, the number of hours of work voluntarily offered is exactly equal to the number of hours voluntarily demanded. An increase in wages would help some, but some others would be unemployed. That is, an increase in wages would make some better off, some worse off. A decrease in wages would cause an excess demand. Thus a change in wages from the general equilibrium level will upset both Pareto optimality and general equilibrium.

Do not hold the idea that Pareto optimality necessarily leads to the maximum attainable welfare or maximum attainable utility of society as a whole. To specify maximum welfare we would have to specify a welfare function for society as a whole. This we cannot do. To be sure, a dictator could specify his country's welfare function. It would probably be his own utility function. Or a society could vote upon all possible organization and distribution. But even this leads to complications. Consider the following simple hypothetical case. There are three individuals in the society who will vote on three possible events, A, B, and C. The preference orderings of 1, 2, and 3 are as follows:

1.   (ApB) (BpC) (ApC)
2.   (BpC) (CpA) (BpA)
3.   (CpA) (ApB) (CpB)

In the table (ApB) denotes that the situation A is preferred to situation B. Note that each individual is rational in the sense that if A is preferred to B and B to C, then A is preferred to C. If this three person society voted upon events A and B, A would get a majority as would B if they chose between B and C. But note that society would vote for C over A even though rationality would imply (ApC). Thus, there can be inconsistency in determining social welfare by voting, even in this simplified example. In any event do not confuse Pareto optimality with maximum social welfare. We simply cannot make interpersonal utility comparisons.

12.4 PERFECT COMPETITION AND SOCIAL WELFARE: A FINAL VIEW

So far we have said that perfect competition will lead to a Pareto optimum, and this is the best economists can recommend. In certain cases, this is not even true. Either perfect competition may break down or the results of perfect competition are not the socially desirable ones. In concluding this book we shall treat these cases briefly, with one tremendous caveat. What we have to say is only an introductory statement. It requires one or more *courses* to treat this problem adequately.

12.4.a—Social Benefits and Social Cost

Let us suppose that commodity prices are given.[5] Each consumer, in order to maximize the satisfaction obtainable from a given money income, sets his marginal rate of substitution between two goods equal to their price ratio. This process—as explained in Chapter 4—generates each consumer's demand curve for each commodity. Summing the individual commodity demand curves horizontally gives the market demand curve for each commodity.

An individual demand curve shows the *marginal valuation* the consumer attaches to the commodity in question. That is, the demand curve shows, at each point, just how much the consumer is willing to give up in order to obtain an additional unit of a good. Thus when summed to obtain market demand, the latter shows just how much the society is willing to give up to obtain one more unit of the commodity. Now since we are discussing demand curves, the amount society is willing to give up is expressed as a price in terms of money. But money represents a general command over all resources and, hence, over all other commodities. Consequently, at each point the market demand curve shows society's marginal valuation of the commodity in question in terms of the available resource base. This marginal valuation is called, at each point on the demand curve, the *marginal social benefit* of the commodity.

Our attention has so far been directed toward the consumer; let us now

---

[5] In the general equilibrium model, prices are variables whose optimizing values are determined within the model. For simplicity, but not of *necessity*, we assume prices are parameters.

turn to the *perfectly competitive producer.* Given commodity price, the producer sets marginal cost equal to price in order to maximize profit. That is, the producer's *marginal private cost* (or supply price) is set equal to demand price, or marginal social benefit.

The implications should be clear. The resources society *is willing to sacrifice* in order to obtain an additional unit of the good precisely equal the amount of resources the producer must, by the given technology, use to produce an additional unit. Other things equal, resources are allocated optimally and society's well-being is maximized.[6]

Now we must deal with this "other things equal" business. We have just said that in competitive equilibrium, the additional resources a producer must use to produce an additional unit of a commodity is marginal cost. But the calculation involves *marginal private cost.* Let us now define *marginal social cost* as the minimum resource sacrifice that society as a whole must make in order to obtain an extra unit of a commodity. Then if marginal private cost equals marginal social cost, resources are indeed allocated optimally.

In this case the competitive pricing mechanism is Adam Smith's "invisible hand." Each consumer simply tries to maximize his satisfaction without regard to the entire society. Similarly, each producer attempts to maximize profit, taking no account of the way in which his actions affect the economy. But the competitive price system leads each person, acting in his own self-interest, to a course of action that benefits society as a whole.

12.4.b—External Economies and the Market Mechanism

In many cases, perhaps in most, there is no reason to expect a divergence between marginal private cost and marginal social cost. In his own self-interest, the producer uses the *minimum* amount of resources technologically required for his output. So, it would seem, marginal private cost is always equal to marginal social cost. There are three situations, however, in which the competitive market mechanism breaks down.

---

[6] This assumes that demand represents marginal social benefit, which in turn assumes that income is distributed in the way society wants it distributed. This may or may not be the case. In an economy characterized by perfect competition, each person receives the value of his marginal product; that is, he receives what he contributes to the total social output. For various reasons, some people are much more productive than others; they consequently receive much more and contribute much more to the formation of market demand. Further, there are "inheritances" or "endowments" of resources that some people receive through no effort of their own. These people also help form demand.

If the ethic of a society is such that the competitive distribution of income is regarded as desirable, demand does represent marginal social benefit. It would certainly not in a *pure* communist society in which the ethic is "from each according to his abilities, to each according to his needs."

12.4.c—Technological Difficulties

The first way in which the competitive market mechanism may break down is by a breakdown in competition itself. Let us suppose there exists a commodity whose production function shows continuously increasing returns to scale. Further suppose that factor prices are constant or that they do not rise fast enough to offset increasing returns to scale. In this situation, the long-run average cost curve is not U-shaped—it is a continuously declining curve.

Suppose such a market is initially organized competitively and has somehow attained a temporary equilibrium. Each firm has an incentive to expand output because: (a) average cost declines as output expands, and (b) each perfect competitor expects his actions to go unnoticed by his rivals. Thus *each* competitor expects to reduce average cost and expand output tremendously (believing all other producers will continue their previous price-output policy).

But what one producer has an incentive to do, all have an incentive to do, and as industry output expands, the industry "slides down" the negatively sloped market demand curve. As this sliding down continues, a point will be reached at which price is less than average cost. Then all firms make losses, and some firms will leave the industry. But so long as the enterpreneur believes *his* demand curve is a horizontal line he has an incentive to expand output so as to reduce average cost; and of course he believes that if he expands enough, he will eliminate his losses.

Again, however, *all* entrepreneurs have the same incentive; and as industry output expands, losses increase. More firms leave the industry. This must continue until the number of firms is so small that each recognizes that its actions *do affect* market price.

The ultimate organization of the market is uncertain. Perhaps "economic warfare" may result, with all but one firm finally eliminated from the market. In this case, monopoly emerges. On the other hand, the last few entrepreneurs left in the market may decide upon the quiet life of collusive oligopoly. As in the Chamberlin model, they decide to "live and let live" and divide the monopoly profit among themselves. In either case, perfect competition breaks down. Marginal cost is set equal to marginal revenue rather than price.

Thus even if marginal private cost equals marginal social cost, the latter is less than marginal social benefit. At the price where marginal revenue equals marginal cost, society is willing to sacrifice more resources to gain an additional unit of the good than is socially necessary (price is greater than marginal social cost). The monopolist or oligopolist, however, will not use these resources because to do so would reduce their profit.

This is the result that always comes about under monopoly or oligopoly. There is an "underproduction" of the commodity in the sense that society is willing to give up more resources than necessary to expand output. But output is restricted to preserve the monopoly profit.

Principle: If there are constantly increasing returns to scale, competition will break down; and the market price mechanism will not allocate resources optimally (that is, the price mechanism will not allocate enough resources to the monopolized sectors).

12.4.d—Ownership Externalities

The second reason why perfect competition may not lead to optimal resource allocation is called ownership externalities. To get at this we must begin with two definitions. An *external economy* is said to exist when marginal social cost is less than marginal private cost. Thus when marginal private cost equals marginal social benefit, marginal social cost is less than marginal social benefit. More resources *should* be allocated to producing the commodity in question, but they are not. On the other hand, an *external diseconomy* exists when marginal social cost exceeds marginal private cost. At such a point, marginal social benefit is less than marginal social cost. An undesirably large amount of resources is allocated to producing the commodity in question.

Definitions: An external economy (diseconomy) exists where marginal social cost is less than (greater than) marginal private cost.

At this stage it is quite reasonable to ask *how* marginal private cost and marginal social cost can diverge. One of the chief answers is "by the existence of ownership externalities." Briefly, this means that there is some scarce resource owned by a person but for some reason, the owner cannot charge a price for the use of this resource. And when prices cannot be charged, misallocation of resources results.

Our discussion to this point must seem murky indeed. From here on we proceed by use of examples, the first of which is the classic example of an ownership externality. Suppose an apple orchardist and a beekeeper are situated side by side. The production of apples, we shall assume, requires labor only. The production of honey, on the other hand, requires the labor of the beekeeper *and* apple blossoms to provide the bees with the nectar used to make honey.[7]

Now put yourself in the position of the apple orchardist. Suppose apple production is perfectly competitive; you determine output so as to make your marginal private cost (labor cost, in this case) equal to price. Apple blossoms are a by-product you own; but you cannot keep the bees out of your orchard and you cannot charge the beekeeper for the nectar

---

[7] In this example, we abstract from the cross-pollenization service provided by the bees.

taken from the blossoms. Thus, the marginal private cost of expanding apple production is the cost of the additional labor necessary to expand production.

Let us now reverse our position and look at the problem from the point of view of society as a whole. Expanding apple production does indeed cost some labor resources that could be used elsewhere. But expanding apple production also means increased apple blossoms and the nectar they contain. Thus an expansion of apple production is accompanied by an expansion of honey production; and honey is a "good" in the sense that it has a positive price.

Let us recapitulate. To the apple orchardist, expanding production entails the marginal cost of the labor involved. To society it does so as well; but society, without further use of resources, gets more honey as a result. Thus the marginal social cost of expanding apple production is the marginal private cost *minus* the value of the additional honey produced. Clearly, society would be better off if more resources were allocated to apple production. But the apple orchardist, looking at competitive prices and his marginal private cost, would never expand production to the socially optimal point.

In this case of ownership externality there is a simple solution, if it can be brought about. Let the apple orchardist buy the beekeeper's business. This "internalizes" the externality in the sense that the orchardist-beekeeper makes the same cost calculation as society does. The owner of this joint enterprise recognizes that an increase in apple production means more blossoms, more nectar, and more honey that *he* can sell in the market. That is, the internal cost accounting of the combined orchardist-beekeeper alerts him to the fact that the marginal cost to his joint enterprise of additional apple production is less than the direct cost attributed to the apple part of his business. Thus a solution to this type of externality problem can be achieved by integrating the firms involved.

Unfortunately, other types of ownership externalities are not so easily resolved; and more unfortunately still, these types are by far the most important. We begin with a rather trivial example and then consider some of the most important problems confronting the American economy today.

Suppose there is a woman who supports herself and her children by doing hand laundry. Being poor she cannot afford an automatic dryer. Consequently, she must hang the clothes in her yard to dry. But a factory is situated alongside; and its smokestack belches forth soot that dirties the freshly washed clothes. The woman must wash again.

This problem is almost insoluble. The factory creates an external diseconomy because the marginal social cost of smoke disposal exceeds the marginal private cost. The factory owner has no interest in buying the hand laundry because he would be confronted with the smoke problem.

The trouble lies in the fact that the air space above the woman's yard is a scarce resource; but she cannot build the equivalent of the Astrodome and charge admission to each bit of soot. She owns a scarce resource, but she cannot charge for its use; hence the factory uses it to her detriment.

The simple example above suggests some situations of much more far-reaching importance. The marginal private cost of dumping industrial waste into a river is very small. The marginal social cost is much greater because of the resources required to eliminate the consequent water pollution. No one "owns" rivers, only the land adjacent to them. Thus in the absence of government action, there is no one to set a price on this scarce resource. With a zero price attached to using rivers and lakes for waste disposal, we face an ever increasing problem of water pollution.

Exactly the same reasoning applies to air pollution. The marginal private cost of disposing of industrial smoke and automobile exhausts is negligible. But when there are many factories and many cars in the same location, the result is smog and air pollution. Again, the cost to society far exceeds the marginal private cost of smoke disposal; and there is no automatic corrective device built into the competitive market mechanism. Some type of external control is necessary if the externality problem is to be solved.

As a final example of this type of externality, let us consider the problem of airport congestion and the ensuing delays in passenger traffic. To an airport authority, the marginal private cost of landing a private plane is much less than the marginal private cost of landing a commercial jet. The control tower time is less, the instrument usage is less, and the impact stress on the concrete is much less. As a consequence, airport authorities charge a landing fee for private planes that is only a fraction of the landing fee paid by commercial aircraft. In a small airport that has but few commercial flights per day, this is a reasonable practice. It is merely price discrimination based upon different price elasticities. With few commercial flights, there is no reason to believe that private aircraft traffic will delay commercial passenger service. Hence marginal private and marginal social cost probably do not diverge.

In large, busy airports—such as Chicago, Atlanta, Washington, and New York—the situation is entirely different. Handling private air traffic causes a significant delay in commercial flights. This does not cost the airport authority or the owners of private aircraft. But it does cost the commercial airlines and the passengers. It costs the airlines mainly in fuel burned in holding patterns and in waiting on runways. It costs the passengers in the inconvenience of delay and the money value of the time wasted. Marginal social cost accordingly exceeds marginal private cost. From society's point of view, too much air space is used by private airplanes because air space is a scarce commodity (resource) that bears a zero price.

12.4.e—Public Good Externalities

The final case to be discussed here is that of public good externalities. This is much more complicated than the other two situations in which there is a breakdown of the market mechanism. One of the main reasons for this is that the experts in the areas of public goods and public choice cannot decide upon the exact definition of a public good. We provide a brief discussion only for the purpose of indicating that a problem exists. Any further analysis must be left to courses in public finance.[8]

For our purposes, we shall define a *public good* as one whose consumption by individual A does not preclude its consumption by individuals B, C, D, and so on. An apple is a private good. If I consume an apple, you cannot consume the same one. Good examples of public goods are open-air concerts and pyrotechnic displays. Within very broad limits, as many people as desire can "consume" the concert or the fireworks. Up to a very limited point, the same applies to public schools, libraries, and so on. In the latter cases a "capacity ceiling" is reached much more quickly.

The problems presented by this situation can only be sketched in a heuristic manner. A minor problem first: In many cases of public goods, it is difficult, if not impossible, to *exclude* people who are unwilling to pay a positive price for the good. In this case, private enterprise would never supply the good. Thus let us suppose that the production of a true public good is organized by a perfectly competitive industry and that exclusion of people unwilling to pay a positive price *is* possible.

If the industry is organized competitively, factor prices and the production function will determine marginal cost for each firm. These marginal cost curves establish the industry supply curve. There is a demand curve for the public good; and the intersection of supply and demand determines a competitive market price. Each firm then equates marginal cost with market price to maximize profit.

Consumers take this price as given and adjust their purchases accordingly. Let *a* be the *public* good *privately* supplied, and let *b, c, d,* and so on be private goods privately supplied. Each consumer arranges his purchases so that the marginal utility per dollar spent on each commodity is the same. Let MU_i be the marginal utility of commodity i and p_i be its price. Using this notation, each consumer arranges his budget so that

$$\frac{MU_a}{p_a} = \frac{MU_b}{p_b} = \frac{MU_i}{p_i} = \frac{MU_d}{p_d}, \text{ etc.}$$

---

[8] There is a good justification for this slight treatment. This is a course in market decision making; that is, how consumers, producers, and resource owners react to the signals given by market-determined prices. The case of public goods typically involves nonmarket decision making, as do some other problems treated by economists.

Now for every consumer, the marginal utility of a dollar's worth of various other commodities is so low that he does not elect to purchase them.

This presents no problem so far as private goods are concerned. If a consumer decides not to purchase a private good, less of the good is produced and fewer of society's resources are used to produce it. The same, however, does not apply to public goods.

For many consumers the marginal utility of a dollar's worth of *a*, the public good, will be so low that he will not purchase it at a competitively determined price. That is,

$$\frac{MU_a}{p_a} < \frac{MU_b}{p_b} = \frac{MU_c}{p_c}, \text{ etc.}$$

The consumer does not choose to purchase the public good at the competitive price, even though he would at lower prices (in the limit, a zero price). In this case, however, when a consumer elects not to consume the good, *none of society's resources are saved* because, by definition, a public good is one that may be consumed in the same amount by all consumers.

Herein lies the problem. Regardless of the total consumption of the public good, the same amount of society's resources must be used to produce it.[9] Now it is reasonable to assume that for consumers who elect not to purchase the public good, the marginal utility of the good is not zero. That is, even though

$$\frac{MU_a}{p_a} < \frac{MU_b}{p_b} = \frac{MU_c}{p_c}, \text{ etc.,}$$

$MU_a \neq 0$. Thus if a zero price were charged these consumers, they would consume the public good. They would be better off, and no one would be worse off because no more of society's resources are used when they consume it.

Principle: If the production of a public good is in the hands of private enterprise, social welfare is less than it would otherwise be because some consumers are excluded from the market when price is greater than zero. Since their consumption of the good is "free" to society in the sense that it entails no further resource sacrifice, society as a whole would be better off if these people were allowed to consume the good at zero price; but under free enterprise, they are not.

This is not an indictment of the free enterprise system. It is merely a recognition of the fact that there are some goods that are not optimally consumed when price is set by the competitive market mechanism.

---

[9] By this we mean that if a public good is produced in a competitive market, demand and supply will determine the equilibrium output. But that output could be consumed by many more people without sacrificing more resources.

12.5 CONCLUSION

In most cases perfect competition, by means of the price mechanism or Smith's "invisible hand," leads to the optimal allocation of resources. In a few instances it does not; and in this section we have merely listed these "perverse" cases. It is impossible to determine empirically how important they are. About the best one can say is that in any economic society there is some role for governmental economic controls; *but* the government's role should be limited to markets where the price mechanism does not allocate resources efficiently. In particular, it should not extend to arbitrary controls over markets where demand and supply is an efficient allocative device. This may seem to be a weak conclusion for an entire textbook. In fact, it is not. The function of microeconomic theory is to determine the relative efficiency of various types of market organization. The chief conclusion is that perfect competition is, in general, optimal. The purpose of this last section is simply to show that there are some situations, whose importance cannot be determined, in which this conclusion may not hold. Generally, however, competitively determined prices in competitive markets allocate resources in something like an optimal way.

Index

This book has been set in 10 and 9 point Caledonia, leaded 2 points. Chapter numbers are in 18 and 24 point Helvetica and chapter titles are in 18 point Helvetica Medium. The size of the type page is 27 × 45½.